Putin

Vladimir Putin has had a major domestic and international impact since his election as Russian President in March 2000 and yet remarkably little is known about the man in the West. *Putin: Russia's Choice*, written by one of the UK's leading scholars of Russian politics, is the first major study of the man and his politics. Richard Sakwa's discussion provides the biographical and political context to explain Putin's astonishing rise from anonymous KGB apparatchik to leader of one of the world's most important and interesting countries.

The book explains Putin's personal and intellectual development and his ability to effect social and political change. Putin's attempt to counter the endemic weakness of the Russian state and to reshape its political system and national identity are explored alongside his economic, social, cultural, regional and foreign policies. The author also examines the close personal relationships that Putin has forged with other world leaders including President George W. Bush, Prime Minister Tony Blair and Chancellor Gerhard Schroeder.

Drawing on both Russian and English-language sources, and providing comprehensive coverage of Putin's speeches, interviews and policy documents, this is the definitive study of the Russian leader.

Richard Sakwa is Professor of Politics at the University of Kent. His recent publications include *Russian Politics and Society, The Rise and Fall of the Soviet Union, 1917–1991* and *Soviet Politics in Perspective*.

Putin

Russia's choice

Richard Sakwa

Routledge
Taylor & Francis Group

LONDON AND NEW YORK

First published 2004
by Routledge
11 New Fetter Lane, London EC4P 4EE

Simultaneously published in the USA and Canada
by Routledge
29 West 35th Street, New York, NY 10001

Reprinted 2004

Routledge is an imprint of the Taylor & Francis Group

© 2004 Richard Sakwa

Typeset in Baskerville by Wearset Ltd, Boldon, Tyne and Wear
Printed and bound in Great Britain by TJ International Ltd, Padstow,
Cornwall

British Library Cataloguing in Publication Data
A catalogue record for this book is available from the British Library

Library of Congress Cataloging in Publication Data
Sakwa, Richard.
  Putin: Russia's choice by Richard Sakwa.
    p. cm.
Includes bibliographical references and index.
  1. Russia (Federation) – Politics and government – 1991– 2. Putin,
Vladimir Vladimirovich, 1952– I. Title.
  DK510.763.S247 2004
  947.086'092–dc21   2003013170

ISBN 0–415–29663–3 (hbk)
ISBN 0–415–29664–1 (pbk)

Contents

List of tables		vii
Preface		viii
Acknowledgements		xi

1 The unlikely path to power   1

The unlikely making of a leader 2
The succession operation 15

2 The ideas behind the choice   34

Who is mister Putin? 35
The Russian 'transition' and beyond 37
Russia at the turn of the millennium 43
Planning for the future 47
The state of the nation 51
The 'normalisation' of politics 53

3 The Putin way   60

Building the Putin bloc 61
Putin and the people 68
Leadership and style 73
Putin's path: towards a Russian 'third way'? 78

4 State and society   83

State and regime 83
State strengthening as politics or law 90
The 'liquidation of the oligarchs as a class' 96
Freedom of speech and the media 103
Judicial reform and human rights 107

5 Restructuring political space   113

Changes to the party system 113
Changes to electoral legislation 118
Parliamentary realignment 119

Regime and opposition 122
Democracy and civil society 125

6 **Putin and the regions**   130
Segmented regionalism 130
The reconstitution of federal relations 135
Establishing the presidential 'vertical' 141
Reorganising federal relations 146
Regional governors and legislatures 152
State reconstitution and federalism 155

7 **Reforging the nation**   161
Images of the nation and symbols of the state 161
Chechnya: tombstone or crucible of Russian power? 170

8 **Russian capitalism**   182
Entering the market 182
Models of capitalism – oligarchical democracy? 190
State, economy and society 201

9 **Putin and the world**   207
The normalisation of foreign policy 207
Putin's choice 215
Practising normality 221

10 **Conclusion**   234

Appendix: Russia at the turn of the millennium   251
Notes   263
Select bibliography   293
Index   296

Tables

1.1	State Duma election, 19 December 1999	22
1.2	Presidential election, 26 March 2000	29
8.1	Economic indicators	187
8.2	Russia's leading financial-industrial conglomerates	193
8.3	Russia's oligarchs	193

Preface

The coming to power of Vladimir Putin at the beginning of the new millennium signalled the beginning of a period of change in Russian politics that could well prove decisive. The choices made in the early years of a century have traditionally established a long-term pattern. In 1703 Peter the Great began the building of St Petersburg and thus signalled the aspiration to modernise the country 'from above' along Western lines. His attempt, as Lenin put it, 'to chase out barbarism by barbaric means' by establishing the city in the marshes of the Neva river established a pattern of forced modernisation that ruptured evolutionary patterns of development. Russia was thrown back into bureaucratic authoritarianism, and the development of inclusive government and popular representation was retarded. A distinctive pattern emerged of modernisation without modernity, adopting a type of superficial Westernisation in forms without the critical spirit that distinguishes Western modernity. In the early nineteenth century Alexander I brought Russia to the front ranks of the European powers, defeating Napoleon's Grand Army in 1812 and then, following the Congress of Vienna in 1815, made it part of the Holy Alliance of conservative powers. The various plans for constitutional reform and debates over how best to Europeanise the country at the beginning of the nineteenth century culminated in the Decembrist uprising in 1825. The choice thereafter, with exceptions, was to try to modernise within the framework of autocratic government, a combination that spectacularly collapsed in 1917. Russia at the beginning of the twentieth century also struggled to define its developmental path, torn between various populist, Slavophile and nationalist ideas on the one hand, and a variety of Westernising theories of modernisation on the other. In the event, in 1917 the choice was made by Lenin and the Bolsheviks in favour of a socialist path of modernisation that later, under Stalin, represented a peculiar mix of Western technical modernisation, again 'from above', while rejecting the Western spirit of modernity. President Boris Yeltsin's reforms in the 1990s once again sought to turn Russia on to a new path by forceful means.

It was this legacy of hybrid modernisation with which Putin was forced to come to terms. Putin considered the communist attempt to modernise the country by revolutionary means as doomed to failure, although he accepted that the Soviet regime between 1917 and 1991 had brought the country some benefits. His view of Yeltsin's reforms appeared to be the opposite; as probably fated to succeed but at a heavy price. Putin's government sought to come to terms with the various developmental choices made in the past. He was faced with a number of stark choices, while at the same time aware that each carried penalties. The choice now was not so much over the direction in which the country should move, since a broad consensus had finally emerged that Russia should become a capitalist democracy integrated with the West. There was less agreement, however, over the methods to be adopted to pursue these goals. Russia sought to find a new path that would break the vicious circles into which the country had been embroiled by its early century choices in the past.

The challenge facing Putin as he took up office as acting president on 1 January 2000 was to overcome not only the legacy of the decade of rapid liberalisation that had followed the fall of the communist system in 1991, but to find a way of combining Russia's distinctive character with what appeared to have become universal norms of democracy and international integration. How could freedom be reconciled with the need to re-establish effective governance, and how could the poor and outcast be protected as the economy shifted towards the market and international economic integration? How could powerful executive authority be reconciled with the development of democracy, pluralism and federalism? The country was far from being a blank slate on which Putin could write at will, but at the same time his choices had the potential to determine the pattern for the rest of the century. It is these choices and the dilemmas that lay behind them that we shall explore in this book.

The intention is to provide three strands of analysis. The first focuses on Putin's personal and intellectual development, with a brief discussion of his childhood and career. The relationship between individual choices and structural constraints must be at the forefront of any political biography. The role of the individual and their ability to effect social and political change will be examined in the context of Putin's leadership qualities, his attempts to build a power base and his relationship with the public. The second theme focuses on broader theoretical questions about the shape of the Russian polity, the way that Putin related to it, and the nature of his leadership. He inherited from Yeltsin a country that had been an independent and sovereign state for less than a decade and which had undergone the trauma of rapid market development. He was also heir to a society that had been ruled by a one-party communist system for over seven decades, and which for most of that time had been locked in conflict with the capitalist world. He was also the legatee of a political culture in which political authority tended to be concentrated, state administration inordinately bureaucratised, and the development of a pluralistic civil society inhibited. This second strand examines the thinking and dilemmas behind Putin's choices and looks at how they worked in practice as he sought to reshape the Russian political system and national identity. The third strand focuses on policy issues, above all on regional, economic and foreign policy. In each area there were fundamental choices to be made but, as with leadership in general, the constraints were real but the decisional factor had the potential to transform the situation.

These three themes interacted to create a fascinating period of political development. There were no easy answers to fundamental questions concerning method and policy, and as a result Putin's choices were characterised by a combination of strategic purpose and tactical flexibility. The legacy of the past certainly acted as one of the most important constraints on development, but at the same time powerful ideas for innovation and change were present. By the end of the book the reader should have a clearer idea of the enormity of the options facing Russia, a sense of the factors that determined Putin's choices, and some indication of how these choices worked in practice.

Richard Sakwa
Canterbury, May 2003

Acknowledgements

The debts incurred in writing this book are numerous. I would like in particular to thank those who have shared their time and expertise with me. I am especially grateful to Mikhail Afanas'ev, Vladimir Amelin, Jonathan Aves, Pavel Baev, Yitzhak Brudny, Philip Boobbyer, Lena Danilova, Artour Demtchouk, Dmitrii Furman, Vladimir Gel'man, Elena Hore, Yurii Igritskii, Mikhail Il'in, Svyatoslav Kaspe, Vladimir Kolosov, Anatolii Kulik, Sergei Markov, Andrei Medushevskii, Lena Meleshkina, Andrei Melville, Valentin Mikhailov, Alexei Mukhin, Oleg Mramornov, Oksana Oracheva, Vladimir Pastukhov, Nikolai Petrov, Yurii Pivovarov, Cameron Ross, Andrei Ryabov, Viktor Rudenko, Elena Shestopal, Louis Skyner, Svetlana Stephenson and Valerii Solovei. Collaboration with the Institute of Law and Public Policy in Moscow, under the directorship of Olga Sidorovich, has been particularly fruitful, and I thank all there who have helped in the development of this work. The faults, of course, remain my own. Craig Fowlie and Zoe Botterill at Routledge have displayed great patience and understanding as work on this book was held up by Quality Assurance Agency Subject Review and the baleful and obviously ridiculous consequences of the Research Assessment Exercise. Living in an age of Straussian Stalinism in Britain has helped put contemporary Russian politics into perspective. I am most grateful for the secretarial and other assistance of Alison Chapman, Ann Hadaway, Jean Hudson and Nicola Huxtable in the Department of Politics at the University of Kent. It is my great pleasure to thank the Nuffield Foundation (Grant No. SGS/00730/G) for their assistance in the preparation of this book.

1 The unlikely path to power

The state whose prospective rulers come to their duties with least enthusiasm is bound to have the best and most tranquil government, and the state whose rulers are eager to rule the worst.

(Plato[1])

Putin's rise to power reflected one of the most unusual political biographies in recent years. Brought up in a communal apartment in Leningrad (from 1991 once again St Petersburg) and an enthusiastic participant in the rough and tumble of childhood play in the city's streets, only slowly did his leadership qualities emerge. Attracted to work in the Soviet Union's secret service, then known as the Committee for State Security (KGB), he went on to win a place to study law at Leningrad State University (1970–75), followed by a career in the KGB (1975–90), the last five years of which he served in the German Democratic Republic (GDR), the communist half of Germany until the fall of the Berlin wall in 1989. The following year entering the service of the former law professor, Anatoly Sobchak, Putin rose swiftly to become his right arm as Sobchak became mayor of the city (1991–96). Sobchak's failure to win a second term in 1996 left Putin at a loose end, until he was offered a job in the Kremlin. Once in Moscow Putin's rise was meteoric, from an official in the presidential administration, up through minister of the service in which he had once worked, now renamed the Federal Security Service (FSB), and then as prime minister from 9 August 1999. On 31 December 1999, by some reckonings the last day of the century and of the millennium, president Boris Yeltsin unexpectedly resigned and Putin took over as acting president until elections on 26 March 2000 confirmed him as president for a four-year term. How did Putin manage to achieve such an astonishing rise to become president of the world's largest country? In this chapter we will examine his background and the decisive moments that led to the presidency, and in the next we will discuss the situation that he faced and the ideas that shaped his politics. By the end of these two chapters we should be able to sketch an answer to the question that greeted his emergence as the leader of Russia: 'Who is mister Putin?'

The unlikely making of a leader

Vladimir Putin was a late child, born into a family of workers on 7 October 1952 in the centre of Leningrad, two tram stops from the central avenue, Nevsky Prospekt and not far from the Griboedov canal. By the time he became president he had spent half his life living in a communal apartment, where several families share basic facilities. In Putin's case, the house at No. 12 Baskov Lane had been built in 1859 and divided into high quality rented apartments. After the revolution the apartments were divided up to house several families, and the Putins moved there in 1944 at the disposition of the factory where his father worked.[2] By the time he was born Putin's parents were already in their forties, and as a late and only surviving child he was considered a 'gift for all their earlier sufferings and deprivations'.[3]

Putin's roots

Putin's paternal grandfather, Spiridon Ivanovich Putin, had been an out-standing cook employed for a time at Lenin's country house (Gorki) and following his death in January 1924 worked for his wife, Nadezhda Krup-skaya, and later on several occasions cooked for Stalin when the latter visited one of his Moscow region dachas (country house). Spiridon later worked at the country house of the Moscow City Committee of the Communist Party of the Soviet Union (CPSU) in Ilinsky, where the young Vladimir visited him. He died in 1965 aged 86.[4] Putin's father, Vladimir Spiridonovich, was born on 23 February 1911 and spent his childhood in the village of Pominovo in Tver *guberniya* (region), while his mother, Maria Ivanovna, was born in the same year (17 October) and lived in the neighbouring village of Zareche, both in the Turginovsky district about 60 kilometres from the regional capital of Tver. Although coming from different villages, the two met in ado-lescence and thereafter proved inseparable and were married at the age of 17 in 1928.[5] Their first son Oleg died before reaching his first birthday. In 1932 the couple moved to Leningrad, and while Putin's mother worked in a factory his father was drafted to serve in the submarine fleet. Just before the onset of the Great Fatherland War the Putins received an apartment in the Stary Peterhof district of Leningrad, where their second son, Viktor, was born. He died of diphtheria aged five in the first year of the blockade and was buried in a communal grave. Maria's mother was killed by a stray bullet fired by the occupiers of Tver region on 13 October 1941, her father died in 1947, while her older brothers disappeared without trace at the front.

Just before Leningrad was surrounded by the Germans Maria had the chance to leave, but she decided to stay since her husband was fighting to defend the city, assigned at first to a demolition battalion of the NKVD and then one of the defenders of the so-called Neva nickel (*Nevskii pyatochok*), a redoubt on the left bank of the Neva river next to Lake Ladoga that the Germans were never able to capture despite repeated assaults, a type of mini-

Stalingrad. Vladimir Spiridonovich in the winter of 1942 was severely wounded by a grenade in this area, and his wife nursed him back to health. On recovering he went to work in the Yegorov engineering plant, at the time making shells. As the days of the blockade stretched towards the accursed nine hundred (1942–January 1944), for lack of food Maria Ivanovna could barely move and only her husband's soldier's rations saved her life. Putin's father remained with a limp to the end of his life. By the time the blockade ended only 560,000 of the city's three million inhabitants remained: over 1.5 million had died of hunger and illness, 200,000 from bombs and shells, and 560,000 had been evacuated. Among those who had survived the whole siege were Vladimir senior and Maria.

By the time Vladimir Vladimorovich was born in 1952 his parents had endured much. His birth symbolised the end of the sufferings of the past and the privations of the war. It is clear from all accounts that they were a close-knit although strict family. Their mutual devotion is commented on by all biographers. His father worked as a toolmaker in the Yegorov plant, by then making railway carriages and from 1968 metro wagons. He was a model communist, genuinely believing in its ideals while trying to put them into practice in his own life.[6] He became the secretary of the Party cell in his workshop in 1947, and in 1948 at the age of 37 took up evening classes and later joined the factory's Party buro. Maria was a devoted Orthodox believer, and although there were no icons in the flat she regularly slipped off to church, which in those days of official atheism and persecution suggested a person with deep-felt beliefs. She ensured that the baby Vladimir was christened, although this was done in secret,[7] and she regularly took him to services.[8] His father, although a communist, knew of his wife's church-going but turned a blind eye.[9] In those days maternity leave was only two months, and Putin's mother worked in a succession of low-skill jobs, in part to allow extra time to spend with her son: a concierge, receptionist at a baker's, washing laboratory equipment. In pre-school years Putin and his mother spent most of the summer in their home village. Later Putin recounts that on the eve of an official visit to Israel his mother gave him his baptismal cross to have it blessed: 'I did as she said and then put the cross around my neck. I have never taken it off since.'[10]

Childhood and youth

On 1 September 1960 Putin started at School No. 193 on Baskov Lane, just opposite the house where his family lived. Before the revolution the school had been a women's *gymnasium*, where Nadezhda Krupskaya had once studied. His form teacher was Tamara Chizhova, whose devotion to the class has been much commented upon.[11] The memoirs of his later teacher of German, Vera Gurevich, reveals that the young Putin was an energetic and strong-willed boy. Putin started learning German in after-school classes in April 1964, and according to Gurevich he had an aptitude for foreign languages. When she started teaching form 5A in September 1964 Putin was one of only a handful in the class of over 45 pupils who was not yet a member of the Pioneers (the Communist pupils' organisation), largely because of his rowdy behaviour. Gurevich, who became a friend of the family, recalls that out of school hours Putin would disappear for hours to play in the courtyard, called by Blotskii his 'window on the world',[12] mostly with older boys.[13] It was this experience of courtyard life that played an important part in shaping Putin's character. Putin was never particularly interested in music and soon gave up classes. However, in sixth grade he started taking sport seriously in the form of sambo and then judo.

It was in this academic year, beginning in September 1965, that his school-work markedly improved, with Putin taking a particular interest in history and literature. In sixth grade, too, Putin entered the Pioneers, and indeed quickly came to lead the class group by popular demand.[14] Already in critical situations his peers looked to him for leadership.[15] In those days one could not join the Komsomol (the Communist Youth League) without having been a Pioneer; and without Komsomol membership the door would be closed to most good higher education institutions and professions. At the beginning of eighth grade Putin entered the Komsomol organisation in a ceremony at the district Party committee. These were highly ideological organisations, but by this time political commitment was typically worn lightly and had largely become a matter of form. Putin's rapid assumption of leadership of his class Pioneer group, it may be noted, was an early indication of the speed with which his career would advance in the post-Soviet era. In summer 1968, after eighth grade, pupils were faced with a choice of where to study further and Putin, rather surprisingly, chose for the final two years to enter a chemistry secondary school (No. 281). Blotskii notes that Putin took the decision on his own: 'It was already a feature of his character: Volodya would announce a decision, but would never explain the reasons for his choice'.[16] He continued with his German studies here. His class teacher, Mina Moiseevna Yuditskaya, who later emigrated to Israel, notes that although a passable scientist Putin was much more inclined to the humanities and Russian history.[17] Having completed ninth and tenth grade, Putin left secondary school in 1970.

After an unsuccessful experiment with boxing, when his nose was broken, Putin in the autumn of 1965 joined the 'Trud' sports club. There he met his trainer, Anatoly Rakhlin, who was to have a profound influence on Putin's development. He began with sambo, and then moved on to judo. As Putin noted 'Judo is not just a sport, you know. It's a philosophy. It's respect for your elders and for your opponent. It's not for weaklings.'[18] In 1973 Putin became a master at sambo, and in 1975 in judo, becoming in 1976 the city champion.[19] Putin travelled throughout the country as part of his team. Sport for Putin was a way out: 'If I hadn't taken up sport, who knows what would have happened. It was sport that took me off the street.'[20] One of his classmates recalls him as 'soft and modest, even shy, but with a character of steel'.[21]

The Putin family shared their fifth-floor flat with two families, including an elderly Jewish couple and their grown-up daughter. The sink and gas cooker were in the corridor, without hot water or a bathroom, and of course there was no lift. Putin was long to remember the stairwell with a metal banister, where the boys hunted rats. At the end of seventh grade in 1967 the old couple in the communal flat finally received an apartment of their own and their room was turned into a kitchen, which became the scene of endless gatherings of Putin's friends.[22] Putin's parents bought a small house in the country (Kingisepp district of Leniningrad *oblast*, a spot where Putin's father had fought in the early part of the war) so as to be able to take the young Vladimir out of the city in the summers. This proved too far from the city so in 1969 it was sold and a closer dacha in Tosno was bought. At this house Putin would gather with his friends to play the guitar, sing songs and listen to records (the songs of Bulat Okudzhava and Vladimir Vysotsky were particularly popular), while in winter it was used as a base for skiing. All would toil round the house, with Putin particularly enjoying chopping wood and fetching water in a churn fixed on a sledge. Later a banya (wooden Russian bathhouse) was built and all enjoyed taking a steam bath. The young Putin was infamous for concocting cock-and-bull while remaining poker-faced and laughing up his sleeve.[23] It was these realities of daily life of the late Soviet period that stamped Putin's character. As Putin put it in his book of interviews, 'I was a pure and utterly successful product of Soviet patriotic education.'[24]

The Brezhnev era (1964–82), the latter part of which was later to be dubbed by Mikhail Gorbachev as the 'period of stagnation', was nevertheless characterised by gradual improvements in standards of living, although by the late 1970s there were growing shortages and ever-lengthening queues. Putin's parents in 1977 saw their own conditions improve as they moved out of the communal flat in Baskov Lane and received a two-room apartment on Stachek Prospect. The smaller room was taken by Vladimir, and thus at the age of 25 for the first time he gained a small corner that could be called his own. By then he had been working with the KGB for two years, but there was no question of him getting a flat of his own. As Blotskii notes, 'In all of his years of Service in intelligence, Vladimir Putin did not receive a single square metre of his own accommodation.'[25] The Brezhnev years represented a period of 'normality' the like of which the Soviet system had rarely known, with the USSR achieving superpower parity in 1975, enjoying the fruits of détente and with relative domestic peace.

It was now safe enough to make anti-Soviet jokes (Putin appears to have been a master at telling *anekdoty*, and indeed all accounts suggest a strongly developed sense of humour[26]), and to read dog-eared copies of banned literature circulating in *samizdat*.[27] Putin by all accounts at an early age had a strong political awareness, enjoying political discussions in which 'he defended Russians and Russia'.[28] As long as people did not engage in unofficial political activity and make political demands of the regime, life in this period of relative non-market prosperity could be good. The premium was not on earnings and work but on social relationships and 'getting' (*dostat'*) rather than buying. His mother in 1972 bought a lucky lottery ticket and won a car (a Zaporozhets, mocked today but a magnificent trophy at the time), and instead of selling it gave it to her son and Putin became the family chauffeur. These fifteen-odd years of calm from the late 1960s to the early 1980s stand in marked contrast to the fifteen years of upheaval from Gorbachev's launching of *perestroika* (restructuring) in 1985, the collapse of communism and the disintegration of the USSR in 1991, and Yeltsin's erratic shift to the market and democracy in the 1990s.

Clearly facets of personal biography shape political preferences, and Putin's generational character is as a person of the 1970s (a *semidesyatnik*), a type that stands in sharp contrast to the previous generation, the people of the 1960s (known as the *shestdesyatniki*). The latter were shaped by Nikita Khrushchev's denunciation of Stalin in his 'secret speech' of February 1956 at the Twentieth Party Congress, and were inspired by a belief in the Soviet system's potential to reform into a more democratic form of socialism. It was this idea that motivated Gorbachev and to which he remained remarkably loyal despite all the vicissitudes of *perestroika*, and an idea that was repudiated by Yeltsin in the late 1980s as he adopted the programme of the anti-systemic 'democratic' movement that called for market democracy of the Western type. As a *semidesyatnik* Putin was influenced by the spy thrillers popular at the time, notably the book (published in 1965) and later film *Shchit i mech* (*Sword and Shield*), about the doings of a Soviet secret agent, and the later television serial *Semnadsat' mgnovenii vesny* (*Seventeen Moments of Spring*), about the Soviet spy Stirlitz working in the foreign ministry at the heart of the Nazi regime. As Putin noted of his fascination with the spy thriller genre, 'What amazed me most of all was how one man's effort could achieve what whole armies could not.'[29] Although both films were deeply patriotic, neither was particularly ideological: the struggle was to defend the Soviet motherland against its various enemies, not to defend the communist regime against its ideological opponents. This relatively non-ideological patriotism shaped Putin's personality and later took him into a career with the KGB. As he noted, 'For better or for worse, I was never a dissident.'[30]

Ambition achieved and lost

Putin was at first interested in studying at the civil aviation academy, but in the end decided that he would try to enter the law faculty of Leningrad State University (LGU). The reason for this choice of academic path is interesting. Putin recounts how when in ninth grade (aged 16) in 1968 he turned up at the reception office of the Leningrad KGB (the KGB under Lenin was known as the 'sword and shield' of the revolution) at No. 4 Liteinyi Prospekt (known as the 'Big House'). He was told, first, that they did not take volunteers (*initsiativniki*), and second, that they only took those who had done military service or graduates. Upon asking what he should study, the KGB officer apparently told him that a law degree would be most appropriate.[31] It was at this time that the new (appointed in May 1967) head of the KGB, Vladimir Andropov, tried to modernise the repressive apparatus by attracting more intellectual and creative graduates into the profession.[32] The KGB was being modernised at the same time as the aspiration to modernise communism itself had been crushed in Czechoslovakia, where just a few months earlier (August 1968) attempts to create 'socialism with a human face' had been stamped out by an invasion of the USSR and its allies. It was a rather romantic representation of the work of the security organs that led Putin to the KGB. Even his parents had no idea about the visit.[33]

Putin acted on the advice and sought to study at LGU. Competition was fierce, with some 40 applicants for every place, and Putin had none of the advantages other more privileged families enjoyed. Nevertheless, through sheer determination in 1970 at the age of 17 he managed to win a place. Putin thus became the fourth Russian leader (after Alexander Kerensky, Lenin and Gorbachev) to be a lawyer by training, and he was the only one of the three to have studied in the law faculty at LGU to finish full-time legal studies: Kerensky had begun studying history and philology before transferring to law, and Lenin had been an external candidate.[34] Putin studied hard and engaged in few extracurricular activities except sport, and in the book of interviews stressed that 'I wasn't a Komsomol functionary'.[35] He continued with his sporting life and in the summers earned money as a building worker. His interest in civil law led him to take the course taught by Sobchak, already a leading lecturer in the department.[36] His Diploma work was on the subject 'Principles of Successful Nations in the International Sphere'.[37] While at university, in March 1973 a tragedy occurred when Putin's close friend Vladimir Cheremushkin, whom Putin had encouraged to take up the sport, broke his neck in a sambo competition and later died.

It was at university that Putin broke off his first engagement, for unknown reasons, at the last moment when all the arrangements had been made, the rings bought and the suits hired: 'The cancellation was one of the most difficult decisions of my life . . . But I decided that it was better to suffer then than to have both of us suffer after.'[38] This was about four years before his actual marriage. Putin's wife, Lyudmila Shkrebneva, was born in Kaliningrad on 6 January 1958, and after a number of jobs became a flight attendant on the local airline. They met in March 1980 when she visited Leningrad with a friend and went to a show by Arkady Raikin at the Lensovet theatre. Later in 1980 she moved to Leningrad and registered to study in the philology faculty of LGU, gaining access through the workers' faculty (*rabfak*), a programme in the last year of its existence that allowed those with a working class background to enter higher education. She majored in Spanish language and literature while learning French as a subsidiary language, and lived in a normal student hostel. They married after a three-and-a-half year courtship on 28 July 1983, when Vladimir was already 30 and working with the first department (intelligence) of the KGB. They went to live with Putin's parents on Stachek Prospekt. Lyudmila graduated in 1986, writing her Diploma dissertation on 'The Participle in Contemporary Spanish'.[39] She later learned German well enough to become a teacher of that language in the early 1990s, and it was at this time on 28 October 1993 that she had a near fatal motor car accident and was saved only by the timely intervention of the surgeon Yury Shevchenko, who under Putin became Minister of Health. Like her husband, Lyudmila is strongly religious, although occasionally attracted to astrology. The role of 'first lady' is not something that particularly attracted her. The Putins' two daughters, Maria (b. 28 April 1985) and Ekatarina (b. 31 August 1986), were named after their grandmothers. They enrolled in Moscow's German school attached to the German embassy, named after the German doctor Friedrich Gaaz who worked in Russian prisons and hospitals in the early 1900s, studying not only in German and Russian but also English.[40] From September 1999 they studied at home. Both play the piano and violin, and are reputed to ski even better than their father.

In his fourth year at university the KGB made contact with him to discuss his 'career assignment', and he was invited 'to work in the agencies'. Putin readily agreed, having 'dreamed of this moment since I was a schoolboy'. On being asked whether he thought of the great terror of 1937 at this time, Putin responded: 'To be honest, I didn't think about it at all. Not one bit. . . . My notion of the KGB came from romantic spy stories.'[41] Work in the KGB at the time was considered a prestigious occupation and the selection was tough. He joined the KGB in the summer of 1975, training for a year in the closed 401st KGB school in Leningrad and then briefly working in the second department (counter-intelligence) before being transferred to the far more prestigious and elite 'first department' (*Pervoe glavnoe upravlenie,* PGU),[42] monitoring foreigners and consular officials in Leningrad. As a KGB operative he also had to join the Communist Party. To his family and friends his cover was that he was a police officer with the CID. At the same time he was allowed to continue with his German language studies in a course that lasted eight semesters, something that was only allowed for officers 'with a future'.

The head of his section noted Putin's 'analytical turn of mind', and recommended him to the prestigious Red Banner (Krasnoznammenyi) Institute in Balashikh in Moscow *oblast,* named after Andropov in March 1984 following his death and now the Foreign Intelligence Academy but then disguised as a research institute of the Ministry of Defence. Only those with strong language skills were accepted, and entrance involved a gruelling selection process. Putin was successful, and started there in September 1984, leaving his pregnant wife in Leningrad. The year-long training was tough at the Institute, including tests for physical stamina and mental endurance. Students were given a code name that began with the same letter as their real name, but could not be too close: Putin became Platov, and not Putilovsky or Putilin.[43]

Putin graduated in July 1985 and was posted to the KGB office in Dresden. East Germany at this time hosted the 380,000-strong Western Group of Forces (WGF). He arrived in August, just at the time that Gorbachev's *pere-stroika* of the USSR began to take off. Thus at the age of 32 Putin came to an East Germany still remaining what Putin himself called a 'harshly totalitarian country, similar to the Soviet Union, only 30 years earlier'.[44] The Stasi (the GDR secret police) ran a vast surveillance network, holding six million files on a population which was not much more than double that. Putin was no super-spy, as the former head of the Stasi, Marcus Wolf, has confirmed, although he was three times promoted during his stay in the country. The KGB offices in Dresden were at No. 4 Angelikastrasse, just opposite the Stasi headquarters. The head of the city Stasi was Horst Bem, one of the hardest of the hard-liners, who committed suicide after the fall of the wall. Putin's job there was 'political intelligence' and to recruit agents to be trained in 'wireless communications', probably to gain access to Western technology and to monitor visitors to the giant 'Robotron' computer factory in the city that supplied the whole socialist camp. Numerous myths have grown up around Putin's work in East Germany, but Putin insists that his work was political rather than technical intelligence gathering.[45] He appears to have had a network of agents across the world.[46] Contrary to much assertion, there is no evidence that he ran a Soviet-German friendship house in Leipzig (there was such an institution in Berlin), but he did visit Bonn frequently. In his leisure time Putin took up fishing so enthusiastically 'that even Germans were amazed at his pedantry'.[47] He took up beer drinking, although Putin was never one to drink to excess, and gained significantly in weight. He forged some close friendships with Germans at this time,[48] which he has maintained ever since.

With the unfolding of Gorbachev's reforms the hard-line regime led by Erich Honecker became ever more isolated. On a visit to the GDR in 1989, paradoxically to celebrate the fortieth anniversary of the founding of the state on 7 October 1949, Gorbachev warned that history punishes those who do not change with the times. Putin may well have been involved in the Soviet plan (operation '*luch*') to replace GDR hard-liners with reformers of the Gorbachev ilk.[49] Mass marches turned into protests, and on the night of 7–8 November 1989 the Berlin wall was breached. Back in Dresden the KGB was burning files on agents and operations so furiously that, as Putin put it, 'the furnace burst'.[50] Shortly afterwards, on the evening of 6 December, the KGB office was besieged by an angry crowd.[51] Putin called on the local Soviet army barracks for help and was told: 'We cannot do anything without orders from Moscow. And Moscow is silent.' It was at this point that Putin realised 'that the country no longer existed. That it had disappeared'.[52] Putin notes that 'intellectually I understood that a position built on walls and dividers cannot last'.[53] Later he argued that he was astonished that 'such a lifeless state form could still exist in Europe at that time'.[54] However, like many of his contemporaries, including the last communist head of Dresden, Hans

Modrow, who after the fall of the wall went on to become premier and tried to establish in East Germany what Gorbachev called a 'humane, democratic socialism', the most bitter disappointment was that no alternative took shape and the Soviet Union made a hasty exit: 'They just dropped everything and went away.'[55] A rather chastened Putin returned from Germany, faced by serious choices about changing his life path.[56]

Second career: city functionary

In early February 1990 Putin returned to St Petersburg and turned down the offer to work at the headquarters of the Foreign Intelligence Agency (SVR) at Yasenovo in Moscow, largely because no apartment was forthcoming. At that time accommodation was more important for the flood of service personnel returning from Eastern Europe and other Soviet outposts than career.[57] Instead he planned to study international law at LGU, hoping to write a doctoral dissertation and move into a new sphere of work, although as one of his friends told him, 'There's no such thing as a former intelligence agent.'[58] At LGU in March Putin was appointed head of the foreign section, *Inotdel*, and thus became assistant rector for international affairs while remaining in the 'active reserves' of the KGB. Putin maintained contacts with friends from the law faculty, and in this way was introduced into the office of Sobchak, the 'democratic' chair of the Leningrad City Soviet from May 1990. The democratic movement in Leningrad was shocked at Sobchak's choice of Putin as his assistant, although Putin had informed him that he was a career KGB officer. When questioned about this Sobchak liked to answer: 'Putin is no KGB operative but my former student.'[59] As for Putin, he entered second city politics, according to one of his friends, out of 'the romanticism of that period'.[60]

The first Russian presidential elections were held on 12 June 1991, when Yeltsin became the country's first president. The first mayoral elections were held on the same day, and Sobchak was elected. He took Putin with him as an adviser, and a fortnight later appointed him head of the newly formed city committee for foreign economic relations with responsibility for attracting foreign investment. Despite attempts to resign from the KGB earlier, when the letter apparently went astray, Putin finally resigned from the KGB with the rank of lieutenant colonel on 20 August 1991, the second day of the attempted coup launched against Gorbachev's reform communism by hard-line conservatives. Putin's choice was unequivocal: 'As soon as the coup began, I immediately decided which side I was on.'[61] Although he notes just how hard the choice was since he had spent the best part of his life with 'the organs'.[62] During the coup Putin managed to reach an agreement with the Leningrad KGB that they would maintain their neutrality, and as a reward Sobchak subsequently appointed him one of three mayoral deputies. With the dissolution of the old order Putin's membership of the CPSU simply lapsed.

Revealing strong administrative talents and loyalty, Putin soon became known as Sobchak's 'grey cardinal', and from March 1994 to 1996 he was first deputy mayor overseeing the law-enforcement agencies and the media. Sobchak refused to sign any documents unless previously signatured by Putin. At the time when Putin was active in the city, St Petersburg became known as the crime capital of Russia. Before going on to head the national privatisation programme in 1992, Anatoly Chubais in 1990–91 was also a deputy to the chair of the Leningrad city soviet, and it was at this time that he got to know Putin. Chubais's privatisation programme allowed a small number of people to become extraordinarily rich. Although engaged in trying to attract investment in the city, no serious evidence of corruption has been found against Putin, although numerous charges have been made against him for his work during this period.[63] In particular, the scandal associated with the issuing of licences (with very high commission charges) to firms as part of a programme in 1992 to sell natural resources abroad to buy food is often mentioned.[64] The planned redevelopment of the area around the Moscow station to build a business, shopping and hotel centre is also cited. As a bureaucrat Putin was known to take shortcuts to achieve a desired result in the fastest way possible, and gained the reputation of being a tough negotiator and a 'strong, effective and pragmatic leader'.[65]

Putin stood loyally by Sobchak as the latter revealed an inability to build consensus, and routinely ended up in conflict with the St Petersburg city council. Contrary to his boss, all the evidence suggests that Putin enjoyed a very good relationship with the city legislature. For the last year and a half of his term in office Sobchak was under investigation, among other things, for allegedly buying an apartment with city funds. Putin at this time was a member of the prime minister's, Victor Chernomyrdin, Our Home is Russia (*Nash Dom – Rossiya*, NDR) party, and in late 1995 led its unsuccessful parliamentary election campaign in the city, for which he was blamed by Chernomyrdin.[66] Despite this, in April 1996 (together with Alexei Kudrin) he was placed in charge of Sobchak's re-election campaign. The election had been brought forward from 16 June to 19 May to shorten the odds for the incumbent, but this did not help. Sobchak was successfully challenged by his other deputy, Vladimir Yakovlev, in a very dirty campaign, with numerous charges addressed towards Putin personally. Putin was no master of electoral 'black PR' (as the sophisticated 'election technologies' are called in Russia), and it was clear that he felt deeply uncomfortable in his role as electoral manager. In a programme at this time Putin called Yakovlev 'a Judas', an epithet that he did not retract later.[67] Sobchak was later forced into exile in the face of corruption charges. On 7 November 1997, Putin organised a covert operation that smuggled him by medical plane to Finland and then on to France. There is clearly a contradiction between Putin's loyalty to his mentor and what could be considered a cavalier approach to the law. Sobchak could only return once Putin was acting president, only to die of a heart attack soon after. Putin's genuine anguish at the funeral of his teacher and sponsor on 24 February 2000 was there for all to see.[68]

Third career: state official

Following Sobchak's defeat Putin made yet another decisive choice: he resigned from the city administration, refusing a job offer from Yakovlev. His willingness to enter a career limbo attests to his loyalty, a quality that would serve him well in the next few years. Putin was now at a loose end, and moved out to his dacha, which he had been building for some years, only to have it burn to the ground six weeks later in August 1996. Putin once again contemplated an academic career, entering the St Petersburg Mining Institute with the intention of completing his Candidate dissertation on the exciting topic of 'The strategic planning of the production of the mineral-raw materials resources of a region during the transition to a market economy'. Putin in Autumn 1996 successfully defended the thesis, analysing how most rationally to exploit Russia's natural resources, and became a Candidate of Economic Sciences (between an MPhil and a PhD).[69] 'Strategic planning' was to be one of the buzzwords of Putin's presidency later, when he set up an institute by that name to advise him, and his conclusion that the country would be best served by establishing vertically integrated companies encompassing whole industries that could compete in world markets was also applied during his presidency.

This period of difficulty in fact proved to be an opportunity for advancement along an entirely different line. Nikolai Yegorov, the head of the presidential administration, planned to give Putin a job in the Kremlin, but as part of the purge of hard-liners following the 1996 presidential elections, in which Yeltsin won a second term, Yegorov was dismissed and replaced by Chubais, who promptly suppressed the post. In the event, with the support of another St Petersburger, Kudrin (then head of the Kremlin's Main Control Directorate), Chubais offered Putin the job of head of public relations. Before he could take up this post, in June 1996 Pavel Borodin, in charge of the Kremlin's property service, brought Putin into the presidential administration, at first as head of the general affairs department and then as his deputy. Borodin was later to face corruption charges associated with the magnificent restoration by the Swiss company Mabatex of the Kremlin halls, notably the one named after St Andrew. Putin for eight months was responsible for managing the vast portfolio of properties abroad (in 1995 there were 715 sites with an income of $10 million per annum), and defending the Kremlin's ownership against other claimants, notably the Ministry of Foreign Affairs.

Thereafter Putin's career went into overdrive through a series of lucky breaks; although this 'luck' was determined as much by character as by chance. On 26 March 1997 he was appointed a deputy to the head of the presidential administration and head of the Main Control Administration

(GKU), probably on the recommendation of the former head, Kudrin, who became a deputy finance minister. The GKU was the successor of the old Party Control Committee, headed for years under Brezhnev by Arvid Pelshe, whose office in Old Square Putin now inherited. His job here was to conduct audits of state agencies, and to help him Putin set up a powerful analytical office, gathering a vast amount of information on misconduct by state officials in government offices and the regions.[70] In his inspection of the state arms agency, 'Rosvooreuzheniya', he found considerable evidence of malpractice, especially in delivery of weapons to Armenia, something that caused a major international scandal. It was at this time that Putin repeatedly stated that the Ministry of Defence could not reform itself.[71] Just over a year later, on 25 May 1998, he was appointed first deputy chief of staff responsible for relations with the regions. It was while working here that he got to know many regional leaders, and learnt that 'the *vertikal*, the vertical chain of government, had been destroyed and that it had to be restored'.[72] From 15 July he headed the presidential commission drafting treaties on the division of responsibilities between the centre and the regions.[73]

Putin's administrative skills and loyalty did not go unnoticed here as well, and on 25 July 1998 he was appointed head of the FSB, a job that he took up most reluctantly: 'I can't say that I was overjoyed. I didn't want to step into the same river twice.'[74] Once again Putin was subject to the endless vetting, the secrets and the closed life. Putin insisted that he returned to head the KGB 'not as a colonel [of the reserves] but as a civilian', coming from a responsible post in the presidential administration, and was thus a civilian leader of the security services.[75] A similar point could be made about Andropov, whose career prior to taking over the KGB had primarily been as a party worker. On 29 March of the following year he was given the additional post of secretary to the Security Council and thus became one of the most powerful men in Russia.

As head of the FSB he proved a tough administrator, launching the eighth reorganisation of the agency in as many years, abolishing two key departments (economic counter-intelligence and defence of strategic sites) and firing ten generals and about a third of its central staff (reducing it from six to four thousand). At the same time he reoriented the service away from its traditional obsession with domestic subversion towards the fight against corruption, organised crime, computer security and work in the regions. The staff reductions were done rather mechanically, letting go those approaching or beyond pensionable age, and thus the most experienced staff were the ones to leave. Putin also impressed his colleagues by declaring that coercive measures alone could not bring about the much desired order to society, and endorsed the development of civil society and pluralism.[76] At the same time, Putin's association with Sobchak won him no friends in the Lubyanka, since Sobchak had headed the parliamentary committee investigating the 'Tbilisi events' of April 1989 and the role of the military and security services in the deaths. To compensate, Putin brought some of his friends in the security services from St Petersburg: above all Victor Cherkesov with whom he had trained (head of the security services in the city and region, whose career in the KGB had begun by persecuting dissidents); and Sergei Ivanov, brought in from the foreign counter-intelligence service (SVR). When Putin moved on he appointed another of his close friends, Nikolai Patrushev (who had already taken his place earlier as head of GKU) to head the FSB. In general, it was clear that the FSB did not welcome Putin to its bosom as one of 'its own', and thus later commentary about Putin being little more than a tool of the security services is wide of the mark.[77]

In all of Putin's postings one detail remained consistent: the wages of his staff were always paid on time.[78] This may not seem such a big deal to Western readers, but in Russian circumstances during the chaotic move to capitalism it was some achievement.[79] By the time that he was appointed prime minister in August 1999 Putin had already gained wide experience: he had travelled extensively across the country as a member of his sports team; he had completed a full-time higher education degree from one of the country's best universities; he had worked for a decade as a security official; he had lived abroad for five years; he had become the second figure in the politics of Russia's second city; he had successfully defended what was effectively a doctoral dissertation; and as a senior member of the presidential administration in Moscow he was already familiar with the problems of the regions, the workings of the government, the presidential apparatus and the security services. He was certainly far from the 'nobody' that some suggested on his appointment to the premiership. He had seen life in many aspects, and had grappled with genuine problems of management and modernisation. The various layers of his personal and professional experience built on each other; it was not in Putin's character to reject the past to move to the future.[80]

Character

Putin was the first Russian leader since Lenin to speak foreign languages, having a good command of both German and English. Apart from his close links with Germany, something that he maintains even as president, Putin had also twice visited America, during his time as Sobchak's assistant, before taking on the leadership. The many times winner of the sambo championships of St Petersburg, a black belt in judo, and with a long record of effective work in the intelligence services, Putin is clearly a man of considerable self-discipline.[81] Even with a full-time job he was able to complete work on his Candidate dissertation. He also showed considerable intelligence and, something that can already be judged from his record in office, significant flexibility. This pragmatism, however, was always constrained and operated within a severe code of what he considered correct behaviour or appropriate politically. According to Mukhin, Putin's character is disposed towards the negotiated solution of conflicts, but that in crisis situations he is willing to take forceful measures. He has a systematic approach to analysing issues, logical while at the same time cautious, combined with an intellectual and non-emotional way of dealing with issues. Hence his phrase (used about those guilty of the bombings in 1999, see below) about 'soaking the bandits in the John' (*banditov i v sortire zamochim*) is not part of his typical vocabulary, and he apparently apologised several times for using such semi-criminal (*blatnoi*) language.[82]

The many biographies that have been published in Russia highlight a wealth of other personal details. For example, Bortsov notes that Putin's star sign is Libra (the scales), the only mechanical astrological representation and, we may add, a symbol that suggests balance and justice. Similarly, in the Chinese calendar Putin is a dragon, the most-favoured in Chinese cosmology and the only mythical creature in that particular bestiary.[83] Putin's character-istic rhetorical turn of phrase has been much analysed, typically answering a question with a question.[84] Talanov characterises Putin as an introvert, while at the same time being of the 'critic' type who tries to avoid allowing psycho-logical conflicts to reach an emotional peak, whereas the 'artist' type tries precisely to bring crises to an emotional climax.[85] Avramchenko, one of the multitude of authors who wrote detailed plans on how Putin could save Russia, characterises him as 'moderate and cautious', while at the same time warning that Putin's insistence on an exclusively evolutionary approach and ban on radical changes would prevent the country moving 'off the path of destruction onto the path of accelerated development'.[86]

Many note Putin's sense of humour. When visiting Martitime *krai* as prime minister in Autumn 1999, the governor Yevgeny Nazdratenko heaped lavish compliments on him, to which Putin replied: 'Yevgeny Ivanovich, you praised me so much that I began to think that I must have died.'[87] Putin's back-ground as part of the 'St Petersburg mafia' provided him later with a pool, although relatively small, of clients and also with an orientation to the world that is Western-oriented and responsive to the real needs of the country. It was this man who was now called upon to ensure stability and continuity in the post-Yeltsin era.[88]

The succession operation

For Schumpeter, the role of the people in a democracy 'is to produce a government', and it is in this light that he provides his classic definition: 'the democratic method is that institutional arrangement for arriving at political decisions in which individuals acquire the power to decide by means of a competitive struggle for the people's vote.'[89] The distorted nature of the competition for the people's vote in the 1999–2000 electoral cycle, however, has led many commentators to suggest that it was less than democratic. Above all, as Schumpeter went on to stress, the people not only vote to elect a government, they must also have the ability to evict it.[90] It is this absence of governmental rotation in the transition from Yeltsin to Putin that casts a shadow over the whole process. Nevertheless, the succession was by no means as easy as it may appear in hindsight,[91] and Putin's character and personal choices played a large part in ensuring its success.

Putin's premiership

The fifth premier in two years, and the third in turn from the security services, Vladimir Putin was soon transformed from adjunct bureaucrat into a relatively independent political figure. On appointing Putin as prime minister on 9 August 1999 Yeltsin had declared him his successor. Experience suggested that this was a precarious position. Already at various points Yeltsin had considered Sergei Shakhrai, Vladimir Shumeiko, Oleg Soskovets, Alexander Lebed, Boris Nemtsov, Sergei Kirienko, Nikolai Bordyuzha, Sergei Stepashin and Nikolai Aksyonenko as potential successors, and all had been found wanting and discarded. Yeltsin had been thinking about the succession since 1991, even when in the pink of health, but with greater urgency after his re-election in 1996 and multiple heart bypass operation that autumn. He set his administration one main task: 'the succession of power through the election of 2000'. They had four years to make sure that in 2000 the new president would be 'a person who would continue democratic reforms in the country, who would not turn back to the totalitarian system, and who would ensure Russia's movement forward, to a civilized community'.[92] The sacking on 23 March 1998 of his long-standing prime minister, Chernomyrdin, as someone in whose hands the country could not be entrusted, was part of the succession operation.[93] The procession of prime ministers that followed – Kirienko (March–August 1998), Primakov (September 1998–May 1999) and Stepashin (May–August 1999) – was in part determined by the logic of the succession. Bordyuzha had served 20 years in the KGB and in September 1998 he was appointed secretary of the Security Council, and four months later head of the presidential administration, an extraordinary concentration of power. Bordyuzha has been described as 'Putin No. 1', but he lacked leadership qualities and proved not up to the task.[94] The economist Alexander Voloshin replaced him as head of the presidential administration, and Putin as chair of the Security Council. The appointment of Stepashin had been quite explicitly a stopgap while preparing the way for Putin.[95]

It is characteristic of Putin to make decisive choices and stick to them, but now the Kremlin's choice was to determine his fate. Yeltsin had first noticed Putin in 1997 when he headed the GKU and then when he was first deputy to the presidential chief of staff, Valentin Yumashev, with responsibility for work with the regions. 'Putin's reports,' Yeltsin notes, 'were a model of clarity,' and he was impressed by the businesslike way that Putin dealt with matters: 'Putin tried to remove any sort of personal element from our contact. And precisely because of that, I wanted to talk to him more.'[96]

Yeltsin was also impressed by Putin's 'lightening reactions', responding calmly to Yeltsin's interjections. So when Yeltsin in the summer of 1998 was looking for a new director of the security services, his choice fell on Putin. Not only had he worked for many years in the security agencies, 'the more I knew Putin, the more convinced I was that he combined both an enormous dedication to democracy and market reforms and an unwavering patriotism'.[97] Yeltsin also appreciated Putin's sense of decency, as when he dismissed numerous officials at the FSB but always ensured that they had a 'soft landing', new jobs or generous pensions. Yeltsin notes that Putin

> did not allow himself to be manipulated in political games. Even I was amazed by his solid moral code ... for Putin, the single criterion was the morality of a given action or the decency of a given person. He would not do anything that conflicted with his understanding of honor. He was always ready to part with his high post if his sense of integrity would require it.'[98]

This was certainly the case when Putin gave up his job in the mayoral administration on Sobchak's defeat in 1996.

On 5 August 1999 Yeltsin summoned Putin and informed him of his decision to appoint him prime minister, and already then intimated that this was just a step on the way to 'the very highest post'. Putin was aware that this would mean harsh political struggles, especially in the forthcoming parliamentary elections. According to Yeltsin, Putin asserted that 'I don't like election campaigns ... I really don't. I don't know how to run them, and I don't like them.'[99] With the bitter experience of unsuccessfully running the NDR's parliamentary campaign in 1995 and Sobchak's 1996 re-election campaign, Putin's comments were hardly surprising, and this attitude was to endure into the March 2000 presidential elections. The conversation ended with Putin agreeing: 'I will work wherever you assign me', reportedly said with military terseness. In introducing Putin to the country on 9 August, Yeltsin spoke of Putin as a 'prime minister with a future',[100] and talked of him as someone 'who can consolidate society, based on the widest possible political spectrum, and ensure the continuation of reforms in Russia'.[101]

Most commentators regarded nomination as Yeltsin's successor as the kiss of death. As Gennady Seleznev, speaker of the State Duma (lower house of parliament) put it, 'If Yeltsin declares someone his successor, it means putting a cross on his political future. This has already happened many times.'[102] Putin himself considered the appointment temporary: 'I thought, "Well, I'll work for a year, and that's fine. If I can help save Russia from collapse, then I'll have something to be proud of." It was a stage in my life. And then I'll move onto the next thing.'[103] Putin's self control was evident at this time; his father had died on 2 August (his mother had died of cancer in 1998), with the funeral taking place three days later. On 16 August the Duma ratified Putin's appointment by 233 votes for, 84 against and with 17 abstentions.[104]

Putin was appointed as a Yeltsin loyalist, and it appeared at first that he would enjoy little more freedom than his predecessors under Yeltsin's overbearing leadership. Like all of Yeltsin's prime ministers, Putin was not given independence to form his own cabinet and instead had ministers foisted on him by the presidential administration. Above all, Aksyonenko, as a first deputy prime minister, openly pursued his own interests and those of the presidential 'family', the colloquial term for the combination of favoured oligarchs, insider politicians, political advisors, and some of Yeltsin's blood family members, above all his daughter Tatyana Dyachenko. On several occasions, as in the displacement of the head of the state's monopoly pipeline company Transneft, it appeared that Putin was ignored entirely. The influence of the most notorious 'oligarch' (a term popularised by Nemtsov in 1997) of them all, Boris Berezovsky, and his ally, Roman Abramovich (known as the treasurer to Yeltsin's family), remained strong. The energy minister Viktor Kalyuzhny and the interior minister Vladimir Rushailo were part of this group. We shall have much more to say later about the 'family'.

Putin, however, soon transcended the limitations of his post. On any scale, his metamorphosis was remarkable, and Putin soon emerged as the leading candidate in the presidential election. His support rose from 2 per cent in August, 15 per cent by the end of September, 25 per cent in late October and an astonishing 40 per cent in late November.[105] At least four factors help explain Putin's astonishing rise. The first is that the Kremlin put its entire weight behind him. His potential presidential rivals, above all Yury Luzhkov, the mayor of Moscow, and Primakov, who had been foreign minister (January 1996–September 1998) before becoming prime minister, were subjected to vitriolic attacks, above all in the various press and television outlets dominated by the Kremlin and its allies, notably by Berezovsky. The Primakov myth that he could become a wise elder statesman restoring the best of the Brezhnev years while ensuring economic and diplomatic success was systematically dismantled, and instead he was portrayed as a sick old man who symbolised the failures of the Soviet system. Although Putin undoubtedly enjoyed overt and behind the scenes official support, it was also during his premiership that the independent NTV station, founded by another of the dominant oligarchs, Vladimir Gusinsky, subjected Putin to an extraordinary barrage of personal attack. With the stakes so high, in late 1999 the pre-presidential campaign on all sides was vicious.

Second, the renewed war in Chechnya turned out at first to be genuinely popular, unlike the first conflict in 1994–96. By the terms of the Khasavyurt agreement of 31 August 1996 the republic gained effective independence. Russian troops were withdrawn and in February 1997, with Moscow's blessing, a former guerrilla leader, Aslan Maskhadov, was elected president. However, in the face of growing lawlessness Russia had since early 1999 been preparing for renewed conflict.[106] The turning point, according to Stepashin,[107] was the abduction on 5 March 1999 of Russia's deputy interior minister, Major-General Gennady Shpigun, who had been dragged off a plane by Chechen insurgents at Grozny airport (his body was found in June 2000). It was clear that Maskhadov was conclusively losing control of the situation in the republic. As head of the Security Council and of the FSB, Putin responded by meeting with Yeltsin on 19 May 1999 and drafting the tough decree 'On Additional Measures to Fight Terrorism in Russia's North Caucasus'.[108] The second war in the event was provoked by the infiltration by Chechen forces (some 1,500 insurgents led by the Chechen field commanders Shamil Basaev and Khattab) on 2 August 1999 into the Botlikh and Tsumadin districts in neighbouring Dagestan, and a few weeks later (5 September) a second invasion by a larger force into the Novolaksk district to the north of the first incursion. The bombing of apartment blocks in Buinaksk (Dagestan) (4 September, 62 dead), Moscow, Guryanov Street (9 September, 100 dead); Moscow, Kashirskoe Highway (13 September, 124 dead) and Volgodonsk (15 September, 19 dead) created a climate of fear and, to a degree, retribution against Chechens, although the involvement of Chechens in these atrocities remains a matter of controversy.[109] The military intervention in Chechnya began on 30 September and was initially envisaged as a limited operation, but after the relatively easy occupation of the northern lowlands spread to the heartlands of Chechnya (Ichkeria) when Russian troops crossed the Terek river in late October.

Two years before the 11 September 2001 destruction of the World Trade Center in New York, the war was presented as a 'war against terrorism', laying the foundations for the later post-September alliance of Russia and the West. Putin later argued that he was willing to lay his career on the line at this time, but had decided 'that my mission, my historical mission – and this will sound lofty but it's true – consisted of resolving the situation in the Northern Caucasus'.[110] Putin's image as an 'iron chancellor' was created and sustained by his uncompromising approach to the Chechen problem. His use of street language in a press conference on 8 September, where as mentioned earlier he used the underworld jargon of 'soaking the bandits in the John', appeared at first as if it would be a public relations disaster, but in the event it only reinforced Putin's image as a man of the people. Far more importantly, at that press conference Putin insisted: 'Russia is defending itself. We have been attacked. And therefore we must throw off all our syndromes, including the guilt syndrome.'[111] Yeltsin gave Putin a free hand: 'I wanted people to start getting used to Putin and to perceive him as the head of state.'[112] Yeltsin explains Putin's surge in popularity in this way: 'Putin got rid of Russia's fear. And Russia repaid him with profound gratitude.'[113]

The third factor is that, unlike his predecessors, Putin soon enjoyed unprecedented power over the policy process, and could take credit for the raft of good economic news that saw the economy grow, living standards rise and more wages paid on time. Although formally liable to dismissal by Yeltsin at any time, Putin in the last months of 1999 acted with extraordinary confidence and independence. He was even allowed oversight over the power ministries, a presidential prerogative, something that no prime minister had

ever been allowed before.[114] Putin was able to transform the prime ministerial office into a quasi-presidential post, eclipsing Yeltsin personally. In the
past whenever any politician threatened to outshine him, Yeltsin sought to
cut his potential rival down to size. On this occasion the Kremlin clearly col-
luded and allowed Putin to dominate the political scene. With Yeltsin's
declining health and vigour, the trend with the last few prime ministers had
been in this direction anyway. All had seen their popularity ratings soar on
appointment, and the office of prime minister (as in other semi-presidential
systems such as France) is the natural springboard for the presidency.

Fourth, Putin appeared able to restore Russia's national dignity, adopting
neither an obsequiously subservient nor an impotently assertive attitude
towards the West but one based on a measured understanding of Russia's
real needs and capacity. As a newspaper article put it, 'Putin must restore
what Yeltsin destroyed: pride to feel part of a great power. Russians want
respect, not sympathy.'[115] It soon became clear to both domestic and foreign
observers that Putin represented a new breed of Russian politician, honest
and intelligent and untainted by any demonstrable corruption. Putin clearly
cared about Russia more than his personal interests. As Kovalev noted, he
represented 'an alternative both to a Communist restoration and the incompetence of "the democrats"'.[116] He quickly came to epitomise Russia, its sufferings and its aspirations and thus he was to become 'the president of
hope'.

The 19 December 1999 parliamentary elections and the succession

On the eve of the parliamentary elections Nikolai Petrov wrote:

> The political era associated with the name of B. Yeltsin is entering
> history. The regime proved unable to reproduce itself, and the change of
> leader will entail the change of the entire political system, based on the
> personal power of that leader.'[117]

There are at least three elements involved here: regime (that is, the political
order created by Yeltsin), systemic reproduction and leadership succession. In
the event, the system was able to reproduce itself, at least politically, by ensuring that the change of leader did not entail a change of regime.

Beneath the endless political crises, sackings, resignations and dramatic
démarches in Russian politics from 1995, when Yeltsin's health had begun
sharply to deteriorate, there lay a more profound struggle for the succession.
By the time of his visit to Uzbekistan in October 1998 it was clear that the
Yeltsin era was over, being held up only with president Islam Karimov's
support. Klyamkin and Shevtsova note that the 1999 election represented 'an
unprecedented campaign' in which the Duma elections became part of a
struggle for far greater stakes.[118] They note that in most transition countries
two electoral cycles are usually considered sufficient to judge whether demo-

cracy is consolidated, whereas in Russia this was the third, and if anything it only raised yet more questions about the nature of the emerging democratic order.[119] Throughout the 1990s elections had been conducted as plebiscites on the nature of the system rather than as a choice between governments; and clearly, to have to choose between regimes effectively deprives people of the choice between governments. The threat from the Communist Party of the Russian Federation (CPRF) was played up for all it was worth. Too often, notably in the 1996 presidential election, people voted through gritted teeth for Yeltsin as the 'lesser evil'. Earlier that year Yeltsin's bodyguard and influential advisor, Alexander Korzhakov, had asked why risk everything for the sake of democracy, and had advocated cancelling the presidential elections.

In the 1999–2000 electoral cycle there were overtones of this, especially since a credible alternative had emerged. In August 1999 an alliance had been forged between Luzhkov's Fatherland (*Otechestvo*) movement, established in December 1998 allegedly to campaign against the influence of the oligarchs, and the All Russia (*Vsya Rossiya*) bloc, set up in April 1999 by a number of powerful regional leaders including president Mintimir Shaimiev of Tatarstan and Putin's old sparring partner, Vladimir Yakovlev, the governor of St Petersburg. At the head of the new Fatherland – All Russia (OVR) bloc stood Primakov, who made no secret of his presidential ambitions. Stepashin's dismissal in early August had in part been provoked by his failure to prevent this challenge to the Kremlin emerging. In response, in September 1999 Berezovsky masterminded the creation of the Unity (*Edinstvo*) electoral bloc (also known as *Medved*, Bear), drawing also initially on regional leaders. A powerful bandwagon was set in motion on to which more and more regional and other leaders jumped, fearing for their positions if they ended up on the losing side after the electoral battles were over. Putin himself declared on 24 November that he would support Unity 'as a private citizen and friend of Sergei Shoigu',[120] the charismatic Minister for Emergency Situations who had been placed at the head of the new party. Its lack of genuine regional depth was reflected in the low number of single-member constituencies that it contested (13 per cent), winning only nine. Unity was unlike the earlier 'parties of power', namely Russia's Choice in the early 1990s, led by Yegor Gaidar (the architect of the first phase of Yeltsin's reforms), and then Our Home is Russia (NDR), because it had been established not as a governing party but as an instrument of electoral competition. Paradoxically, it went on to form the basis of a loyal bloc of deputies in the third Duma (2000–03), and thus did effectively become the governing party.

Putin in the December 1999 Duma elections sought to present himself as a symbol of confidence and stability, promising to maintain Russia's system of power and property while radically renovating the state system and developing political and legal reform. Putin committed himself to not amending the existing constitution, although he argued that some institutional innovation could take place without necessarily changing the constitution itself. How this would be converted into policy, however, remained to be seen. The election campaign, as noted, was marked by the brutal denigration of the Kremlin's opponents, above all Luzhkov and Primakov. The media was used in ways that suggest that the election, while relatively free, was not altogether fair. Together with the emergence of the Unity bloc, the election was signific- ant for the emergence of a new liberal bloc, the Union of Rightist Forces (*Soyuz pravykh sil*, SPS), bringing together nine small liberal parties and associations led collectively by Nemtsov, Gaidar, Irina Khakamada and the former prime minister Kirienko. Putin had not explicitly endorsed Unity, but stated that 'as a private citizen' he would be voting for it. The SPS had also attached itself to Putin's coat-tails, supporting the war in Chechnya, and the Kremlin had reciprocated by indicating support for them. The result (see Table 1.1) suggested a vote of confidence in Putin and provided a launch pad for the presidential campaign.[121] Although the communists emerged with a plurality of seats, the pro-Putin government bloc led by Unity enjoyed a comfortable majority. As Igor Shabdurasulov, who had managed Unity's election campaign on behalf of the Kremlin put it, 'The new State Duma will be of a principally different character. A peaceful revolution has taken place in Russia.'[122]

Table 1.1 State Duma election, 19 December 1999

Turnout
- Out of some 108 million Russian electors, over sixty million voted, a turnout rate of 61.7 per cent, comfortably exceeding the minimum 25 per cent requirement.
- An additional 1.2 per cent of the electorate cast invalid votes.

Result

Election association or bloc	Party List (PL) vote (%)	PL seats	Single Member Districts (SMD)	Total
Communist Party of the Russian Federation (CPRF)	24.3	67	47	114 (25.9%)
Unity (*Edinstvo*) or Bear (*Medved*)	23.3	64	9	73 (16.6%)
Fatherland (*Otechestvo*)/ All Russia (OVR)	13.3	37	29	66 (15.0%)
Union of Right Forces (SPS)	8.5	24	5	29 (6.6%)
Zhirinovsky Bloc (LDPR)	6.0	17	0	17 (3.9%)
Yabloko	5.9	16	4	22 (4.5%)
Others and 'against all' (3.3%)	18.7	–	–	26 (24%)
Independents			105	105 (23.8%)
TOTAL	100	225	199	450

Sources: *Vestnik Tsentral'noi izbiratel'noi komissii Rossiiskoi Federatsii*, No. 1 (91), 2000, p. 231; *Nezav- isimaya gazeta*, 30 December 1999, p. 1; The results can also be found at the Central Electoral Commission's website: http://www.fci.ru/.

Yeltsin's resignation and the succession

The success of the hastily-assembled pro-Kremlin electoral association Unity opened the way for the unexpected *dénouement* of the succession operation – Yeltsin's resignation on 31 December 1999. The process was carefully planned since, as Yeltsin admitted, 'there was no precedent for a voluntary resignation by Russia's head of state', and he clearly enjoyed taking everyone (including his closest associates) by surprise.[123] He had first intimated his plan to Putin two weeks earlier, on 14 December at his Gorki-9 residence. On being told that Yeltsin planned to make him acting president, Putin's immediate reaction was to say, 'I'm not ready for that decision, Boris Niko-layevich.' Putin's hesitation, according to Yeltsin, was not a sign of weakness but 'the doubts of a strong person'.[124] After Yeltsin had insisted that 'The new century must begin with a new political era, the era of Putin', the latter had finally agreed.[125] They met again, this time in the Kremlin, on 29 December to arrange the details of the transfer of power, including the passing over of the nuclear suitcase. Yeltsin noted that Putin appeared 'a different man. I suppose he seemed more decisive', and Yeltsin notes how pleased he was with the way that the conversation went:

> I really liked Putin. I liked how he reacted, how he corrected several points in the plan – everything was clear and precise ... Strictly by the law, accurately, and dryly, we were implementing the article of the Russian constitution concerning the transfer of power.[126]

Putin would be acting president until pre-term elections were held within the mandated three months.

In his speech on 31 December, first broadcast at noon Moscow time and repeated hourly thereafter, Yeltsin spoke of his desire to have established the precedent of the 'civilised voluntary transfer of power' after the presidential elections set for June 2000, but 'Nevertheless, I have taken another decision. I am resigning.' There was now no danger of Russia returning to the past, and thus, Yeltsin argued, 'I have achieved the main task of my life' and he did not want to impede the smooth transition to a new generation of politicians. There was 'No reason to hang on to power when the country had a strong person worthy of becoming president'. He also asked for forgiveness: 'Not all our dreams came to fulfilment ... we thought we could jump from the grey, stagnatory totalitarian past to a light, rich and civilised future in one leap. I believed that myself ... But it took more than one jump.' He stressed that he was not resigning for health reasons. After the speech the nuclear suitcase was passed to Putin and, as a last gesture on leaving the Kremlin, he gave Putin the pen with which he had signed so many decrees and laws and said, 'Take care of Russia.'[127]

Yeltsin's resignation broke the Soviet tradition of leaving office feet first, but it still remains a mystery. On the surface, the version presented by Yeltsin does make sense. The Duma elections had created a solid pro-government bloc in parliament and strengthened the position of the Kremlin's designated successor, Putin, while weakening all main competitors. Yeltsin had achieved his goal of creating a political conjuncture that allowed him to leave the political scene without fear for himself or for his political achievements. It was also clear that Yeltsin had been rapidly losing his physical powers, and thus his explicit statement that he was not resigning on health grounds reflected only his pride. There remain suggestions, however, that Yeltsin's resignation was not entirely his personal choice. Was he pushed by powerful figures in the Kremlin, seeking to capitalise on Putin's popularity and alarmed by Yeltsin's physical and mental deterioration? Equally alarming was the continuation of the investigation into various corruption charges swirling around the Yeltsin family, above all those associated with the Mabatex construction company that had spent some half a billion dollars on the refurbishment of the Kremlin halls. Borodin, in charge of the Kremlin property management department, allegedly siphoned some of the money into his pockets and that of Yeltsin's blood family. Did the 'men in grey suits' suggest to Yeltsin that it would be in the best interests of his family and himself to resign and accept the generous terms of the settlement or face a very uncertain future? Putin's first move, indeed, as acting president on 31 December was to sign a decree granting Yeltsin and future Russian presidents immunity from criminal prosecution, arrest, search or interrogation. The former president was entitled to 75 per cent of his monthly salary, state protection for himself and his family, and access to VIP lounges in Russia's airports, railway stations, ports and airports.[128]

While the interests of the country may have been served by Yeltsin's premature exit, democracy was not best served by the timing. As Yeltsin himself admitted in his resignation speech, his premature exit meant that Russia would not see one democratically elected leader transfer power to another in direct accordance with the stipulations laid down in the constitution. Instead, there was an attempt to pre-empt the choice of the voters by transferring power to a regime nominee for whom the most benign political environment had been established. Fearing that Putin's popularity would begin to wane if the elections were held at the stipulated time in June, they were moved forward to March. For Alexander Zinoviev, the whole business was little more than a 'political coup', insisting that 'there was no reason for Yeltsin to leave his presidential post just a few months before official elections'.[129] In a sad reminder of the way that life imitates art, the words of the popular anecdote come to mind: question, 'What is democracy in Russia?'; answer, 'Yeltsin's right to nominate his successor.' Even this is perhaps not the worst outcome. As the journalist Yulia Latynina put it:

> The system of succession that will guarantee the Kremlin's victory is a
> very positive development. For, in circumstances where the authorities
> and their opposition are equally corrupt, a corrupt regime based on suc-

cession is preferable to a revolutionary corrupt regime, whose ascension to the throne is accompanied by the hollow grunting of pigs rushing to the trough – and who, amid the cries of 'bribe-takers to jail', make the same pie all over again.[130]

According to Sergei Kovalev, the human rights campaigner and liberal deputy, the Kremlin simply selected Putin to become Russia's leader and then manipulated the political process to ensure that the voters formally elected him:

> Putin is the creation of a closed and non-transparent political system. The procedure of the elections simply rubber-stamped a decision that had already been taken by behind-the-scenes plotters. That is all.[131]

The war in Chechnya was used to rally society around the designated heir, although this was a high risk strategy since there was the obvious danger that this could rebound against the Kremlin 'selectorate' itself. The first Chechen war had turned out to be deeply unpopular, and there was great danger for Putin in yoking his political fortunes to the renewal of war, however great the provocation.[132] In fact, Putin's victory represented far more than the manipulations of the Kremlin or the temporary advantage accruing from the pursuit of what was perceived to be a tragically necessary war. For good or ill, it reflected the nature and desires of the Russian people:[133] in looking at Putin, they saw themselves.

The 26 March 2000 presidential election

The physical contrast between Putin and Yeltsin could hardly be stronger: one in the prime of life, physically in top shape, logical and calculating; while the other had a towering presence but was in physical decline, more spontaneous and intuitive. The choice had been made for a change of generations in a context in which all strong characters who could overshadow Yeltsin personally had been marginalised. This meant that by the time that the succession became an urgent issue, there were few politicians of significant stature who were credible candidates for the presidency. The question, moreover, is not just one of personalities but also concerns the nature of the system. Although Yeltsin throughout his leadership remained remarkably consistent in his broad strategic goals, the day-to-day management of affairs was erratic and shaped by a Byzantine struggle between court politicians. These two factors – the lack of credible alternatives within the camp of the reformers and the tactical irresponsibility of the Yeltsinite elite – facilitated Putin's path to power. From the first days of his appointment as prime minister it was clear that a leader had emerged who was ready, if not willing, to take responsibility for the fate of the country. Putin was far more than 'A political myth created by specialists in PR'.[134] Medvedev quotes Georgy Plekhanov's well-known thesis about the role of personality in history: when social needs and national interests cannot be met without the emergence of a hero, someone who sees further than others and acts as the crystallisation of the needs of the epoch, then such a hero usually appears.[135] In Putin's case, the need was 'to put an end to the time of troubles (*smuty*) and the transitional period, that had already lasted ten years'.[136]

While in 1996 the contest polarised around Yeltsin and his veteran opponent Gennady Zyuganov, the head of the main opposition party, the CPRF, and represented a plebiscite on the continuation of reforms, by the time of the 2000 presidential elections such a primitive (even though politically highly effective) bipolarity was a thing of the past. The law on presidential elections, signed by Yeltsin before he resigned, stipulated that candidates had to collect 500,000 signatures (one million in normal circumstances), a requirement that thinned the field somewhat. Candidates also had to provide detailed financial information about themselves, their spouses and children. Eleven candidates cleared the hurdles to enter the race, but if none won more than 50 per cent of the vote in the first round then a second run-off election between the two top candidates would be held three weeks later. Given Putin's strong support right across the political spectrum, it was clear that high turnout would benefit him. The worst scenario as far as he was concerned was that complacency over the certainty of victory would keep voters at home for turnout to fall below 50 per cent (in which case the election would have been declared invalid and a rerun held four months later). The rather passionless campaign threatened precisely this outcome.

Putin's campaign was managed by the deputy head of the presidential administration (on leave), Dmitry Medvedev, who had been Putin's assistant throughout the Sobchak years. Other members of the presidential staff also helped: Alexander Abramov took responsibility for relations with the regions; Vladislav Surkov dealt with relations with parliament; and amongst the many from Yeltsin's old team was Igor Shabdurasulov. Numerous political consulting firms were hired, notably Gleb Pavlovsky's Foundation for Effective Politics.

A number of prominent politicians pulled out of the race even before it had begun. Notable in this respect was Primakov, the veteran Soviet-era politician who as prime minister had reinvented himself as a politician free from the fog of corruption swirling round the presidential administration, and thus had emerged as a popular alternative. Equally Luzhkov, the charismatic mayor of Moscow, decided that it would not be wise to challenge the power of the Kremlin. This left a rather diminished field. No Russian election would be complete without Vladimir Zhirinovsky, the head of the misnamed Liberal Democratic Party of Russia, and although initially disqualified by the Central Electoral Commission (CEC) he was later reinstated by the Supreme Court. Putin's main rival, however, was Zyuganov, although it was clear that some of the communist vote was drifting to Putin. Even the candidate Aman Tuleev, governor of Kemerovo region, who had stood down in the 1996 election in favour of Zyuganov, stated that in these elections he would throw his support behind Putin in the second round as a man of 'higher qualities' than Zyuganov, particularly in areas 'as professionalism, statehood, power and personality'.[137] Another serious candidate was Grigory Yavlinsky at the head of the liberal party Yabloko. This group had crossed the five per cent representation threshold in the December 1999 parliamentary elections but with a decreased vote, and now Yavlinsky's image of permanent opposition and increasingly mystical abstraction did him little good in the campaign.

Most of the other contenders were 'vanity' candidates in one way or another. The former Prosecutor-General Yury Skuratov, who had been dismissed by Yeltsin (although only after three refusals by the upper house of parliament, the Federation Council) for pursuing corruption investigations with perhaps too much vigour in 1999, sought to draw attention to the injustice of the case against him and to corruption. The leftist-nationalist film director Stanislav Govorukhin sought to rally the people to the idea of a great Russia. Samara governor Konstantin Titov represented the liberal part of the Russian political spectrum. Despite endless talk the previous year that the regions were storming the Kremlin through various electoral blocs, Titov ended up the only serious regional leader to withstand the fires of the parliamentary election with his reputation intact. He remained, however tenuously, the only real candidate for the role of leader of the regions.[138] He was, however, unable even to gain the undivided support of his own party, with a number of groups within the SPS alliance declaring themselves in favour of Putin.[139] Other candidates were the Chechen businessman Umar Dzhabrailov (the part owner of the Slavyanskaya Hotel implicated in the controversy surrounding the murder of the American businessman Paul Tatum, and later manager of the giant Rossiya hotel), Alexei Podberezkin at the head of the Spiritual Heritage organisation and former Zyuganov guru, and Ella Pamfilova, former minister for social affairs and head of the Movement for Civil Dignity. The former deputy head of the presidential administration, Yevgeny Savostyanov, pulled out at the last minute.

The election, however, was perhaps most notable for who did not stand. We have noted that Primakov, who had appeared unstoppable a mere six months earlier, had seen his fortunes sink rapidly, while Luzhkov by the summer of 1999 had intimated that he would step out of the presidential contest. Alexander Lebed, once the great hope of authoritarian reformers, had decamped to Krasnoyarsk *krai* where, as governor from 1998, he faced a host of problems that ruled him out as a serious presidential contender. His death in a helicopter crash on 28 April 2002 means that we shall never know whether he would have been able to become a General Charles De Gaulle, a marginalized leader returning in triumph to the centre of political power. A possible future challenger to Putin had gone. As the Putin bandwagon gathered speed Luzhkov provided one of the most important endorsements for the new leader. On 15 March 2000 Luzhkov gave Fatherland's official blessing to Putin's campaign. Although Fatherland set a number of conditions, above all the preservation of democratic freedoms, an end to the political and economic ascendancy of the oligarchs, strengthening the state, and commitment to improving conditions in the social sphere, science and culture, these were not 'conditions' in any real sense since the endorsement preceded agreement on their acceptance and were thus designed to save face. Thus one of the most important potential competitors for the presidency succumbed to the Putin effect.

The most difficult thing for most candidates was that Putin's own programme, in so far as he had one, encompassed almost every conceivable shade of opinion and thus allowed no space for a coherent alternative. As Luzhkov put it following the congress of Unity in late February, Putin's address on that occasion contained 'quotes, nearly intact', from Fatherland's documents.[140] Putin, moreover, enjoyed the advantages of incumbency of not only one post but two, as acting president and prime minister, and thus he was far from an ordinary candidate. These 'asymmetries' in the campaign were much remarked upon and led to fears that Putin harboured dictatorial ambitions. In addition, Putin appeared reluctant to provide details about his programme. Meeting with students on 8 February 2000 he stated that he would not hurry to publicise his election platform, lest it 'comes under attack'. He noted that 'As soon as you make it public, they will start gnawing at it and tearing it to pieces.'[141] This was certainly an interesting approach to campaigning in a democratic election.

His *Open Letter by Vladimir Putin to the Russian Voters*, published on 25 February 2000, was the closest Putin came to an election manifesto. He noted:

> Our first and most important problem is the weakening of will. The loss of state will and persistence in completing things that have been started. Vacillation, dithering, the habit of putting off the hardest tasks for later.[142]

The letter contained important general principles about the need to improve the economy and people's living conditions, but was short on specific policies. The Centre for Strategic Development, the think tank headed by Putin's colleague from St Petersburg, German Gref, that Putin had asked to produce a long-term programme for Russian development, had not been able to produce a detailed programme before the election. Above all, with such a towering pre-eminence enjoyed by Putin and the weakness of all the other candidates, there was a danger of over-confidence and deafness to the views of others. The problem is not unique to Russia but can take particularly morbid forms here since the checks and balances against the abuse of power are so weak.

One factor in Putin's victory should be stressed. Putin proved a masterful image maker. In Chapter 2 we will discuss his *Millennium Manifesto*, a document published in the last days of 1999 outlining his views on the Soviet past and his hopes for the Russian future. This was joined in early 2000 by the publication in book form of a series of interviews conducted over several days by Nataliya Gevorkyan and colleagues in one of Putin's state dachas.[143] They showed Putin's human side and offered an appealing updating of the log cabin to White House motif, although in this case it was from communal apartment to the Kremlin. The dynamic sense of rapid upward social mobility achieved through one's own efforts, aided admittedly by a great deal of luck and, latterly, official sponsorship, struck a chord in Russia's long-suffering population. The book showed Putin as a man surrounded by a loving family, with his wife Lyudmila and two daughters, and all the trials and tribulations attending the collapse of the Soviet empire when serving as a KGB officer in the GDR. Clearly, passages had been deleted or amended by the Kremlin minders, and Putin's image was carefully moulded. Putin was one of the new breed of politicians of that time, such as Bill Clinton in America and Tony Blair in Britain, for whom news management often acted as the substitute for policy, and where policy development remains shrouded in a dense fog of spin and show. Popularity for these 'post-modern' politicians is nurtured and tended like a delicate plant, with focus groups, private polling and the manipulation of information.

While the overall result (see Table 1.2) may have been a foregone conclusion there were at least three interesting subordinate outcomes. The first was

Table 1.2 Presidential election, 26 March 2000

Turnout
- Registered voters: 109,372,046
- Turnout: 75,181,071 (68.74 per cent)
- Total valid ballots: 75,070,776

Result Candidate	*Percentage*	*Number of votes*
1 Vladimir Putin	52.94	39,740,434
2 Gennady Zyuganov	29.21	21,928,471
3 Grigory Yavlinsky	5.80	4,351,452
4 Aman Tuleev	2.95	2,217,361
5 Vladimir Zhirinovsky	2.70	2,026,513
6 Konstantin Titov	1.47	1,107,269
7 Ella Pamfilova	1.01	758,966
8 Stanislav Govorukhin	0.44	328,723
9 Yury Skuratov	0.42	319,263
10 Alexei Podberezkin	0.13	98,175
11 Umar Dzhabrailov	0.10	78,498
Against all candidates	1.88	1,414,648

Sources: *Vestnik Tsentral'noi izbiratel'noi kommissii Rossiiskoi Federatsii*, No. 13 (103), 2000, pp. 63–5; *Rossiiskaya gazeta*, 7 April 2000, p. 3; The full results are in *Vestnik Tsentral'noi izbiratel'noi kommissii Rossiiskoi Federatsii*, No. 16 (106), 2000.

Note: The percentages are calculated from the total vote.

the size of Putin's majority, and above all whether he would be able to win on the first round. Most polls suggested that this would be possible, and in the event was achieved, although with only a small margin above 50 per cent. An outright win endowed Putin's presidency with the sort of legitimacy that Yeltsin had enjoyed following his first-round victory in June 1991, but the small margin somewhat tempered the triumph. The second aspect was the degree to which this was a 'clean' election. There have been allegations that in some regions, for example Saratov, votes were transferred from other candidates to Putin, while in Dagestan over half a million votes may have been added to Putin's total, while in many places the bank of 'against all' votes may have been raided to Putin's advantage.[144]

The third interesting question about the outcome was whether the main challengers, Zyuganov and Yavlinsky, would be able to hold on to their electorates and leadership. Zyuganov's continued claim to leadership of the left would have been threatened by a humiliating defeat. Only two-thirds of the electorate that had voted for the CPRF in December 1999 cast their votes for Zyuganov in March, while a fifth voted for Putin. Already Tuleev during the campaign, as we have seen, was openly contemptuous of Zyuganov's leadership. In the event, Zyuganov's strong showing (29.2 per cent), improving on his party's performance (24.3 per cent) in the December 1999 Duma elections, meant that he was able to fight off all challengers for the leadership of the left. However, his vote did not match the 32 per cent he received in the first round of the 1996 elections, let alone the 40 per cent he won in the run off, and thus suggested a secular decline in the communist vote that condemned him forever to second place. In particular, he lost ground in traditional communist strongholds. In the second round in 1996 Zyuganov came first in 32 of Russia's 89 regions, whereas in 2000 Putin came first in all but five regions. In Kemerovo Tuleev won handsomely, leaving Zyuganov victor in only four (the republics of Adygeia, Chechnya and Altai, and Bryansk *oblast*). As for Yavlinsky, his leadership of the liberals had been challenged by Titov, calling on him to withdraw from the race, while Stepashin, although a member of Yabloko, openly declared his support for Putin. Despite fighting his best electoral campaign by far, Yavlinsky emerged with a reduced vote in comparison with 1996 (5.8 per cent as opposed to 7.3 per cent) and found his position as the putative leader of the democratic camp much weakened. Coming third in his home region of Samara, trailing behind Putin and Zyuganov with only 20 per cent of the regional vote, Titov resigned as governor soon after the election, but was then 'persuaded' by a mass upsurge of popular support to stand again in rescheduled gubernatorial elections.

It is clear that Putin did have a solid political base. Surveys during the Duma election revealed that the majority of SPS voters supported Putin for president; 'supporters of the right saw Putin as their natural ally', and thus the SPS leadership's alliance with Putin was more than a political calculation but reflected the aspirations of SPS voters themselves.[145] The SPS leaders, moreover (and in particular Chubais), saw in Putin a powerful ally who could strengthen their position. The SPS strategy of support for Putin, including his controversial policy in Chechnya, reflected the dilemma of the liberals throughout the era of post-communism in Russia: lacking a hegemonic social and electoral base of their own, they sought to use the presidency as an instrument to pursue their goals. Although not as prominent as in 1996, Chubais provided critical support for Putin's presidential bid.

Although Putin emerged in the first round with the level of support that Yeltsin had achieved in the second round in 1996 (53.8 per cent) they were drawing on somewhat different constituencies. Putin was able to win greater support from rural areas that had formerly been the bedrock of the communist vote, but he fared worse in the city of Moscow, winning only 46 per cent of the vote compared to Yeltsin's first round 61 per cent and second round 74 per cent in 1996.[146] In his hometown of St Petersburg, however, Putin romped to victory with 62.4 per cent of the vote. While the dichotomy between a 'red belt' (a swathe of regions in central and south Russia that had traditionally voted for the communists) and the rest had been maintained in 1996, by 2000 it had eroded to the extent that Putin could win in the traditional heartland red belt region of Krasnodar *krai*. If in the 1996 election 60 per cent of the military vote in the first round went to Alexander Lebed, and in the second round half went to Zyuganov, in 2000 about 70 per cent went to Putin.[147] He also gained the support of Russian citizens with the right to vote abroad. In the Ukraine there were 36,000 registered Russian voters, a large proportion of them in the Crimea. Of the 20,631 people voting here, 17,820 (86.3 per cent) voted for Putin and only 1,321 (6.3 per cent) for Zyuganov, and in districts where only Black Sea Fleet personnel were registered, Putin's vote was slightly higher at 88.8 per cent, compared to only 4.9 per cent for Zyuganov.[148] The relative uniformity of Putin's support across Russia reflected the success of his strategy of appealing to all classes, social forces and ends of the political spectrum. It is clear that Putin's constituency was a broad one.

Surprisingly enough, in the context of the Chechen war, is the extent to which Putin drew support from the liberal wing of the electorate: the young, educated and economically successful.[149] Putin's electoral and political base was broad, and certainly did not depend on the fate of the war in Chechnya alone. While the war was certainly used by Putin and his campaign managers to demonstrate his qualities as a resolute and committed leader, Putin garnered far more support than that generated by the war alone. As Henry E. Hale put it, 'Russians clearly want a strong leader, capable of bringing order to their tragically unpredictable lives.'[150] Russians certainly wanted a strong and not corrupt leader, but they also wanted a democratic one.[151] At least some of Putin's popularity was derived from the post that he occupied rather than from the policies that he pursued. It also built on Yeltsin's support base, a remarkably consistent and stable electorate committed to Yeltsin's programme of market reform and liberal internationalism, if perhaps committed with rather less enthusiasm to Yeltsin personally. Yeltsin's winning coalition remained remarkably consistent over the years. In the June 1991 presidential election he received 45.5 million votes, in the April 1993 referendum his policies were endorsed by 36.5 million people, and in the second round of the 1996 presidential elections he received 40.2 million votes. As Brudny puts it,

> a solid and stable majority of Russian voters rejected communist and virulent nationalist appeals to end the economic and political reforms enacted during Yeltsin's era despite economic dislocation, an increase in crime, and the blatant corruption which accompanied them.[152]

Putin had refused to publish a detailed programme during the campaign, and held himself above the fray, acting as if he was not a candidate himself. In his press conference on election night (the first of the entire campaign) Putin declared that he considered campaigning an 'absolutely dishonest business', because 'you always have to promise more than your rivals, in order to appear more successful. And I couldn't imagine myself promising something, knowing that the promises could not be kept'. He insisted that he had kept himself aloof because 'it freed me from the necessity of misleading enormous masses of people', and thus he took pride in not reducing his candidacy to the level of that of his opponents.[153] Thus the whole electoral process was dismissed as somehow not worthy of an honest leader. Putin did, however, praise the opposition politicians who, in his opinion, took a constructive position regarding his policy in Chechnya, or who supported him in the elections. He singled out in particular Zyuganov, Luzhkov and Primakov – the three people who had been credible competitors for the post of president. This was quintessential Putin, and reflects the code of honour in judo where the hand of friendship is extended to the defeated rival.

Others were rather less impressed. The Yabloko deputy, Sergei Mitrokhin, took a sceptical approach to the elections: 'One way or another, we will not be having elections in March but a plebiscite on an already designated successor.'[154] Yeltsin as we have seen had already suggested as much in his resignation speech. The reasons for Putin's victory, however, derived not simply from manipulation and the creation of the most benign environment possible for anointment through the ballot box. He represented the widespread yearning for stability in a society traumatised by disintegration and decline. In that context, Putin's 'anti-political' approach to the election, in which he waged a 'non-campaign', made sense.[155] A greater danger, however, lurked behind this approach, and that was the repudiation of politics itself as the mode of adjudication between interests and concerns in society. An anti-political approach can easily slip into populism, where the single will of society is represented by the charismatic leader without the necessity of mediating political institutions. It also allows administrative rationality to subvert the clash of views and political pluralism. This was certainly dangerous in conditions where Russia's 1993 constitution rendered the president virtually an 'elected tsar'.[156]

*   *   *

Putin's path to power cast a shadow over his leadership, but this was compensated by the relatively strong endorsement that he received by winning the presidential election in the first round. By any standards Putin's meteoric rise was astonishing. He seemed to be the living embodiment of the way that education acts as an escalator of social mobility. At the same time, his career in the KGB reflected both the crisis and opportunities in the late Soviet system. This was a time of growing disenchantment with the idea of communism, the decay of public administration as time servers ruled the roost at home, and abroad the image of the Soviet Union was damaged by foreign adventures that culminated with the invasion of Afghanistan in December 1979. For an ambitious person like Putin a career in the KGB, an organisation that enjoyed the reputation of being one of the few untarnished bodies remaining, offered a way out. The degree to which Putin took into account the horrors that the KGB's predecessor organisations had inflicted on the Soviet people is unclear. Putin had also engaged in two other careers before entering the presidential race. It was this man that the Russian people chose to lead them into the new millennium.

2 The ideas behind the choice

One repays a teacher badly if one remains a student.

(Nietzsche[1])

We noted in the Preface that choices made in the first years of the century have proved decisive. The pattern, however, was modified with the launching of Gorbachev's *perestroika* in 1985. In the next six years the country was faced with fundamental choices about how to develop. Gorbachev himself drew on a long and deep current of reform communism, an idea that had blossomed in the Prague Spring of 1968 when Alexander Dubček had sought to establish 'socialism with a human face'. The Warsaw Pact invasion of August 1968 had put an end to these hopes for a generation, and when Gorbachev sought to revive them two decades later it appeared that the historical moment for them had passed. *Perestroika* was accompanied by an intense debate over choices, including such fundamental questions as the balance to be drawn between the plan and the market, liberal pluralism and socialist values, Party direction and democracy, and this was reflected in numerous works of the time that suggested choice.[2] At the same time, a powerful current argued precisely that Russia had no choice except to rejoin the West on the basis of shared democratic and market values.[3] The emergence of Russia as an independent state in December 1991 only exacerbated the debate between those who accepted this relative lack of choice and the nationalists, leftists and even some liberals (various brands of liberal statists and liberal patriots) who insisted that Russia must find its own path. Yeltsin's choice in the 1990s for Russia to take the path of liberal democracy, neo-liberal capitalism and international integration was contested. It was against this background of a country divided over its own identity and its role in the world that Putin came to power. The early twenty-first century, like so many times before, was for Russia yet another liminal period, a time when many options seemed open and in which the country's leadership was well aware of the epochal choices facing them. In this chapter we will examine the ideas and debates that attended Putin's coming to power, beginning with some divergent views of what Putin represented and a brief discussion of the nature of the system that he inherited.

Who is mister Putin?

Putin had come to power reflecting the contradictory aspirations of a broad majority of the Russian electorate, and it remained unclear exactly what his policy preferences and political style would be. Having risen rapidly to supreme power in Russia, his track record was episodic and there appeared to be no consistent thread to his work. Although a flood of speeches and materials about his life soon appeared, there remained something hidden in his character and his precise leadership intentions. It was for this reason that the question posed at the head of this section sounded so insistent.[4]

Views about what Putin represented differed sharply. For the philosopher and writer Alexander Zinoviev, Putin coming to power represented 'the first serious attempt of Russia to resist americanization and globalization, which comes from the country's internal needs'. Zinoviev projected on to Putin his own hopes, but he recognised, like so many of his countrymen, that Putin had unusual characteristics: 'I have a feeling that neither the West nor the predecessor of Putin who made the appointment realized the potential of that man', and he warned that if the matter had been delayed the West could well have tried to prevent Putin from taking the office.[5] For Zinoviev the key tasks facing Putin were:

> Strengthening the basic results of the anti-communist coup of the Gorbachev-Yeltsin period, complete the formation of a post-Soviet social organism, overcome the glaring defects of the Yeltsin regime, normalise the living conditions of the Russian population in the framework of the new social organism, and normalise the position of post-Soviet Russia in the global community.[6]

Alexander Solzhenitsyn took a rather more nuanced view, distinguishing between Putin's platform and his personality. According to him,

> Putin's platform comes from Yeltsin and his entourage, the corrupt bureaucrats, the financial magnates. They are united by one great fear: that people will take from them everything they have stolen, that their crimes will be investigated and that they will be sent to jail.

Solzhenitsyn excoriated Putin's first official act as interim president that granted Yeltsin and his family immunity from prosecution. As for Putin's personality, Solzhenitsyn argued that

> He is in many ways a puzzle. We don't know how he will act as president. He stands at a cross-roads. Either he can give in to his sponsors and lead the country inevitably to its ruin – and him with it – or he can break with clan loyalty and pursue his own policies.[7]

Either Putin would cast out on his own and repudiate Yeltsin and his legacy, or he would be swallowed up by the corruption and self-seeking greed of the Yeltsinite clan. In the event, Putin did neither. He did not openly repudiate the grouping that had brought him to power, but neither did he become their instrument. Instead, he navigated a difficult path in which his own policies could gradually take shape within the framework of the system he inherited.

The dual nature of Putin's personality and leadership have been much commented upon. An editorial in *The Guardian* noted that: 'Our pre-election question, "Who is Vladimir Putin?", may now be confidently answered. It transpires that he is two quite different people wrapped into one.'[8] One face, allegedly, would engage with the West to create a business-friendly democracy committed to open markets, while the second face was turned inwards and revealed an uglier aspect, seeking to impose discipline and order by authoritarian means. There are elements of truth in this portrait, but the division is not so much a contrast between domestic and foreign policy but runs through all of Putin's policies simultaneously. This contrast was not just a facet of Putin's personality but reflected the nature of the system that he inherited. More than that, the order that Putin tried to install was not antithetical to democracy but sought to inculcate respect for law and observance of the constitution.

Given the highly concentrated nature of Russian politics, much depended on Putin's personal choices. To characterise these we can identify two elements in his political identity that coexisted uncomfortably. The first was his 'neo-Soviet' facet, his nurturing in the late Soviet years when he imbibed the values, with all their contradictions, of the period, and then his 15 years of service in the Soviet intelligence agency. This neo-Sovietism is at odds with his 'post-Soviet' identity, marking an unequivocal break not only with communist ideology (there appears to have been not much of that even in his neo-Soviet characteristics), but also in attitudes towards power, property and Russia's status in the world. Putin, like the philosopher Nikolai Berdyaev, considered the October 1917 revolution as the only way of preserving the country 'in those circumstances', although he condemned the Bolsheviks for becoming excessively ideologised and rabid centralisers.[9] Putin's post-Sovietism recognises not only that the Soviet Union was a failed utopian experiment (this is accepted even within the framework of his neo-Sovietism), but also accepts that this failure was rooted not only in the inadequacies of communist ideology but also in Russia's typically exaggerated views of its abilities, capacities and importance. Putin's neo-Soviet face sought to restore dignity to the past and tended towards administrative methods rather than fully endorsing political pluralism and the clash of views. This was balanced by Putin's post-Soviet stance, imbibed as a student in the 1970s and probably reinforced by his years in Germany where he saw the old system collapse, then reinforced by his career as Sobchak's deputy in St Petersburg. Putin helped turn the city towards capitalism when he promoted international economic integration. His background as a denizen of this city also disposed him to a Western orientation. These two faces allowed Putin within the space of a few weeks to inaugurate a plaque in the Lubyanka honouring Andropov, the head of the KGB from 1967–82, and then place flowers at the grave of Andrei Sakharov, one of the most outstanding liberal dissidents and victim of Andropov's 'second cold war' of 1979–82. Mommsen reflects the contradictions in her evocatively titled article 'The Sphinx in the Kremlin',[10] and like the two-headed eagle that looks both East and West, that became Russia's state symbol, Putin looks both backwards and forwards.

These two facets can also be seen as authoritarianism versus liberalism, or statism versus pluralism. In structural terms, there was a conflict between attempts to *rationalise* the system without fundamentally changing the traditional pattern of personalised, dominant and often arbitrary leadership, or to *reorder* governance to make it genuinely more inclusive, law-based and democratic. The dichotomy was one between attempts to *reconcentrate* state power and the struggle to *reconstitute* it on the basis of the rule of law and the writ of the constitution. Putin's reform project and leadership was torn between these tendencies (which we shall explore later), but ultimately such an approach suggests a misleading polarity, as would any attempt to suggest a stark contrast between his authoritarian and nationalist instincts and his democratic and Westernising ideas. Later we shall see how these facets in his political identity sometimes clashed, but we shall argue that ultimately a new synthesis emerged that transcended these rather stereotypical stances. Mister Putin was more than just a product of his past and circumstances but was a dynamic political actor able to respond to new challenges and to learn from experience.

The Russian 'transition' and beyond

In the twentieth century Russia had endured two experiments with modernisation from above: the Soviet attempt to achieve accelerated development through the planned economy; and the neo-liberal reversion to perhaps excessively free markets in the 1990s. While very different in character, for those at the receiving end both were traumatic. Putin tried to move Russian politics away from these 'extraordinary' times towards a routine politics that could incorporate change but within the bounds of the constitution and law.

Extraordinary politics

The whole epoch of Soviet power can be considered a period of 'extraordinary politics'. If we define normal democratic politics as the relatively open-ended debate over alternative policies within the framework of the rule of law and certain guaranteed rights for individuals, then clearly the 'ideological' politics pursued by the Bolshevik regime in Russia was dominated by a contrasting set of values determined by the over-riding goal of 'building communism'. The definition of communism remained the prerogative of the high priesthood of the communist regime, and it was this combination of ideology and exclusive organisational rights on which the power of the communist order was based. Gorbachev's attempts to 'normalise' this system during *perestroika* between 1985 and 1991 included the renunciation of the claim to ideological leadership, let alone invincibility, and at the same time he attacked the powers of the *apparat* as part of his attempt to introduce a degree of political pluralism. Instead of achieving some sort of stable reformed socialist 'normality' the system crashed. Gorbachev's great achievement, however, had been to bring to an end the period of Bolshevik extraordinary politics in a remarkably peaceful manner.

Following *perestroika* and the end of what some have called the seventy-four-year period of emergency between 1917 and 1991, however, there was no simple return to 'normality'. The foreign minister Andrei Kozyrev, for example, argued that there could be no 'returning to a normal economy' because Russia had never known anything other than the totalitarian distribution of resources.[11] The Russian government under Yeltsin committed itself to the rapid transformation of the country. The government sought to take advantage of what Leszek Balcerowicz, the finance minister and architect of Poland's economic 'shock therapy' from 1989, explicitly termed 'extraordinary politics', the moment following the fall of communism when society expects radical changes.[12] In Poland this period of high legitimacy for fundamental reform lasted some three years, whereas in Russia it barely survived a few months. The neo-liberal reforms launched by Gaidar's radical government in the first days of 1992 soon ran into bitter opposition and by mid-year had been severely modified. The extraordinariness of the Soviet period had been perpetuated in new forms by the post-communist leadership.

Although extraordinary politics of the Balcerorowicz sort soon came to an end, politics in the Yeltsin years were anything but 'normal'. Following the breakdown of the first set of post-communist Russian political institutions in September–October 1993, when Yeltsin forcibly dispersed the legislature based in the Russian White House, a new constitution was adopted in December 1993 that lay at the basis of the system inherited by Putin.[13] For many, however, the consolidation that took place after 1993 has not been that of the independent institutions of democracy but of an excessively powerful presidency. In the economy a distinctive hybrid system emerged that appeared to borrow the pathologies of both the planned and market systems. Despite Yeltsin's rhetorical, and in many ways genuine, commitment to market reform, the 1990s were characterised by the emergence of a hybrid economic system. In politics, sharp polarisation between 'democrats' and an eclectic communist–nationalist anti-Western group meant that elections were less about changing governments than referenda on the very nature of the system that was to be built. Politics remained axiological, in the sense that ideological issues remained in the forefront. Yeltsin's presidency remained a 'regime of transition', devoted to the systemic transformation of the society and the marginalisation of opponents. Although the aim of Yeltsin's reforms was the creation of a capitalist democracy, his methods were divisive and on occasions flouted basic democratic norms and appeared to be an inverted form of the authoritarian order that it sought to overcome. This characteristic is highlighted, for example, by Reddaway and Glinski, who subtitle their major analysis of the Yeltsin years 'market Bolshevism against democracy'.[14] Their work stresses the continuation of extraordinary measures that flout legality and which allow the government to position itself above the laws that it seeks to impose on the rest of society.

The revolution from above

In one of the most detailed analyses of Russia's fifteen-year revolution that began in 1985, Gordon Hahn argues that the result was not democracy but an illiberal system. Instead of being a 'revolution from below' (although he notes that there had been elements of popular mobilisation), Russia had endured a 'bureaucrat-led revolution from above':

> Russia's revolution from above involved the mass cooptation and incorporation of the former Soviet party-state's institutions and apparatchiks into the new regime. These institutions and bureaucrats constrained the consolidation of democracy and the market by bringing their authoritarian political culture and statist economic culture into the new regime and state, producing to date an illiberal executive-dominated and kleptocratic and oligarchical political economy.[15]

The institutions of the state in Russia, according to Hahn, were taken over by a group of radicals led by Yeltsin, who then 'proceeded to carry out a creeping bureaucratic revolution against the central Soviet party-state machine',[16] and, it may be added, against Gorbachev's vision of a humane, socialist and reformed Soviet state. Although they are modernising, revolutions from above are liable to lead semi-authoritarian, or at best semi-democratic systems. According to Hahn they

> produce a state with very little autonomy from the former ruling class and the most powerful economic interests left-over from the *ancien regime*, producing non-liberal, oligarchic 'state capitalist' economies in which economic elites maintain close ties to government, rent-seek and foster corruption.[17]

Although undoubtedly elements of this are present in Russia, the key question is the degree of autonomy enjoyed by the government and its ability to exercise state power in ways that run counter to the immediate interests of the nascent capitalist class. This class gradually transformed from 'red directors' and holdovers from the bureaucratic order of the past into players in the global economic order. In other words, to what degree was Putin an independent political actor or was his freedom of political manoeuvre excessively constrained by the oligarchic-bureaucratic structures bequeathed to him by Yeltsin? Putin's struggle to strengthen the state, as we shall see, was primarily intended to reduce its dependence on the powerful economic interests that had been spawned by the anti-communist revolution while at the same time strengthening the presidency. The aim was to increase the state's autonomy and the presidency's ability to pursue policies that represented what he considered to be the interests of the country as a whole rather than that of the new capitalist–bureaucratic elites.

Michael McFaul argues along similar lines in suggesting that rather than a liberal democracy emerging in Russia, by the early years of Putin's rule it had become an 'electoral democracy'; one where the forms of democracy and electoral competition were preserved, but which had failed to gain the real spirit of democratic accountability and leadership turnover.[18] As far as he was concerned, this outcome derived not from the actions of any particular individual or set of policy preferences, but from the sheer scale of the changes required and the finely balanced relationship between those pushing for democratic change and the institutions and individuals who could take advantage of the residues of the old system. The emergence of an electoral democracy was not predetermined by Russian history or political culture, in his view, but by the confrontational, imposed and protracted transition itself, traumatised above all by the moments of institutional failure in August 1991 and October 1993. For McFaul, the 'scars of transition' include a number of institutional problems: 'a superpowerful presidency, a weak party system, an under-developed civil society, and the erosion of the independent media, the rule of law, state capacity, and center-regional relations', quite apart from ambivalent attitudes towards democracy by elites and the people.[19] There are elements of truth in all of this, but the traumatic birth of Russian democracy should not detract from the very real democratic gains achieved in a remarkably short period. After all, not only Russia bears the 'scars of transition'. France endured De Gaulle's *coup de main* in 1958, and as late as 1968 Ralf Dahrendorf had very real doubts whether democracy had sunk into German popular consciousness.[20] One of Putin's central goals was to transform the democratic capitalist project from a state of emergency into an everyday part of Russian normality. Democracy was to be 'naturalised', that is, to be made part of Russia's natural order of things.

The return to normality?

Normality is always relative, and when we use the term the intention is not to suggest that somewhere (other than in the realm of theology) there is some perfectly normal state. Our measure of normality is derived from Russia's own traditional sense (expressed most forcibly by Peter the Great) that its development has in some ways been 'deviant' from a standard set in Western Europe, and in recent times more broadly in 'the West'. We are also well aware that the standard of normality set in the West is deeply problematic; after all, Emile Durkheim was convinced that the Western European pattern of development over the last half millennium has been deeply morbid, if not pathological, a view that this author shares. At the same time, the development of a set of liberal rights, democratic methods, the rule of law and the individual right to economic self-affirmation (including property rights), as codified in the European Convention on Human Rights and subsequent protocols, defines a normality that, while failing to achieve medieval or Marxist visions of the unity of the social, political and religious, do offer a viable model of civilisation. It is to this 'normal' civilisation that Russia under Putin aspired. As Maly puts it, 'For the majority of Russians today "normality" is defined on a scale borrowed from the West'.[21]

The approach to reform under Putin moved away from systemic transformation towards system management. This suggests that politics has finally become 'normal', in the sense that larger constitutional questions over the shape of the polity have now given way to governmental management of mundane policy questions. The period of constitutional politics, predicted by Dahrendorf to last 'at least six months',[22] in Russia effectively lasted about a decade but now gave way to the hard work of 'normal politics'.[23] The question of regime type has been resolved and the basic choices between institutions of government have been decided. Schumpeter argued that a successful transition occurs when 'abnormality is no longer the central feature of political life; that is, when actors have settled on and obey a set of more or less explicit rules'.[24] For the authors of a landmark study of democratisation, 'normality, in other words, becomes a major characteristic of political life when those active in politics come to expect each other to play according to the rules – and the ensemble of these rules is what we mean by a regime'.[25] Russia under Putin finally had a chance to move away, as Kaspe puts it, from its 'permanent condition of being "post" something or other'.[26] A transition is over when the initial period of uncertainty associated with regime change comes to an end, and in Russia we appear to have reached this point.

This return to 'normality', an approach that was explicitly taken up by Putin, is tempered, however, by at least two other processes. The first is the strong and explicit project of a 'return to normalcy'. The notion of a return to normalcy was the slogan popular in the United States after the First World War and reflected the desire for peace of a nation tired of military exertions. The idea has also been applied to the period of recuperation in the USSR following victory in the Fatherland War.[27] In the Russian context today the politics of normalcy reflect a country that endured over a century of revolutionary, military and secret police depredations. The attempt to link up with the past, to restore the torn fabric of society, to draw on intellectual traditions and cultural values of yesteryear, all reflect this post-traumatic pursuit of a usable past as the grounding of the present. Putin's pragmatic approach is rooted in the explicit attempt to base Russia's politics of the twenty-first century in the repudiation of 'revolutionary' and 'shock therapy' politics of the twentieth. He is in effect saying to the Russian people: 'The period of emergency is over. Carry on with normal lives'. Putin's identification with the politics of normalcy was one of the most potent sources of his enduring popularity.

Putin's politics of normality and a 'return to normalcy', however, are accompanied by disturbing overtones of 'normalisation', the term used to describe the pacification of Czechoslovakia following the Soviet invasion in 1968. The concepts of 'managed' and 'guided' democracy are openly proclaimed by some of Putin's advisors as preferable to the unpredictability and disintegrative trends so evident under Yeltsin's leadership in the 1990s. A whole raft of terms have been devised to describe the state of affairs in countries like Russia where the formal institutions of democracy are vitiated by informal practices that subvert their impartial operation. O'Donnell's concept of 'delegative democracy',[28] Zakaria's notion of 'illiberal democracy'[29] and Diamond's idea of 'electoral democracy' (which we have already mentioned, p. 40) are among the best known. This post-communist normalisation is very different to that imposed on Czechoslovakia by Gustav Husak in the wake of the Soviet invasion, yet in certain respects the attempt to subvert the free operation of politics and the accompanying dialectic of coercion, consent and consumerism, the three Cs of late communism, find some echoes today.

A benign version of this would be the comparison with De Gaulle, who after 1958 managed to achieve the rapid modernisation of French political institutions and the economy by combining a regime of personal power and managed democracy. Similarly, following Mao Zedong's death in 1976, Deng Xiaoping shifted China away from the revolutionary path of modernisation towards a distinctive communist-led capitalism. Another comparison is with Alexander III, who succeeded to the Russian throne after the assassination of the 'tsar-liberator', the reformer Alexander II in 1881 and proceeded to impose stability by repressive means. In 1917 the symbol of the failure of Russia's first transition to democracy had been Kerensky, and some suggested that Putin could become the gravedigger of Russia's second attempted transition. The comparisons between Kerensky and Putin are even deeper: both had been born in St Petersburg, both studied in the law faculty of St Petersburg University, the careers of both developed with dizzying speed, and both enjoyed phenomenal popularity at first as they stood for 'war to victorious conclusion' and attempted to strengthen the state (Kerensky by reimposing the death penalty). However, while Kerensky had become a noted democrat, Putin went into the security services, and Kerensky was a better public orator. By July 1917 Kerensky's popularity had fallen dramatically and by October he was overthrown by a 'third force', the Bolsheviks.[30] An even more malign comparison is with

Andropov, who followed his stint as head of the KGB by becoming the successor to Brezhnev as General Secretary from November 1982 until his death in February 1984. The model here is an authoritarian modernisation from above, seeking to impose social discipline by coercive means while recognising the need for economic reform.[31] As Pechenev notes, there is an obvious lack of comparability between Putin and Andropov, since the latter was 'neither a liberal nor a democrat (in the contemporary sense of these words) and not even a "secret" (as many people in Russia today affirm) communist reformer'.[32] Andropov had, however, been able to establish the legend that the KGB was the least corrupt and best informed agency in the decaying Soviet Union, one that was not entirely devoid of truth.

Putin's approach, characterised by the pursuit of a politics of normality, is thus riven by contradictory ideas and processes. The most glaring one is the tension between trying to achieve a genuinely *ordered* system, where democratic institutions work largely free of political constraints and are accountable to the people, and a system that tries to impose *stability* from above by managing political processes, and thus impeding the free operation of political institutions. The contradiction between order and stability is one that has deep roots in Russia. Too often a genuine political order (*Ordnungspolitik*) has been reduced to *poryadok*, the coercive imposition of stability. This was the case with Brezhnev's stagnation, a peculiar type of late Soviet politics of stability and normality that proved to be far from stable and a 'normality' that turned out to be unsustainable, hence clearly abnormal. The fundamental tension in Putin's politics was the desire to create a self-sustaining system that did not require 'manual control', and the fear that such an autonomous system would spin out of control. It was not clear whether Russia's Thermidor, the post-revolutionary attempt to achieve 'normalcy', would find an adequate balance between normality (order) and normalisation (stability).

Russia at the turn of the millennium

In Russia history appears too often as a crushing weight rather than as a garb to be worn triumphantly. Before the country can move forwards, it needs to digest the past. This was reflected in Putin's 'manifesto' to which we have referred before. Posted on the internet on 28 December 1999, the document laid out in systematic form the thinking that would underlie his presidency.[33] The document was prepared by members of Gref's Centre for Strategic Development, but we know that Putin carefully went through the draft and added his own comments and corrections.[34] The document thus provides a genuine insight into his thinking. Three days later, on the last day of the year and by some reckonings the last day of the century and millennium, Yeltsin in his New Year address announced to a surprised people that he was giving up office and transferring presidential responsibilities to the prime minister. Putin had already been informed about the planned changes, and thus knew that his message would indeed act as a type of manifesto for his presidential campaign.

The formal name of the missive was *Russia at the Turn of the Millennium* and was significant not only for its content but also for the form in which it was presented. By posting it on the government web site before publication in the press, Putin appeared to be making a statement about technical innovation and signalling his acknowledgement of the importance of communication with the people. This was campaigning of a new sort, however, based not on the soapbox and the electoral stump, but as the elucidation of a personal revelation and its transmission to the people. This quasi-religious approach to news management would characterise Putin's later relationship with the media, and indeed his approach to politics in general. In this case it was not so much that the medium was the message, but that the message reflected the inter-relationship of the personal and the epochal.

Putin outlined not only the challenges facing Russia but also sought to characterise the nature of global transformations taking place at that time, above all the shift towards post-industrial patterns of development. Under communist rule in the twentieth century Russia had fallen far behind, Putin argued, and things had been made much worse by the drastic reforms of the 1990s when under Yeltsin the country had been wrenched from Soviet-type socio-economic development and thrown in at the deep end of capitalism. The neo-liberalism predominant in that decade repudiated any significant managerial role for the state; Russia had moved from one extreme to another. After the fall of the communist system in 1991 Russia moved from a state-dominated system to its opposite, accompanied by a reduction in its GDP of 42 per cent and leading to the country's GNP, as Putin pointed out, becoming ten times smaller than that of the USA and five times smaller than China's.[35] The economy was characterised by low investment, labour productivity and wages, with a pitiful volume of foreign direct investment (FDI). Russia was paying the price for the distorted pattern of Soviet development, above all excessive attention to raw materials and defence industries and the neglect of information technologies and the service sector, but also for its own 'mistakes, miscalculations and lack of experience' in the transition itself.[36] However, Putin insisted, Russia had now 'embarked upon the highway that the whole of humanity is travelling'. In other words, Russia had shed the communist illusion that it had found a viable alternative modernity to that practised in the West. For Putin, there was no alternative to the market economy and democracy. Thus a whole epoch had come to an end in which Russia, like Germany earlier, had sought a distinctive *Sonderweg*. This represented a choice of fundamental significance. The essence of Putin's path was that there was no special path for Russia, as the ruins of 1945 had demonstrated for Germany earlier, but only accommodation to the mainstream of global developments.

As for his understanding of the communist epoch in Russia, Putin argued that it 'would be a mistake not to recognise the unquestionable achievements of those times', but he insisted that 'it would be an even bigger mistake not to realise the outrageous price our country and its people had to pay for that social experiment'. In words that echoed in a remarkable way Solzhenitsyn's assertion that communism represented 'a mad dash down a blind alley', Putin went on to argue:

> What is more, it would be a mistake not to understand its historic futility. Communism and the power of the Soviets did not make Russia a prosperous country with a dynamically developing society and free people. Communism vividly demonstrated its inability to foster sound self-development, dooming our country to lagging steadily behind economically advanced countries. It was a blind alley, far away from the mainstream of world civilisation.[37]

This was the first lesson to learn from the past and reflected the authentic voice of a man of the 1970s. It was closely associated with a second lesson concerning the way that change should be achieved. One of the strongest motifs in Putin's thinking in this document and later is the repudiation of revolution as a mode of political action in favour of 'gradual, prudent methods':

> Russia has reached its limit for political and socio-economic upheavals, cataclysms, and radical reforms. Only fanatics or political forces which are absolutely apathetic and indifferent to Russia and its people can make calls for a new revolution. Be it under communist, national-patriotic, or radical-liberal slogans, our country and our people will not withstand a new radical break-up. The nation's patience and its ability to survive as well as its capacity to work constructively have reached the limit. Society will simply collapse economically, politically, psychologically, and morally.[38]

Putin would return to this theme repeatedly later on, as we shall have occasion to note, and reflects his commitment to a politics of normality.

A third lesson emerged out the previous two: Russia should find its own path and reject 'experimenting with abstract models and schemes taken from foreign textbooks'. The reforms of the 1990s were thus placed in the same category as the communist experiment that they sought to overcome: both had been characterised, according to Putin, by 'The mechanical copying of other nations' experience ...'.[39] This assertion clearly modifies the earlier repudiation of special national paths. The power that lies in this apparent contradiction is derived from the attempt to move away from excessive borrowing of foreign models while at the same time trying to avoid falling into the opposite extreme of repudiating the value of international experience.

This search for a distinctive Putinite 'third way' characterised his leadership (see Chapter 3). We may also add that the attempt to transcend the contradictions that characterised Russia's history, notably between the

internationalist utopianism that lay at the root of Marxism and the nationalist messianism that the ideology turned into under Stalin, was the source of
much of Putin's power. Elements of both remained in many post-communist
Russian political movements, including to a large extent in the CPRF led by
Zyuganov. At the base of Putin's policies and what we shall describe as his
'third way' lies the idea of a grand transcendence of so many of the conflicts
that had both shaped and torn Russia in the modern era. We may note here
yet another very particular one that emerges out of his biography. In 1721
Peter the Great had moved the capital from Moscow to his new creation, St
Petersburg, and thus set in motion a centuries-long rivalry. Lenin had moved
the capital back to Moscow in 1918, and thereafter the northern city, living
under the name of Leningrad between 1924 and 1991, had been overshadowed. Putin conducted much of his diplomacy from St Petersburg and
ensured that it became the home of a number of inter-state organisations.
Putin was not able to overcome the rivalry between the two capitals, but he
certainly ensured a more balanced appreciation of the political significance
of both. The celebration in 2003 of the three hundredth anniversary of St
Petersburg, by then a city with five million inhabitants (not very far short of
Moscow's eight million), appeared a moment of reconciliation not only
between the two cities but also between Petrine and Muscovite Russia.

A number of other themes emerge from the *Millennium* address that later
characterised Putin's leadership. One of these is the attempt to forge a
national consensus to avoid once again dividing the country over basic values
and orientations, as it had been after 1917 and in the 1990s. Putin was
unequivocal in opposing 'the restoration of an official state ideology in any
form' and insisted that 'there should be no forced civil accord in a democratic Russia', although he stressed the importance of achieving 'social
accord on such basic issues as the aims, values, and orientations of development'.[40] These could be achieved on the basis of traditional Russian values.
Here he listed a number: *patriotism*, that should be free of 'nationalist
conceit' and instead serve as the inspiration for making the country 'better,
richer, stronger and happier'; *the greatness of Russia*, and here Putin insisted
that 'Russia was and will remain a great power'; *statism*, one of the most controversial of Putin's arguments (that we will discuss later); and *social solidarity*,
whereby 'the striving for corporate forms of activity have always prevailed
over individualism. Paternalistic sentiments have deep roots in Russian
society'.[41] Although Putin's programme represented the transcendence of
historical contradictions, here we apparently find one in his own thinking:
between the values of liberal individualism and statist collectivism. How this
was resolved, if it was, we shall see later.

The restoration of the state lay at the centre of Putin's activity as president. In his manifesto he insisted that

> Russia will not become a second edition of, say, the US or Britain, where
> liberal values have deep historic traditions. Our state and its institutions

and structures have always played an exceptionally important role in the life of the country and its people.... Russians are alarmed by the obvious weakening of state power. The public looks forward to a certain restoration of the guiding and regulation role of the state, proceeding from Russia's traditions as well as the current state of the country.[42]

This did not represent a repudiation of liberal values, as some commentators have argued, but instead suggested that these values had to be adapted to Russian conditions. In later sections of the article Putin placed a strong state at the centre of his programme, but insisted that this had nothing in common with the totalitarianism of the past: 'A strong state power in Russia is a democratic, law-based, workable federal state.'[43] This was to lie at the basis of economic and other policies. Putin did not seek to find a middle path between, on the one hand, capitulation to Western values and, on the other, totalitarianism, since his choice was unequivocally that of Western market democracy. The problem was not in the lack of definition of the end, but in the means.

From the above it is clear that it was not so much the changes pursued by Putin that were so radical, since in many respects they continued the work of his predecessor, but the way in which they were conducted. Putin set himself the task of repudiating the sharp turns and revolutionary breaks that characterised so much of Russian history. In their place, he sought to achieve a type of politics of normality. This indeed is one of the most paradoxical features of Putin's leadership: its very ordinariness represented a radical break with the past. At the same time, the attempt to reconcile the past with a future-oriented strategy meant that Putin's politics were imbued with a post-Soviet face while often taking on a neo-Soviet aspect. These two facets, however, were not necessarily in tension with each other, but on the contrary it was the very force of this contradiction that acted as the source of much of Putin's power.

Planning for the future

Putin came to power with his own ideas about how to deal with the problems facing the country. At the same time, he sought to harness academic expertise to devise appropriate strategies. To this end, as noted, the Centre for Strategic Development, headed by the Petersburger German Gref, was established on Putin's initiative in December 1999. It was set an ambitious task: to devise a strategy for Russia's development over the next 10–15 years. Members of its Advisory Board included the economists Yevgeny Yasin, Vladimir Mau, Lev Okun'kov and Andrei Illarionov (who had by the end of the 1990s become bitterly critical of Yeltsin's macroeconomic policy and later became one of Putin's key economic advisors).[44] In an interview Gref suggested that the strategy of the Centre was based on the idea of developing a 'special', if not 'third way', for Russia.[45] Soon after the presidential elections Gref noted that 'Putin's position is quite radical and we must think about how to resolve the tasks before us'.[46] The unknown Putin soon revealed himself to be a liberal reformer. The need to move from a relatively self-regulating political system to a more directed system was vividly reflected in Gref's proposals for the reform of the structure of the presidential administration:

> At present, the social and political situation in Russia can be characterized as self-regulating and self-governed. The new President of the Russian Federation, assuming he really wants to ensure order and stability in the country for the period of his rule, does not need a self-regulating political system. He needs a political structure (institution) within his administration, which will be able not only to forecast and engineer desirable political situations in Russia, but also to provide operational management of political and social processes in Russian Federation and in the countries of the near abroad.[47]

The core of this new and more directed system, as we shall see, was the presidency. Gref later became the minister for trade and industry, a probably conscious effort to reproduce on a more modest scale the Japanese experience, where the famed MITI (Ministry of International Trade and Industry) acted as the powerhouse for Japan's rise from post-war destruction to the world's second economic power. In the event the reports produced by Gref's centre played only a marginal role in detailed policy formation, with the initiative passing firmly to the government headed by Mikhail Kasyanov, but Putin's attempt to broaden the debate over policy options and the use of think tanks indicated at least a recognition of the need to have a variety of sources of information and policy options.

Under Gorbachev and Yeltsin a vigorous public sphere had emerged, and Putin now sought to use the intellectual energy available. One of Russia's leading think tanks is the Council for Foreign and Defence Policy (CFDP). Established in the early 1990s to provide strategic guidance and recommendations to the presidency and headed by Sergei Karaganov, the CFDP brings together an illustrious cast of academics and former politicians. In anticipation of a change of leadership, from late 1998 the council commissioned a major study of the problems facing Russia, designed explicitly as a programme for the new president. The report was published in 2000, just in time to fall into the hands of the new leader, and dealt (in its own words) not only with Russia's eternal question of 'what is to be done?', but focused above all on 'how it is to be done'.[48] The CFDP, Karaganov insisted, was a civil society association, and the 300 or so citizens who participated in the various discussions that produced the report sought to help the state and society devise a strategic concept for the country's development. The report covered all aspects of Russian policy, and below we will give no more than a brief indication of its main ideas. We do not know the precise impact that the report had on Putin, but it is clear that he took its main lessons to heart and in a quite remarkable way his policies addressed the concerns voiced in this report.

In his introduction Karaganov listed the ills besetting Russia as it entered the new millennium: the failure of the reforms begun in 1992, the weakness of the state, the gulf between state and society and between the regions and the centre, and the decline in Russia's foreign policy position. All this he argued required a drastic change in the country's model of development. The experts were agreed: the country found itself in a dead end: 'if the ruling class does not find in itself the strength to lead society towards a change of power and model of development, then Russia was doomed to decay and destruction.'[49] Russia, he insisted, should stop 'struggling against the phantoms and shadows of the past',[50] and for this reason there would be no special study of 'the Russian idea', the endless metaphysical search for the meaning of Russia, and instead 'the ruling class, all of society, must engage in self-limitation' and understand the need to renounce grandiose and unsustainable ambitions and focus on the real problems facing the country.

This rather pessimistic tone was reflected in the discussion on the state of democracy in Russia, with the general view being that Russia, at best, was an 'unripe (or immature) democracy', with the absence of some key elements of a more developed democracy and with far too many 'superfluous' features, many of them inherited from the late totalitarian period.[51] While, for example, the country may in the early 1990s have been federalised, it was on the basis of the Soviet pseudo-federal territorial divisions. Territorial decentralisation verged on the feudalisation of the country. In case after case, above all with the military, the creation of new institutions was accompanied by the survival of the old. Behind the façade of reformed institutions 'there lie hidden Soviet, if not Stalinist, administrative practices'.[52] Everywhere there were 'grey zones where the rule of law confronted the world of informal relations, where the law is silent'.[53] Authority was unconsolidated, and thus power was unable genuinely to become state power.[54] These problems in political development had provoked three major problems: the inability to achieve sustained economic development and the rational use of resources; the failure to defend the country's position in the world; and the difficulty in convincing society that democracy 'to the greatest degree reflects the interests of each and everyone, and thus gaining public support for democratic transformations that would ensure their practical irreversibility in Russia'.[55] Polls on the question of whether people preferred 'order', even if it necessitated some infringements on democracy, had been conducted since 1992, and some 70–80 per cent consistently considered order the priority.[56] When the question was posed differently, however, a strong majority also favoured the retention of democratic freedoms.[57] In this context, the idea of a 'strong state' has to be treated with caution: the only effective way forwards was for it to be both ordered and democratic. Despite attempts to manage political pluralism and the public sphere, it was this that Putin tried to do.

As for foreign policy, the report was scathing about Russia's conduct in the 1990s:

> The main thing is that the country's political class does not understand and does not want to understand obvious truths. Russia did not lose the 'cold war'. It emerged from it with honour. But because of mistaken policies, unsteadiness, the traditional expectation of miracles, the almost deliberate weakening of the state, the endless postponement of hard decisions, *we lost the post cold war world* [italics in original], snatching defeat from the jaws of victory.[58]

Among its many prescriptions, the chapter insisted that the country should normalise its relationship with the Group of Eight leading industrialised nations (G8),[59] something that Putin did at its meeting in Japan in July 2000, and in July 2002 at the G8 meeting in Kananskis in Canada Russia was accepted as a full member and invited to host the 2006 summit.

Corruption was identified as one of the main challenges facing the country and could only be tackled by a reform of public administration. Transparency International identifies Russia as one of the most corrupt in the world; in 1999 and 2000 ranking 82nd among 99, but in 2001 ranking 79th out of 91 and by 2002 rising to 71st out 102. Although there is plenty of venal corruption (bribe taking and the like), there is also systematic corruption arising out of the inter-penetration of private and public affairs, the 'merging (*srashchivanie*) of the state apparatus and private capital'.[60] Under Stalin a powerful network of criminal gangs emerged harnessed to the state, but in the post-Stalin years they became a virtual 'state within the state', gaining enormous economic power as a result of Gorbachev's reforms. Under Yeltsin there was a virtual fusion of economic and political matters as business and the state effectively became one.[61] The notorious example was Boris Berezovsky, dubbed by Khlebnikov the 'Russian Rockefeller'.[62] By the time Putin came to power, by some estimates up to 40 per cent of business was part of the 'shadow economy', employing over 8 million people.[63] Whole regions appeared to have fallen into the hands of organised criminal gangs, notoriously Primorsky *krai*, the port and its infrastructure in Astrakhan *oblast*, and the oil and gas industries in Tyumen *oblast*.[64] One of the cardinal aspects of Putin's strengthening of the state was precisely to differentiate it from direct economic influence. Karaganov's report recognised the high degree of segmentation in the country, requiring differentiated anti-corruption strategies at the departmental, sectoral and regional levels.[65]

As for the crucial question of constitutional reform, the report noted the 'dialectical unity' between two opposed ideas: 'the need to ensure the stability of the basic law; and the need to introduce amendments, changes dictated by life itself.'[66] The report rehearsed all the fundamental arguments for and against changing the constitution, but in the end plumped for some mild corrections:

There are two conclusions: either do everything possible to ensure that the authorities fulfil to the letter constitutional norms and raise their political and legal culture, or to render the constitution less 'dependent', stricter, remove some of its most glaring faults. It is clear that to achieve cultural change could take decades. This is an argument to introduce certain changes to the constitution.[67]

The authors however did not recommend converting Russia from what was effectively a presidential republic into a parliamentary one, and indeed insisted that such calls were extremely dangerous: 'A parliamentary republic is a one-wheel cycle, a presidential republic is a bicycle, while a presidential-parliamentary one is a tricycle, the most stable.'[68]

The state of the nation

The *Millennium Manifesto* and the *Strategy for Russia* document provide two fundamental starting points for analysis of the challenges facing Putin's leadership as he assumed office. In this section we will use his annual state-of-the-nation messages to the Federal Assembly (the two houses of parliament – the Federation Council and the State Duma – taken together), which reflect changing priorities and concerns. Putin's annual address acted as a moment to take stock of his ideas and priorities. These speeches served as programmatic documents, but of course they also served to justify policies to the public. In examining them we should be aware that they were not exactly manifestos, yet they do reflect the evolution of Putin's thinking.

In his first state-of-the-nation speech on 8 July 2000 Putin focused on his favourite theme, the need to 'strengthen the state' and to establish 'a single vertical line of executive power' while pursuing liberal economic reforms. He dismissed 'speculation about dictatorship and authoritarianism' and stressed instead that his purpose was to create an 'effective and a democratic state ... capable of protecting civic, political and economic freedoms'. He condemned the 'unreasonable level of taxation' and conceded that the state had contributed to the development of corruption, capital flight and the shadow economy because the rules were vague and ill-defined. Russia was continuing to lose ground economically, despite some economic growth, and was in danger of becoming a third world state. More than that, the Russian nation was threatened with extinction if policies did not change. Although the rudiments of a democratic state had been built 'quite often the distance separating laws from real life is too great'. So far only the outlines of civil society had developed and now 'patient work is required to make society the government's equal partner'. Russia had been unable, Putin insisted, 'to combine patriotic responsibility with what [Peter] Stolypin [prime minister between 1906 and his assassination in 1911] described as civil freedoms'. Putin sought to restructure political space by sponsoring the development of political parties as 'a constant link between the people and the authorities'.[69] The speech outlined a strategy for the reform of Russia that he proceeded to implement.

Perhaps Putin's most radical address came on 3 April 2001. He began by looking back on the fulfilment of his earlier plans to reorganise federal relations, insisting that 'the period of the erosion of statehood is behind us'. He now talked about the development of judicial reform and the improvement of the quality of legislation. Along with the shadow economy, he argued, 'a kind of shadow justice had emerged' for those who had lost faith in the official system. The status of judges needed to be improved. In the economy capital flight was continuing (some $20 billion a year) and the country was 'still living predominantly in a "rent-based" rather than a productive economy'. An 'equilibrium' point had been achieved in the economy based on inactivity, provoked not only because of 'resistance to reform on the part of the bureaucracy' but the system itself was based on receiving what Putin called 'status' rent (bribes and compensation). Administrative reform was urgent, he argued, to focus on scaling back the bureaucracy. The number of civil servants, he noted, had increased from 882,000 to over a million. Putin once again reiterated his belief that 'a state's efficiency is determined not so much by the amount of property it controls as by the efficacy of political, legal and administrative mechanisms for observing public interests in the country'. On foreign policy he failed to mention the US and instead prioritised relations with the European Union (EU). He stressed the importance of economic factors in foreign policy.[70]

His speech on 18 April 2002 came in the wake of the 11 September events, and he took full credit for having made possible the creation of a 'durable antiterrorist coalition'. Russia was 'building constructive, normal relations with all states in the world'. Judicial reform had moved forward, with most of the necessary acts and laws adopted, but the whole system needed to be made more humane. The focus of the speech, however, was on economic matters. Putin's insistence on the need to improve people's standards of living reflected his frustration that so little had been done in this sphere, although he did stress some of the government's achievements. He noted that in 2001 economic growth had continued, real incomes had risen by 6 per cent and unemployment fallen by 700,000. This meant a return just about to the level of 1998, before the financial crash in August of that year had nearly halved people's real incomes. There was still a long way to go before they reached the 1990 level, before the fall of communism and the disintegration of the USSR. Putin expressed dissatisfaction with the government's forecast of an economic growth rate of between 3.5 and 4.6 per cent, although this figure was probably a realistic one and he did not put forward any new ideas about how higher targets could be achieved. This part of the speech reflected Putin's traditional face, where planning served the function of exhortation and encouragement. However, elsewhere in his speech the post-Soviet face was much in evidence, especially in his stress on the need to limit the state's role in the economy and his excoriation of government bureaucracy, warning that 'the habits of the command system persist' and urged serious administrative reform. This was balanced by his call for reform of the natural monopolies, the need to support science, and for the state to manage its property more effectively. At the same time, Russia's integration into the global economy remained at the heart of Putin's economic agenda. Overall, there remained many grey areas in Putin's strategy for economic development and in his view of the proper role of the state.[71]

Putin's address in 2003 was postponed because of the war in Iraq and, it appears, because of his refusal to accept the complacency in some of the earlier drafts. As head of the executive the president had to take responsibility for the actions (or inaction) of the government. Earlier speeches had stressed the stabilisation of the system and the introduction of order, together with specific concrete measures (the payment of wages, the indexation of pensions, encouragement of small businesses and the like), in contrast to Yeltsin's abstractions like building the market and democracy. After ten years and more of upheaval, society wanted 'no more revolution, but calm and considered movement forward'.[72] In his speech of 16 May Putin condemned complacency and warned of the dangers of stagnation. He warned that despite certain achievements the economic fundamentals were still 'very weak', with the country burdened by uncompetitive industries, excessive reliance on temporarily favourable international economic circumstances, administrative inefficiency and a declining population. He categorised the economic achievements as 'very, very modest', and set a ten-year target of doubling GDP. As long as the economy was not put right, Russia would not be able to become a rich and powerful country again. He warned that terrorism 'threatens the peace and security of our citizens', and insisted that the Russian army should be professional and well-equipped to defend the country. He praised those Chechens who voted in the March 2003 referendum in favour of remaining an 'inseparable part' of the Russian Federation, and insisted that the people of Chechnya should be given the chance to lead 'normal, human lives'. He warned against parliamentary populism in the forthcoming Duma elections, while welcoming them as a new stage in the development of the country's multiparty system. Most significantly, he looked forward to a 'professional and efficient government relying on the parliamentary majority' being formed after the elections.[73]

The 'normalisation' of politics

We have suggested above that Putin explicitly put an end to talk of 'transition' in Russia, and this was accompanied by an attempted 'return to normality'. Although Putin's election did not at first represent a rupture in the constitutional order, his policy innovations and leadership style effectively marked the beginning of a distinct era. It is still too early to provide a full analysis of this new period or to discern the underlying significance of the events, but it is already abundantly clear that Putin's programme of 'normal' politics, accompanied by attempts to rebuild the state, reflected the underlying values of the society, the aspirations of the political elite, and was perceived to correspond to the needs of the country.[74] In this section we will draw together some of the threads of Putin's thinking about normality and note the effect on his policies.

Putin's leadership represented a search for normality, a return to normalcy, but the elements of normalisation allowed an ambivalence to be drawn about whether his politics represented order or stability. The concept of normality as we apply it suggests a certain naturalness of political debate and choice of policy options, relatively unconstrained by the formal imposition of ideological norms. For Vitaly Tretyakov (the former editor of the leading liberal patriotic paper *Nezavisimaya gazeta*), this naturalness was defined by the 'objective predetermination [*predopredelennosti*] of what happens' within the framework of a set of norms and, 'clearly, within the limits of these norms'.[75] Putin's strategic goal of modernisation of the economy was accompanied by the attempt to consolidate society. Although these goals were not always compatible a common principle underlay both: the attempt to avoid extremes in policy and to neutralise extremist political actors. Putin's speeches and interventions are peppered with the concept of 'normality'. For example, in his greeting to the delegates to the constituent congress of the Unity party in February 2000, Putin argued that it would be 'normal' for Russia to have a three- or four-party system, instead of the 150-odd registered at that time.[76] The 'normalisation' of Russia was also a process proceeding at the international level, with the US State Department, for example, in February 2001 abolishing its special section on Russia and reducing it to a sub-unit of the European department. At all levels a process of 'naturalising' politics was taking place, repudiating the extraordinary and extra-legal, and at the international level the emergency and the confrontational.

Putin is a reformer, but his approach to change is no longer one of systemic transformation but of system management. This is reflected in a number of features. The first is the refusal to accept changes to the constitution. This was highlighted in his very first policy statements, although repeated rather less frequently thereafter. Instead, institutional development, as with the establishment of the seven federal districts (see Chapter 6), has assumed para-constitutional forms. Although the system of federalism, as outlined in the constitution, has been modified by the establishment of these districts, the change is portrayed as affecting the organisation of executive power and thus not requiring constitutional amendment. Another case of para-constitutional change is the adoption of the law on the merging of subjects of the federation and the incorporation of new subjects. It should be noted that the constitutional order in all democratic societies evolves as a result of legislative activity and changes in political practices, but there comes a point when quantitative changes, to use Marxist terminology, require a qualitative re-adjustment of constitutional doctrine. In the Russian case this would probably be necessitated by attempts to extend the presidential term to seven years, or to make the government and prime minister directly responsible to a parliamentary majority. However, in Putin's first term there was no indication that he favoured such changes.

The second feature of Putin's politics of normality is the refusal to reverse the results of the privatisations of the Yeltsin years, above all in the mid-1990s. The refusal to re-open the question of the legality of earlier privatisations is often interpreted as a token of Putin's pusillanimity in the face of the entrenched interests of 'the family', the combination of powerful business people, politicians, members of the presidential administration and blood members of Yeltsin's entourage. It can also be seen as a refusal to engage in another social revolution. Putin accepted that Yeltsin's 'revolution from above' laid the foundations of a market economy and established the basis of a bourgeois social class in which democracy could be rooted. Putin also accepted that a wholesale review of the corruption and outright theft that accompanied this process would be socially divisive and disruptive. Only clearly provable criminal cases, he insisted, would be investigated. Putin thus exposes himself to the charge of prosecuting those who made their fortunes in the era of wild capitalism, the so-called oligarchs, on a selective and politically biased way. It also made him extremely cautious in pursuing privatisations, as in the repeated back-pedalling over attempts to privatise parts of RAO UES (United Energy Systems), the electricity monopoly.

The third feature is Putin's insistence in the foreign policy sphere that Russia should be treated as a 'normal' great power. This was most vividly seen at the G8 summit in July 2000 in Okinawa and Miyazaki, when Putin successfully convinced the other seven world leaders that Russia should be treated as just another country, asking neither for exceptions nor expecting any favours. On numerous occasions thereafter Putin argued that Russia's foreign policy should serve the country's economic interests, a policy that was evident in debates over the union of Russia and Belarus. In general, while regretting the disintegration of the Soviet Union, Putin accepted that the break-up was irrevocable and thus jettisoned illusions about the recreation of some sort of unified successor state based on the Commonwealth of Independent States (CIS). Only now, after the revolutionary transformations of the Yeltsin era, could politics at home and abroad become genuinely pragmatic. The word comes from the Greek *pragma*, meaning 'deed' or 'action', and in Putin's Russia deeds were cautious and actions tailored to Russia's real capacity.

The fourth feature, following on from the above, is the explicit repudiation of revolution as an effective form of achieving positive political change. Putin's leadership is 'revolutionary' in its explicit repudiation of revolution and extraordinary politics, and thus can be classified as the delayed fulfilment of the promise of 1989, the anti-revolution that puts an end to the whole cycle of emancipatory revolutionism inaugurated by the universalistic radicalism of the Enlightenment.[77] The fall of communism entailed the rejection not only of a specific revolutionary ideology, but of the revolutionary method (with its violence, polarisation and destructiveness) in its entirety. This was the promise of 1989 in Eastern Europe, and it was also reflected in Russia. Already Yeltsin had argued that 'Russia was tired of revolutions. It was tired of the very word, which implies either rebellion or a social cataclysm by an unseen force and means destruction and famine', and thus the country was opposed to the idea of 'class warfare' or 'social struggle' as part of what he called his 'radical reforms'.[78] By eschewing a revolutionary transformation, both Yeltsin and Putin were to make peace with the existing social order, and thus to bring Russia's long cycle of revolution to an end.[79]

On numerous occasions Putin returned to the point and it acts as a *leitmotif* of his thinking. There may well have been an element of self-preservation involved here, because as a former agent of the previous regime's security agency he was potentially culpable, but his arguments are much more profound than this. In his *Millennium Manifesto* he noted that the communist revolutionary model of development not only had not delivered the goods, but could not have done so. In his state-of-the-nation speech on 3 April 2001 he sought to break the vicious cycle of revolution and counter-revolution, reform and counter-reform:

> We are not afraid of change and must not avoid it. However change, whether in politics or administration, must be justified by the situation. No doubt public apprehensions and fears do not appear out of nowhere. They emerge from the long-established logic that revolution is usually followed by counter-revolution, reforms by counter-reforms and then by the search for those guilty of revolutionary excesses and by punishment, all the more so since Russia's historical experience abounds in such cases. As I see the matter, it is high time to say firmly that this cycle has ended. Enough is enough! There will be no more revolution or counter-revolution.[80]

He then insisted that 'Russia and its people require firm and economically viable state stability and we should long ago have learnt to live according to this normal human logic'. In his question and answer session with the Russian people in December 2001 Putin once again returned to the theme: 'As one of my acquaintances said, "Russia in the past century over-fulfilled its plan for revolutions." I hope that in the twenty-first century there will be no revolutions, that things will only be positive.'[81] In an interview shown on Russian TV (RTR) on 7 October 2002, his fiftieth birthday, Putin said: 'I would like to remind you that I am a lawyer and I think that one's actions should be based on law, and not revolutionary expediency.'[82] It is this nuance that represents an epistemological break of enormous proportions between Gorbachev and Putin, and reflects the gulf that separates their respective generations. If Gorbachev in power reflected the preoccupations of the *shestdesyatniki*, the children of the Twentieth Party Congress, the thaw, Khrushchev's destalinisation and its associated aspirations for reform communism, then Putin is a *semidesyatnik*, a product of the 1970s and Brezhnev's stagnation.

Associated with the above, a fifth feature of Putin's politics is the tension between stability and order. This was a feature of Brezhnev's rule that in the end gave way to stagnation. Stability is the short-term attempt to achieve political and social stabilisation without having resolved the underlying problems and contradictions besetting society. Thus Brezhnev refused to take the hard choices that could have threatened the regime's precarious political stability, and thus his stability gave way to stagnation. Order in this context is something that arises when society, economy and political system are in some sort of balance. To a large extent an ordered society operates according to spontaneous processes, whereas in a system based on the politics of stability administrative measures tend to predominate. As Samuel Huntington noted, political order in changing societies sometimes requires the hard hand of the military or some other force that is not itself subordinate to democratic politics.[83] Putin on a number of occasions explicitly sought to distance himself from this sort of tutelary politics. For example, in his question and answer session with the Russian people on 19 December 2002, in response to a query about how the excesses of the media could be curbed, he insisted that 'it is impossible to resolve this problem, *to resolve it effectively that is* [italics added], simply with some kind of tough administrative measures'. This was linked in his view to the fact that the old Soviet-style politics that treated the whole population as infants was no longer viable since society had matured: 'our whole society is becoming more adult'.[84] Rather than seeing politics as a cultural struggle to impose a single truth, Putin appeared to accept a more pluralistic vision of societal diversity. As we shall see, however, it proved difficult to give adequate political form and expression to this diversity.[85]

There are many other features of Putin's politics of normality that could be identified. Let us note in conclusion to this section perhaps the most important and the source of all the others: Putin's attempt to reconcile the various phases of Russian history, especially over the last century. Tretyakov talks in terms of 'the attempt to restore the links of time disrupted by Yeltsin',[86] but the problem is far more far-reaching than that. In his New Year message to the Russian people on 31 December 2000 Putin noted that it had been 'a year of cheerful and tragic events' but above all had seen the emergence of 'distinct elements of stability'.[87] The day before at a Kremlin reception he noted that the adoption of the anthem (see Chapter 7) represented 'an important indication that we have finally managed to bridge the disparity between past and present', adding that 'one cannot be in permanent contradiction with one's own history and the destiny of one's own country'.[88] Putin sought to put an end to this 'permanent contradiction', one that some see as having been imposed on Russia at the dawn of the modern era by Peter the Great's attempts to impose modernity by unmodern means. Since then, it could be argued, Russia had been living in a type of 'permanent transition' (with transition here defined as the attempt to impose models of modernisation devised elsewhere). This long transition, Putin suggests, has now come to an end.[89] Putin has repudiated the idea of Russia as an alternative type of modernity, and to myths of unrealised alternatives in Russia's history.[90] As far as Putin is concerned, the revolution is over and it is time for Russia to start living in the present. This means a very different appreciation of historical time and developmental paths.

At the same time, the 'what country are we living in?' question appeared also to be resolved. Pavlovsky, the *éminence grise* if not Svengali of the new regime and the head of the Effective Policy Foundation, argued that Putin had put an end to the question of the USSR. 'Today the army in Chechnya,' he insisted, 'is victorious under the Russian flag, whereas in the previous war the Soviet army lost.'[91] Russia still hesitated to allow the formal demarcation of borders with countries like Ukraine, but under Putin the Yeltsinite 'smaller Russia' policy triumphed, although this did not mean the relinquishment of the new country's assertion of its alleged great power interests in the former imperial sphere. It did mean, however, that these national interests were now defined in terms of Russia's own needs, above all the pursuit of economic advantage. Although never losing sight of larger security and other interests, Putin explicitly espoused the 'economisation' of Russian foreign policy (see Chapter 9).

All of the above suggests that politics have now become 'normal', in the sense that larger constitutional questions over the shape of the polity have now given way to governmental administration of more mundane policy questions and the management of a functioning market economy based on private property and international economic integration. However, while a sense of normality has undoubtedly returned to Russia after nearly 15 years of post-communist revolutionary upheaval, quite apart from the preceding century of revolutionary 'extraordinary' measures, there are also some disturbing overtones of 'normalisation'.

*   *   *

The essence of Putin's political programme was the attempt to construct a dynamic and future-oriented politics of the centre. By definition, such a programme is in danger of becoming amorphous to the point of meaninglessness; but it does also have the potential to transcend traditional divisions and to lead the country on to a balanced developmental path conforming to native traditions while encouraging integration into the international community. The sharp polarisation that attended Yeltsin's rule has given way to an explicitly consensual and 'centrist' approach. The nature of this centrism is not simply an avoidance of the extremes of left and right but a radical centrism tailored to Russian circumstances. This radical centrism and the 'normal' politics with which it is associated, however, are beset by a number of fundamental contradictions, above all between the recognition of the necessity to encourage civic activism and attempts to control this activism, between the attempt to develop the rudiments of a liberal economy and society while strengthening the role of the state, and between institutionalising the powers of democratic accountability while engaging in personalised leadership activism. There could be no simple 'return to normalcy' in Russia, since Russia's normality has always been accompanied by elements of the emergency and the improvised. Putin's great aspiration was that at last Russia could enter a period akin to the normality enjoyed by the capitalist democracies of the West. We shall see below the degree to which his hopes were fulfilled.

3 The Putin way

Democratic socialism is not a middle way between capitalism and communism. If it were merely that, it would be doomed to failure from the start. It cannot live by borrowed vitality. Its driving power must derive from its own principles and the energy released by them.

(Aneurin Bevan[1])

In Chapter 2 we explored some of the thinking about the problems facing Russia on Putin's accession and the choices facing him. Here we will look more closely at Putin as a politician, examining the opportunities and risks that he confronted. He was constrained by the legacy of the past and the political and social order that he inherited, but as an active political agent he was able to shape agendas and build a political machine of his own. The development of Putin's own power base reflected his broader political role. While Yeltsin's rule can be understood as a period of 'permanent revolution', Putin now assumed the role of consolidator, the Napoleon (not necessarily on horseback) to Yeltsin's Robespierre. During the presidential campaign in 2000 Zyuganov had already called Putin a 'little Napoleon', and as Pavlovsky stressed, a Napolean does not emerge out of nowhere, and not everyone could become a Napoleon.[2] Like Napoleon, Putin sought to rebuild the state and incorporate into the new order the progressive elements of the revolutionary epoch necessary for social development while discarding the excesses and the revolutionary froth. Putin adopted the key test of such a consolidating role, the so-called 'zero-option'; the prohibition on the redistribution of property and the legal persecution of those involved in the privatisation excesses of the past. Putin also favoured the larger zero option: the crimes and repression of the Soviet period were to be put to one side for the sake of social harmony. The Soviet and Yeltsin revolutionary periods now gave way to one of post-revolutionary consolidation.

Building the Putin bloc

Putin's career reflected the enormous changes that had taken place in Russian society following the onset of *perestroika* in 1985. As Medvedev points out, Yeltsin could only challenge Gorbachev because he had belonged to the party elite for 20 years, whereas Putin was an outsider.[3] Adopted by the Yeltsin elite, he nevertheless remained an independent politician. Putin's refusal to launch wholesale investigations into the past can be interpreted as a pragmatic response to political weakness, but it also indicated a normative strategy of reconciliation and consensus-building. Putin considered not only the Yeltsin chapter as closed but also the whole Soviet period that preceded it. Putin's choice, rare for Russia, was in favour of social and political reconciliation; but it was a choice constrained by the circumstances in which he came to power and by the realities of the country he was destined to rule. Yeltsin had achieved a political revolution but had built the new system on traditional social foundations. Much of the old elite remained in office since the system, to use Huntington's terms, had been transformed rather than replaced.[4] At a certain point tensions between Putin's policy preferences and the constraints imposed by the inherited structure of social and bureaucratic power could come into contradiction. There is in addition the possibility that Putin had promised Yeltsin not to conduct wholesale personnel or policy changes for a certain period of time, and there is some circumstantial evidence to support such assertions.

Emerging as an unexpected president, Putin did not have a shadow government waiting to take over. The key problem facing him was the lack of a reliable team of his own and hence, according to Reddaway, he was forced to become a balancer of elite factions.[5] On several occasions Putin remarked, 'we have no personnel' (*'U nas net kadrov'*). According to Hahn, 'The logic of *nomenklatura*-led revolution from above predisposed the new regime to turn to *ancien regime* softliners in the hope of regaining the state's autonomy lost under nomenklatura capitalism.'[6] This dynamic had already come into play in the last few weeks of Kirienko's government in July 1998 in the attempt to appoint as economics minister Yury Maslyukov, a former member of Gorbachev's government and still a member of the CPRF, to what was meant to be a liberal government. The process had been marked much earlier, above all with the appointment of Primakov as foreign minister in January 1996, and then as prime minister in September 1998 as part of the regime's attempt to stabilise the system after the partial default of August. It was during Primakov's premiership that the assault against the most prominent of the oligarchs, Berezovsky, was first launched through an investigation into alleged money-laundering when he was at the head of Aeroflot, but in the event it was Primakov who was dismissed in May 1999.

Although Putin was to draw liberally on members of the old Soviet ruling class, above all its security apparatus, to staff his administration, they were typically kept far away from the management of the economy. The presidency itself was sustained by an unstable mix of Yeltsinite officials (some of whom were associated with the 'family'), a newer generation of reform-minded St Petersburg officials (many of whom had been associated with Putin personally), and people from the military and security services, the *siloviki*.[7] Former KGB workers are known as *chekisty* (taking their name from Lenin's secret police established in December 1918, the Cheka), and this group was one of Putin's main sources of personnel, in particular those whom he had known during his years in Leningrad. There appeared to be a fundamental rivalry in the Kremlin between the 'old Muscovites', members of Yeltsin's 'family', and the Petersburg newcomers (the '*Pitery*'), who themselves were divided into economic liberals (many of whom had worked with Putin in the city administration) and *chekisty* (from the first stage of his career). The Muscovites were represented by the head of the presidential administration Alexander Voloshin and his deputy Vladislav Surkov, while the key *Pitery* included the chief secretary Igor Sechin, deputy head Victor Ivanov and the lawyer Dmitry Kozak, also a deputy head of the presidential administration. Outside the Kremlin the *Pitery* included Sergei Pugachev, the head of Mezhprombank, who enjoyed close ties with Putin from their St Petersburg days. Pugachev provided financial support for the *Pitery*, while his association with the Orthodox Church earned him the moniker 'the Christian oligarch'.

The *Pitery* provided many of the liberals in Putin's administration. The head of Putin's campaign team, Dmitry Medvedev, was one of Putin's main advisors in the Kremlin. The two had worked together in St Petersburg as part of Sobchak's administration. The promotion of St Petersburgers, even if they may not have been native sons or daughters of the city (the so-called 'Moscow St Petersburgers' like Valentina Matvienko, born in Moscow but who had made her career in St Petersburg, and sponsored by Putin in the St Petersburg gubernatorial elections in 2000 and 2003) underlined the continued importance of the *zemlyachestvo* (friendly ties between people coming from the same homeplace) in Russian politics.[8] There were even rumours that Putin had plans to move some federal institutions to St Petersburg, including the State Duma, the Federation Council and several ministries, but in the event Putin remained committed to Moscow remaining the undivided capital of the country.

There were also a number of 'clans' that remained outside the Putin 'bloc', notably Luzhkov's power base in Moscow, Yakovlev's team in St Petersburg and some other powerful regional power constellations. By contrast with Primakov, Putin went out of his way to demonstrate his openness to enter into dialogue with regional elites, and Unity (later United Russia) became the organisational expression of this. The core of United Russia was regional officialdom, with the 39 founding governors (mostly not of the first rank) in autumn 1999 swelled by new cohorts once the success of the body became clear. United Russia looked as if it could become the core of a presidential catch-all party with Putin at its head. This is something that Yeltsin had always avoided doing on the grounds that he was 'president of all Russians', fearing that he would himself be constrained politically. Although careful not to rupture relations with the regions, Putin moved forward to strengthen the powers of the central government in the regions and to ensure the uniform implementation of the constitution. (We shall discuss this in greater depth in Chapter 6.)

The presidency in Russia is directly responsible for some fifteen ministries, above all the so-called power ministries (defence, security, MVD and the like, the *siloviki*) together with foreign affairs. Ministers in these fields report directly to the president. The prime minister manages the economic and social bloc of ministries. The premier in Putin's first term, Kasyanov, was a holdover from the Yeltsin period, and his apparent lack of reforming zeal led to accusations that the economy was doomed to enter another period of stagnation. In fact Kasyanov was far from being a tool of the increasingly mythical 'family', and proved an able and loyal ally to Putin. Despite repeated rumours that Kasyanov would be sacked, he remained Putin's prime minister in his first term. Although Putin's personal ratings remained high, those of his government were weaker. This did not prompt major governmental reshuffles, and in this area as in others Putin preferred an incremental and piecemeal approach. It was not clear what a team of his own liking would look like. The government itself, according to Nemtsov, could be considered a 'coalition oligarch-liberal government', which he suggested would inevitably be torn apart by internal differences between the two rival groups.[9] This did not happen, but there were tensions within the government, above all over the most appropriate economic policy.

There is an important difference between coalition-building, which in Western democracies usually takes the form of a stable alliance based on the mutual self-interest of identifiable political forces, and consensus-making, the attempt to draw people into a common project or around a common policy. The only time that coalition building had been attempted in post-communist Russia was in 1992, when Yeltsin sought to gain the support of party leaders for reform and in his struggle with parliament. The political system emerging out of the defeat of the old parliament in October 1993 and enshrined in the December 1993 constitution focuses all fundamental political processes on the president. In the context of a weak party system and a hegemonic presidency, coalition building can at best be marginal. Instead, under Putin the presidency tried to rally individual political leaders, social and political groupings and interests, as well as the public at large, to its cause. Putin's power was based not on a formal coalition of political groupings but on his ability to draw forces in under the wing of the hegemonic presidency. This worked as long as he remained a popular and effective leader, but some sharp setback in policy or a loss of nerve could see the Putin consensus dissolve.

One of the key tests of Putin's leadership was how he would relate to Yeltsin's elite: would Prince Hal turn against Falstaff? Many insisted that

'Putin is no more than a tool of oligarchical capital and at the same time the hope of those who wish to see the strengthening of nomenklatura capitalism.'[10] Andrei Ryabov, an analyst with the Carnegie Moscow Centre, took a more nuanced view in arguing that 'Yeltsin's style was feudal, but it worked. And now Putin is trying to completely change this relationship between the state and the elites, No one knows what the new relationship will look like.'[11] The Kremlin elites that had propelled Putin to power certainly tried to achieve the perpetuation of Yeltsin-style politics, 'Yeltsinism without Yeltsin'. Putin's policies did not challenge the economic and political privileges and semi-feudal power of the neo-nomenklatura elite, but Putin was more than simply a representative of one of these factions or trapped by balancing between them. He clearly represented a more enlightened and developmentally progressive group disgusted at the rapacity and short-termism of the dominant Yeltsinite faction, willing to see the golden goose that was Russia die as they stuffed their pockets full of the pickings from the dying body.

Although an effective consensus builder, there were at least two potential constraints on Putin's policies. The first was dependence on the oligarchs, the backbone of the old Yeltsin regime and the power base of the Muscovites. These elites were focused on the so-called 'family', the group of Kremlin insiders that included the head of the presidential administration, Voloshin, the oligarchs Berezovsky and Roman Abramovich, Moscow banker Alexander Mamut, former Yeltsin presidential speech writer Valentin Yumashev, Boris Yeltsin's daughter Tatyana Dyachenko, and Pavel Borodin, the former head of the Kremlin's 'property department', who became state secretary of the Russia–Belarus Union in early 2000 on Putin's recommendation. Voloshin had once been Berezovsky's business partner and had then become presidential chief of staff under Yeltsin, a position that he continued to hold under Putin. Despite endless rumours about Voloshin's dismissal, he had become the core of Putin's team, in part because of his phenomenal stamina and ability to devour work.[12] In late 1999 and early 2000 it certainly appeared that Putin was constrained by the oligarchs, with Berezovsky and Abramovich taking advantage of the presidential election campaign to seize control of the bulk of Russia's extraordinarily profitable aluminium industry.[13] The oil and aluminium oligarch with close ties to the family, Abramovich, appeared untouchable, as did Mamut, although later Berezovsky's political influence was destroyed. In numerous interviews it was Pavlovsky who invented the idea of a struggle between the '*siloviki*' and 'the family' as a way of explaining the difficulties and impediments in the way of implementing Putin's policies.[14] According to Petr Kozma, the family are a group of opportunists ready to turn their coats to remain in power.[15] That is probably the case, but the group, however amorphous, did place a constraint on personnel changes.

It was Voloshin who allegedly countermanded Putin's attempts to appoint his St Petersburg colleague Kozak as Prosecutor-General. Instead, the acting Prosecutor-General, Vladimir Ustinov, was confirmed in his post, and thus one avenue whereby the excesses of the Yeltsin years could have been exposed was closed off. As one commentator put it, with Ustinov's appointment 'any lingering doubts that Putin was an unwilling captive of the Family were dispelled'.[16] The acting prime minister, Kasyanov, who had traditionally been close to the Yeltsin insiders, was confirmed as prime minister following Putin's formal inauguration as president in May 2000. However, things were far more complicated than that. Putin at this time was able to ensure the dismissal of family-member Viktor Kalyuzhny as fuel and energy minister, replacing him by the little-known Alexander Gavrin, suggesting at least an awareness of the need to show independence in forming the government. This independence gradually grew during the term of his first administration. By the end, few suggested that Putin was not his own man. There was to be no Yeltsinism without Yeltsin.

It would nevertheless be very difficult for Putin to distance himself from 'the family', even if he wanted to. Pavlovsky, after all, argued that Putin had been selected by the family 'not only according to the principle of loyalty, but [of] ... dependence'.[17] The precise nature of this 'dependence' was unclear: was there some sort of deal whereby Putin guaranteed no major personnel changes in the first year of his leadership? As it happens, Putin dismissed the Yeltsin-era defence and interior ministers the day after he had served a year in office. Rumours abounded that the Yeltsinite elite held some sort of *kompromat* (compromising material) against him, to be held as insurance that he did not trespass against their interests. This could help explain why Putin at times appeared so irresolute. As Yevgeniya Albats put it: 'Putin, weak and inconsistent as he has seemed up to now, is being torn apart by the two loyalties he inherited: first to the corporation, the brotherhood, the KGB which made him a man; second to "the family" which made him president'.[18] Perhaps the gravest danger that Putin faced in his early period of rule was that these two elements would come into conflict with each other.

In the short term, one of the immediate consequences of Putin's policy of consensus was his insistence that there would not be another grand redistribution of property. Instead, Putin drew a thick line under Yeltsin's own possible misdemeanours and those of the class that had profited from his rule. Putin's first official act as interim president had granted Yeltsin and his family immunity from prosecution. Putin's adoption of the 'zero-option' represented a deliberate act of social reconciliation. It was motivated by practical considerations, but it also had a normative basis: putting an end to Russia's endless cycles of revolutions and counter-revolutions. This issue was particularly important in the context where some 60 per cent of the population according to one poll favoured the administrative confiscation of the wealth of the 'new Russians'.[19] Instead of the stark choice posited by many of either breaking with the Yeltsin family or remaining a dependent politician, Putin finessed the problem. He remained true to his commitments to Yeltsin and continued his policies, but during his presidency the conduct of politics changed dramatically. As Putin put it in his 24 June 2002 extended press conference, 'we are developing the country on the base that was established by the previous political leadership headed by the first president of Russia Boris Nikolaevich Yeltsin'. Pressed on his personal relations with Yeltsin, since the latter had been insisting on speedy union with Belarus, Putin answered, 'He has his views on that question, and I have mine.'[20]

If 'the family' and their associated oligarchs was one constituency that constrained Putin's freedom of action, another was that exercised by what we may call the national security establishment. In theoretical terms, Putin was heir to the Andropov tradition of attempting to modernise an ailing system by the firm hand from above, the model of authoritarian modernisation. In this context many have talked about the 'securitisation' of appointments, if not of the system as a whole. Putin certainly drew on the security establishment and his old roots in St Petersburg; and in many cases the two groups coincided. According to one estimate, almost 40 per cent of the high posts in the early days came from the FSB,[21] and this trend was continued thereafter. A number of near contemporaries of Putin from his time as a KGB officer in Leningrad enjoyed close personal links with him and gained influence. The key figures were Putin's long-time associate with a record of twenty years in the intelligence service, Sergei Ivanov, Putin's replacement as head of the Security Council and appointed defence minister on 28 March 2001; Nikolai Patrushev, Putin's successor head of the FSB; and Victor Cherkesov, Putin's envoy (*polpred*) in Northwest Russia. Ivanov rejected the argument that men from the security services had come to power, while at the same time denying that the Security Council was in any way becoming a shadow cabinet or a Politburo, insisting that it was and would remain a consultative body doing no more than preparing proposals for the president on strengthening national security.[22] Although the Security Council was given extraordinary powers to be applied during states of emergency, comparisons with the Politburo of old are rather far-fetched. Its influence has tended to rise and fall depending on the status of its secretary. When Ivanov was appointed defence minister the SC once again sharply declined in significance.

The military was granted considerable latitude in the second Chechen war from September 1999. Already there was evidence, however, that Putin sought to trim the effective veto exercised by some of the security hard liners in foreign policy. In February 2000 he effectively sidelined hawks like Leonid Ivashov, head of the Defence Ministry's foreign affairs department, and General Kvashnin, the Chief of the General Staff, to allow a meeting with Lord George Robertson, the head of Nato. Soon after, in an interview with the BBC on 5 March 2000 Putin even went so far as to entertain the possibility that one day Russia might join Nato, albeit on 'equal terms' (see Chapter 9). Like Yeltsin earlier, rhetorical support for the military was not translated into concrete policies, and the military as an institution continued to decline under Putin. Severe cuts in numbers were accompanied by continued moves away from a conscript to a fully professional service. An unintended but no less important consequence of this was the continued demilitarisation of

Russian politics, although in terms of personnel the presence of military and security officials continued to increase. This, however, reflected less the militarisation of domestic politics than the civilianisation of the military. This was reflected in the appointment of Ivanov to head the defence ministry in 2001, the first civilian (although with a security background) to become defence minister since the Brezhnev period.

The debate continues over whether security and military personnel in office means the militarisation or 'securitisation' of politics in its entirety. The security component of the Putin bloc was itself far from homogeneous, and its support for Putin was at best conditional. An interview with Valery Velichko, the president of the State Security Veterans Association, was revealing. He noted:

> Yes, we did help him [Putin] during a first stage, during the election campaign. But now, it's time to wait. Putin can go one way and continue working for the Family . . . Or he can work for the state. Or he can work for himself. For the moment he hasn't shown anything yet.[23]

Velichko was an adherent of the Andropov approach to change, hoping for an evolutionary course like China's that developed a market economy while maintaining the communist regime. There is no evidence that Putin shared such an approach. The Andropov way was not the Putin way.

The Putin bloc remained a broad church, reflecting Putin's past, but its disparate nature was reflected in certain policy areas (above all the economy) by a loss of coherence. In general, although sharp policy disagreements swirled around Putin, it is only with great difficulty that these debates can be mapped directly on to factional struggles, such as Muscovites against *Pitery*, *chekisty* versus liberals. Putin did turn, as we shall see, against some of the more odious oligarchs, but worked happily with the rest. He did not become a captive of any particular grouping, such as the security establishment or the St Petersburg liberals, but allowed room for manoeuvre. At the same time, the composition of the ruling elite changed under his presidency, with the proportion of women and intellectuals falling, while those from the regions and the security services increasing.[24] Putin's skill as a political tactician is perhaps best revealed in the way that he was able to draw the fire of the communists in parliament by offering them a disproportionate share of committee chairs and powers in the new Duma in January 2000, and then encouraging a breakaway grouping of moderates led by the speaker, Gennady Seleznev. The rump CPRF was left alienated and angry, but relatively powerless, and when a reshuffle of portfolios came later, the communists lost their positions. As for popular support, it was clear that Putin nurtured the public as a farmer tends his stock, never pushing policies (such as reform of municipal services) so far or so fast as to add significantly to the burden of public misery. Putin, however, was no populist, pandering to the whims of public opinion and the often vengeful, xenophobic and angry moods to which the public is prey when whipped up by the 'birdseed' press in societies that feel under siege from crime, migratory and other pressures. Putin was certainly no Alexander Lukashenko, whose brand of populism in neighbouring Belarus was based on sensitivity to popular prejudices and a crude disdain for representative institutions, the courts and for all political institutions that could in any way limit the power of the presidency. More than that, in Russia the rudiments of a middle class had developed, and provided the bedrock for the politics of normality propounded by Putin. According to Maleva, about 20 per cent of Russian families could be considered middle class.[25]

Although subject to constant sniping from elite groups and the media, Putin's qualities were recognised by the people, and this was reflected in a remarkably sustained high level of poll ratings. Popular support, in turn, provided Putin with an important political resource in his struggles against opponents and in pushing through his reforms. However, his resolute yet accommodating political style began to provoke comparisons with Gorbachev: the 'Gorbachevisation' of Putin's leadership was taken to mean a style where rhetoric substitutes for action and crucial decisions are delayed. This is unfair to both Gorbachev and Putin, since both tried to rule by consensus, although willing to take hard decisions when required. Putin's power base was built on three key elements: the family cum oligarchs, a disparate group of St Petersburg economic liberals, and *siloviki*. It is clear, however, that none of these three existed as a coherent force. Like any democratic politician Putin had to take into account the interests of various constituencies, the fluctuating balance of political forces, and arbitrate between different policy choices.

Putin and the people

The entrenchment of the 'transitional winners' and their resistance to the reassertion of national state interests was an important constraint on Putin's power, but to overcome this obstacle Putin posed as the champion of the interests of 'transitional losers', the great mass of the people who had seen their living standards eroded, wages left unpaid, pensions falling into arrears, and their savings lost. While Putin's policy attitudes have indeed been popular, Putin was far from populist himself. Neither was he simply the product of 'virtual politics', the passive beneficiary of the manipulation of political consciousness, processes and institutions by various powerful interests. These 'political technologies' are indeed highly developed in Russia, and a whole industry has developed bringing together academics, opinion polling experts and political aspirants, and they were particularly active in the 1999–2000 electoral cycle.[26] Yet Putin's political charisma and programmatic identity cannot be reduced to this, and without a popular sense of a determined personality with a vision for Russia's future, no amount of manipulation would have ensured victory. In addition, Putin did largely deliver on his election promise to pay wages and pensions on time, and this was no small achievement.

Despite continuing debates over public attitudes towards core values of democracy, tolerance, pluralism, the West and the like, it is clear that the country which Putin came to lead suffered from a lack of confidence in the new order and public institutions. Some 80 per cent of the population appeared dissatisfied with democracy, a figure higher than the CIS average (75 per cent) or that typical of the EU (50 per cent).[27] In spring 2001 just two per cent of the population thought that Russia was a democracy, while 21 per cent thought the country was moving in that direction and 27 per cent considered Russia more democratic than it had been in the Soviet era (although 17 per cent took the contrary view).[28] Questioned on the level of trust in institutions, churches came out top with 19 per cent evincing full and 28 per cent some trust. Second came the armed forces at 14 and 36 per cent, respectively, while near the bottom came the government at 7 and 24, parliament at 2 and 14, and political parties at a miserable 2 and 9 per cent, respectively.[29] Despite polls showing a clear popular distrust of the new democracy, when it came to elections participation has been remarkably high. The 54 per cent of eligible voters turning out in December 1993, 64 per cent in 1995 and 62 per in 1999 suggests that scepticism is tempered by a certain commitment. In presidential elections turnout was even higher: in 1991 75 per cent; in 1996 (first round) 70 per cent, and second round 69 per cent; and in 2000 69 per cent.

The central question on coming to power was whether Putin and his allies would challenge the Yeltsinite socio-political settlement, above all the bureaucratised neo-nomenklatura regime that had emerged in the 1990s that benefited from a country stuck half way between the plan and the market. To what extent did Putin have an independent political base? The answer to this question is crucial to understanding the room for manoeuvre that Putin had as president. As we saw in the previous section, the Putin consensual bloc was fragmented and lacked a single coherent programme. Pavlovsky raised the basic question: 'We are trying to determine now whose victory was the victory of Putin. On whom should he now rely?' He dismissed Unity as an adequate political base, and came up with the unexpected answer: 'The masses, which were not allowed to emerge on the political scene after 1991–93, have surged onto it today. And Putin is their leader.' He went on:

> One can argue in what sense he is the leader – the leader of the party of power or the leader of the opposition. I believe that those who chose Putin regard him as the leader of the opposition who seized power in Russia. For Putin's majority Putin is the leader of the party of opposition to the old regime.[30]

Putin's rise, in other words, can be seen as a distinctive variation on the theme of a revolt from below, reflecting spontaneous revulsion against the venality of the Yeltsin years while not rejecting the basic principles that Yeltsin's leadership had espoused. Putin's popularity was based at least in part on favourable comparisons with his predecessor, but also on a more positive projection of popular aspirations, hopes that were not totally devoid of rationality. In particular, the Putin bloc was anchored in the aspirations of the younger generation, who were more likely to support market reform, democracy and integration with the West than other age groups.[31]

Sooner or later there was a danger that the public would tire of the relentless projection of the Putin personality in the media. As the years passed it became clear that this would come later, if at all. According to poll results Putin's popularity remained remarkably stable. After his first 100 days in office the ARPI Agency of Regional Political Studies revealed that some 54 per cent still evaluated him positively, giving rise already at this early stage of talk of a 'teflon president'.[32] One reason for Putin's popularity, of course, was that he was not Yeltsin. Between 1994 and 2001 the percentage of people holding Yeltsin personally responsible for the troubles of the 1990s nearly doubled from 18.1 to 34 per cent.[33] The basic feeling that Russia had become a happier place since Putin's accession remained. Two years into his leadership a growing number were positive about the system of government that he headed, although at 47 per cent this was still a minority. At that time 72 per cent rated the old communist system positively, by far the highest positive ranking in any of the non-CIS post-communist countries.[34] The shaky foundations of the new order was reflected in the astonishing figure that half of Russia would approve of the closing down of parliament, and just over one-fifth thought that it could happen.[35] While trust in the political institutions of democracy was low throughout the region, in Russia it was lower still, with only 7 per cent trusting parliament and the same number parties.[36] Not surprisingly, both Yeltsin and Putin ran as independents.

Putin's approval rating in the first three years of his leadership remained at a remarkably high and consistent level, with between 65 and 73 per cent whose attitude remained positive.[37] In contrast to Yeltsin's frequent absences 'working on documents', Putin did not have a single day off sick in the first three years of his presidency.[38] Polls consistently found Putin's performance rated excellent by between 37 and 50 per cent of respondents, while another 36 to 48 per cent considered his performance satisfactory. On the third anniversary of his election in March 2003 39 per cent found his performance excellent or good, another 46 per cent considered it satisfactory, and only 11 per cent thought that he worked badly.[39] A poll taken at the same time revealed that 38 per cent felt more positive about Putin than they had done on his election, 52 per cent the same, and only 10 per cent worse. The reason for this was a strong sense (61 per cent) that Putin had managed to fulfil many of his plans during his presidency, while only 10 per cent felt that he had fulfilled none. As for his independence as a decision maker, 61 per cent thought that he was influenced by other people while 37 per cent thought that he was his own man. A related question asked whether he was more independent now than three years earlier, and 66 per cent thought that he was more independent while 26 per cent thought that he was as independent as before. The response to the related question of whether Putin put his own popularity or the interests of the country first saw nearly 60 per cent agree with the latter proposition, while 28 per cent thought that he cared more for his popularity.[40]

Richard Rose and associates have argued that a president's popularity that is 'a mile wide' on election day can prove ephemeral, and examine the degree to which Putin's popularity may well have been an inch deep.[41] In the event Putin's popularity proved rather more enduring, but the approach does draw attention to the decidedly mixed approval ratings for his performance and that of his government on a number of policy issues. Approval of the work of his cabinet fell from 57 per cent to 39 per cent in June 2000 alone, due apparently to the failure to end the war in Chechnya and fears that inflation was once again on the rise.[42] In December 2002 only 33 per cent thought that Kasyanov handled his job well, while 27 per cent thought not. The performance of his government was rated similarly, with only 24 per cent thinking it was doing a good job while 37 per cent thought its performance bad.[43] In general, as noted, trust in political institutions in Russia scores poorly, highlighting the gulf between trust in the president and the political system that he headed. Polls suggested a relatively low belief that Russia had become a democratic system.[44]

Putin's achievements in the sphere of foreign policy and democracy tended to gain more positive than negative ratings, but on issues such as whether Putin had been able to restore order to the country, limit corruption, improve the economy or resolve the Chechen crisis, then the negative ratings predominated.[45] For the majority of the population, trying to survive on small pensions and miserly wages, the big questions of macroeconomic policy, judicial reform and the like appeared very distant, especially since their personal contacts with the courts and other authoritative bodies tended to be dispiriting if not outright corrupt. Asked what they would ask Putin to do if presented with the opportunity, 47 per cent said 'raise living standards', 21 per cent 'establish an effective management system', 12 per cent 'stimulate economic development and employment', while only 2 per cent said 'end the Chechen war' and the same number focused on 'foreign policy'.[46]

The near mythical status of the 'Putin phenomenon' aroused much resentment, but it would not be fair to say that it was achieved by the deliberate suppression of the status of alternatives.[47] Putin's popularity was sustained in part by the absence of anyone else who came even close to him in trust ratings. Throughout 2002 Putin was trusted by about 40 per cent, with Zyuganov coming a distant second at 10 per cent, followed by Shoigu, Zhirinovsky and only then Kasyanov at 5 per cent.[48] In the same poll Shoigu's Emergency Situations Ministry came out well on top by respondents when asked to rate which ministries best executed their duties, and he was considered by far (41 per cent) the best performing minister, followed way below by Igor Ivanov (the foreign minister) at 13 per cent. Although Putin's general approval rating remained astronomically high, this was not, as Elena Shestopal puts it, 'hypnotic blindness' but was tempered by an awareness, and indeed criticism, of his shortcomings and a recognition of his unattractive qualities.[49] Putin's electoral attractiveness remained high and victory in the 2004 presidential election seemed assured.[50] There appeared to be no alternative candidate who could seriously challenge him.

Another factor maintaining Putin's popularity was that he became more adept at managing crises. One of the greatest tests to Putin's leadership in the early period was the sinking in the Barents Sea of the *Kursk* nuclear submarine on 12 August 2000.[51] The craft had only entered service in 1995 and was considered the most modern and reliable in the submarine fleet. The explosion that tore the craft apart and killed 118 submariners was caused by the leak of highly unstable hydrogen peroxide torpedo fuel. A first explosion then provoked a far more powerful blast in the nose of the submarine that sent it to the bottom. This was admitted only two years after the sinking by the government commission headed by Ilya Klebanov. Earlier various explanations had been advanced, including the idea that the *Kursk* had been struck by either an American or British submarine, or that a rocket from a nearby Russian battleship participating in the same military exercise may have been responsible. Putin's failure to break off his holiday on the Black Sea immediately drew much criticism, as did the extended delay before the offers of foreign help were accepted.[52] Putin later fulfilled his promise that the craft would be raised and the sailors given a proper burial. By the time of the Dubrovka theatre siege in October 2002 (for more on this see Chapter 7) he was able to project an image of resoluteness and humanity, although chaos among the emergency services after the storming of the building caused many additional deaths. On the evening of 26 October, at the end of the three-day siege in which 129 out of the 800 hostages had died, largely because of the carelessness of the rescuers, Putin addressed the people:

> We succeeded in doing what seemed almost impossible – in saving the lives of hundreds of people. We showed that Russia cannot be forced to her knees. But now, first of all, I would like to address the relatives and friends of those who have perished. We could not save everyone. Forgive us.[53]

The fact that a large group of armed Chechens could capture a building in Moscow revealed the relative powerlessness of the state and the advanced decay of its institutions, and thus only reinforced Putin's exhortations to strengthen the state.

Putin's resilient popularity could be taken as a sorry reflection of the condition of Russian politics, when so many of the population projected their hopes on one individual. As Avtandil Tsuladze put it, 'Putin appears to be the last hope of society for the preservation of stability.'[54] Putin can be seen as representative of the type that has a long pedigree in Russian history, the decisive leader who forges the nation's consolidation in a time of crisis. This usually took place at a time of a foreign threat, accompanied sometimes by internal disintegration. In Putin's case, the main threats were domestic. Putin's rise to power can be considered a type of 'revolt of the masses' against the venality and greed of the Yeltsin years. In this context it was perfectly logical for the reform of the federal system to be one of Putin's first priorities. It was an attempt, in the words of Andrei Ryabov, 'to bring more order and justice into society, since the arbitrariness of the regional barons is there for all to see'.[55] Equally, the struggle for 'social justice' meant for many an assault on the extra-democratic privileges of the oligarchs. However, if he failed to deliver, popular disenchantment could well take dangerous forms. Putin did not enjoy a stable power coalition, and some of the liberal economic reforms entailed harsh social consequences and for this reason Putin was most cautious in implementing them. This in turn meant that the reform impetus threatened to stall, provoking the danger of yet another period of stagnation, which in turn would have deleterious social consequences.

Leadership and style

Leadership is an essential, although often neglected, aspect of any democratic system. As Schumpeter argued,

> The classical theory [of democracy] did not do this ['give proper recognition of the vital fact of leadership'] but ... attributed to the electorate an altogether unrealistic degree of initiative which practically amounted to ignoring leadership. But collectives act almost exclusively by accepting leadership – this is the dominant mechanism of practically any collective action which is more than a reflex.[56]

Putin's presidency is a classic case where individual leadership can stamp its preferences on a period, although of course constrained by the conditions of that time. In addition to the important role of leadership in all democratic societies, there are factors particular to Russia. It is often argued that Russia has a cultural predisposition towards strong personalised leadership. In post-communist Russia this aspect of the country's political culture was boosted by the weakness of formal political institutions and the under-development of societal representation, above all the relatively inchoate nature of the party system. In addition, the numerous crises affecting the country increased support for resolute leadership.

In this context the notion of charisma has particular relevance, although distinct types of charismatic leadership can be identified. Eatwell distinguishes between *coterie charisma*, in which a leader inspires devotion among a relatively small inner core of followers; *mass charisma*, whereby the leader is able to generate broad popular sentiments; while the phenomenon of *institutional charisma* suggests that a charismatic bond may develop between an institution, such as a political party or even the presidency as an abstract symbol of power, and its followers.[57] The charismatic bond, moreover, can be either affective or based on rational calculation.[58] Putin's charisma was distinctive but clearly of the mass type. He was a strong leader with a vision for the country's future that made him 'the president of hope'.

Archie Brown has drawn the contrast between 'transformational' leaders, who change not just policy but the system as well, with 'transactional' ones, who may well achieve major policy changes but who remain within the bounds of the existing order.[59] He recognises that the characterisation of any particular leader depends on the categories of transformation that are chosen, and in our case this is particularly important. Putin repudiated the revolutionary approach to political change, but this does not automatically make him a transactional leader. He worked within the parameters of the system inherited from Yeltsin, but at the same time he transformed the way that it operated. Paradoxically, Putin's repudiation of revolutionary methods made him one of Russia's most profound revolutionaries, wreaking a greater transformation of Russia's culture of politics than many a more obviously revolutionary predecessor.

Putin's first period in power was marked by a flurry of activity, with attacks launched on a number of fronts simultaneously – against the regional barons, the oligarchs and the media. Important constitutional issues appeared to be resolved by bullying tactics and administrative means. The strategic wisdom in becoming embroiled in so many conflicts simultaneously was questionable. Even with popular support, Putin's skills as a political manager would be crucial in seeing his changes through. When faced with strong opposition, however, Putin tended to conduct an orderly retreat. Putin retreated, for example, when it became clear that the electorate would reject his favoured candidate (Matvienko) against the incumbent, Yakovlev, in the St Petersburg gubernatorial elections of 16 May 2000. Too many such retreats could dent the 'aura of invincibility' that had built up during his premiership and early presidency, and in later years Putin was careful to prepare the ground before launching a policy – perhaps too cautious, hence the charges of the 'Gorbachevisation' of his leadership.

The appearance of apparent policy reversals led the *Kommersant* weekly business magazine to editorialise about 'The weakness of the firm hand'.[60] The case could be made with equal conviction that Putin's leadership style reflected the firmness of the weak hand. It is clear that authoritarianism without a bedrock of institutional support can prove ephemeral. The possible social and institutional bases for authoritarianism in Russia would include the security establishment and the military, together with some alienated intellectuals, but there is no evidence that Putin sought to forge such a coalition. It is unlikely that the authoritarian populism practised by Lukashenko in neighbouring Belarus could be transferred to Russia. There is no serious evidence that Putin sought to establish an alternative system to the representative democracy that had emerged in Russia in the 1990s; but, equally, his commitment to democratic values would only be proven by the flourishing of media freedom, the rule of law and ultimately the greatest challenge, the democratic rotation of the highest political office in the land in free elections. While the legitimacy of democracy in Russia was undermined by its association with economic failure, social hardship, criminality and waning prestige on the world scale, opinion polls still showed a strong core of support for basic democratic principles. Indeed, if the main criticism of government in the early period of Putin's leadership was that it was not strong enough, by the end of his first term the main charge was the Russian state was not democratic enough. A sea of change in the terms of discourse had taken place.

Putin's room for manoeuvre was limited by the existing socio-political and socio-economic structure. Did the pattern of property, privileges and power established under Yeltsin allow scope for radical political intervention and change? It soon became clear that an activist presidency could mobilise the population and state loyalists against the venality of the Yeltsin regime in the name of Russia's honour and dignity. Putin found many to support such a reconstitution of the state and law and order. However, while Putin could use the presidency as instrument for change, its power was constrained by Putin's lack of an organised mass political base. While Unity was potentially such a movement, this would take a lot of time to create as a genuine mass movement. The merger of Unity with Luzhkov's Fatherland party in early 2002 to create United Russia (*Edinaya Rossiya*) represented no more than one step in the creation of an effective presidential party.

Putin carefully managed his relationship with the press, and thus with the people. On 18 July 2001, a year and a half after the last one, Putin held an extended press conference, with some 500 domestic and foreign correspondents in attendance. Putin argued that his main achievement in office was the maintenance of 'stability and a certain consensus in society' that would allow the country's political and economic modernisation. He became angry when asked about the mopping-up operations (*zachistki*) in Chechnya, but was able to turn questioning about the status of the oligarch Berezovsky by asking 'Boris Berezovsky – who is that?' into humour. Berezovsky had accused Putin of harbouring authoritarian tendencies and planned to establish an opposition party (later called Liberal Russia). Putin called Berezovsky an 'irrepressible, indefatigable man', always 'appointing someone or overthrowing someone'.[61] In his similar press conference held a year later on 24 June 2002 Putin was more measured in his comments on Chechnya; clearly, he had learnt to control his emotions on this question. He was asked several questions about his relationship with Yeltsin. By then Yeltsin's health had dramatically improved and he sought once again to find a role for himself, and was not backward in making his views known on issues such as unification with Belarus. On being questioned about this Putin clearly revealed that a chill had entered into his relations with Yeltsin.

Certain familiar elements of a mini cult of the personality began to emerge, with Putin's portrait obligatory in all offices of the presidential administration and often in government departments. Whereas under Yeltsin portraits of Russian artists or historical leaders (usually Peter the Great) hung in the space vacated by Lenin, now Putin's features adorned the walls of the bureaucracy. Kemal Ataturk had had to work long and hard to become 'father of the nation', while Putin seemed to have adopted the pose *ex officio.* A spate of books on Ataturk reflected the comparison.[62] From this perspective, Putin's 'dazzling' foreign policy persona was no more than a manoeuvre to give him time to consolidate power at home. Putin's vigorous style gave rise to the accusation that he was guilty of a neo-authoritarian style of governing. He was even called by some a 'soft dictator'. His assertions about the need for a 'dictatorship of law' revealed perhaps more than he intended. The frontal assault on the old system of federal relations meant the developing constitutional order was less able to incorporate perhaps necessary correctives from the regional leaders themselves. The 1993 constitution had established a strong executive and it has been argued only formalised traditional Russian patterns of centralised and personalised governance.[63] Yeltsin's style of government had been highly personalised,[64] and this was accentuated by Putin's activist leadership style.

There was a tension in Putin's approach to leadership between traditional patrimonial and personalised facets and the attempt to achieve more rational, impersonal and ordered administration. Some have stressed the origins of Putin's thinking in Andropov's plans to achieve an authoritarian modernisation of the country, and have argued that the increased role of security and military officials in Putin's new elite would give rise, to use Marc Raeff's phrase, to a 'well-ordered police state'. Such an approach misses the fundamental novelty of his leadership. Putin sought more than just a rationalisation of power, but a fundamental reordering of administration. Unless we adopt what would probably be the untenable position that all of Putin's speeches, declarations and exhortations were no more than a cloud of propaganda designed to put people off the track of his real ambitions, we have to take at more or less face value his understanding that governmental relations had to be placed on a more formal and institutional basis and operate according to the dictates of the constitution, and that this reordered administration had to be embedded in political pluralism and a free society. There were no end to the contradictions accompanying the implementation of this programme, but we need to be clear that this was the strategic direction in which Putin sought to take the country. In recognising this, as so often, the wisdom of the Russian people was far greater than many of the professional pundits.

Was Putin weak or strong? Despite his great rhetorical vigour, Putin's position at times appeared weak and inconsistent, torn as he was between the security apparatus and the 'family' that had made him.[65] It was clear that he came to power with the support of 'the family', but although he did not become their prisoner, he was clearly constrained by the interests that it represented. Putin clearly tried to broaden his political base. He invited Primakov and Luzhkov on trips abroad, and in general sought to ground his leadership in a broad consensual bloc. Relations within the bloc were personal and largely based on loyalty. Putin's personal preference was to soften the edges of conflicts where possible, as in his pattern when dismissing someone from one post to offer them another. This was the case with the governor of Maritime *krai*, Yevgeny Nazdratenko, and it was also seen most spectacularly with General Gennady Troshev in late 2002. Having been dismissed from the command of the North Caucasus Military District when he refused to take up the command in Siberia, Troshev a few months later popped up as head of the Cossack affairs section of the presidential administration.

This was a pattern of behaviour that was in keeping with that exhibited earlier. Putin may well have been a product of the Soviet system at its most stable and most decayed, yet he emerged with a set of standards about personal and institutional behaviour that transcended the venal careerism and sycophancy that typically characterised the late Brezhnev years. An exemplary case of this is the incident recounted by the former prime minister, Primakov. On his dismissal from the premiership in May 1999 most of his former colleagues quickly sought to distance themselves from him, whereas Putin came over with the FSB Collegium to offer sympathy. As Primakov put it, this showed 'Putin to be a decent man'.[66] Despite his failed plans to contend for the presidency Primakov refrained from criticising Putin personally. He was appointed chair of the Russian Chamber of Commerce and Industry, a body that sought to encourage small and medium business, and as such Primakov became an important figure in the Putinite establishment.

Whatever the problems with Putin's style of leadership, it was clear that he was a conviction politician. Putin remained loyal to a core set of beliefs about the type of state and society he wished to see established in Russia. The danger here was his convictions could get the better of his political judgement, and thus instead of instilling order it was possible that he would provoke chaos. To avoid this, Putin at times was forced to trim his convictions, leading to charges of inconsistency and weakness. Although it appeared that Putin would be tempted by grandiose visions of becoming 'the father of the people', in the event he proved to be a level-headed politician committed not to personal aggrandisement but to the development of the country. As with few other politicians, it was clear that 'what you saw, you got'. His speeches and declarations had not been an elaborate screen to mask personal aggrandisement, the defence of favoured oligarchs or the remnants of the Yeltsin 'family', but a genuine attempt to modernise the country and to resolve the problems of the past not by employing the methods of the past but to apply a forward-looking agenda of social, political and economic liberation *for all*. His aim, like that of his great hero Ludwig Erhard,[67] was capitalism with a human face, but the establishment of the Rhineland model of capitalism in Russia was to prove beyond his powers.

Putin's path: towards a Russian 'third way'?

The etymological root of the name 'Putin' derives from the word 'put'', meaning path, and many commentators have enjoyed the play on words in talking of 'Putin's path'. In this section we shall indeed argue that Putin sought to find a distinctive route for Russian development but he categorically refused to be limited by one single path to the shining future. As a Putin aide put it early in his presidency, 'There are a mass of pathways (*tropinok*), and the task is to keep moving in the right direction.'[68] At the same time, the stress in this book is that there were choices to be made, although these were not taken in a vacuum. Already in the early 1990s the main liberal organisation, building on the broad Democratic Russia coalition established in 1990, was Russia's Choice (*Vybor Rossii*), headed by the architect of Russia's neo-liberal economic reforms, Gaidar. By 1993 this body had transformed itself into the party Russia's Democratic Choice. The first name appeared to be a conscious decision to stress the alternatives facing Russia, while the second emphasised that with the fall of communism the only possible choice was democracy.

Reinventing the centre

Although Putin was promoted as the representative of the Kremlin, it is remarkable how quickly and convincingly he was able to disassociate himself from the Yeltsin legacy. Putin's political and programmatic innovations, although broadly in keeping with the general thrust of Yeltsin's reforms, broke sharply with the methods employed and the style of rule. In his *Millennium Manifesto* Putin talked frankly about Russia's comparative economic backwardness and condemned not only the faults of the Soviet system but challenged its status as a modernising regime. He stressed that an enormous effort would have to be undertaken to put Russia back in the front rank of developed powers, but insisted that Russia would have to do this in its own way. The precise nature of the increased role of the state in the economy remained unspecified, but the need for a new industrial policy to develop key branches of the economy and to stamp out corruption was stressed. As for politics, the manifesto stressed the traditional role of the state in Russian life but insisted that this was complementary to the development of democracy and human rights. There are fundamental theoretical questions to be explored when we look at the way that Putin put this into practice.

In his manifesto and in later speeches Putin was clearly trying to move beyond traditional amorphous definitions of centrism towards a more radical future-oriented model. How different this was from Primakov's centrism is a matter of dispute. Putin in the 1999 Duma elections sought to present himself both as a symbol of confidence and stability, promising to maintain Russia's system of power and property while radically renovating the state system and promoting political and legal reform within the framework of the existing constitutional settlement. Putin committed himself to the maintenance of the existing constitution unchanged, although he allowed that the position of the government could be strengthened but that it should find support not just in parliament or in the form of the presidency but in 'the widest spectrum of forces . . . in the country as a whole'.[69]

Victor Sheinis argued that victory in the December 1999 Duma elections went to the 'quasi-centre'.[70] The basic policy orientation of this quasi-centre, insofar as it has one, he argued, is right wing economics and left wing politics: economic liberalism accompanied by statist great power politics. Privatisation and other economic reforms would continue, but also the continued iron grip of the bureaucracy over the 'market'. According to him, the 2000 presidential elections revealed 'the minimal movement towards a self-sustaining civil society' and 'the separation of the political class from the deep layers of society'. This gulf between the power system and society was something noted by many other commentators. This is why Sheinis' notion of a quasi-centre is so suggestive. It does not come from a historical convergence on the centre ground of policy, but from the opportunistic cooptation of political actors and ideas to ensure regime survival. Our argument is that under Putin a new type of centrism emerged, with a positive dynamic but also retaining some of the problems associated with centrist politics in general. In studying the development of centrist politics, therefore, we should examine the degree to which they represent a genuine dynamic politics of the centre or whether they are no more than the lowest common denominator typical of quasi-centrist approaches.

The sharp polarisation that attended Yeltsin's rule gave way to an explicitly consensual and 'centrist' approach. Putin's centrism was not simply an avoidance of the extremes of left and right, of backward-looking traditionalists and nationalists or teleologically-inspired Western-oriented modernisers. His centrism sought to generate a radical centrism of the type espoused by 'third way' thinkers like Giddens,[71] although Putin's third way is tailored to Russian circumstances.[72] At the heart of this programme was the attempt to increase the autonomy of the state from socio-economic and bureaucratic interests. For Kaspe the essence of Putin's centrism was that it was removed from the field of party politics, and elevated the presidency to a degree even above the political field.[73] While this could appear to be little more than an attempt at authoritarian consolidation, the struggle to provide governmental coherence and to enhance state capacity are the essential base for any democracy. Political rights have to be accompanied by an adequate level of personal and social security for people to enjoy those rights. The contrast between democracy and order is to some degree a false one, since the one without the other is impoverished. However, the personification of political power and the attempt to legitimise the presidency by its association with supra-democratic values raised all sorts of problems of accountability and responsibility.

Jowitt has argued that in the context of the strong 'Leninist legacies' in Eastern Europe traditional attempts to strike a balance between economic development and democratic participation may not be effective. Liberal authoritarianism may well be a more 'desirable alternative' and a 'more practical response than the utopian wish for immediate mass democracy in Eastern Europe'.[74] It is precisely this tension between the authoritarian reimposition of stability and democratic anarchism that Putin sought to finesse. Behind the talk of 'guided democracy' and 'manipulated democracy' (to use Sergei Markov's term) there lies the classical problem identified by Huntington in his classic work: how to maintain political order in changing societies.[75] Putin provided a new approach to the problem of institutionalising order between the old-fashioned establishment of a repressive stability system and the anarchy in social relations that characterised early post-communist Russia. The key point was precisely the institutionalising of order, to make it not something external but vital to the very operation of the system. In short, the aim was to achieve the internalisation of authority where power moved from being despotic and arbitrary to becoming infrastructural and legitimate. The aim was to shift from power to authority. Between radical liberalism and restorationist authoritarianism there is perhaps another way, and this was now sought by Putin.

The politics of Russia's third way emerge out of traditional 'centrist' positions but the degree to which they represent a development of them is unclear. Putinism reflects the political amorphousnous of the quasi-centre but at the same time potentially transcends it. Putin himself remained an enigma. It was clear that support for Putin in the 1999 Duma elections was not based on any real appreciation of his policies, since other than the vigorous pursuit of the war in Chechnya, it was unclear what these policies were, especially in the economic field. Instead support went to mythologised conceptions of what he was taken to represent: youth and vigour in contrast to Yeltsin's senescent debility; the impersonal pursuit of Russian national goals as opposed to selfish and irresponsible pursuit of enrichment and aggrandisement of personal power by Yeltsin and his acolytes; the continuation of economic reform accompanied by a crackdown on corruption, lawlessness and banditry; good relations with the West based on genuine partnership rather than Russian kowtowing to Washington. Some of these representations turned out to be accurate but, perhaps more importantly, the extraordinary speed and scale of the rise in his popularity reflected an awareness that Putin offered at last a way out of the short-termism, corruption, venality and incompetence of the Yeltsin years.

Liberal conservatism

Does Putin's centrism reflect a distinctive type of Russian third way or is it little more than a manipulated and opportunistic quasi-centre? A genuine 'third way', *à la* Giddens, is derived not simply from the repudiation of idealised notions of left and right, reflected in traditional class politics, but from attempts to create a genuinely radical politics of the centre. This is not a trivial political project, although much of the writing and commentary about the subject is indeed trite. The argument here can be reduced to the following: while the 'third way' in the West is an attempt to come to terms with the apparent exhaustion of traditional social democracy and represents an attempt to renew it, Russia's third way, or genuine politics of the centre, is drawn from an older tradition, liberal conservatism. Writers like Peter Struve and Semyon Frank are drawn on to sustain the emerging consensus over a Russian 'third way' based on support for the reconstitution of state authority and patriotism while continuing market reforms and international economic integration.

Although Von Mises always argued that there was no 'third way' or 'third system' between the Soviet and the American forms of social organisation, today with the end of the cold war and the ideological confrontation between East and West, the possibility of testing out a variety of paths is now more relevant than ever. We do not need to think in terms of only a 'third' way, of course, since there is no reason not to think in terms of a fourth, fifth and ever more ways. However, in our conception the notion of a third way is specific to the attempt to overcome the traditionally polarised nature of Western European and Russian politics: between socialism and capitalism, between market and non-market, between individualistic and collectivist approaches to social development; and between universalism and particularism. In that sense, a third way represents not an abstraction but a very specific response to Russia's self-identity and problems of development today.

Yanov has identified a battle between two Russias. The first is the liberal one, inalienably part of Europe, what Alexander Yanov has calls Decembrist Russia.[76] The second Russia is one where geopolitical considerations rule supreme and trample the development of civil society, one based on the striving to achieve the restoration of territories, like the Crimea and Sevastopol, confrontation with the West and autarchic economic policies. This is the Russia that Yanov dubs Slavophile. Again, in this sphere as in others, Putin sought to overcome this sterile confrontation of tired stereotypes to forge a new forward-looking identity. Putin's third way, moreover, had little in common with those advocates of self-limiting *perestroika* who sought to find a third way between outright liberal democracy of the Western sort and the neo-Stalinist inertia of the Brezhnev era.

One can identify a whole series of attempts to find new solutions to old problems. Twentieth-century Russia, for example, has been torn between revolution and stagnation, a phenomenon that was repeated in miniature during Yeltsin's rule. Beginning with a revolutionary break in the first years of the 1990s, under Chernomyrdin there were pronounced tendencies towards stagnation. Could Russia now find a new way between revolution and stagnation that would allow the country to embark on a balanced developmental path? The broader context of Russia's third way is the depoliticisation of the political, the attempt to present tough policy choices as above politics and in the realm of an uncontestable common sense. Structurally, Putin's third way also borrowed from Tony Blair's, using think tanks and policy institutes to devise new approaches. As in Britain, the third way in Russia promised to be eclectic, borrowing ideas freely from all corners of the political spectrum.

*   *   *

In a presidential system the leader inevitably has to try to be all things to all people, at least during the first term in a fixed two-term system. As we have seen, in his election campaign in 2000 and thereafter as the elected president Putin quite consciously tried to avoid confrontation and sought to rule by consensus. This allowed his critics to accuse him of political chameleonism, changing his colours to suit the occasion. We have argued that what may have looked like political indeterminacy in fact reflected a normative commitment to something akin to a distinctive Russian third way. The third way approach is liable (as Polly Toynbee wrote of Clinton) to be a way of 'ducking tough choices, appeasing and eschewing ideology until he was left with none. He could always spin a mean speech, but fine words were a substitute for action'.[77] It is also a way of healing the terrible divisions that had scarred Russian political life for over a century. Putin's market-oriented moderate centrism, combining a commitment to democracy with the appeal to strong leadership while drawing on both Slavophile and Westernising ideas, may well have looked like an unstable syncretic mix, but it did at least offer an alternative to the failures of the past. The essence of Putinism as a political programme is the attempt to construct a dynamic and future-oriented politics of the centre: by definition, such a programme is in danger of becoming amorphous to the point of meaninglessness; but it does also have the potential to transcend traditional divisions and to lead the country on to a developmental path conforming to native traditions while encouraging integration into the international community. Putin's presidency demonstrated the role that individual leadership plays in history. Putin's emergence as leader was structured by the needs of the Yeltsinite succession; but the character of his leadership was contingent on nothing more than the quirks of his character. Thus the fate of nations is decided.

4 State and society

> I believe that one of the main purposes of the state is to create rules – universal rules – in the form of laws, instructions, and regulations. And secondly, to comply with these rules, and guarantee their compliance.
>
> (Vladimir Putin[1])

In the post-communist period the hypertrophy of Soviet power gave way to the atrophy of the Russian state. In every sphere the ability of government to impose its will on society, to extract adequate resources and to sustain the symbols of legitimate power weakened. Putin's immediate and intense concern to revive the Russian state emerged directly from his own background as witness to the dissolution of the ideological structures that had sustained authority for so long and to the disintegration of the muscle power of government. The overriding theme of much of Putin's writings and speeches, as we have seen, was the need to restore the ability of the state to act as an independent political force, no longer at the mercy of oligarchs, regional bosses or foreign interests. However, a newly energised executive authority, even if its aims were benign, entailed the danger of recreating the traditional system of mono-centric power.

State and regime

François Mitterrand referred to the post of president, as created by De Gaulle in 1958, as a 'permanent *coup d'état*', and shortly before his death he warned that French political institutions 'were dangerous before me and could become so after me'.[2] Many felt that this warning was no less appropriate for Russia.[3] The presidency there overshadowed all other political institutions, to the degree that Klyamkin and Shevtsova called it an 'elected monarchy'.[4] The paradox under Yeltsin, however, was the emergence of a strong presidency in a weak state, something that created a whole range of power asymmetries and distortions. This was not a problem unique to Russia. As Stephen Holmes has argued, the 'universal problem of post-communism is the crisis of governability produced by the diminution of state capacity after the collapse of communism'.[5] The creation of the presidency in the first place had been intended to compensate for the weakening power of the Communist Party, and now it filled the vacuum created by the ebbing of state authority and the weakness of civic initiative.

Development and the state

State development in the post-communist world faces distinctive challenges. Russia is not only a hybrid system in terms of democracy and authoritarianism, but is also one torn between the market and state patronage. Class and state power is highly fragmented, with the regime mediating between the former communist officialdom, the old economic monopolies, the rising oligarchical financial-industrial business interests, and sectors of the economy integrated into the international economy. It is indeed the absence of a hegemonic class that inhibits the development of an accountable regime, as Miliband has argued.[6] Where state power relies on a narrow group which is dominant but far from enjoying social and ideological hegemony, an authoritarian outcome is likely. As Fatton writes of the African context, 'The non-hegemonic status of the African ruling classes deprives the state of the relative autonomy that makes reform possible, despotism unnecessary, and liberal democracy viable.'[7]

Under Yeltsin the state lost both administrative capacity and steering capability. The government's failure to cut subsidies to loss-making enterprises meant that the budget deficit grew ever larger. The government began to borrow money in the form of GKOs (treasury bills). First issued in May 1992, the number of GKOs rose astronomically to reach $70 billion by May 1998, or 17 per cent of the country's GDP. This was accompanied by continuing inflation and the impoverishment of salary earners, provoking widespread corruption. The symbolic and practical low point of this period was the partial default of Black Monday, 17 August 1998. Although some of the causes of this financial crash lie in 'contagion' from the East Asian economic problems from October 1997, for the most part the crisis was 'made in Russia'. The government defaulted on its GKOs while also declaring a moratorium on debt repayment on all foreign loans. More broadly, in conditions of institutional decay many of the normal functions of the state deteriorated. Russia became at best a weak democratic regime, where social interests gained direct access to the state. The exploitation of connections with government officials proved to be one of the most lucrative economic resources, allowing insider deals in the privatisation process, in gaining export licences and in carving out spheres of risk-free enrichment through the use of state funds designated for wages, social needs and welfare payments. The country's leadership was weak and devoted itself largely to personal enrichment, while the elite grouping around Yeltsin (the family) by the end focused on saving itself.

The potential and formal powers of the state, however, remained enormous, and now someone had come to the helm strong and healthy enough to use them. Under Putin the reconstitution of the state became the central theme of his programme. This was recognised by no less a figure than the oligarch Berezovsky. Speaking on 23 February 2000 in his constituency (he had been elected a Duma deputy on 19 December 1999), Berezovsky said, 'For the first time in 15 years, power in Russia is being consolidated.' He noted that 'a new stage of creating a strong state has begun. Russia will have neither a strong army nor a strong society without consolidating power'.[8] At that time he rejected claims that totalitarianism was being revived in Russia,[9] although later (after Putin had targeted him as one of the most dangerous oligarchs who had abused access to the corridors of power) he was to argue precisely the opposite. Nevertheless, there cannot but be profound ambiguities between liberalism and state strengthening.

Putin sought to restore the state at a time when its role appears to be undermined by globalisation at the international level and by the strivings for sub-national autonomy. In this context the concept of state redundancy has been advanced to suggest that the functions traditionally fulfilled by the state could more properly be achieved by other actors. In the Russian context in the 1990s this took an extreme form, in the belief that the market could more effectively achieve economic rationality than state interventionism. This may well be the case in the abstract (but even in the most neoliberal of economies the regulatory role of the state is increasing), but loosening the tentacles of state domination over the Russian economy took the form of the loss of state capacity in its entirety. By the end of the 1990s even the most ardent supporters of the market realised that things had been taken too far: no shortage of commentators began to bend the stick back in the other direction. The theme of the 1997 World Bank report, *The State in a Changing World*, reasserted the role of the state in economic and political development: 'Good government is not a luxury – it is a vital necessity for development.'[10]

In the Russian context state reconstitution would appear to enjoy advantages not available to countries still in the throes of the early stages of development. The Russian state has not collapsed, and in certain areas retains the ability to mobilise resources to pursue policies, if not effectively, then at least vigorously. Russia has enormous reserves of intellectual potential, a trained administrative elite and the basic infrastructure of a modern state. Russia suffered not so much from a crisis of the state as a crisis of governance. Clearly, they cannot be separated, yet they are analytically distinct. The remedy for one problem is not the same as that for the other. Improvement of governance requires political institutionalisation, that is, the process whereby organisations, procedures and norms not only acquire legitimacy and stability but are conducted within the framework of law and in the spirit of state service. The response to a crisis of the state, by contrast, can take numerous forms, not all of them compatible with constitutionalism and the rule of law. In the transition from communism many had called for a 'firm hand', even of the Pinochet type where in Chile political liberty was traded in exchange for economic growth. Others have stressed the Bonapartist features of Putin's rule, a system defined in Marxist terms as 'an authoritarian government that temporarily gains relative independence and reigns above the classes of society, mediating between them'.[11] Medushevsky, for example, has developed this model, with the appointment of the *polpredy* acting as the functional equivalents of the Napoleonic prefects.[12] For Lukin, the key point was to end 'the excesses of the "democratic revolution" while preserving its major achievements'.[13] Putin, as we have argued earlier, certainly scraped off the revolutionary froth and tried to restore order, strengthen the constitutional state and improve the quality of governance, but these ambitious 'post-revolutionary' tasks were entwined with the problem of the nature of the power system.

Regime politics

The constitutional order enshrined in the December 1993 constitution is focused on the presidency. When the president is weak, so is governance. The effectiveness of the state is dependent on the strength of the presidency in general and on the character of the incumbent in particular. It is this entwining of institutional and personal factors in a weak constitutional order and under-developed civil society that gives rise to what we call regime politics. A regime here is defined as the network of governing institutions that is broader than the government and reflects formal and informal ways of governing and is usually accompanied by a particular ideology. The regime in Russia is focused on the presidency but is broader than the post of president itself. It can be seen as a dynamic set of relationships that include the president, the various factions in the presidential administration, the government (the prime minister and the various ministries), and the informal links with various powerful oligarchs, regional bosses and other favoured insiders.[14] Our model of Putin's presidency suggests a tension between the presidency and the regime, in which the former sought to gain greater autonomy from the latter by relying on a revived constitutional state and a reinvigorated civil society and popular support.

At the heart of the regime system that emerged under Yeltsin was the oligarchy and its allies, which represented a fusion of financial and industrial capital with direct access to government. The traditional distinction between the market and the state was eroded, and lobbying interests enjoyed an extraordinarily close relationship with government. Russian politics became characterised by the salience not so much of the formal institutional structures of government and management but by informal relationships. Above all, given the weakness of the state, the emergence of what might be termed quasi-state actors became particularly important. For example, the banks (including the Central Bank), and the large energy companies (above all Gazprom and Unified Energy Systems – (UES)), acted as substitute sinews of the state, providing financial resources not available through general taxation, and serving as indirect enforcers of federal policy, while at the same time ensuring that federal policy was not hostile to their interests. A type of 'state' bourgeoisie emerged, dependent on access to the state, rather than a more independent entrepreneurial bourgeoisie (for more on this, see Chapter 8).

Personalised leadership inhibited the development of institutions. The political regime was focused on Yeltsin and his family and operated largely independently from the formal rules of the political system, whose main structural features were outlined in the constitution. Behind the formal facade of democratic politics conducted at the level of the state, the regime considered itself largely free from genuine democratic accountability and popular oversight. These features, as Hahn stresses, were accentuated by the high degree of institutional and personal continuity between the Soviet and 'democratic' political systems. While a party-state ruled up to 1991, under Yeltsin a regime-state emerged that perpetuated in new forms much of the arbitrariness of the old system. Both the regime and the constitutional state succumbed to clientelistic pressures exerted by powerful interests in society, some of whom (above all the so-called oligarchs) had been spawned by the regime itself. These constituted a fluid ruling group. We have suggested earlier that the 'family' represents one of the factions in the regime; another is the *Pitery* brought in by Putin to establish a power base of his own.

The regime in Russia, where legitimacy is ultimately derived from the ballot box, is caught, on the one hand, between the legal order represented by the state (the formal constitutional institutions of administration and the rule of law), and, on the other hand, the system of representative institutions (above all political parties) and accountability (primarily parliament). The regime acts as if it stands outside the political and normative principles that it has formally sworn to uphold, but at the same time is constrained by those principles. It is as much concerned with its own perpetuation as the rational administration of the country. For comparative purposes it should be noted that similar regimes relatively independent of the constitutional constraints of the rule of law and of popular accountability had emerged in post-war Italy and Japan, and in general appear to be a growing phenomenon in post-cold war political systems.

Regime politics in post-communist Russia, therefore, is not like traditional authoritarianism, and the regime could not insulate itself from aspects of modern liberal democratic politics such as media criticism, parliamentary discussion and, above all, from the electoral cycle. The regime looked in two directions at once: forwards towards democracy, international integration and a less bureaucratised and genuinely market economy; while at the same time it inherited, and indeed perpetuated and reinforced many features of the past – bureaucratic arbitrariness in politics and the economy, a contemptuous attitude to the citizenry, knee-jerk anti-Westernism, pervasive patron–client relations, Byzantine court politics and widespread corruption. Only when the regime is brought under the control of law and the constitution and within the ambit of political accountability can Russia be considered to have achieved democratic consolidation. This would be a revolution every bit as significant as the fall of communism itself in 1991, and was the main challenge facing Putin's presidency. It is this process that we call the reconstitution of the state (see below), literally rendering the political process and regime actors subordinate to the legal constitutional system and responsive to the needs of citizens. What Max Weber had called sham constitutionalism was to give way to real constitutionalism where political institutions are subordinated to the rule of law and where human and civil rights are defensible by law.

Pluralistic or compacted statism

While the presidency under Putin sought to carve out greater room for manoeuvre, Putin was hesitant to subordinate the regime entirely to the imperatives of the constitutional order or to the vagaries of the popular representative system (elections). Yeltsin earlier had feared that the untrammelled exercise of democracy could lead to the wrong result, the election of a communist government that would undo the work of building market democracy, threaten Russia's neighbours in pursuit of the dream of the reunification of the USSR, and antagonise the country's Western partners. It was for this reason that factions in the regime had called for the 1996 presidential elections to be cancelled. The dilemma was not an unreal one, and reflected the regime's view that the Russian people had not yet quite matured enough to be trusted with democracy. Like the Turkish military and the army in some Latin American countries, the regime considered itself the guardian of the nation's true ideals. This was the ideology explicitly espoused by some of the regime's policy intellectuals such as Gleb Pavlovsky and Sergei Markov, and it was not entirely devoid of rationality. However, we know that whenever the military acts against democracy as the 'saviour of the nation' the results are usually the opposite of those intended, and the regime's mimicry of the military stymied the development of a political order robust enough to defend itself against the enemies of democracy.

Thus when Putin undertook the task of rebuilding the state he was torn between a number of imperatives. The first and most obvious was his intention to clean up the regime's own act, to put an end to the most extravagant corruption and free access to political power by the oligarchs. This he managed to achieve, as we shall see, relatively quickly. The next task was to ensure the unimpeded and universal application of law throughout the whole country. While this began to rein in the regional barons, in certain cases (and above all in Chechnya) the writ of law was far from uniform. The predominance of the regime itself was not challenged, while within the regime Putin sought to broaden the autonomy of the presidency. While Putin stressed the strengthening of the state, too often it appeared that his interpretation of state strengthening was synonymous with the consolidation of the regime, and within the regime, the enhancement of the presidency. This was a strengthening that itself was more based on control and loyalty rather than trust. As McFaul put it,

> it would be wrong to conclude that Putin is an 'anti-democrat'. The Russian president is simply too modern and too Western-oriented to believe in dictatorship. Rather, Putin is indifferent to democratic principles and practices, believing perhaps that Russia might have to sacrifice democracy in the short run to achieve 'more important' economic and state building goals.[15]

The resurgence of the state was thus torn between two forms, each of which gave rise to a distinctive type of statism. The first takes Putin's commitment to the maintenance of the principles of the existing constitution at face value, and accepts that the attempt to apply constitutional and other legal norms across Russia in a uniform and homogeneous way represents a genuine attempt not only to undermine the neo-medieval features of governance that had emerged under Yeltsin but also reflected a commitment to liberal universalism. From this perspective, we can describe the process as the *reconstitution* of the Russian state. Putin's statism represented an advance for democracy in the sense that the application of the law would be the same for all, including regional bosses, oligarchs and, presumably, the regime and presidency itself. This is very much a normative (that is, legal and constitutional) reconstitution of state power. The type of system that emerges out of this is a *pluralistic statism*, a democratic statism that defends the unimpeded flow of law and individual rights while respecting the pluralism of civil society and federal norms. Pluralistic statism takes as genuine Putin's commitments in his *Millennium Manifesto*, his state-of-the-nation speech of 8 July 2000 and many other statements arguing that a strong state should be rooted in a liberal economic order and a vibrant civil society.

However, the selective approach to the abuses of the Yeltsin era, the attack on segmented regionalism that threatened to undermine the development of federalism, and the apparent lack of understanding of the values of media freedom and human rights, suggested that Putin's reforms could become a general assault on the principles of federalism and democratic freedom. The dependence of the presidential regime on 'power structures', as part of an unstable alliance of the presidency, certain oligarchs and the power ministries suggested that another, less benign, form of statism could emerge. We call this the *reconcentration* of the state to distinguish it from the reconstituted statism described above. State reconcentration gives rise to *compacted statism* in which the rhetoric of the defence of constitutional norms and the uniform application of law throughout the country threatens the development of a genuine federal separation of powers, media and informational freedoms, and which establishes a new type of hegemonic party system in which patronage and preference is disbursed by a neo-nomenklatura class of state officials. There were many indications that United Russia sought to become the core of a new patronage system of the type that in July 2000 was voted out of office in Mexico after 71 years.

From the very first days of his presidency Putin drew on constitutional resources to re-affirm the prerogatives of the state vis-à-vis segmented regional regimes. The struggle for the universal application of the rule of law, however, threatened to intensify at the federal level the lawlessness that characterised so much of regional government. Yeltsin's personalised regime represented a threat to the state, but its very diffuseness and encouragement of asymmetrical federalism allowed a profusion of media, regional and other freedoms to survive. Putin's new statism carried both a positive and a negative charge: the strengthening of the rule of law was clearly long overdue; but enhancing the powers of the regime and the presidency was not the same as strengthening the constitutional rule of law. The weakening of the federal pillar of the separation of powers was not likely to enhance the defence of freedom as a whole. The key test would be whether the revived presidency would itself become subordinate to the new emphasis on 'the dictatorship of law', and thus encourage the development of a genuine ordered rule of law state, or whether it would attempt to stand aloof from the process and thus once again perpetuate the traditions of the 'revolution from above', if only to put an end to the revolution, and thus perpetuate typical patterns of stability politics.

State strengthening as politics or law

Putin's approach was characterised by a combination of institutional and programmatic innovation combined with constitutional conservatism. In his state-of-the-nation speech of 8 July 2000, Putin argued that Russia must not remain a 'weak state', asserting that 'the only realistic choice for Russia is to be a strong country'. In his speech he stated:

> We have to recognise that the state itself was largely responsible for the growing strength of the unofficial, shadow economy, the spread of corruption and the flow of great quantities of money abroad. . . . An inefficient state is the main reason for our long and deep crisis – I am absolutely convinced of this.

Responding to criticisms that his attempts to remake the state could give rise to authoritarianism, he insisted,

> The battle between strong power and freedom is an old one, and at the moment this debate is giving rise to almost daily speculation on the themes of dictatorship and authoritarianism. But our position is clear. Only a strong and democratic state can defend the civil, political and economic freedoms of the population.

Putin emerged as something akin to a Jacobin or French republican state builder: seeking to ensure the universal and equal application of the constitution and the laws, accompanied by the homogenisation of political space and the establishment of a stable set of political institutions. The concept of institution here encompasses not just administrative structures but also the formal and informal 'rules of the game'.[16]

Law, regionalism and the state

At the heart of Putin's statism was the universal applicability of law. Although the phrase 'dictatorship of law' became peculiarly Putin's own, it was a term first used by Gorbachev on 13 February 1991.[17] Putin first used the phrase in his speech to a conference of chairs of regional courts on 24 January 2000, and the idea was at the heart of his early programme of state reform. A week later Putin argued: 'The dictatorship of law is the only kind of dictatorship which we must obey', insisting that freedom without law and order 'inevitably degenerates into chaos and lawlessness'.[18] In his 8 July 2000 speech he argued that 'an era is beginning in Russia where the authorities are gaining the moral right to demand that established state norms should be observed' and that 'strict observance of laws must become a need for all people in Russia by their own choice'. In an interview soon after he insisted that he sought to put an end to the situation in which Russians appeared to have become subjects of different regions rather than citizens of a single country.[19] This applied as much to economic as to civic life. Putin insisted that he was determined to put an end to the curtailment of economic freedoms in certain regions, where business was divided up between clan members and where the media and civil organisations were persecuted. Thus a secondary theme of Putin's statism was the restoration of coherence in central-regional relations. In his 8 July 2000 speech he stressed that 'competition for power' between the centre and regional powers has been 'destructive', and he argued that 'we have to admit that [Russia] is not yet a full-blown federal state'. Instead, Russia had 'created a decentralised state'.

The inefficiency of the Russian state derived from its peculiar development both as a continuation and a modification of the Soviet model. Russia in the early 1990s retained many of the features of the territorial organisation of the Soviet state, above all the dual federal system based both on territory and on ethnicity, with the latter reflected in the 21 ethno-federal republics. The system was modified to the extent that the old system of Communist Party regional first secretaries was abolished, but functionally their role was perpetuated by the emergence of powerful chief executives in each region. On top of this, Yeltsin in a rather half-hearted way and Putin with greater vigour sought to impose a quasi-Napoleonic system of prefects (presidential representatives) to supervise the work of regional executives. This hybrid system, however, lacked all functional unity and instead resorted to the use of administrative means to exert political control over recalcitrant governors. Lines of responsibility between Moscow and the regions became confused and the whole system lacked an institutional focus that would allow regional communities to regulate their relationship with the state in a harmonious manner.

The unformed nature of Russian federalism meant that relations between the centre and periphery remained contested, and were viewed through the prism of a constant struggle for advantage between the two levels of governance, weakening both. The system was highly inefficient in both political and administrative terms, with the inefficiencies rooted in patterns of historical evolution and partial adaptation to the norms of democratic federalism in the post-communist years. The Russian state, in its imperial and Soviet guises, had traditionally maintained a strongly centralised structure, and elements of this were perpetuated in the new conditions. However, a tendency that had already been evident under Brezhnev now became much stronger, namely the need for the centre to bargain with regional elites, who were thus able to negotiate advantageous deals and to consolidate clientelistic patterns of rule.[20] The attempt to maintain central management in the old authoritarian style in fact weakened the centre by preventing the emergence of a new federal model based on new lines of responsibility and accountability.

In other countries where there has been a similar stalemate between the centre and the periphery clientelistic patterns have emerged to overcome the blockage. The state itself in countries like Italy was manipulated to the advantage of regional elites.[21] If the system under Yeltsin was very much focused on the presidency and his own personality, the development of greater institutionalisation under Putin provided the opportunity both for a more ordered system but at the same time did not put an end to the parallel development of extra-legal relations between centre and periphery. The development of a national party system began to displace local elites as the main mediators between the centre and periphery. However, the new system only provided the framework for new forms of clientelism and the privatisation of state power.

From regime to governance

The reconstitution of the state became the central theme of Putin's programme. For the first time in fifteen years, power in Russia was being consolidated. There were, however, profound ambiguities between state strengthening and liberalism, between the rationalisation of power and its reordering. We have argued that state strengthening has two faces: one sees state power being rationalised through reconcentration to emerge as a force in its own right and pursuing its own interests against those of the market, society and the individual; whereas the second face is a liberal one whereby the state is reordered through reconstitution to assume its proper role as the defender of individual liberties, rights of property and acts as regulator of market relations. The former would be a 'well-ordered police state', whereas the latter would be a pluralistic society. As Stephen Holmes has argued, there is no more powerful defender of human rights than a strong liberal state.

The key element was the 'statising' of politics, that is, bringing all social actors with the purview of the law and limiting personalised regime-type rule focused on the presidency. At the same time, this statisation would have to take legal forms. The precise strategy adopted to a large extent depends on the diagnosis of the problem itself. Much discussion has been focused on a simple polarity between Russia as a weak state, unable to enforce its laws, collect adequate taxes to sustain its administrative coherence or to defend its citizens (at the extreme, this view considers Russia a 'failed state'), or Russia as a relatively strong state able to impose its will brutally in Chechnya, erode media and political freedoms, and reassert its authority vis-à-vis the regions.[22] Our model of a regime-state has tried to avoid such over-simplifications, arguing instead that there is a complex interaction between the type of politics associated with the regime and the legal-constitutional resources available to the state. The normative resources available for the state to reassert itself vis-à-vis the regime are immeasurably greater than the opportunistic exploitation of transitional opportunities by the regime. The nature of presidential power is itself highly ambivalent, of course, since it has been both the core of regime politics while at the same time representing the potential transcendence of the corrupt, personalised and self-seeking politics associated with the regime.

Whether this would take the form of political authoritarianism or legalism was unclear. There were no shortage of politicians in Russia arguing that the slide into lawlessness and banditry had gone so far that Russia has become not only a state with gangsters but a gangster state by its very essence. On the basis of such an analysis it is quite easy to envisage a scenario where state reconstruction could take place on the basis of an authoritarian programme of 'law and order', although the result clearly would be neither, except in a superficial sense. The state would be reconstructed politically, but not in the normative constitutional sense (the 'stability' regime, defined above). The 'Westernising' programme of state reconstitution on the basis of law, pluralism and accountability would be reversed, and in its place there would be more authoritarianism, isolationism and Slav nationalism.

In the event, the 'Westernising' programme of state reconstitution on the basis of law, pluralism and accountability continued under Putin. Despite much talk of Russia as a 'failed state', it was clear from the early days of Putin's presidency that the state retained adequate resources to restore some sort of social *stability*, but whether it could achieve a more profound and sustained *order* was another question. Putin rejected the Andropovist scenario where authoritarianism is moderated by a progressive understanding of developmental tasks. Putin instead talked about building a 'strong' state, one that would not only be genuinely constitutional but also able to defend the broader principles of constitutionalism. This ordered state would develop stable and predictable administrative structures and reduce the power of traditional personalised leadership. The aim was for a state to emerge committed to the inculcation of liberal and democratic values, the principles of Russia's membership of such bodies as the Council of Europe, and with the constitution the genuine cornerstone of public life. The 'monarchical' elements of rule that had been so pronounced under Yeltsin were tempered by the development of a more ordered system of power.[23] Under Putin a state emerged that began to pull Russia out of its centuries long 'transitional' status and achieve some sort of ordered 'normality'. However, the fundamental contradiction between the need for strong leadership to establish a system where strong leadership was no longer required was not resolved.

As a result, many critics argued that Putin's statism had compacted elements, representing no more than the rationalisation of traditional authoritarian and personalised patterns of rule. In response to Putin's state-of-the-nation speech of July 2000, the president of Chuvashia, Nikolai Fedorov, noted that Putin's statism left out many factors:

> when he says 'the state' he means only the president and the Kremlin, but he does not see the parliament, the judicial power in the real meaning of the words. Words have one meaning, deeds have another, and they are absolutely opposite so far.[24]

The warning against compacted statism was clear, and was one sounded by others at this time. Thomas Graham, for example, noted that 'Judicial independence did not even merit a mention' in his speech.[25] Putin's definition of the state was an idiosyncratic one, seemingly referring to that part of government that was under his direct control.[26] From this perspective, the strengthening of the state could be seen as little more than the consolidation of Putin's power; and seen logically from Putin's perspective the two could easily become indistinguishable. More than that, if we accept that excessively close ties between power and property had characterised Yeltsin's regime politics, then Putin's programme of state strengthening could be considered as little more than reinforcing the power element in the power-property relationship rather than breaking the pernicious tie that was at the root of so much corruption in post-communist Russia.

In all post-communist countries there has been a tension between expedience and law, sometimes taking crude and overt forms but everywhere shot through with ambiguities. These ambiguities are most visible when it comes to decommunisation, lustration and restorative justice. Active decommunisation is easily turned into another weapon in political struggle, whereas a policy of 'letting sleeping dogs lie' allows those guilty of mass murder to escape unpunished. The very crime itself tended to disappear in the rhetoric of overcoming the divisions of the past, and for many in the older generation Leninist and Stalinist repression was viewed as unavoidable collateral damage in the great project of communist construction and victory in the war. The worst thing, of course, is when the dogs of old regime revanchism are not sleeping but straining at the leash to take revenge for their defeat in 1991. This is the case with parts of the barely reformed security agencies, elements in the military establishment, and the mood among many rank-and-file members of the CPRF and other leftist and nationalist parties. Russia had nothing like the truth and justice tribunals of some other post-authoritarian systems. The lack of decommunisation, seen most vividly at the time of the fiftieth anniversary of Stalin's death in 2003, allowed the communist period to relegitimate itself in the eyes of millions and weakened the foundations of the new democratic order.

The hybrid nature of the new order was nowhere more vividly manifest than in the contrast between the formal commitment to democracy and the market, and the great Soviet administrative dinosaur on which the new democratic order was precariously perched. In the post-communist era the state bureaucracy had grown enormously: if in 1990 the whole Soviet administrative apparatus, including central, regional and local government and the ministries, numbered 662,700,[27] by 2000 the bureaucracy in Russia alone numbered over a million *chinovniks*. This great army may well have been the core of Putin's social basis of support but it also represented a major political challenge. As Tretyakov put it, 'This leviathan (the state bureaucracy) must be subordinated to Goliath (the president).'[28] Plans for administrative reform moved forwards only very slowly, however. Reforms were designed to achieve the functional restructuring of state service by reducing the number of state agencies and the size of the bureaucracy. One plan in early 2003 talked of reducing the number of ministries from 24 to 15–17, while the economic development ministry divided the 5,000 functions performed by the state into three categories: setting regulations, applying regulations, and providing state services, and examined those that could be abolished.[29] In his address to the Federal Assembly on 16 May 2003 Putin once again lambasted the Russian bureaucracy that had 'proved ill-prepared for working out and implementing the decisions appropriate to the country's present needs', although it had known how to 'accumulate administrative clout':

> The powers of our bureaucracy are still vast. But the number of powers it possesses do not match the quality of government. I have to stress that the source of this is nothing other than the superfluous functions of state government bodies. And yet, despite the huge numbers of functionaries, the country has a severe dearth of personnel at every level and in all government structures. There is a dearth of modern managers, of efficient people.[30]

In the 1990s Russia became a dual state, with the institutionalised state undermined by the arbitrariness of the personalised regime. This was far from being anything like the totalitarian systems of the earlier part of the century. The regime may have been arbitrary in some policy areas, above all in its personnel policy, but it was mostly not above the law. It certainly manipulated the electoral system to its advantage, but it did not suspend the electoral process or simply reduce it to a 'balloting charade'. It was clear that Putin believed that only an evolutionary approach to Russia's problems could transcend and heal the wounds of the past and move from regime to governance. With the basic institutions in place, Russia did not need any more revolutions. It did, however, require reform.

The 'liquidation of the oligarchs as a class'

Yeltsin's rule was marked by the paradoxical contrast between the introduction of the institutions of a modern representative democratic state and their simultaneous emasculation. This contradiction was forcefully reflected in the development of the presidency itself; as an institution it flowered and became the centre of Russian political life, but as an organisation it was weakened by Yeltsin's personalistic style of leadership. The key test of Putin's leadership was whether he would be able to depersonalise political relationships and allow a genuine institutionalisation of the political process to prevail. As part of this the state needed to be differentiated from economics. As Thomas Graham notes, 'The trouble with this approach [the various attacks on the oligarchs] is that it is still unclear whether the Kremlin is taking true aim at the structural conditions that gave rise to the oligarchs in the first place'. These structural conditions, in his view was 'the intertwining of power and property', something that stymied the development of both effective governance and efficient markets.[31] Only the clear separation of business from government would break the system that had given rise to oligarchical capitalism in Russia in the first place. For that an independent judiciary, a streamlined bureaucracy and more honest policing was required.

Struggle against the oligarchs

During the election campaign and in his state-of-the-nation address on 8 July 2000, Putin talked of the need to break the cosy relationship between big business and government. During the presidential campaign in early 2000 Putin had talked, in language reminiscent of Stalin's plan in 1929 to 'liquidate the kulaks as a class', of his aspiration to 'liquidate the oligarchs as a class', stressing the need to create a level playing field.[32] His central idea was that special interests, above all the oligarchs, should be kept 'equidistant' from the government. No longer were a select group of oligarchs to have privileged access to the corridors of power. In other words, they were no longer to be allowed to exercise class power over the state, or indeed, to hold the state hostage whenever the regime needed financial or other support at election time. As with so many of Putin's other ideas, this approach was undoubtedly correct in conception, but its application fell short of its aspirations. Selective attacks against certain oligarchs were not able to eliminate the regime's dependence on the business interests that had been spawned in the comprador phase of Russia's capitalist development.

Within months of his election Putin launched a campaign against some of the beneficiaries of the market free-for-all of the Yeltsin years. The first to feel the cold wind was the Media-Most empire headed by Vladimir Gusinsky, the company that owned a string of newspapers but above all the NTV television station, one that had been sharply critical of Putin. The Media-Most offices were raided on 11 May, and on 13 June Gusinsky was arrested (while Putin was in Spain) and jailed for four days, and thereafter feared for his life. (We shall have more to say about this when we discuss the media below.) Soon some of the country's biggest businesses came under scrutiny of state agencies investigating alleged tax evasion and the legitimacy of privatisation deals. The companies affected included Gazprom, Norilsk Nickel, Lukoil, and the biggest car manufacturer, Avtovaz. Norilsk Nickel had fallen into Vladimir Potanin's possession as a result of the notorious 'shares for loans' deals of 1995–96, and now the authorities called for the repayment of $140 million in compensation for his alleged underpayment when the plant was privatised in an auction that he had helped organise. The inclusion of Avtovaz in the list suggested that the campaign was beginning to affect members of the 'family', the group of powerful politicians and oligarchs grouped around Yeltsin personally, since the mightiest of them all, Berezovsky, had gained his first millions by association with the hugely loss-making car company through his car dealership business, Logovaz. Berezovsky had moved on and his interests had diversified to include Aeroflot, natural resources and the media (including a 49 per cent stake in the main TV station, ORT).[33] As Berezovsky put it in June 2000, the way that business had been conducted in the last decade meant that no one 'could survive a serious government effort to find something to charge them with'.[34]

In July 2000 Putin criticised 'people who feel comfortable in conditions of disorder, catching fish in muddy waters and wanting to keep things as they are'. Yeltsin himself had occasionally talked in these terms, and as prime minister Primakov had launched an investigation against some business leaders, notably Berezovsky and Alexander Smolensky. In April 1999 Berezovsky had been charged with 'illegal business activity', but these charges were dropped in November (when Putin was already prime minister) because of a lack of evidence linking him to the Aeroflot case. The investigation into Berezovsky's activities when Aeroflot's cash flow fell into his hands, passing through a Swiss intermediary, had been conducted by Yury Skuratov when he was Prosecutor-General, but Skuratov was dismissed from his post in Yeltsin's last year.[35] Berezovsky used his businesses as cash milch cows, running their capitalisation down close to zero. For example, Berezovsky had obtained Sibneft in 1995 at a deep discount, and although it produced 40 per cent as much oil as Surgutneftegaz, the market capitalisation of the latter (one of the best-managed oil majors in Russia) was eleven times higher. Berezovsky was always more interested in politics than business.

Berezovsky's behaviour, as always, was marked by audacity and cunning. Having won a Duma seat in the December 1999 parliamentary elections in the single-member constituency of the North Caucasian republic of Karachaevo-Cherkessia, Berezovsky gained immunity from prosecution, unless the Duma itself voted to strip him of that immunity – something that was not unlikely given the depth of his unpopularity. In a typically brazen move, he announced on 17 July 2000 that he planned to resign his Duma seat in protest at the 'authoritarian' trends in Putin's government,[36] saying that he did not want 'to take part in the destruction of Russia and the establishment of the authoritarian regime'.[37] He described the guarantee of immunity as worthless, which in his case it probably was since, as noted, most deputies would have been only too glad to see him face the consequences of his economic asset-stripping and political adventurism.[38] His official letter of resignation was submitted on 19 July and highlighted three issues: the attempt to rein in regional leaders; the criminal cases opened against a number of businessmen; and the lack of attention devoted by Moscow to the problems in Karachaevo-Cherkessia. At this time he called for an amnesty for all past economic crimes, denouncing the anti-corruption drive as 'an orchestrated campaign, directed at destroying major independent businesses',[39] and arguing that 'Everyone who hasn't been asleep for the past 10 years has willingly or unwillingly broken the law.'[40]

Berezovsky moved into opposition to Putin, condemning his reforms of the regional system, and announced the creation of a new party made up largely of regional governors only a few months after he had created one for Putin (Unity).[41] Berezovsky argued that Russia needed 'a constructive opposition', or 'the process of centralisation will inevitably begin'.[42] Berezovsky furthered his party-building efforts by bringing together a group of like-minded deputies in the Duma to create a new faction, later to be known as Liberal Russia. This was intended to become the kernel of an anti-Putin coalition. Berezovsky still enjoyed control of ORT to exploit popular fears about Putin. In an interview on 27 June 2000 he argued: 'All the decrees, all the laws proposed by Putin are directed at again enslaving people. People were given a whiff of freedom, and now they are to be forced to their knees again.'[43] Similarly, on announcing his intention to resign from the Duma, he declared that he wanted to have no part in the 'destruction of Russia and the imposition of authoritarian rule'.[44] He condemned the Duma, calling it 'the Kremlin's legal department that obediently follows all orders and instructions'.[45] On resigning Berezovsky announced that he planned to merge all the media that he owned into a single media holding to be run by Shabdurasulov, the former head of Russian Television (RTR) and then member of the presidential administration.[46] The very idea that Berezovsky could consider bringing ORT formally into his stable only confirmed his dominance over the channel, the only one able to be received throughout the CIS and the Baltic region. Soon afterwards, however, Berezovsky was forced to negotiate the sale of his 49 per cent stake in ORT.[47] In November 2000 he went into 'exile' in London and focused on the development of the oppositional Liberal Russia party, a party from which he was expelled on 9 October 2002 because of his overtures to the communists and nationalists.

The attack against certain oligarchs was interpreted by many as an oblique attack against media freedom. Gusinsky joined Berezovsky in his condemnation of Putin's government. He asserted that the anti-oligarch campaign signalled the end of the democratic freedoms that Russia had enjoyed in the 1990s. As he put it, 'In Russia there used to be a police regime. It disappeared temporarily and now it is being rebuilt'.[48] Gazprom, headed at the time by Rem Vyakhirev, had provided considerable financial backing for NTV, and many considered that this was the real reason for the firm coming under investigation.[49] Indeed, it was documentation dealing with the company's links with Gusinsky's Media-Most that were seized when its headquarters were raided on 11 May 2000. Similarly, Vagit Alekperov, head of Lukoil, was associated with a number of television stations and held a joint stake with Potanin, head of Norilsk Nickel, in the liberal daily *Izvestiya*. At the same time, some of the other oligarchs, like Roman Abramovich (the head of the oil group Sibneft) appeared to avoid scrutiny. Not only that, Abramovich and his aluminium associate Oleg Deripaska were able during Putin's rise to power, as we have seen, to amass an empire that brought 70 per cent of Russia's aluminium industry under their control.

Seventeen leading businessmen, including Vyakhirev and Alekperov, wrote a collective letter to the Prosecutor-General protesting against the arrest of Gusinsky and warning that democracy was in danger. They noted that Gusinsky's arrest sent a negative signal to the business community in Russia and abroad. Putin was prepared to engage with these concerns, and a round table was arranged with some of the leading oligarchs. This was not the action of a dictator. The dilemma was neatly captured by Dmitry Furman:

> In the abstract, Mr Putin's campaign against the illegal activities of various oligarchs and their apparently illegal influence is completely acceptable and essential for the democratic development of Russia. . . . But the struggle is taking place in the context of an undemocratic, authoritarian regime. The logic of this campaign seems to be an attempt to liquidise [sic] any political or economic power that asserts its independence from the Kremlin.[50]

Putin himself put a very different slant on events. In his interview with *Izvestiya* on 14 July 2000 he defended actions by the tax police and the federal Prosecutor-General's office against companies like Media-Most, Avtovaz, Lukoil and Potanin's Interros group. He insisted that 'the state has the right to expect entrepreneurs to observe the rules of the game', and he insisted that the state 'would act more vigorously towards the environment in which business operates. I am referring first and foremost to the tax sphere and the restoration of order in the economy'.[51] Putin insisted that all the oligarchs would be kept at equal arms length from the government. By turning Berezovsky and Gusinsky into the Empson and Dudley of his regime, Putin sought to warn the rest that a new leader had arrived.

The new rules of the game

The main charge against Putin was the selective nature of the campaign, provoking the suspicion that it was directed not so much against corruption as against his critics and opponents, and above all those who threatened his political pre-eminence. However, while the attack was undoubtedly selective, it was far from arbitrary. Putin targeted those who had flaunted their closeness to power in the most provocative manner, or had allegedly abused their dominance of the media. Putin was setting the rules of the political game, and in attacking a few oligarchs he was disciplining the rest. There was an implicit threat: toe the line if you wish to keep the assets 'gained' in the 1990s.[52]

Putin's attempts now to end the asset stripping mentality of the Russian economy and to bring some of its exponents to court signalled a sea change in the legal environment. Foreign investors were encouraged by his actions to enter the Russian market now that the political protection of the state had been withdrawn to cover the irresponsibility of some of Russia's key economic players. Oligarchs like Berezovsky had long warned of the danger from the left, epitomised above all by the return to power of the communists, but he now found himself outflanked on the right, by the presidency in alliance with the security establishment. However, pervading the apparent anti-oligarch campaign there hung the suspicion that one set of tycoons was using the law and the presidency against another set, and thus to corner the market. In particular, Roman Abramovich, who in early 2000 had participated in the creation of a holding that controlled most of Russia's aluminium production, was known to covet Norilsk Nickel and Gusinsky's NTV. Other oligarchs, notably Mikhail Fridman at the head of the Tyumen Oil Company (TNK) and Mikhail Khodorkovsky of Yukos Oil turned over a new leaf and gradually brought their companies up to international levels of corporate governance. They willingly accepted the new rules of the game and thus went on to become key figures in the new era.

The significance of Putin's anti-oligarch campaign, however, was deeper. It signalled that at last the economy would be differentiated from politics. The shadowy half-world of the 1990s, when the country appeared stuck midway between the plan and the market to allow rent seeking and asset stripping, now gave way to a more robust and less arbitrary market environment. A classic case of the blurring of the boundaries between politics and the economy was the career of Potanin in government (as a deputy prime minister) from August 1996 until March 1997, a time when he apparently was able to ensure preferential treatment in his bid for the giant Svyazinvest communications company in September 1997, a deal that was subsequently unpicked by his rivals (above all Berezovsky) with even greater influence over the 'family' at the head of the Russian state.

In keeping with Putin's consensual approach and at the same time reflecting his desire to remove big business tycoons from direct political access to government, twenty-one top figures of Russia's business elite met with the president on 28 July 2000 to lay down the ground rules of relations between the government and business. This was not the first meeting brokered by Nemtsov between the business elite and the Kremlin. In September 1997, in the wake of the Svyazinvest privatisation scandal, the top oligarchs had been invited to meet Yeltsin to lay down the rules of engagement. Not much had come out of that meeting, and the Kremlin now sought to ensure that the business leaders did not gain the impression that they were equal political interlocutors with the elected presidency.

The aim of the July 2000 meeting was to establish a level economic playing field in which the role of the state as referee would be enhanced and respected. The attendees were an eclectic group, but equally notable were the absentees.[53] The agenda was established by Nemtsov, the leader of the liberal Union of Right Forces (SPS) Duma faction. He insisted that 'The business and power should not attack or blackmail each other, they should be partners working towards the economic recovery of Russia.'[54] The business leaders presented a three-point declaration to the government: first, for the Kremlin to declare a moratorium on any investigations into the legitimacy of privatisation over the past decade and not to initiate any redistribution of former state property; second, the business community must undertake to play by the rules, pay taxes and scrupulously obey the law; third, the government must rid itself of corrupt bureaucrats, while the business tycoons on their part must undertake not to use government institutions or bribe state officials to fight their competitors.[55] As many noted at the time, however, the link between power and property was hardly challenged by such an extra-constitutional 'pact', which in any case left out some of the key players.

The modification of Yeltsin-style regime politics, however, was accompanied by fears that democracy would be swept away at the same time. Gusinsky argued that a 'police regime' was being established in Russia, and said that he feared for his life. He asserted that Putin had turned against him after Media-Most began criticising the war in Chechnya. He added that one of the reasons he had become a 'victim of persecution' is that Russians 'try to destroy' rich people, whom (he argued) they inherently envy and hate, and because he was a Jew.[56] Tretyakov provided a more subtle analysis of the situation. Several logical approaches, he noted, were in conflict here: while the Kremlin still saw the world in terms of the traditional nation state, the owners of NTV saw the world like any transnational corporation, above all one concerned with the media, as a single borderless sphere of economic activity.[57] At the same time, given the rather amorphous nature of most Russian parties, Gusinsky's media empire had become effectively the leader of the opposition to Putin, subjecting his actions and motivations to sharp criticism. When the interests of the state are seen as synonymous with those of the government, any criticism of the government can be seen as anti-state. As Tretyakov put it, Media-Most from the Kremlin's perspective was 'a radical opposition political party disguised as a media holding'.[58]

As long as Putin's anti-oligarch campaign was conducted by the presidency, the core of the old regime system of relations, there could be legitimate questions about its political selectivity. Putin's methods in dealing with oligarchical power were criticised. Instead of using the courts, he relied on strong-arm tactics led by the MVD, the FSB and the Prosecutor-General. Only when the anti-corruption campaign was conducted by a demonstrably free and independent judiciary would fears that it was designed to further political ends be allayed. There were signs of this in the enhanced role played by the Audit Chamber, an independent body authorised to monitor the use of federal budget funds and headed in Putin's early years by the former prime minister and one time head of the FSB, Stepashin. In July 2000 the Audit Chamber began to investigate the 51 per cent state-owned UES, the electricity monopoly, and alleged that in the period when UES was partially privatised between 1992–98 shares had been improperly sold to foreigners (who were allowed no more than a 25 per cent stake in the company) and was part of the general attempt to defend the interests of minority shareholders.[59] It appeared that it would only be a matter of time before the anti-corruption campaign would come knocking at the door of Chubais, the head of UES but formerly the architect of privatisation. Chubais, moreover, had played a prominent part in arranging the finances of Yeltsin's re-election campaign of 1996, and before that had organised the loans-for-shares scheme of 1995. As noted above, Norilsk Nickel had fallen into Potanin's hands as a result of this scheme at a time when Chubais' ally, Alfred Kokh, had been head of the State Privatisation Committee (Goskomimushchestvo).

Although formally elected by the people, Putin was perceived to be the instrument of a narrow 'selectorate', namely 'the family' that had acted as a 'collective Yeltsin' in his final period of illness and stagnation. Thus the key question in the anti-oligarch campaign was whether the crackdown was part of a genuine anti-corruption campaign or simply an instrument for Putin to gain some extra room for manoeuvre. As long as prominent Yeltsin-era oligarchs thrived it would appear that the close relationship between business and politics had not been untangled; only another layer of complexity added. In the event, Putin's new rules of the game opened the way for Russia's oligarchical (or comprador) capitalism to be transformed into a new system. The conglomerate-dominated Russian economy remained highly concentrated but its relations with government were more formalised and distant. Putin met regularly with business leaders in round tables of the sort held in July 2000, but the days of oligarch dominance were over. Many companies saw improved corporate governance, greater transparency in financial process, greater economic competitiveness and an orientation towards profit rather than rent seeking. The Russian version of the multinational company had arrived, known as the financial-industrial conglomerate (FIC), about which we shall hear more in Chapter 8.

Freedom of speech and the media

Putin's presidency was accompanied by persistent fears for the preservation of media freedom. A warning issued by Putin's campaign headquarters on 4 March 2000 threatened 'an asymmetric response to acts of provocation' by the mass media, the rather more robust Russian version of New Labour's rapid rebuttal unit in the 1997 British general election. The persecution of the Radio Liberty reporter Andrei Babitsky, the environmental reporter and retired Navy captain Alexander Nikitin, of the popular muckraking reporter Alexander Khinstein and others, all appeared to signal the end of the luxuriant but riotous profusion of press liberties that had emerged in the late 1980s and grown rankly under Yeltsin. Much of it, however, had become bent to the will of the oligarchs. The lack of a strong independent financial base and the weakness of the heavily monopolised advertising market meant that in the 1990s the state tutelage of the Soviet period was gradually exchanged for conglomerate dominance. Some independent radio stations and print publications did survive, but their existence was precarious.

Babitsky had been arrested in Chechnya on 16 January 2000 and then held incommunicado for a month before being exchanged for some Russian prisoners to the Chechen insurgents. On his release in Dagestan, he was accused of having false documents and was banned from leaving the country. In an extract from his forthcoming book published in *Kommersant-Daily* on 10 March 2000 (the later book text lost some of the toughness of the newspaper version) Putin was harsh about Babitsky ('observe the laws of your country if you are counting on those laws being observed with respect to you') and former KGB agent Oleg Kalugin was described by Putin as a 'traitor'. However, when questioned about the propriety of appointing Pavel Borodin state secretary of the Russian–Belarusian Union before a full investigation of the allegations of his corruption while at the head of the Kremlin property division, Putin noted that 'there is a golden rule, a founding principle of any democratic system. It is called the presumption of innocence'.[60] As Yevgeny Kiselev noted during NTV's influential *Itogi* current affairs programme two days later, this smacked of double standards: Babitsky and Kalugin were branded traitors and enemies, while others enjoyed the presumption of innocence.

The information regime imposed on reportage of the second Chechen war took contemporary Western informational practices in times of warfare to new extremes. It appeared that any non-official reporting of the war could be construed as 'anti-state activity'. Khinstein had written an article in *Moskovsky Komsomolets* suggesting that the Kremlin had been involved in high treason. The response was not long in coming, being dragged out of bed and attempts made to section him in a psychiatric ward, claiming that he had incorrectly filled out his 1997 driving licence application by not fully declaring his mental health history. The raid by masked tax police on the offices of Gusinsky's NTV, the only national independent TV station, on 11 May 2000, followed on 13 June by his imprisonment for four days, suggested a sustained assault against press freedom. A collective editorial of the democratic *Obshchaya gazeta* warned that Putin was building a 'dictatorship': 'It seems that the consolidation of ever more power in the hands of the president is not intended to implement some policy, since no policy unconnected with the consolidation of power itself has yet been announced, but has become an aim in itself.'[61]

It was unlikely that Gusinsky was any more corrupt than other oligarchs, but he was the head of an independent media company that was critical of Putin and 'the family'. NTV had been established in 1993 and during the first Chechen war from 1994 had provided vivid critical commentary on federal actions, but in 1996 it had thrown in its lot with the regime as Yeltsin sought re-election. As with so many others, the head of the station at the time, Igor Malashenko, argued that compared to the threat of a communist comeback, Yeltsin represented the lesser evil. By the time of the 1999–2000 parliamentary and presidential elections, however, an air of hubris hung over the station. The personal attacks on Putin were quite vicious, although probably no less nasty than the attacks on Luzhkov and Primakov made, for example, by Sergei Dorenko on the Berezovsky-dominated ORT. In short, the sphere of the mass media was ripe for reform by the end of the 1990s, but a spirit of obsequiousness began to creep in that stifled some of the exuberance of earlier years.

In his first address to the Federal Assembly on 8 July 2000 Putin insisted that 'without truly free media Russian democracy will not survive, and we will not succeed in building a civil society'.[62] In that speech he warned that many TV stations and newspapers promoted the political and commercial interests of their owners, arguing that some media engaged in 'mass disinformation' and were 'a means of struggling against the state'. There could be few clearer examples where Putin's post-Sovietism – the acceptance of media pluralism and recognition that media freedom is the cornerstone of a democratic society – was at war with his neo-Soviet reactions, suggesting that the media in some way was guilty of 'anti-state' activities. In an interview soon afterwards Putin insisted that the building of a strong and effective state must not lead to the violation of civil freedoms, and that Russia must not become a police state. Even here, though, there were echoes of his neo-Sovietism, reflected in his argument that democracy in post-Soviet Russia, imposed from above, had almost led to chaos.[63] Already at this time some commentators (for example, Kiselev) argued that Putin was strengthening his personal power rather than the power of the state and called Putin 'the chief bureaucrat in our country'. Kiselev went on:

The president has different ideas to ours about what the state is and what its interests are. I think Putin is trying to imitate Louis XIV, who said 'L'etat c'est moi'. Putin's address yesterday made it clear that what he means by strengthening the state is strengthening his personal power. He didn't say a word in his address about developing parliamentarianism, nor developing local self-government, nor developing an independent judiciary, nor reforming the prosecutor's office, which has of late become the absolute shame of the Russian state. . . . What we understand by the state is not a bureaucratic machine headed by a former member of the power structures and security services, but a democratic Russia with its people.[64]

On 3 April 2001 a new management was installed at NTV and one of its first acts was to cancel the *Itogi* programme. Kiselev then went on to become part of the consortium that took over TV6.[65] The station then broadcast as TV Centre (TVS) under the supervision of a loyal board of directors headed by Primakov. The end of the old lively NTV was a great loss (especially the fine programmes of political analysis introduced by Svetlana Sorokina), but it should be noted that the crude attacks that it indulged in on leaders would never be countenanced in the West. In the United States the president is treated with great respect, if not deference, whereas the vicious attacks (from all sides) in the Russian media reflects the coarsening of the Russian intelligentsia.

Pressure on radio was also evident in the case of the Ekho Moskvy station, which had made a name for itself as fiercely independent. The old team was disbanded, but then a new group of independent journalists were allowed to take over. The new-style NTV was not immune to political pressure later either, and the loyal owners Gazprom Media sacked the station's new manager, Boris Jordan, in January 2003 at the Kremlin's instigation because of the way that the station had covered the Dubrovka theatre siege a few months earlier. Although Putin vetoed legislation adopted by the Duma in the wake of the October siege, which severely limited the reporting of terrorist actions and banned broadcasts of their statements, as 'too draconian', it was clear that he had strong views on the proper limits of media behaviour. Putin's strategy was to set out the parameters of acceptable journalistic behaviour, but then to allow a degree of freedom within these approved limits. As in his dealings with the oligarchs, the intention was to establish the rules of the game and use a few select cases to discipline the rest. This encouraged pre-emptive obedience and the imposition of self-censorship for fear of transgressing the bounds.

The State Press Committee had been upgraded in July 1999 into a ministry, and it now began to show its teeth. The press minister, Mikhail Lesin, moved aggressively to implement a 1998 law on licensing of publishing activity. The law at first had been implemented only partially, focusing on the terms of an earlier law that required only registration; now the ministry insisted on both registration and licensing. The new rules were a potentially powerful club against press freedom. As he warned, 'If one strictly follows the letter of the law, we could have shut you all [the media] down a long time ago.'[66] He insisted that all Russian print media would have to be licensed and would have, once the procedures had been established, between six months and a year to comply. Although formally a court decision was required to take away a licence, the law allowed the ministry to suspend a publication for six months for a violation of any law, which would be tantamount to closing it down.[67] In a situation where some 80 per cent of all printing presses and 90 per cent of all TV and radio transmitters are state-owned, the scope for state interference is considerable. Government subsidies for the regional media were no longer to be funnelled through regional government bodies but directly from the federal budget. The scope for administrative intervention in press freedom on the basis of these regulations posed a significant threat to the freedom of the press. Most regional media was highly politicised, either acting as the mouthpiece of the governor or being used instrumentally by the opposition, and thus only in some metropolitan areas (where independent sources of funding, including foreign, were available) were the principles of accuracy and unbiased reporting observed.

The *glasnost* (openness) of the Gorbachev era appeared to have given way to *neglasnost*. In a policy that smacked strongly of attempts by some Third World countries backed by the Soviet Union in the 1970s to establish a New International Information Order (NIIO), that would have limited the free flow of information to defend countries from the dominance of US media interests, Russia under Putin developed the idea of 'international information security'. In a paper submitted to a Council of Europe conference in Krakow in June 2000, the government argued that countries should have 'equal rights to protect their information resources and vital structures from illegitimate use or unauthorised information intervention'. The paper reflected the themes formalised in the Information Security Doctrine, adopted in June 2000 by the Security Council, headed by Putin's long-time associate Sergei Ivanov, and decreed into force by Putin on 9 September 2000.[68] The doctrine applied the ideas of the National Security Concept (see Chapter 9) to the information sphere. The doctrine argued that the Russian media could pose a threat to Russia's national security by publishing 'untrue or biased' information. Ivanov himself noted that in many of Russia's regions residents could not exercise their right to free information because of the lack of access to television and newspapers (he cited the examples of Dagestan and Chechnya). The aim of the doctrine, he insisted, was to keep secrets tight while not threatening freedom of speech and the press.[69] The doctrine was a combination of the trivial, the malicious, the paranoid and the pointless. It was an example of Putin's neo-Sovietism at its worst.

Such themes were echoed in Putin's state-of-the-nation speech of 8 July 2000; while claiming to support a free press and to oppose censorship, he accused some media of generating 'mass disinformation' and even worked to undermine the state. The implications of this were made explicit in an interview shortly afterwards, where he questioned whether the Russian media were truly independent given the dominance of oligarchical interests: 'They fight more for maintaining their influence on the state than for freedom of speech and the press.' He added, however, that he considered the conflict between the media and the authorities 'artificial'.[70]

By 2003 national newspapers represented only 15 per cent of titles, with 3,500 regional and city newspapers in the country and with 20 new mass media outlets registered every day. In March 2003 there were 6,715 electronic, 38,060 printed and 933 online periodicals registered in the country.[71] Media developments can be interpreted differently. Putin repeatedly insisted that the building of a strong and effective state must not lead to the violation of civil freedoms, and that Russia must not become a police state. Under Yeltsin most of the press and much of the electronic media had fallen under the influence of the individual oligarchs, who then proceeded to use the media as a weapon in their struggle against each other and to influence the policies of the state. Putin now set his face against the abuse of media freedom by regional barons and oligarchs, but this did not mean that he tried to restore the genuine independence of the media. The aim of the new Information Doctrine advanced by the Security Council was to ensure a balance between state security and media freedom, but it was clear that when it came to a trade off between the two, the former would win. Fortunately the doctrine was to play little role in shaping the future of the media. Under Putin there was an attempt to free the media from the grip of the regional barons and oligarchs, but it would certainly be an exaggeration to argue that diversity and pluralism now flourished. As in all the developed societies in the early twenty-first century, the media was driven ever more by ratings and subservience to corporate advertisers. Even the BBC lost some of its public broadcasting ethos, so it could hardly be expected that ORT would be able to adopt such standards. Not only the regime but the lack of diverse sources of funding became the greatest threat to the freedom of the media.

Judicial reform and human rights

The personalised and arbitrary nature of Yeltsin's rule was nowhere more in evidence than in the judicial system. Despite endless plans, the Russian judiciary until well into the post-communist era remained stamped by its provenance in the Soviet era, something that was reflected in the low level of judicial defence of citizens' rights and freedoms. As a law graduate Putin was acutely sensitive of the role that law plays in shaping social relations. Sharlet however argues that Putin's 'politics of law' was used as 'an instrument for re-engineering the distribution and flow of political power'.[72]

Reform of the legal system

The 1993 constitution established a unified national system of the administration of justice. The judicial system includes the procuracy, the *arbitrazh* courts (dealing with disputes between economic and other legally-constituted organisations), and the normal criminal courts with the Supreme Court at its head. The Constitutional Court of 19 judges gives judgements interpreting the writ of the constitution in specific cases. The national judicial system acted as a barrier, however weak in some places, to the emergence of regional despotism. It was this obstacle to the medieval fragmentation of law that Putin sought to strengthen.

In all, by 2003 eleven major laws had transformed the judicial environment, with attempts to provide adequate funds to ensure the effective implementation of the reforms. The overall scheme of the reforms was master-minded by Dmitry Kozak, Putin's colleague from St Petersburg who had failed to become Procurator-General in 2000, when faced by the hostility of the family. The judicial reforms were designed to improve guarantees for the human and civic rights of individuals and the economic rights of citizens. The intention was to move from the Soviet-style system where the system was weighted in favour of judges and prosecutors and based on an inquisitorial ideology towards a more adversarial system where the rights of the defendant and the courts were more evenly balanced.

A landmark in the new system was the introduction of a new Criminal Procedure Code (UPK), which came into effect on 1 July 2002. The new UPK, which was part of a far broader reform of the legal system, represented a major overhaul of Russia's criminal justice system intended to defend the individual from the arbitrariness of the state. The rights of defence lawyers were increased, periods in remand were cut, and the use of jury trials was extended. Under the new law it is the courts and not the prosecutors who sanction searches, arrest and detention for longer than 48 hours, a measure that was bitterly resisted by the procuracy. Trials *in absentia* were abolished. The new Code grants detainees the right to a two-hour meeting with a lawyer before being questioned, and can only be remanded for two days without an extension granted by a judge. The rules governing the use of evidence were also modified to make it easier to challenge the state's evidence and that of the police. The context was a court system marked by corruption (with Russians allegedly spending some $400 million a year in bribes to courts), the falsification of evidence and excessive brutality that at times became torture. The system of jury trials, which had for a number of years been limited to nine regions, was gradually extended to the rest of the country, although a lack of funds delayed its widespread introduction. The aim was to increase the acquittal rate, which had traditionally run at a miniscule fewer than half of one per cent whereas in Western Europe it is about 15 per cent and in the United States 25 per cent.

The new Code sought to reduce the number of people in pre-trial detention (about quarter of a million in 2002), who often faced years in limbo before being brought to trial. Lengthy gaol terms were imposed for relatively minor offences. With over a million people incarcerated, Russia's prison population was far higher *per capita* than in all Western countries except the United States. At the same time, the government increased the number of judges from the 17,000 when Putin assumed the presidency to about 20,000 and raised their salaries four-fold. The aim was to ensure their independence and to increase their accountability by the adoption of new procedures for bringing miscreant judges to book. Although the power of judges vis-à-vis prosecutors had increased, the establishment of a 'qualifications commission', which hires and sacks judges, appeared to increase the dependency of judges on the executive.

On the same day as the introduction of the new UPK, a new Administrative Violations Code came into effect. It imposed or increased fines for non-criminal offences such as traffic violations, bootlegging, prostitution, swearing in public or failing to carry a passport. At the same time, a new law on the *advokatura* came into effect on 1 July 2001, while the powers of the arbitration courts (*treteiski*) were enhanced to provide a venue for the non-state resolution of commercial conflicts. New rules were adopted to ensure the enforcement of the decisions of the Constitutional Court. The issue of the death penalty remained vexed, with the moratorium imposed by Yeltsin following Russia's accession to membership of the Council of Europe in 1996 still in place, but this had not been formalised in the UPK or by law because of opposition in the Duma and public opinion. Putin made known his personal view that the death penalty should be abolished by law, even though 80 per cent of the public supported its retention.

Although there has been justified criticism directed against the Russian judicial system, much commentary has been exaggerated. The common image of Russian judges as incompetent and corrupt is very far from the mark. As Kathryn Hendley and Peter Murrell, for example, demonstrate in their study of the workings of the *arbitrazh* court system, these courts were remarkably effective in disputes between businesses, although the implementation of decisions remained a problem.[73] In addition, when the state is a party to business disputes there have been concerns about the impartiality of judgements. In general, the court system increasingly fulfilled its role as contract enforcer and as an instrument for conflict resolution, leading to a decline in the use of violence as a way of achieving these aims. Russia's murder rate (34 per 100,000 people), however, remained the second highest in the world, behind South Africa and triple that in the United States, with a quarter of the 33,500 murders in 2001 remaining unsolved.[74] It was for this reason that public opinion sought to visit the retribution of the death penalty on perpetrators of the most heinous crimes. In general, although there have been major changes in the legislative sphere, achievements in the field of enforcement have lagged behind. The system that Vladimir Pastukhov calls bi-legalism remains in force, with 'official' and 'unofficial' law competing with each other.[75]

Human rights

However effective the national judicial reforms, as long as the war in Chechnya continued Russia would stand indicted of monstrous violations of human rights. Russia was condemned by the Parliamentary Assembly of the Council of Europe (PACE), with its voting rights suspended for six months in the second half of 2000, while domestic bodies, like the Moscow Helsinki Group in its annual human rights report (as in the one issued on 9 July 2002) condemned the systematic use of torture and extra-judicial executions.

A number of landmark human rights cases caused considerable concern. Alexander Nikitin had faced charges of divulging state secrets in contributing to a report, based on openly-available documentation, to the Norwegian environmental group Bellona on the environmental dangers posed by rusting nuclear submarines in the Barents Sea. Acquitted by a St Petersburg court in December 1999, his case was only finally closed in September 2000 by the refusal of the Supreme Court to reverse the acquittal. The military journalist Grigorii Pasko was subjected to an equally long drawn-out series of trials and postponements over charges, first made in 1997, that he had committed state treason by disclosing information about the environmental dangers posed by the Pacific Fleet to the Sea of Okhotsk. The treason conviction on Pasko aroused particular controversy. On 25 June 2002 the Supreme Court's military section upheld the conviction, and although soon pardoned Pasko refused to accept that he had been guilty of any crime. A number of other cases, above all that of the academic Igor Sutyagin, added to popular concerns about human right. It was not clear whether these cases were the exception, with the security services lapsing back into old habits, or whether they were becoming part of the new rules of the game.[76] As in other spheres, were a few exemplary cases intended to act as a warning to the rest?

The troubled passage of the law on alternative civilian service (ACS) can also be held to account as part of the infringement of the human rights declared in the constitution. The law adopted in July 2002, to come into effect on 1 January 2004, was the harshest of all those proposed to the Duma and faithfully reflected the concerns of the military. Applicants for ACS have to prove to the conscription commission that military service is against their convictions. ACS will normally be served outside the applicant's region of residence. ACS in civilian bodies lasts 42 months (for those with higher education, 21 months), while in military bodies it lasts 36 and 18 months, respectively. With the adoption of the law, those who had served on an informal experimental ACS scheme in Nizhny Novgorod were forced to undertake military service. The punitive nature of the ACS law led many liberal deputies in the Duma to amend the law to allow men to undertake ACS in their home regions.

The Presidential Human Rights Commission's annual report under Vladimir Kartashkin had often been hard-hitting documents. In July 2002 he was replaced by another respected activist and Duma deputy, Ella Pamfilova.

She had been a vociferous critic of the conduct of the 1994–96 Chechen war. On her appointment she insisted that her main aim was to help people 'defend their rights in a civilised manner and to protect them from the caprices of bureaucrats and other people'.[77] Russia also had a Human Rights Ombudsman, one of the three posts in the gift of the Duma (the other two are the heads of the State Bank and the Audit Chamber). Oleg Mironov was chosen for a five-year term in May 1998, and lamented the fact that he had only been received once by Putin, soon after the latter's election.[78] His annual reports were particularly critical of judicial abuses of human rights, above all in Chechnya. The president also appointed a special representative for human rights in Chechnya, in the first instance Vladimir Kalamanov and then in July 2002 an ethnic Chechen, Abdul-Khakim Sultygov, who had previously been secretary of the joint Duma–PACE working group on Chechnya. Despite the 'Chechenisation' of the post, there remained considerable doubt whether it would become more effective. On the very day that the armed forces attacked the offices of Memorial in Grozny, 18 July 2002, the leading Russian human rights organisation published a list of 447 persons who had been seized by the federal forces and then either directly murdered or had 'disappeared'.[79]

There remained considerable concerns about the human rights situation in Russia. In 2001 the FSB regained the right, lost by the KGB in 1988, to 'consider evidence supplied by anonymous sources'. The introduction of the infamous Information Security Doctrine in 2000, warning among other things that foreign countries were trying to dominate the global information sphere and to 'force Russia out of domestic and international information markets', could not but raise alarm because of its tone as much as its substance. In Chechnya mopping-up operations (*zachistki*) continued and the list of settlements suffering from the sad litany of beatings, tortures, disappearances and murders grew ever longer: Sernovodsk, Assinovskaya, Kurchaloi and more. While Chechnya by the late 1990s had indeed sunk into 'total lawlessness', to use Putin's expression, it is hard to see that these operations contributed to the restoration of 'constitutional order'. However, fears that Putin's KGB background would entail a 'creeping statism' that would destroy independent NGOs and lead to the imposition of a new, modernised, totalitarianism proved exaggerated.

*   *   *

Between civil society and the state a relatively autonomous power system emerged, a special type of regime, which was largely independent and unaccountable to the former and parasitic on the latter. The regime is located between the constitutionality of the state and accountability to the people. Putin's greatest achievement was to regularise the relationship between the regime and the state, but there remained a gulf between the regime and society. Civil society associations, above all trade unions and the media, were not adequately integrated in forming the social order while retaining their independence. There were fundamental tensions in Putin's state building strategy between a liberal and a more authoritarian approach. We characterise this contradiction as one between the reconstitution of the state, on the basis of law and the supremacy of the constitution, and reconcentration, where pluralism is undermined and social activity subordinated to the interests of the governing group. Putin's reforms sought to remake the state; but they also carried the danger of limiting the hard-won freedoms of Russia's untidy, unfinished but genuine democratic revolution of the 1990s. Putin may just be able to reconcile order and liberty, and thus complete the programme outlined by Peter Stolypin at the beginning of the century, but this time in a democratic form. What the autocracy and the communist regime failed to do may just be within the country's grasp today: to become a free, democratic and ordered state. Unfortunately, a new Leviathan could also be born.

5   Restructuring political space

> History proves all dictatorships, all authoritarian forms of government are transient. Only democratic systems are lasting.
>
> (Putin[1])

The parliamentary elections of December 1999 acted as the launch pad for Putin's presidential campaign in early 2000. The Kremlin had been able to beat off the challenge posed by various regionally based parties led by the likes of Luzhkov and Primakov, and in its place had created its own organisation, Unity, that not only countered the threat but also acted as the core of a pro-presidential bloc in the third Duma (2000–03). More broadly, many observers noted that civil society was weak and was unable to constrain the actions of the political authorities. As a recent work put it: 'Civil society remains in an embryonic condition and can only to a very limited degree define the domestic or foreign policies of the state ... there is a gulf between the views of the elite and the majority of the population on a number of questions.'[2] While the first part is undoubtedly correct, the idea of a vast gulf between the views of the elite and the people was probably exaggerated – or so it appeared as Putin's leadership progressed. What is beyond doubt is the lack of a single Russian political identity, with enormous social polarisation, a relatively small middle class and at least a third of the population below the poverty line. Some parts of the country were torn by actual or potential ethnic conflict, and in some of Russia's furthest regions (and some not so far away) Moscow's authority rang as a distant bell. At the heart of Putin's state building project was the attempt to homogenise political space and to stamp the Kremlin's authority on political processes everywhere. How he tried to do this and to what extent he succeeded we shall examine below.

Changes to the party system

The development of a national party system was undermined by the ability of regional executives to control patronage and to influence electoral outcomes. The use of so-called 'administrative resources' by central and regional authorities, above all the manipulation of the 'virtual' world of the media and public relations, tended to set up a parallel sphere of politics that by-passed parties. Russia's party system in any case had developed in a peculiar way, with no shortage of parties but few enjoying extensive and consistent support.[3] Russia's political parties did not legitimise the authority of the government, while the executive authorities at both the regional and federal levels strove to remain independent of parties. Nevertheless, while it is common to berate the flaws in Russian party development, the distance that it had travelled in a relatively short time since the official end of the Communist Party's monopoly in February 1990 is impressive. Party systems in the mature democracies, moreover, are subject to increasing fluidity, seen with particular force in the collapse of the *partitocrazia* (partitocratic) system in Italy in 1992, and the defeat (if only temporary) of the hegemonic Liberal Democratic Party in Japan in 1993.

In Russia there are plenty of signs of an emerging pattern of partisan alignment, with a relatively consistent third of voters supporting the communists, about a quarter supporting a variety of liberal groupings, a large 'marsh' (*boloto*) in the centre, accompanied by a relatively high level of party recognition. The system, however, remained relatively fluid, characterised as a 'floating party system'.[4] There were few institutional barriers to the entry of new parties leading to Russia's rapid transformation from a one-party state in the Soviet period to a state that by any reckoning had too many parties.[5] The December 1993 Duma elections were contested by 13 associations, a number that had risen to 43 for the 1995 elections before falling back to 26 in 1999. By July 2001 Russia had 199 officially registered parties and movements. This confirms Scott Mainwaring's observation that, despite the many challenges to them, parties 'have continued to be the main agents of representation and are virtually the only actors with access to elected positions in democratic politics'.[6] Putin's reform of the party system sought to consolidate this prerogative of parties while reducing their number and making them genuinely national organisations. Whether he could also make them genuinely representative bodies with party elites responsive to the views of the membership and accountable to the social interests that they claimed to represent was another question. In numerous polls parties came out as one of the least trusted institutions, and at the same time as one of the most corrupt.[7] At the same time, a study showed that in 2000 only 0.7 per cent of respondents were members of a political party or organisation, while only 0.3 per cent considered themselves activists.[8] Total membership of all Russia's multitude of parties and organisations was no more than a million, about 1 per cent of the adult population. Thus party life was very much an elite affair.

Putin had enjoyed, as we have seen, an unspectacular career as a party member and official. In 1991 the Communist Party had left him, rather than him it, and later he joined the emerging 'party of power', Russia's Choice, and then he moved on to the new party of power, Our Home is Russia (NDR). In May 1995 he was elected chair of the St Petersburg branch of

NDR and entered the party's political council, a position of which he was relieved in June 1997.[9] Despite this, Putin has been a consistent advocate of enhancing the role of parties in Russian politics. In his state-of-the-nation speech of 8 July 2000, Putin suggested that 'perhaps only public and political associations should have the right to nominate candidates to the post of head of state'. The aim was to stimulate the development of a party system that had rather more impact on the political process, above all the selection of leaders. Berezovsky, however, argued that if such a plan was implemented, 'democracy will shrink in Russia'.[10] In the event, one of the central changes of Putin's early period in office was reform of the normative framework governing party life. The central act of this was the July 2001 law on political parties, which supplanted the much-amended 1990 law on civic associations. There had been periodic attempts in the 1990s to adopt a law on political parties, notably in July 1995 when the Duma got as far as adopting a law, but this had been vetoed by the Federation Council. In December 2000 the presidential law on political parties, largely drafted by the Central Electoral Commission, was published, to receive its first parliamentary reading in February 2001. The bill was subject to over a thousand amendments, but the presidential version remained substantially intact.[11]

At the heart of the new law was the attempt to create a system consisting of fewer parties but with all of them becoming national in scale. They must have a membership of no fewer than 10,000, with a minimum of 100 members in at least 45 regions, and 50 members in each of the remaining 44. This replaced the old minimum party membership of 5,000 to be registered as an 'electoral association'. The concept of 'national' comprised not only the idea of geographical reach but also how representative they were to be. Parties are not allowed to appeal to sectional interests, and those advancing religious, racial, ethnic and professional causes are forbidden. Russian parties are thus prohibited from drawing on the power of the cleavages that have shaped Western party systems. Although it is possible to fight for broad social welfare issues, parties drawn from a single occupation are not allowed. Collective membership is banned. While not explicitly forbidden, regional parties are effectively ruled out by the rules on membership. There are numerous rules on funding, including provision for state support for parties that receive 3 per cent of the proportional vote, win 12 single-mandate seats in parliamentary elections, or 3 per cent of the vote in presidential elections. Parties that fail to gather 2 per cent of the vote will have to return the money for the free airtime on state radio and television stations that they received during the campaign. Failure to pay will mean disqualification in the next election. The law on parties was reinforced by a federal law stipulating that regional parliaments have to be formed on the party principle, which came into effect in July 2003 (see Chapter 6).

Complex rules govern the registration process by the Ministry of Justice, including the need for a founding congress with at least 150 delegates from at least 45 regions. The founding congress elects the party's leading bodies and adopts a programme. The party is then registered nationally, followed by the registration of its regional branches with local divisions of the justice ministry, and finally the central ministry validates the completion of the process. After registration the ministry continues to monitor observance, and has the right to suspend a party found to be contravening the rules. Suspension cannot take place during an election, and those parties that have entered the Duma on party lists cannot be suspended within five years of their election. Parties have the right to appeal to the courts against suspension, and the final ruling on dissolving a party is taken by the Supreme Court. Parties not only have the right but *must* contest elections, and not only at the national level (parliamentary and presidential) but also at the regional (gubernatorial and legislative) and municipal. At the same time, parties are the *only* organisations allowed to contest elections. Civic associations may join an electoral bloc with parties, but cannot advance their own candidates.

The registration process following the adoption of the law saw a restructuring of the party scene. Even established parties had to go through the registration process. Many of the smaller parties disappeared from view, while others had a struggle to establish themselves in the new system. Plenty of anomalies were revealed. For example, Alexander Chuev's Christian Democratic Union was refused registration on the grounds that it was sectarian, although Christian Democracy is one of the dominant political trends in many Western European countries. Berezovsky's Liberal Russia was initially refused registration because of an alleged lack of precision in its regulations. By mid-2002 56 party congresses had been held and 23 parties had been registered, of which only eight had completed the re-registration of regional branches (they had to have branches in at least half the regions). By mid-2003 the Ministry of Justice had registered 51 parties. The law had certainly not created a two-party system, but it had at least clarified what was a party and what was not.

A law 'On Counteracting Extremist Activity', sponsored by the president, banning organisations found to have committed 'extremist activity' was adopted by the Duma in June 2002. The bill covered religious, social and other organisations and the media. The definition of 'extremist activity' proved controversial. Article 1 of the law defined it as:

> the planning, organisation, preparation for or execution of actions aimed at the forcible change of the constitutional order or violation of the territorial integrity of the Russian Federation; the undermining of the security or the assumption of the governing powers of the Russian Federation; the creation of illegal armed formations; terrorist activity; the incitement of racial, ethnic or religious discord or social discord in connection with violence or calls for violence; humiliation of national dignity; the organisation of mass unrest, hooliganism or acts of vandalism motivated by ideological, political, racial, ethnic or religious hatred towards a particular social group; the propaganda of exclusivity, superi-

ority or inferiority of citizens on account of their attitude towards religion, social status, race, nationality, religion, or language.[12]

This would appear to adopt an attitude of robust liberalism: rights can be exercised as long as they do not infringe the rights of others. However, the procedures associated with the implementation of the provisions of the law raised some disquiet. A whole organisation could be liable to prosecution or banned if any of its sub-divisions were found guilty of extremism, as defined above. An initial warning is sent if any part of an organisation commits extremist activity (Article 7). If a leading member of an organisation makes extremist statements without stating that these were their personal views, then the organisation has to denounce the statements or actions of the person (Article 15). The 1997 law on religion was modified by the passage of this law, to replace the grounds for the banning of a religious organisation with the above definition of extremist activity; the grounds were thus expanded from actually carrying out actions to planning or making calls for this activity.

The law on parties will change the way that parliament works. The party principle will become more deeply entrenched and a clearer division between government and opposition should emerge. Regional assemblies will enter more fully the national political arena since national parties will figure more prominently in their work. Putin's attempt to radicalise the centre means that the traditional centrist 'party of power' has the potential to become a classic ruling party. In the early 2000s this meant United Russia, combining the administrative resources of the state and an ideology of liberal patriotism, and from 2002 there was much discussion, harking back to Primakov's premiership, of forming a government based on the dominant party. However, United Russia remained bound hand and foot to the governing regime and had failed, by the time of its first crucial test in the December 2003 parliamentary elections, to transform itself into a powerful independent, although pro-government, party. Putin tried to activate a radical centre, possibly even against the flailing party of power.

There is no reason to doubt Putin's commitment to 'strengthening the role of parties in political life'. In his state-of-the-nation speech in May 2003 he noted: 'I believe it possible, taking into account the results of the forthcoming election to the State Duma, to form a professional and efficient government based on the parliamentary majority.'[13] Putin's reforms had the potential to transform Russia's political space, but for that regime management of political processes would have to give way to the autonomy of a genuinely competitive political market place. It was not clear that Putin was quite ready for that – or indeed whether the country was. A powerful group around Putin, bringing together *siloviki* and liberals, feared that the passage of a constitutional amendment allowing a party or coalition of parties to form the government and nominate the prime minister would deliver the country into the hands of the oligarchs.[14] A competitive party system began to emerge, but parties are still not adequately embedded in the country's social structure, they do not effectively represent social interests, they are not yet genuinely national in scope, they do not legitimise power and they do not directly form governments.

Changes to electoral legislation

Following every cycle since competitive elections were introduced in Russia at the beginning of the 1990s the electoral legislation was modified to incorporate the lessons learned. A working group in the Central Electoral Commission was established by presidential decree on 26 August 2000 to examine revisions to the electoral code, work that took into account the changes introduced by the new law on parties. A new framework law on elections for parliament and the presidency was adopted on 12 June 2002, with specific laws for each being signed into law by Putin in December 2002 and January 2003, respectively, and the whole package came into effect on 14 July 2003. He also signed into law the use of the automated vote counting system 'Vybory'. Thus the normative framework for the next electoral cycle, with parliamentary elections on 7 December 2003 and presidential elections on 14 March 2004, was in place, unusually, well before the elections themselves.

In keeping with the aim of raising the status of parties, only national parties now had the right to nominate candidates in federal and regional elections. It was still possible to create political blocs, but these are now limited to three members, of which at least one had to be a political party. Individual citizens can still nominate themselves for office, but groups of voters are now deprived of this right, although in local elections non-political groups can still nominate candidates. Thus (starting with the 2007 parliamentary election) voter groups will no longer be able to nominate candidates, and instead only candidates proposed by parties and individuals are allowed. The others have to collect two million signatures, with not more than 50,000 from any one region, a tough task for any party. There are much stricter rules requiring the full disclosure of a candidate's sources of financial support, a measure that will discourage independent candidates (those not belonging to a political party), while at the same time putting off candidates sponsored by criminal or other shady networks. Those parties that do enter parliament will enjoy a number of new benefits. They will be financed from the state budget according to the number of votes that they receive, and their candidates in later elections will not have to gather signatures or provide a deposit to participate. The law stipulated that at least three party list groups would have to enter the 2003 Duma (up from the minimum of two earlier). In the 2007 elections a new barrier of 7 per cent will be in place, and irrespective of the number of votes they obtain a minimum of four parties will enter parliament. In regional elections, too, at least half of the seats in regional legislatures have to be elected through party lists.

Those parties crossing the 5 per cent threshold to enter the Duma (it was anticipated that about five of the 30-odd groups participating in the 2003 election would achieve this) would also be able to nominate their presidential candidate directly. Parties and blocs nominating a presidential candidate will gain extra free newspaper space and airtime, in addition to that granted to all candidates. Half of this will go to candidates and half to the nominating parties, thus giving an advantage to party-nominated candidates. The aim clearly is to focus political competition on probably no more than five major parties. These parties are intended to act as a counter-weight to regional executives if they are able to establish a powerful presence in regional legislatures, and at the national level they will counteract the influence of the oligarchs. One of them could sooner or later become the presidential party.

More broadly, the ability of electoral commissions and the courts to interfere in the electoral process by refusing to register or by disqualifying candidates was restricted. In past elections, especially at the regional level, there had been some infamous cases when leading candidates had been removed from the ballot by the courts at the last moment. The most notorious was when the governor of Kursk *oblast*, Alexander Rutskoi, was struck off the list on the day before the election in October 2000. Now the causes that could provoke such actions have been pared down, and the right to cancel a candidate's registration for violating electoral legislation has been granted exclusively to the courts. This prerogative is itself limited and has to be done by a lower court at least five days before the election. In keeping with the general trend of trying to limit political arbitrariness at the regional level, the rules for forming electoral commissions changed. Regional and local government authorities no longer form the commissions, and instead higher level electoral commissions form the district, territorial and ward electoral commissions as well as nominating their chairs (in the past the commissions had elected their own chairs). Regional and local government administrations establish the respective regional and local commissions as in the past, but these commissions now have two members appointed by the higher commission and the chairs of these commissions are chosen on the recommendation of the higher commission. The aim was to reduce the influence of regional and local governments on electoral commissions. As in other spheres, centralisation was intended to promote rather than to undermine democracy.

Parliamentary realignment

Many commentators have suggested that Russia has a 'superpresidential' system, with the corollary that the executive enjoys a complete dominance over political life. Although Russia's presidency does have extensive powers, governing in partnership with the cabinet of ministers and the prime minister, it certainly does not rule alone. The legislature in Russia is far from marginal, and indeed, with Putin enjoying a working majority after December 1999, his reforms proceeded not by decree but through an enormous body of legislative activity. The degree to which the lower house (the State Duma) and the upper house (the Federation Council) of Russia's bicameral Federal Assembly can impose limits on presidential power and effectively hold it accountable, however, is another matter. The structure of the Duma, according to Ostrow, with its unlinked dual-channel design and poor coordination between the party and committee systems, reduces its ability to act as an effective check and balance on executive power.[15] Thomas Remington, however, has argued that the legislature has been able to act as effective partner to the executive and thus the decree powers of the presidency have not been used to subvert the legislative process.[16] He notes that 'A sign of the end of the revolutionary era is the fact that the Kremlin is pursuing this policy agenda through legislation rather than by decree.'[17]

As in many other countries, parliament's standing in public opinion was rather low, based on a lack of public confidence in the competence and honesty of legislators. There was a widespread perception that many criminals had entered political life, and used the shield of parliamentary immunity to protect themselves against prosecution. Despite some infamous cases where this indeed had taken place, this was far from being a mass phenomenon.[18] One of the changes introduced by the new Criminal Procedure Code of July 2002 (see Chapter 4) was that parliamentary deputies lost their blanket immunity from criminal prosecution. A case can now be brought against a deputy without first having to obtain parliament's permission. Despite its poor image, the Duma since its first convocation in 1994 had produced an impressive body of legislation; during the Second Duma (1996–99), for example, over 500 bills were passed and signed into law by the president, and much of this (some 122 laws) was significant legislation of enduring importance.[19]

Although the 1999 elections delivered a solid block of pro-presidential legislators, no party or group enjoyed an absolute majority (over half of the 450 seats), let alone a two-thirds constitutional majority. This had been the case in the first two Dumas as well, and this explains the marked non-majoritorian features of the Duma's internal organisation. The Council of the Duma, which sets the legislative agenda, is comprised of all the party leaders with equal voting rights, irrespective of the size of the party group. Posts in the Duma's two-dozen odd committees are divided between the parties on a proportional basis, although the chairpersonships are highly prized and in January 2000 were divided up between the Communists and Unity in a way that led to a walk-out and protests by the other groups. On 4 April 2002 a reshuffle (probably Kremlin-inspired) saw the Communists losing the leadership of seven of its committees, and their resignation from the others as they went into open opposition to the presidency. This in turn provoked a split in the CPRF as speaker Seleznev refused to resign his position, and following his expulsion on 25 May from the CPRF he redoubled his efforts to develop his own party, Rebirth of Russia, on the basis of his 'Russia' movement. At the same time, both the Council and the committees are subject to votes on the floor of the house, and thus rank-and-file deputies are able to exert considerable influence over the legislative process.

The base of presidential support in parliament was the Unity grouping, established to provide political support for Putin. Vladimir Zhirinovsky's Liberal Democratic Party of Russia (LDPR) also tended to vote loyally with the president. Although the leader of the CPRF, Zyuganov, made many criticisms of Putin's leadership, the Communist faction in the Duma effectively became part of the governing coalition in the first year of Putin's presidency. This was already in evidence in Putin's support for Seleznev continuing as speaker in the Third Duma, and then in the deal struck on 18 January 2000 between the CPRF and Unity for the division of committee chairs and vice-speaker posts. Thereafter the CPRF moved into opposition, in the first instance to the Kasyanov government rather than to the president himself, tabling a no-confidence motion in the government in March 2001. The CPRF now argued that 'the lower house has turned into a branch of the government'.[20] By 2002 the CPRF looked increasingly prey to damaging splits, with Seleznev and some colleagues expelled from the CPRF, weakening the party as a political force (although Seleznev's group remained marginal). Thus Putin enjoyed a co-operative parliament, something that had eluded Yeltsin after 1992. The Duma broadly backed Putin's 'consensus' government, providing legislative support for his initiatives in federal, economic and foreign relations.

The United Russia party, formed in late 2001 by a merger of the Unity and Fatherland groups, was represented in the Duma in early 2003 by the Unity faction (82 seats) and the Fatherland-All Russia faction (52). It could also count on the support of some of the Russia's Region faction (55 votes) and also the People's Deputy group (55 seats). With this solid bloc of votes behind them, combined with the fact that centrists now enjoyed the chairmanship of all significant committees and domination of the lower house's administrative apparatus, one could fairly say that Putin had tamed the Duma, a dominance reinforced by changes to the Federation Council that will be discussed in Chapter 6. Ranged against this dominant coalition were the now militantly oppositionist Communists (82 seats) and Agrarians (43), while Zhirinovsky's Liberal Democrats (13), SPS (32) and Yabloko (17) remained independent. The Kremlin played an active part in managing its faction in the Duma, seen in the change in the leadership of the United Russia group in November 2002 when the ineffectual Alexander Bespalov was replaced by the interior minister Boris Gryzlov.

With a working majority to support presidential policy, the legislative activity of the Duma in the early 2000s went into overdrive. Legislation in the early Putin presidency was largely initiated by the executive; some 72 per cent of all bills in spring 2000, for example.[21] In the session ending in July 2001 the emphasis was on reform of the federal system. Some 200 pieces of legislation had been voted upon, including a wide range of Kremlin-sponsored bills designed to reform Russia's political and economic system. These included revisions to the land and tax codes, and a number of 'debureaucratisation' measures, including reducing the number of activities requiring licences from some 500 to 104, and the adoption of the law on parties. In the following year the emphasis was on reform of the judicial system and extending property rights, above all of land, with major laws passed: the Land Code, the Labour Code, the Criminal Procedure Code, and the Administrative Code. All of this was in fulfilment of Putin's promise, at his first press conference as head of state, that his aim was Russia's 'modernisation'. The theme was taken up again a year later at a press conference on 18 July 2001 when he argued that this legislative activity marked a significant step towards 'the modernisation of the state's economy' and represented a 'substantial contribution toward the improvement of the country's political system'.[22] In the three key areas of the economy and property rights, federal relations, and the judicial system, substantial blocks of laws had been adopted. As time passed, of course, there were fewer items of landmark legislation. Critical voices, however, argued that much of this legislative activity lacked sufficient time to be improved by parliamentary debate, and indeed that the Duma had become little more than an extension of the Kremlin, a 'transmission belt' rubber-stamping its initiatives and thus confirming the views of those who argued that Russia had become a 'managed democracy'.

In the run up to the 2003 elections the CPRF and United Russia were running head to head. Putin's own position was unclear, since like Yeltsin before him he refused to join a political party. Although United Russia fought hard to become the official presidential party, Putin refused to commit himself unequivocally and kept his options open. He was happy to work closely with many from the SPS, with two of Chubais's associates working in key ministerial posts, Alexei Kudrin and German Gref. Other parties, like Novgorod governor Mikhail Prusak's Democratic Party of Russia, Gennady Raikov's People's Party and Sergei Mironov's Party of Life could be taken up by the Kremlin at any time to act as the vehicle for its ambitions. The Yabloko party headed by Yavlinsky by 2003 also appeared to enjoy the Kremlin's favour; the regime had clearly calculated that a Duma without a solid liberal bloc would be less legitimate, if rather more manageable.

Regime and opposition

What was the nature of the political order that became consolidated under Putin? Many adjectives have been used to qualify the broadly democratic institutional structure that took shape. Most convey the sense of a 'managed democracy' or of 'controlled pluralism'. Choices remain, votes can be cast in a relatively free, and even fair, manner, but the options are constrained by an authority standing outside of the system that regulates the choices and which is not subject to the power of the choice made. We have called this the regime, focused on the political institutions of the presidency but rather broader than the president alone, standing between the impartial operation of the constitutional state and the exercise of popular sovereignty through the ballot box and representative institutions. However, we should be careful to separate process from outcomes. As for process, the regime under Putin sponsored changes to the party system, electoral legislation and much more, and this can be seen as an indication of 'managed' democracy,[23] but it could also be interpreted as an attempt to improve the competitive nature of Russian politics. As for outcomes, while there is undoubtedly evidence of administrative intervention in the electoral process, it would be an exaggeration to argue that electoral outcomes are entirely 'managed'. The democratic process is not managed by some force standing outside democracy. The Putin regime was certainly an active political player, fighting to get its candidates elected in regional and other elections, but this is no more than what the American presidency and other democratic leaders have traditionally done. Is there something fundamentally different going on in the Russian case, other than Russia simply having been a democracy for a much shorter period of time? On this views differ both in Russia and among foreign observers.

The role of opposition parties was particularly difficult in the Putin era because of his political polymorphousness. As Nemtsov noted 'Putin has amazing communicative qualities. . . . When he is with me he is a rightist, but when with Zyuganov he is a leftist.'[24] The main criticism directed against Putin by the CPRF under Zyuganov was not that his government subverted democracy but it did not deliver the desired social and economic goods. The CPRF found itself caught between moving further towards social democracy (a path advocated by Seleznev, the economist Sergei Glazyev and one of the CPRF's most important sponsors, Gennady Semigin), in which case it could find itself merging with the regime, or moving into extreme opposition. In the event the CPRF under Zyuganov kept to its ineffectual 'third path'. The relative passivity and lack of intellectual sharpness in the CPRF's opposition to Putin meant that Zyuganov can be considered a co-architect of the Putinite stabilisation; and for this reason the ruling elite sought to maintain a strong left-wing but ineffectual presence in parliament. As Medvedev notes, 'Putin was able to do what Yeltsin could not: eliminate the "irreconcilable" opposition.'[25]

It was left to the 'democrats' to carry the banner of real opposition. Yavlinsky was convinced that Russian democracy under both Yeltsin and at first to a lesser extent under Putin was largely a sham, a view no doubt encouraged by the failure of the system to make him leader. He insisted that 'political time in Russia is flowing backwards'; a 'guided democracy' had emerged in which 'the bosses remain in power regardless of the will of the voters'.[26] Although Yavlinsky's Yabloko had been in permanent opposition to Yeltsin's regime, he later modified his position towards Putin's government and at various points argued that it should be given a chance to prove itself. Many of his ideas were in any case incorporated into the government's programme, although he retained his reservations. For example, he agreed that governors should be dismissed from their posts if they violated laws or the Russian constitution, but insisted that this should be only done on the basis of a court decision. As he argued, 'The actions that are being undertaken can make sense only if the independence of the judicial system and mass media is strengthened simultaneously.'[27] As he put it on another occasion, 'A repressive police state is no alternative to a semi-criminal oligarchy. Pinochet is not an alternative to Yeltsin.'[28] Yavlinsky was careful not to attack Putin personally, but his condemnation of the system that had been created in Russia intensified during Putin's tenure. He insisted that the power system sought to establish a controlled or managed democracy in which a democratic façade covered the Kremlin's ambition to create a single power centre. In this system the State Duma and other democratic institutions played a largely decorative role. As far as he was concerned, 'the parliament has been completely transformed into a puppet of the executive branch'.[29] He insisted that Yabloko's unification with SPS would be problematical since Yabloko prioritised individual rights and liberty and had a different relationship with the political authorities, and this was reflected in rather different electorates. Coordinated work in the Duma, in the form of a joint inter-factional council, was possible, but even then the two factions did not always vote in the same way.

The SPS in the early period tried both to ride with the horses and run with the hounds, declaring itself part of the 'ruling opposition'.[30] At first supportive of Putin, Nemtsov's criticisms became increasingly harsh as he sought to establish the SPS's independent political credentials. He argued that

> Putin has built a controlled democracy in Russia – with state-controlled TV, with Chechnya, and by extorting budget funds from the regions. He is turning the Federation Council into a 'House of Lords'. . . . Controlled democracy has its own internal logic. The screws can only be tightened . . . in the long run, the strategic choice of Russia is at stake: a choice between democracy and dictatorship.[31]

The SPS had long argued that Putin's programme was basically theirs, and were particularly keen to take credit for the land code allowing the sale of land and for the judicial reforms. However, Nemtsov berated the SPS for having failed to prevent the establishment of 'managed democracy':

> I mean the staking on bureaucratic capitalism: the president is depending exclusively on the bureaucratic and power elements and is giving the bureaucracy, which he himself came out of, carte blanche. I also mean Chechnya, where the force variant is being insisted upon exclusively with maniacal stubbornness. I also mean the 'cleansing' (*zachistka*) of the parliament, both the upper and the lower chambers. I mean the centralisation of both the budget and [state] power, the sharp violation of the balance of power in general.[32]

Nemtsov also criticised 'the practically complete monopolisation' of national television, and argued that Kozak's commission examining local government (and regional) reform in fact represented 'the destruction of local self-government' to strengthen 'the vertical of power'. Nemtsov argued that Putin had inherited 'oligarchic capitalism', and all that he had done was to remove two of the most odious from the arena (Berezovsky and Gusinsky) but left the rest to rule the roost. Putin remained a slave to the family and the *siloviki* leading, in Nemtsov's view, to the construction of bureaucratic capitalism in Russia that squeezed small and medium businesses and impeded the creation of a strong middle class.

Democracy and civil society

Pavlovsky, one of the main ideologists of the revived regime, insisted that it was not so much the authorities that represented the 'empire of façades', but society and its institutions, which he argued were 'dreadfully weak' at all levels, and thus there were no serious interlocutors in society with whom the authorities could interact. He argued that there were 'no institutions of local government capable of taking responsibility at the local level'. As far as he was concerned,

> The social milieu is fragmented. Democracy does not work without 'political publicity', which ensures contacts between members of society, between cultures varying territorially and ethnically, between the author-ities and the common people. Social life has been divided and monopo-lised by small groups of people, engaged in their own actions – self-presentation, self-aggrandisement, show-politics. . . . Our parties have no political will to work with the masses.

The vacuum created by the waning of the communists was being filled by various extremist groups, skinhead-type organisations often working with the local police in various rackets: this, Pavlovsky insisted, was also a type of 'civil society'. Despite the fact that there were some 300,000 non-profit organisa-tions in Russia, it was difficult to work with most, above all human rights activists, since they appeared too ready to condemn the authorities for undermining freedom rather than working with them: 'You need to create these liberties first':

> Crazed envy between organisations has been prominent in Russia. In the social sphere the authorities have been searching for anarchists, spies and rebels, even though ordinary citizens have settled down long ago and do not want to shake up the state. A dissident conspiratorial mindset exists among the human rights activists: supposedly, we know for sure – there is a group within the Kremlin where plans to eliminate rights and liberties are being developed. The only disputed point is whether this

group is headed by Putin, or he is only condoning its actions. What kind of social partnership can be created in this atmosphere?[33]

Pavlovsky nevertheless recognised that a certain demarcation line between the state and its citizenry had been established across which the state at its peril would transgress: it would be impossible to abolish elections, since at least three-quarters of the population reject the idea that state officials should be appointed; restrictions on freedom of movement or travelling abroad would be unacceptable to society; as would the banning of commerce and freedom of speech; and even, surprisingly enough, the banning of unpopular parties would be hard. This does not stop the authorities meddling with the internet, the media and education; and of course, some popular 'victories' (as in the maintenance of the death penalty and hostility to migrants) can be illiberal and destructive.

We have cited Pavlovsky at length since he raises a number of important issues: the ambivalent nature of civil society; the degree to which democratic freedoms had become a popular value that could not be easily withdrawn; society itself was weak and unable to defend its own interests coherently and positively; the old dissident mindset, dating from the period when dissidents were the only civil society, still considered the authorities as the enemy (hence the difficulty in establishing a partnership); society itself was prey to morbid pathologies that could only be dealt with through state action; and the reluctance of political parties to take responsibility for trying to shape social processes by building strong organisations rooted in civil society.

This is not the place to discuss at length the meaning of civil society but simply to note that the core meaning, derived from Roman notions of society, is based on the idea of a partnership between individuals of equal legal status. From this, a 'civil society' is a legal and political order in which individuals interact with others, sometimes in groups, but retain their own identity and interests, as opposed to a system based on kinship, hierarchy, tradition, patronage or power. Political theorists like John Locke took this further to include the consent of the ruled, and in contemporary understandings the emphasis is on a network of civic associations outside the control of the state, guaranteed by law, and with the ability to promote their programmes and pursue their interests.

Although in the late communist years a conflictual model of state and society relations predominated, the early post-communist years reasserted the idea of a necessary partnership. However, in some regions state failure and corruption has encouraged the idea that civil society should make up the shortfall and itself assume the burden of delivering welfare and other traditional state functions.[34] Although in Russia the NGO network has developed enormously since the fall of communism, only the state can deliver extensive welfare goods: the state still performs its traditional functions, although not very well. If civil society can be measured by the quantitative development of public and associational life, then Russia has all the hallmarks of having one. However, measured more qualitatively, above all in terms of the autonomy of social actors, their ability to intervene effectively in decision making processes, to mobilise public opinion in a way that can change the approach of public authorities, the reach of the public sphere in all the far-flung regions of the country, and indeed in the ability of civil society to modify traditional notions of public order, to ensure the impartial application of law, and to ameliorate its own pathologies, then civil society in Russia can be found wanting.

The nascent democracy furthermore, according to commentators such as Shevtsova, was further undermined by the reassertion of state power and the regime's attempts to control social and political processes.[35] The debate over Putin's political reforms was at its most acute over plans to hold a Civic Forum where the country's myriad social and human rights organisations could engage in dialogue with the regime. Would participation in the forum threaten NGOs with co-optation, or would participation in fact broaden the engagement of the government in supporting the development of civil society? That, at its most simple, was the debate that raged in the months before the forum was actually held in November 2001. The fact that Pavlovsky and Markov were the main organisers of the Civil Forum did not help matters, since they had been identified, however unfairly, as the proponents of 'managed democracy'. Markov insisted that the presidency's demonstrative support for NGO development would strengthen the hand of civic and social associations in the regions, and later evidence suggests that the argument was a valid one.

Despite endless assertions about the weakness of civil society in Russia, the enormous development of the NGO sector reflected a strong current of civic activism. The announcement of the Forum's organising committee on 11 October stressed that 'civil society in Russia exists and is developing', noting that according to some estimates about one million people worked in NGOs, and that the social, legal, medical, cultural, educational and other services offered by NGOs directly affected about 20 million people. The aim of the Forum was to provide 'serious discussion of paths of development for civil society in Russia and its relationship with state power'. It was for this reason that representatives from all three branches of the state would attend the event. The committee sought to allay fears that the Forum would turn into a 'parade of loyalty' to the government. The committee ended by declaring that 'Civil society is neither a vassal of power nor its opponent'.[36]

The Civil Forum on 21–22 November 2001 sought to address the vexed question of relations between the state and civil society. In his speech on 21 November Putin argued:

> We have a good chance of combining the forces of the state with the energy of a democratic society. We should not get carried away, but we are making some progress already. The time is coming when being a Russian citizen will be prestigious. . . . Civil society should have its own

foundations, it should feed on the spirit of freedom. Only then will it become civil society. No, our civil society is not yet formed, but I do not think that there is a country where civil society has been formed the way it should have been. This is a necessary and continuous process in democracies, and in Russia it is only beginning.[37]

The experience of some third world countries suggested that civil society should 'give up on the state', since the state was predatory and incompetent. Putin forcefully rebutted any such arguments, but at the same time insisted that civil society could not be created 'from above'. Instead, he called for a partnership of the state and civil society to seize the 'historical chance', otherwise both would find themselves on the 'margins (*zadvorkakh*) of civilisation'. This was a theme to which he returned in his annual address to parliament on 16 May 2003:

> We often talk about the greatness of Russia but a great Russia isn't just a great state. First and foremost, it is a modern, developed society, one that won't come about of its own accord. A fully-fledged and developed civil society will only emerge in conditions where there is a drastic reduction in the functions of the state apparatus, where mistrust between various groups in society is surmounted and, most importantly of all, it will only be possible if there is national unity in assessing the strategic objectives the country faces. The creation of conditions such as these, without the active involvement of political parties, is impossible.[38]

Democracy is as much about cultural attitudes to power and authority as it is about institutions. Russia clearly now has the whole gamut of democratic forms, but the spirit with which they operate is not yet imbued with those 'habits of the heart' that Tocqueville insisted were essential for the democratic operation of a polity. The problem lies not only in what some have argued to be flaws in Russian democracy's institutional design, with an overweening presidency, or the emergence of a relatively autonomous regime between the state and the people, but also with the characteristics of political society as a whole. Russia still lacked an opposition that could monitor authority and inform citizens, it remained difficult for voters to assign responsibility for policy outcomes, and the electoral process could only imperfectly vote incumbents out of office. As the Eurasia Party chairman, Alexander Dugin, put it, 'Our political system has been created in haste, constantly assimilating absolutely immature players. . . . Russian people believe, feel and judge according to other standards rather than those offered by political parties and political technologists.' As Dugin insisted, 'Mr Putin basically stands alone as a party. Contrary to United Russia, he epitomises a real political party, representing the historical interests of a social and national majority.'[39] To paraphrase Bertold Brecht, lucky the nation to have such a one-person party; but sad that it needed one. The restructuring of political space under Putin moved in the direction of creating the instruments of popular representation and accountability, but it remained to be seen whether the authorities would allow them to be used – against themselves.

*   *   *

Under Yeltsin and Putin Russia developed as, at least, three orders superimposed upon each other. The first was the traditional statist one (Napoleonic or Andropovist) in which the emphasis is placed on the power vertical. In this model, whenever a potential autonomous centre of power, official or civil, emerges, the Kremlin moves to co-opt or suppress. The second is the world based on patronage and patrimonial relationships, in which horizontal networks create clusters that become remarkably impervious to the impartial operation of law and political power. The strongest of these developed in economic society, where the fusion of bureaucracy and oligarchical networks even began to shape political space, enjoying far greater financial and media resources than political parties. These informal relationships were particularly strong in the regions. The third political order is that of liberal democracy, based on normative principles of universal citizenship, the electoral constitution of power and legal and political accountability. To a degree Putin used the first and the third to counter the powers of the second. There remain disagreements, however, over how to evaluate the balance between these two. Many critical voices suggest that the first order greatly overshadows the third to establish a self-perpetuating ruling corporation, a type of elective monarchy that has not destroyed the patronage order but rendered it subordinate to the bureaucratic-authoritarian regime. Comparisons have been drawn with Italian *transformismo* of the 1870s–1880s where expedience ruled the practice of government and support was solicited from all quarters. The basis of government was enlarged to include those among the opposition ready to 'transform' themselves into supporters of the government. In Russia critics argue that the lack of independent democratic institutions and the presidency's attempts to bring all political processes under its control sapped the energies of the fledgling democracy that had emerged under Yeltsin. A more nuanced view would suggest that one of the conditions for the development of vigorous political and civil associations was the reassertion of an ordered state system. Putin's restructuring of political space can be found somewhere in between these two views.

6   Putin and the regions

When the state strengthens, the people become enfeebled. (*V Rossii, kogda gosudarstvo krepnet, narod chakhnet.*)

(Vasily Klyuchevsky)

The strengthening of central authority was at the heart of Putin's reform of federal-regional relations and reflected debates and concerns that had long been aired. As noted, the reassertion of the prerogatives of the state could take either pluralist or compacted forms. It was not clear, however, whether even reconstitution could be contained within the framework of federalism. There were fears that renewed state activism would lead to defederalisation, that is, the erosion of the separation of powers between the central authorities and the regions. The creation of seven federal districts, each headed by a presidential representative (*polpred*), to establish a presidential 'vertical' of power appeared to undermine regional autonomy. This regional autonomy, however, in the Yeltsin years had often taken undemocratic forms: instead of federalism a type of segmented regionalism had emerged. The lack of accountability of many regional 'barons' allowed the establishment of a variety of authoritarian systems. Although the regional leaders had adopted certain neo-feudal traits, as a collective institution they nevertheless represented one of the most effective constitutional constraints on the powers of the Russian presidency and central state.

Segmented regionalism

In the 1990s the old hyper-centralised Soviet system gave way to the fragmentation of political authority and contesting definitions of sovereignty.[1] Attempts to build federalism from the top-down were countered by the regions which managed, de facto if not yet *de jure*, to ensure a significant bottom-up devolution of power.[2] Under Yeltsin a complex and unstable balance was drawn between the prerogatives of the centre and the de facto powers of the regions. The tension between central and regional claims concerned not only practical issues of governance and finances, but also focused on fundamental competing sovereignty claims. The evolving practice of 'asymmetrical federalism' affected the very definition of the state. A distinctive type of segmented regionalism emerged as Russia in effect fragmented along the lines of the 89 regions, with the federal authorities in effect becoming a ninetieth and being forced to bargain with what the 1993 constitution called the 'subjects of the federation'.[3] This segmentation arose from the way that national groups and regions had been incorporated into the Soviet order, and this legacy now cast a long shadow over the system that followed, a vivid example of path dependency whereby earlier decisions about institutional arrangements foreclose later options. Segmental incorporation now gave way to segmented regionalism. Under Yeltsin the federal authorities at the centre entered into asymmetrical bargaining relations with the subjects of the federation, one of which (Chechnya) claimed outright independence, while Tatarstan for a time became an autonomous enclave within Russia. Under Yeltsin Russia appeared to turn into a federation of mini-states, many of which were little dictatorships in which press freedom and human rights were abused by regional leaders.[4]

The Yeltsinite regional bargain basically suggested to the regions and republics that they had a free hand as long as they did not threaten secession.[5] As in the Ottoman and Habsburg empires, local privileges were granted in return for loyalty. The development of civil society was inhibited since these were privileges granted not to individuals but to corporate groups. The free hand extended to the manipulation of elections (until the abrogation of the results of the elections for the head of Karachaevo-Cherkessia in May 1999, no election result had been rescinded), allowed the political elites of titular ethnic groups to consolidate their dominance and permitted various types of authoritarian regimes elsewhere. In the context of the segmentation of regional politics, the individual had few recourses.[6]

Mikhail Alexseev notes that 'The specter of regional separatism has haunted Russian politics since the collapse of the Soviet Union in 1991.'[7] Segmented regionalism was underpinned by competing sovereignty claims. On 5 August 1990, on a visit to Kazan, Yeltsin had urged the federation subjects to 'take as much sovereignty as you can swallow'. In the years that followed the crisis of the state and economy allowed some of the republics to expand their de facto sovereignty by adopting laws that created a legal space that became increasingly distinct from that established by Moscow. At the head of this process were Tatarstan, Bashkortostan, Khakassia and Yakutia, quite apart from the open insurgency in Chechnya. The unifying role of the military was lost, and indeed, the army became increasingly dependent on the regional authorities. The federal authorities were unable to guarantee basic civil rights in the regions, and even lost control over regional branches of its own state agencies, of which there were between 36 and 54 (depending on the size of the region) employing a total staff of 380,000. As Smirnyagin notes, 'This giant army of federal employees has long functioned as if no one was in charge.'[8] The local branches of the procuracy, the MVD (internal

ministry) and other ministries fell into the hands of governors and local presidents. Only the KGB's successor, the Federal Security Service (FSB), was
able to withstand 'capture' by regional authorities.[9]

Segmented regionalism in Russia appealed to the language of federalism
but in practice undermined the capacity of the state and the legal-normative
prerogatives of the federal authorities. Undoubtedly elements of federalism
emerged, but in a highly ambiguous way. Part of the ambiguity derives from
the historical legacy. The Soviet institution of ethno-federalism provided
Russia with two very different constituent elements: the republics based on a
titular nationality (or group of nationalities in the case of Dagestan,
Kabardino-Balkaria and others) based on a specific territory; and regions
based on territory alone. This provided a powerful impetus to the segmentation of regionalism along the lines of this division. A second historical factor
promoting segmentation was the weakness of autonomous rational bureaucratic administration and civic association in the regions themselves, a factor
stemming from both the Tsarist and Soviet past. In other words, Russia's
ambiguous legacy of state development, in which the government (or
regime) tended to act as the substitute for legal-rational administrative governance, on the one hand, and the stifling of autonomous associational life in
society itself, on the other, led the regime to substitute for the state and
society. The attempt to establish a federal system in a context where civil
society is weak and modern administrative structures under-developed could
not but exaggerate the autonomy of regional leaders, and encouraged them
to view themselves as quasi-sovereign actors, a tendency reinforced in the
ethno-federal republics by the appeal to the national histories of the titular
nationalities.

Post-communist Russian regionalism expressed specific bureaucratic and
social interests that became increasingly deeply entrenched, deploying political resources against the centre and other federal subjects to ensure
freedom of action to attract investment (above all foreign) and to exploit
regional resources, and to ensure relative autonomy from popular accountability (by diminishing the authority of local legislatures, manipulating electoral contests and by establishing regional 'parties of power'). Although the
regional institutions of the USSR created powerful patronage and political
networks, their persistence was determined by specific regional coalitions
able to exploit the new political and economic conditions.[10] The under-
development of political institutions and personalised patterns of leadership
left regional elites unaccountable to local electorates and relatively immune
from central supervision. They were left to enjoy the gains that they had
made in the early phase of anarchic marketisation.

Regional segmentation took a number of forms. The most dramatic manifestation of federalism à la carte were the 46 power-sharing treaties signed
between the leaders (not, it should be noted, by the subjects as a whole) of
42 regions and the federal authorities, beginning with the first signed with
Tatarstan in February 1994 and the last signed with Moscow city in June

1998. When initially mooted in the early 1990s by Sergei Shakhrai, the adviser to Yeltsin on federal issues, the idea had been to have only three with the most intractable problems: Tatarstan, Chechnya and Kaliningrad. The treaties formalised the emergence of asymmetrical federalism where the rights of separate regions were negotiated on an ad hoc and often conjunctural basis. The terms of many of these treaties, especially various annexes and annual supplements, were not made public, but their net result was to accentuate the asymmetries in federal relations. The bilateral treaties allowed customised deals between the centre and the subjects, and to that degree Yeltsin had a case in arguing that they 'strengthened Russian statehood',[11] yet they could not but undermine basic principles of constitutional equality and political transparency.

At least 50 of the 89 local constitutions and charters contradicted the federal one, while a third of local legislation violated in one way or another federal legislation. The constitutions of Bashkortostan and Tatarstan and the regional charter of Tula *oblast* were exemplary cases of subjects claiming rights not allowed for in the national constitution, derogating from the principle of equality between subjects of the federation. Legal space was also fragmented. According to the Justice Ministry, an examination of 44,000 regional legal acts, including laws, gubernatorial orders and similar documents, found that nearly half did not conform to the constitution or federal legislation.[12] In June 1999 the first serious attempt to redress the situation was the adoption of the long-awaited law 'On the Principles of Dividing Power between the Russian Federation Government and the Regions', that Putin helped draft.[13] It stipulated that all new federal and regional laws had to be adopted in conformity with this law, and that all previously adopted legislation and treaties had to be brought into line within set periods. The law formalised the procedures for the adoption of power-sharing treaties, stressing above all that everything was to be done openly, thus forbidding secret clauses and sub-treaties.

The asymmetry in federal relations was reflected most strongly in budgetary matters. The principles underlying inter-regional transfers have been the subject of considerable controversy,[14] with a large margin of error.[15] The complex allocation of tax revenues at the point of collection and from the federal budget became the defining indicator of Russia's failure to establish itself as a genuine federation. The whole notion of 'donor' or 'subsidised' region depends to a large degree on definition. By May 1999 there were only 13 donor regions,[16] but this did not mean that all the others were recipients: about a third received nothing from the centre. In addition, the various bilateral agreements allowed differences to emerge in the amounts of tax revenue transferred to the centre. Tatarstan, for example, passed on only 50 per cent of its VAT revenues to the federal budget, while other regions transferred 75 per cent of what is the most effectively collected tax in Russia. The fundamental fact of fiscal dependency for most remained, although the degree to which the centre used the system of transfer payments for overtly political purposes has been contested.[17] Daniel Treisman argued that during Yeltsin's rule transfers were used as 'bribes' to encourage loyalty among the more fractious regions rather than as 'rewards' for those who demonstrated loyalty.[18] Others have argued, however, that transfers to a large degree were not used politically but reflected relatively objective criteria of need rather than a mechanism of punishment and rewards.[19] Regions dependent on the centre for subsidies, whatever their political complexion, were forced to establish good relations with the Kremlin to ensure the continued flow of financial resources. Moscow's enduring control over the allocation and disbursement of funds to the regions is the main cement holding the federation together while at the same time undermining genuine regional autonomy.

The growing economic divergence between regions provided an economic basis to federal asymmetries. Some regions have access to world markets through the sale of energy, raw materials or basic finished industrial goods, giving them an independent resource in the federal bargaining game. In this context, it is difficult to talk of 'the regions' as a single unified actor, since that would suggest unified and purposive collective action that would be far from reality. Segmented regionalism was reinforced by the ability of regional leaderships to take advantage of the opportunities opened up by the transition process itself. Non-governmental actors, moreover, were an increasingly important element framing Russia's political and economic space. The large energy producers and primary materials exporters negotiated directly with subject-level leaderships, and indeed appeared to conduct their own foreign policies. The sectoral fragmentation of Russia, with powerful lobbies enjoying direct access to government at all levels, was reminiscent of the old Soviet economic ministries.[20]

Some regions sought to become international actors in their own right. Between 1991–95 alone, Russian regions signed over 300 agreements on trade, economic and humanitarian co-operation with foreign countries, undermining Moscow's monopoly on foreign relations and shifting attention away from high diplomacy to the pressing needs of Russia's regions. While some regions inhibited problem-solving, particularly those in the Far East that opposed the border agreement with China, others like Karelia, Pskov and Kaliningrad acted to stabilise their regional foreign relations. Over half of Russia's regions are borderlands, and need the support of the federal authorities in dealing with their neighbours. On the broader stage, Russia's domestic religious and ethnic balance is an important factor in foreign policy. During the Kosovo war of 1999, for example, president Shaimiev of Tatarstan threatened to send Tatar volunteers to support the Moslem Albanians if Russian nationalists assisted the Serbs, while in the Iraq war of 2003 Tatar volunteers gathered to defend Iraq from coalition forces. Some 20 million people have some sort of Islamic heritage and it is the country's fastest growing religion. This factor in Russia's Balkan and larger Middle Eastern policy making affected policy, in particular when the Moslem Central Spiritual Board in Ufa declared a *jihad* against the coalition forces during the second Iraq war in 2003. The preferences of Russia's regional leaders are part of the complex tapestry of Russia's foreign relations. To coordinate regional and federal foreign policy, in October 1997 the Duma adopted a law ensuring that regional authorities liaised with the Foreign Ministry over any negotiations with a foreign government.[21] A special department was established by the ministry dealing with inter-regional affairs with branch offices in regions and republics that were particularly active in foreign affairs. The principle that only the federal government had the right to sign international treaties (*dogovory*), however was jealously guarded, and upheld by numerous judgements of the Constitutional Court.[22]

In the regions an extremely heterogeneous pattern of regime types emerged, ranging from the relatively democratic in Perm, Novgorod, Arkhangel, Samara and St Petersburg, to the outright authoritarian in Primorsky *krai* under Nazdratenko and Kalmykia under president Kirsan Ilyumzhinov. Peter Kirkow identified the emergence of a type of local corporatism in the regions (on evidence drawn largely from Primorsky *krai*), marked by 'the institutional entanglement of politics and economics'.[23] In other words, regional regimes emerged that paralleled the emergence of the regime at the centre. There was also diversity in types of state-political structure. Udmurtia was a parliamentary republic (until a referendum in early 2000), Samara is a fully-fledged presidential republic, Dagestan is governed by a form of consociational democracy in which a State Council tries to balance and represent the ethnic diversity of the republic, while Moscow city replicates the 'super-presidentialism' of the central government. This diversity in part reflects local traditions, the dynamic of elite relations, and the ethnic and social composition of a particular republic, and in turn affects policy outcomes. It is most unusual to have such a great variety of regime types and governmental structures in a democratic federation, and is reminiscent of the way that the diversity prevalent in the United States before the Civil War allowed many non-democratic systems to flourish. It certainly impeded Russia's development as a democracy. Segmented regionalism cut across all processes of state building, undermining the emergence of a unified national market, legal space and Russia's coherence as an international actor. It is against this segmentation of political, economic and juridical development that Putin set his face.

The reconstitution of federal relations

Instead of an ordered federal separation of powers, the country fell prey to spontaneous processes of segmented regionalism. The development of asymmetrical federalism may well have provided a framework for the flexible negotiation of individual tailor-made solutions to Russia's diverse ethnic and political composition,[24] but it failed to do this within the framework of universal norms of citizenship. Instead, segmented regionalism fragmented the country economically and juridically. By the end of Yeltsin's presidency Russia was not only a multinational state, but was also becoming a multi-state state, with numerous proto-state formations making sovereignty claims vis-à-vis Moscow.[25] The country was increasingly divided into segments, with regional leaders themselves deciding if and when they would obey the constitution. Part of the problem was that the constitution was not always clear in pursuing a consistent model of federal relations, with a large sphere of policy consigned to the joint jurisdiction of regional and central authorities.

This was the situation facing Putin on coming to office, and at the top of his agenda was the reorganisation of federal relations to reverse the leakage of sovereignty from the centre to Russia's sub-national units. In the presidential election he had won a decisive victory in the great majority of Russia's regions, and this gave his reforms a degree of popular legitimacy. His experience working in the presidential administration in 1997–98 clearly influenced his thinking on the problem, but he also drew on a much more deep-seated sentiment that had been apparent since the early 1990s about the need for a 'strong centre'.[26] According to one study, 49 regions in the 1993 elections had favoured the centre reasserting itself against regional fragmentation.[27] Segmented regionalism had emerged as one of the greatest threats to the political integrity of the country, but the reassertion of the central state in the name of uniform administration and the unimpeded writ of law were uneasily squared with demands for a genuine devolution of authority to the regions. Was there a way of making the two processes – state reconstitution and federal decentralisation – not only compatible, but actually mutually supportive? Could Putin find a new balance in relations with the regions that would guarantee the sovereignty of the central state in the spheres that properly belonged to it, while providing for the devolution of sovereignty where appropriate?

We have argued that the resurgence of the state was torn between two forms: compacted statism, using the rhetoric of the defence of constitutional norms and the uniform application of law throughout the country but threatening the development of a genuine federal separation of powers; while pluralistic statism defends the unimpeded flow of law and individual rights while respecting the diversity of civil society and federalist norms. Nowhere was this tension more manifest than in the reform of the federal system. In part this was because the 1993 constitution is capable of varying interpretations, above all between a permissive and a constrictive reading of federal relations. The permissive interpretation sustains *pluralistic* statism; while a more constrictive reading gives rise to *compacted* statism. It is compacted not so much because of any notional agreement between the parties, although as we shall see this element does play a part, but above all because through compaction, a concept rather broader than centralisation, the relative pluralism, media freedom and regional diversity that had emerged under Yeltsin was threatened. Thus when Putin set about what he insisted was the reconstitution of regional affairs, ambiguities in the 1993 constitution and the readiness of the Constitutional Court to back his interpretation of its provisions concerning federalism, means that our distinction between reconstitution and reconcentration is eroded. In federal affairs, even reconstitution could take on the guise of reconcentration. As during the Soviet years, there was a danger that the system would become federal in form but unitary in content.

The reassertion of constitutional authority carried a positive charge for many living in the regions. The legacy and practices of segmented regionalism had given rise to unequal and partial citizenship. To counter segmented ethnic and regional incorporation, Putin proposed the universal application of laws and constitutional norms to promote the development of uniform citizenship. It is for this reason that Putin's initiatives were welcomed by regional democratic movements, hoping that the president would force regional leaders to live up to international standards of human rights and democratic accountability.[28] The strengthening of the independence of the judiciary represented an important step on this road. Putin's declarations in defence of constitutional principles encouraged oppositionists in some of Russia's regions to protest against the development of local authoritarian regimes. A joint letter to Putin of various oppositional groupings in Tatarstan, including communists and some nationalists, expressed their concern that 'Tatarstan's constitution, laws, and political leadership violate the Russian Constitution'. The letter argued that the power-sharing treaty between Tatarstan and the federal government failed to address the contradictions between federal and republican laws, allowing the latter to violate the former. The growth in Shaimiev's personal power was condemned while the rights of the population were restricted. The letter also argued that the republican legislative branch had no authority at the local level since local legislators were controlled by mayors directly appointed by Shaimiev. Local judges, moreover, were dependent on republican and local authorities and could not independently evaluate citizen complaints that their rights were being violated. The text warned that the residents of Tatarstan no longer felt that they were residents of Russia. In conclusion, the groups called on Putin to appoint a presidential representative in the republic, something that Yeltsin had never done.[29] The letter was evidence of pressure 'from below' for the reconstitution of state authority to defend the norms of universal democratic citizenship throughout the Russian Federation.

In his 8 July 2000 state-of-the-nation speech Putin stressed that 'competition for power' between the centre and regional powers has been 'destructive', and he argued that 'we have to admit that [Russia] is not yet a full-blown federal state'. Instead, Russia had 'created a decentralised state'. Putin's response to segmented regionalism was, literally, to *reconstitute* the state; that is, to place the constitution at the centre of relations between the centre and the regions. The aim was to achieve constitutional federalism rather than the ad hoc asymmetrical federalism that had emerged under Yeltsin. At the heart of Putin's reform of federal relation was the attempt to ensure that the writ of the constitution ran unimpeded throughout the territory of Russia. In his book *First Person*, Putin had stressed the importance of an independent judiciary together with greater federal control over the regions,[30] and now he began to implement this programme. In numerous speeches Putin stressed the need to

> guarantee all citizens equal rights and equal obligations. We want to
> ensure the undeviating observance of Russian laws throughout the terri-
> tory of the country so that the rights of citizens are observed equally
> strictly in Moscow and in any other region.... We are striving to
> strengthen and consolidate the state as the guarantor of the rights and
> freedoms of citizens.[31]

As he put it in another interview at that time, 'the establishment of a single legal space' involved 'not only the equal application of federal laws in the localities, but also the strict correspondence of normative acts adopted there to the constitution'.[32] At the rhetorical level, therefore, the reassertion of federal law did not threaten the development of federalism but instead sought to ensure that Russia became a single legal space, with the principles of legality and individual rights enshrined in the constitution enforced throughout the country. This legal offensive against segmented regionalism sought to bring regional charters, republican constitutions and all other normative acts into conformity with the constitution and federal law. However, the struggle for the 'dictatorship of law' entailed a degree of cen-tralisation that could be construed as an attack on the devolved prerogatives of federal subjects.

Already in early 2000 the Chair of the Supreme Court, Vyacheslav Lebedev, announced that henceforth all courts – from the top down to the regional and lower courts – were to be financed solely from the federal budget. The aim was to eliminate the courts' financial dependence on regional governments, something that obviously compromised their independence. At the same time, the salaries of judges were to be raised to improve their level of 'professionalism' and 'honesty'.[33] The federal authori-ties at this time won a court victory that allowed courts of general jurisdiction (with the Supreme Court at the apex of this system) to rule on the constitu-tionality or illegality of regional constitutions and laws.

In his broadcast of 17 May 2000 Putin noted that 'a fifth of the normative acts adopted in the regions contradict the country's basic law, and the consti-tutions of the republics and the charters of the regions diverge from the Russian Constitution'. Regional governments had until October 2000 to bring regional laws into accordance with federal norms. Putin insisted that his measures 'fully fit into the framework of the existing constitution'. He noted that some had urged him to take even more radical action, including the direct appointment of governors. He insisted that he believed in the con-tinued election of regional heads since this had become 'part of our demo-cratic constitutional order'. Putin insisted that the strengthening of the state was not to be interpreted simply as an authoritarian reorganisation of the state capacity, above all its coercive resources, but was associated with a concept of individual security. As he put it in his concluding remarks in his broadcast of 17 May:

> Dear citizens, you know as well as I that the weakness of power affects above all millions of common people. The price of state disorder is personal insecurity, threats to property, housing and ultimately our future and that of our children. This is precisely why we need strong and responsible authorities.... That is why I was elected Russian president, and it is this policy that I intend to pursue firmly and consistently in the future, just as we are doing today.[34]

The struggle to bring regional legislation into conformity with federal norms began with decrees issued on 11 May 2000 demanding that Bashkortostan, Ingushetia and Amur bring their regional laws in line with the Russian constitution and federal legislation.[35] On 16 May another decree was issued with respect to Smolensk *oblast*.[36] Bashkortostan was the most egregious case of divergence from federal norms, and the decree now ordered the republic to amend its constitution and regional laws, above all provisions concerning citizenship and the powers of the republican president, including the stipulation that the republican president must speak Bashkir (effectively excluding the candidacy of a representative of the large Tatar and Russian communities in the republic). The republican constitution had authorised regional participation in international alliances and organisations, as well as permitting agreements with foreign partners and the exchange of diplomatic representatives. The republic's constitution contained articles that overstepped 'the limits of joint jurisdiction' and ran 'counter to the foundations of federal arrangements, including principles of the spread of the Russian Federation's state sovereignty to its entire territory'.[37] Bashkortostan now turned out to be the most resistant to bringing its constitution into line with that of Russia, fearing that doing so would reduce Russia once again to a unitary state.

In a decision adopted on 7 June 2000 the Constitutional Court declared unconstitutional the sovereignty declarations adopted by most of Russia's republics.[38] The ruling dealt specifically with the case of Gorno-Altai, but clearly had wider implications. In its judgement, the Court took a rather narrow state-centred view of sovereignty, arguing that 'the constitution of the Russian Federation does not allow any kind of state sovereignty beyond the sovereignty of the Russian Federation', and went on to assert that 'the subjects of the Russian Federation do not have sovereignty, which from the start belongs to the Russian Federation in general'.[39] The ruling against any devolution of sovereignty to the republics was justified on the grounds of equity: it would, they insisted, be unfair for such an imbalance to persist vis-à-vis the other subjects of the federation (reflecting a classic postulate of the French republican tradition). In a further ruling the Constitutional Court supported the Putinite principle that only the federal government had the right to establish courts and determine criminal procedures, thus denying the regions the right to set up their own courts or to establish rules for their operation.

The stick, bent so strongly towards the republics in the period of the 'parade of sovereignties' in 1990–91, was now pushed back the other way. As suggested above, however, the defence of centralisation to ensure the uniformity of law and legal standards throughout the federation ran perilously close to becoming defederalisation. The presidential representative to the Constitutional Court, Mikhail Mityukov, noted that the judgement discussed above 'drew a line as it were under the so-called ideology of the sovereignisation of the subjects of the federation. Their sovereignty is not unlimited'. However, in stressing that their sovereignty 'has limits, strictly defined in the country's Basic Law',[40] he implicitly accepted the concept of shared sovereignty. Putin himself conceded, in a brief visit to Kazan on 23–24 June 2000, that the normative reconstitution of the state was not all a one-way street, and that while regional laws had to be brought into conformity with federal legislation, in some cases regional laws might be superior to federal norms, in which case the latter should be brought into line with regional practices.[41] Regions like Bashkortostan insisted that its republican laws corresponded more closely to the standards of European law than did the Russian constitution, and condemned Russia's development as a 'unitary enclave state'.[42] The case of land ownership and sale was a major case where regional legislation had moved far beyond the restrictions exercised at the federal level, and would be very difficult to reverse. Above all, the status of Russia's regions was not clearly defined in the constitution, while there were numerous ambiguities concerning the delineation of competencies between the centre and the regions and over the definition of the sphere of joint authority. The regions began to call for constitutional amendments that would clarify the rights and the status of the regions.

Putin's response to regional segmentation was to appeal to the principle of 'the dictatorship of law', and in particular the unimpeded flow of constitutional and juridical authority throughout the territory of the Russian Federation. We have noted earlier that this was in keeping with the Jacobin tradition of state building. However, French unitary centralism in a federal state raises it own problems. Sub-national sovereignty claims are rendered illegitimate, even though federalism as a principle is all about shared sovereignty. Fundamental issues were obscured by Putin's attempts to reconstitute the state, above all the question of the form of state sovereignty. Was Russia to become a genuine federation, in which law would be defined in accordance with the normative spatial division of sovereignty; or would it take the form of de facto regionalism, where an effectively unitary state grants rights to devolved units, in which case a very different definition of sovereignty would operate. To what degree would the experience of the regions be taken into account in reconstituting a *federal* state?

Establishing the presidential 'vertical'

The centrepiece of the new 'state gathering' policy was Putin's decree of 13 May 2000 dividing Russia's 89 regions into seven larger administrative districts.[43] Although the head of the presidential administration's department responsible for relations with the regions, Anton Fedorov, insisted that the reform would not 'in principle' affect the existing territorial-administrative divisions within Russia,[44] the establishment of an administrative layer between the federal centre and the regions could not but reduce the significance of the latter. The new federal districts (FDs) were to be headed by presidential envoys (*polpredy*) appointed by the president, thus undermining the principle of regional democracy, and were directly subordinate to the president. The aim was to restore the 'executive vertical', but in effect a 'triangle' was established with the new FDs added to relations between the regions and Moscow. The *polpredy* were now to organise the work of federal agencies in the regions, with particular attention on the law enforcement bodies, monitor the implementation of federal policy, provide the federal authorities with information on what was going on in the regions, and to advise and make recommendations on federal appointments. They were also to work with the eight existing inter-regional associations to devise social and economic policies, although the fact that the borders of the two entities do not coincide makes such a 'coordinating' role extremely difficult. The envoys were given far greater powers than the old representatives,[45] talking now of 'monitoring the implementation' rather than facilitating the observance of federal laws, decrees and presidential instructions.[46]

The old system of presidential representatives was abolished. They had been appointed in some eighty regions, and had significantly failed to restore presidential authority; indeed, many had been 'co-opted' by the very regional authorities that they had been intended to monitor. Attempts to bolster their powers in 1997 had achieved little. The new system makes the emergence of regional 'policy communities' more difficult since each of the new presidential envoys is responsible for a dozen-odd regions, to which they send their own 'inspectors'. As well as trying to ensure regional conformity to national laws, the reform also had a straightforward administrative rationale: to stop the 'capture' of federal agencies by regional executives, who had often supplied the former with offices, transport and other facilities. The aim was to reassert central control over its own agencies. Just as Putin sought to roll back 'state capture' in the centre against the overweening powers of certain oligarchs so, too, state capture in the regions was to be reversed. Nevertheless, it was unclear how the new system would be an improvement on the old. The powers of the new 'governors-general' remained vague, although intended to coordinate the work of federal agencies in the regions. It remained to be seen whether federal agencies in the regions could now be re-subordinated to a cash-strapped Moscow.

The new federal districts largely coincided with those of military districts, suggesting a certain 'militarisation' of federal relations. With only two exceptions (Nizhny Novgorod instead of Samara, and Novosibirsk instead of Chita), the new federal centres coincided with the headquarters of the military districts.[47] No less significantly, the borders of the seven federal regions corresponded exactly with the districts of the Internal Troops of the Interior Ministry (MVD). It was, moreover, noteworthy that no ethnic republic was made the centre of a federal district. The seven presidential representatives appointed on 18 May, moreover, reinforced the military/security tone to the measure. Only two were fully civilian figures: Sergei Kirienko and Leonid Drachevsky.[48] Many of their staff as well came from military or security background. The precise chain of subordination also remained a vexed question, resolved by Putin's decree of 30 January 2001 that placed the seven presidential representatives directly under chief of staff Voloshin, ensuring that the main territorial administration retained its role. The representatives sought expanded powers to control budgetary flows and even to establish their own governments, but their efforts in this direction were curtailed. The envoys officially were guided in their work by the constitution, federal laws, presidential orders and the instructions of the chief of staff. They became members of the Security Council and met regularly with the president, although the detailed workings of the FD administrations remained shrouded in secrecy. The degree to which they would become political actors and economic managers in their own right rather than simply overseers remained open.

There had long been arguments in favour of reorganising regional governance to create a few giant macro-regions. In the run-up to the 2000 presidential elections, for example, Eduard Rossel, the governor of Sverdlovsk *oblast* (who had remained neutral in the 1999 parliamentary elections) called for a reduction in the number of federal units. He suggested that the existing eight inter-regional economic co-operation associations could become the organisational base for the future federation.[49] Putin in 2000 adopted a variant of such an approach. The economic associations had been established in the early 1990s to coordinate the actions of their members, and thus to increase their leverage, but in the event they had failed to act as cohesive collective bargaining agencies. During Primakov's premiership the heads of the associations had joined the presidium of the government, a practice continued during Stepashin's premiership. Although of great symbolic importance it was of little practical consequence. With Putin's reorganisation of the country, the existing inter-regional associations lost much of their *raison d'etre*. The most active of these associations, the Siberian Accord and Great Volga, were forced to redefine their functions. They had traditionally acted as little more than a governors' trade union, although providing a useful channel of communications between the centre and the regions. While Drachevsky worked closely with Siberian Accord, Petr Latyshev considered Great Urals (*Bolshoi Ural*), headed by his rival, Sverdlovsk governor

Eduard Rossel, as a political threat. Everywhere the inter-regional associations sought to find a new role alongside the federal districts.

The FDs were created by presidential decree rather than through a law or constitutional amendment, and thus the juridical basis for the new system remained precarious. Their creation was para-constitutional in the sense that they represented a change to the constitutional order without changing the letter of the constitution. Any attempt formally to 'constitutionalise' the change would be fraught with difficulties, given the complexity of changing the constitution. In principle, since the change affected only the president's own administration and did not alter the powers of the governors or restructure the Russian Federation itself, the constitutional question was avoided. The *polpredy* report directly to the president, and they in turn appoint inspectors to each of the regions within their jurisdiction. While the reform signalled that Yeltsin's tolerance of diversity and asymmetry in federal relations was over, it did not yet indicate that an effective way had been found of ensuring effective national governance and the subordination of the whole country to the constitution. The measure appeared to be a halfway house on the way towards the fulfilment of Solzhenitsyn's (and indeed Zhirinovsky's) plan for the 'gubernisation' of Russia, that is, the re-establishment of the unitary system of government based on the 78 *guberniyas* into which the Russian empire had been divided before 1917. Towards the end of Putin's first term there was much discussion about moving to a new stage by creating 28 large *guberniyas* based simply on territory, with ethno-federalism to give way to national-cultural autonomy. It remained unclear whether these 28 super-regions would be part of a federal system of *zemli* (like the *Länder* in Germany), as discussed in various constitutional drafts in the early 1990s, or part of a unitary Russia, as before 1917. The attempt to 'de-ethnicise' Russian federalism, however, is fraught with danger and if mishandled has the potential to destroy the country.

The seven FDs gradually came to be filled with content and took on a range of political and administrative functions. They can be seen as part of a long Russian tradition of appointing governor-generals, as outlined in a book edited by one of the new-style governors, Victor Cherkesov.[50] The main focus of their political work was involvement in regional, above all gubernatorial, elections, although their efforts met with variable success. One of their most important administrative tasks was to coordinate the federal agencies and to rebuff regional state capture. On 31 July 2000 Putin ordered the MVD to reorganise some of its key departments, with new offices in charge of preliminary investigations to be established in each FD. Putin's press service insisted that this would provide 'additional guarantees for the protection of the individual' as well as protecting the state from criminal elements.[51] Putin had stressed that the FSB was directly subordinate to Moscow and should at most inform regional leaders of its actions. The FSB remains rigidly unitary and hierarchical, unlike the MVD and Procuracy. At this point, however, Putin did not seek to deprive governors of their constitutional right to approve appointments of local police chiefs, judges and procurators, although there were moves in this direction later. Important federal-level agencies like the treasury and the tax ministry all adapted to the new structure of government. Similarly, the Procurator-General set up office in each of the new federal districts, as did the justice ministry and the judicial system as a whole with the aim, in the words of Krasheninnikov, to 'strengthen federalism and legality on the entire territory of the Russian Federation'. Innumerable 'colleges', commissions and councils were established to coordinate federal administration and personnel policy at the regional level. The dominance over regional branches of federal agencies assumed by regional bosses during Yeltsin's presidency was now countered. In addition, the Soviet practice of rotating the postings of public servants was restored to ensure the homogeneity of public administration and thus to reinforce the powers of the central state.

A crucial task of the federal districts was to bring regional legislation into line with federal legislation. Federal District branches of the justice ministry examined regional legislation to ensure that it complied with federal norms.[52] The influence of vested regional interests was diluted as the supremacy of federal legislation was asserted throughout Russia. The representative in the Central Region, Georgy Poltavchenko, for example, with a staff of 40 people in Moscow and 3 to 4 in each of the other 18 regions in his federal district, drew up an inventory of regional laws to check their conformity with federal norms. He noted that, while the situation was generally positive, some 140 regional laws and acts did not correspond with federal legislation.[53] In addition, he condemned the Moscow authorities for failing to end the registration (*propiska*) system, imposing restrictions on movement that had already been judged illegal by the Constitutional Court.[54] It seemed at times that no sooner was one law or regional constitution amended to bring it into conformity with federal legislation than another was adopted that no less egregiously flouted federal norms.[55]

Among the other tasks assumed by the FDs were a number of economic ones. Comparative studies with China suggest that political centralisation actually enhances 'market preserving federalism'.[56] The main concern of the envoy in the Northwest Federal District, Cherkesov, was the reform of the economy and countering the powers of the regional elite.[57] He devoted considerable attention to affairs in St Petersburg, and ensured that Putin's old rival, Yakovlev, was not able to run for a third term. The basis of Cherkesov's power was an analytical service that helped forge a powerful Federal District political team.[58] Cherkesov was the first of the envoys to be replaced when on 11 March 2003 he was appointed the government's drug tsar at the head of a new agency. His replacement, Matvienko, had tried to run against Yakovlev in the 2000 gubernatorial race. The envoys played an active role in trying to attract investment, above all from abroad. A fourth and no less important role was to delineate the powers of the federal, regional and local authorities. Reform of local government was seen by some as part of a pincer movement from above and below in cutting the regional authorities down to size.

The revocation of the bilateral treaties was also part of the process of ensuring more rational and uniform regional administration. In his state-of-the-nation speech on 18 April 2002 Putin noted that of the 42 regions that had such agreements, 28 had already revoked them.[59]

An intriguing aspect of the reform was whether a measure designed to enhance the unity of the country could well inadvertently hasten its fragmentation. By creating seven powerful new units Putin may well have established the framework for seven new countries, each with the resources able to sustain statehood. The seven super-regions began to take on the attributes of mini-states, including the establishment of replicas of the Federation Council in the form of councils of heads of regional executive and legislative bodies, as well as councils of regional governors (smaller versions of the State Council), together with councils for local self-government and expert consultative and scientific research councils.[60] Poltavchenko in the Central District took this furthest, with the establishment of a council bringing together all the heads of administration of the eighteen regions within his jurisdiction. The brief of the new council was to focus on economic issues, but it also provided a forum for the discussion of broader political issues. Kirienko in the Volga district established a coordinating council for the chairs of regional legislatures to coordinate the drafting of regional legislation and to assist with the implementation of Putin's demand that regional laws should conform with federal norms. Conflicts between the federal centre and the regions were now to a degree displaced to the level of relations between the federal districts and individual regions. The FDs acted as a buffer and intermediary in relations between the federal centre and the regions. They played an active part in regional elections, above all for the governorships. In the 2002 electoral round, for example, about a third of governors were replaced, with a number of incumbent governors being dissuaded or blocked from running again.[61]

Putin's reforms to the federal system were based on a complex system of supports and alliances and it would be a great simplification to suggest that they have 'failed'. Officially, the *polpredy* were part of the federal level of government and were not intended to govern but to supervise (*kontrol'*) the work of federal bodies in the regions. In practice the FDs fundamentally changed the dynamics of regional politics, effectively curbing the political pretensions of the governors to be national players and depriving them of control over federal administrative agencies in the regions. In many ways the envoys were remarkably effective, forcing legal changes, providing a forum for macro-regional coordination, resolving a number of cardinal administrative and personnel issues and emerging as active political players. It was unlikely that they would be abolished quickly. They also provided the president with a chain of support, especially in the management of the security and legal systems at the regional level, which balanced the powers of the presidential administration that had been inherited from Yeltsin. The establishment of the FDs had been followed by massive personnel turnover in the federal agencies, above all the regional heads of the security services. The 200,000 strong Internal Troops of the MVD saw army officers loyal to Putin appointed to their head, and thus an embryonic Praetorian guard was in the making. The FSB and the Federal Tax Police (part of the *siloviki*) in this area as in others were the source of many of the new appointments, helping to create a single line of command. If the Soviet era had been characterised by parallel administrative structures, those of the Party and the soviets, the recreation of a new parallel 'power vertical' in the shape of the *polpredy* suggested that the administrative practices of the old Party-state was once again being mimicked by the new regime-state.

Reorganising federal relations

Soon after the announcement of the creation of the federal districts, in a televised address on 17 May Putin announced that he would submit a package of laws to the State Duma designed 'to strengthen and cement Russian statehood'.[62] 'The common task of all these acts,' according to Putin, 'was to make both the executive branch and the legislative branch truly working, and to fill the constitutional principles of the separation of powers and the unity of the executive vertical with absolutely real content.'[63] The origins of Putin's federal reforms lay in the various debates since the mid-1990s, but he now gave these ideas flesh through three bills at this time and a number of other measures.

Re-forming the Federation Council

The first convocation of the Federation Council (FC), the upper house of Russia's bicameral federal assembly, in 1993 had been formed by direct election in the regions, but a law adopted in 1994 had made the heads of the regional executive and legislative branches directly members of the upper house. Now Putin was suggesting a return to a variant of the earlier system, to allow the senior figures to 'concentrate on the specific problems facing their territories'.[64] The Federation Council was to be composed of two permanent representatives from each region, one nominated by each region's executive branch and one by the legislature. The new 'senators' were to be delegates of the regional authorities rather than popular representatives.

Although Putin made some concessions, with some thirteen amendments approved, the overall package was in line with his aspiration to create a full-time working upper chamber. The passage into law of even this rather half-boiled measure was subject to extensive bargaining, with three Duma votes in support of Putin's measure being over-turned by the Council, leading to the formation of a conciliatory commission. On 19 July 2000 the compromise bill was approved by the Duma and on 26 July it was adopted by the upper house by the surprisingly large majority of 119 votes in favour and 18 against, with four abstentions.[65] The vote did not so much reflect the senator's enthusiasm for the reform as acceptance that any contrary vote would simply be over-ridden by the Duma. The law conceded that a governor's appointment of a representative could be blocked by a two-thirds majority in the regional legis-lative assembly within two weeks. Dismissal was also to be approved by a two-thirds majority of the local legislature. Regional legislatures were able to nominate and recall their delegates according to their own procedures. Agreement was also reached over a 'soft turnover' of Federation Council members, with governors leaving the Federation Council as their terms expired or by 1 January 2002 at the latest. A large number of governors faced election in Autumn 2000, and were not able to return to the upper chamber.

The new representatives were to be dismissed in the same way as they were selected. The current members of the Federation Council who were not members of local legislatures lost their immunity from criminal prosecution after 1 January 2002. With the regional leaders in the conciliatory commis-sion having won the right to recall their representatives, the latter were ren-dered not much more than puppets. According to Andrei Ryabov, 'With this law, they [the governors] lost nothing but prestige.'[66] Luzhkov insisted that replacing the regional leaders with representatives in the Federal Assembly was the first step towards abolishing the Federation Council altogether: 'After they change the make-up of the chamber, it will become clear that no one needs a branch of power with no authority and that it should be abol-ished.'[67] The reform of the Federation Council demonstrated Putin's pecu-liar mix of strength and weakness. He achieved the reform that he desired, above all achieving a full-time upper legislative chamber and the more realis-tic separation of powers (by removing the heads of the regional executive branch from the national legislature), but in doing so conceded much. Luzhkov's fears were not without substance, and the new Federation Council had to fight to regain its authority, while some even called for its abolition.

The creation by presidential decree on 1 September 2000 of a para-constitutional consultative body known as the State Council under the president seemed to be a step towards abolishing the Federation Council. The State Council is made up of regional leaders, allowing them to retain direct access to the national leadership. Since the body is consultative, its cre-ation did not require amending the constitution. The State Council appeared a sop to the regional leaders displaced from membership in the Federation Council. Its presidium consists of seven regional leaders serving for six months each, one from each federal district. It meets in plenary session once every three months to discuss two main topics, usually prepared by commissions headed by a presidium member. The State Council took on functions that were the prerogative of parliament, including discussing regional and federal reform, but its views lacked legislative force.

Important questions about the constitutional status of the new-style Feder-ation Council remained. The upper chamber according to the 1993 constitu-tion has the right to declare a state of emergency, to authorise the use of the military abroad, to appoint and remove the Prosecutor-General, and many other important functions. With the new assembly made up of nominated figures, was it appropriate for these tasks to remain with the assembly; would it not be better for them to be fulfilled by the Duma? A constitutional amendment would be required to make the change, yet Putin in his first term avoided talk of amending the constitution. The reform raised important institutional questions, as well as equally important political ones. As the president of Chuvashia, Nikolai Fedorov, noted at the time, 'the bill causes a destruction of the system of checks and balances, and is very dangerous for democracy'.[68] In the long run there could well be a return to a system of direct elections to the upper chamber, as it was between 1993–95.[69]

The chairman of the Federation Council, Yegor Stroev, had long argued in favour of constitutional reform, but Putin's plans were not to his liking, in particular the establishment of the State Council, whose relationship with the existing two houses of parliament is unclear. He praised the stabilising role played by regional leaders, in particular after the crisis of October 1993 and then again after the financial collapse of August 1998, insisting that it was in the regions 'where Russia's strength lies'. He insisted that neither parliamentary house quarrelled with Putin's main argument that a system of power had to be built: 'Russia must be a federal, democratic, unified country where all laws are the same for all citizens, whether they live in Chechnya, Tatariya, or Orël Oblast.'[70] The head of the Main Territorial Administration in the presidential administration, Sergei Samoilov, suggested that the new State Council would fulfil important functions, such as key appointments and the declaration of war and states of emergency, and conceded that such a drastic shift of responsibilities away from the Federation Council would 'require some legislative changes or amendments to the constitution'. However, he was in no hurry to see the constitution amended, insisting that 'the constitution has sufficient political and legal flexibility'.[71] Indeed, at this time Fedorov, together with some like-minded senators, sought to appeal against the reforms of the Federation Council to the Constitutional Court, insisting that the changes entailed a 'revision of the existing constitutional structure of the Russian Federation'.[72] With the replacement on 6 December 2001 of Stroev by the Petersburger and Putin ally Sergei Mironov as speaker of the upper house, the Federation Council was brought firmly within the ambit of the presidential bloc.

Dismissal and dissolution

A second bill sought to provide a mechanism whereby the heads of regions could be removed and regional legislatures dissolved if they adopted laws that contradicted federal legislation. Although in principle the courts already enjoyed the power to dismiss governors, two court decisions were required stating that the governor had violated federal law. The attempt to strengthen this right proved extremely difficult, especially since it had to be approved by the Federation Council, the very body whose membership was under threat.

The bill sought to give the president the right to dismiss governors who violated federal laws on more than one occasion. In introducing the bill, the presidential representative in the Duma, Alexander Kotenkov, averred that 'at least 16 governors' faced the prospect of criminal prosecution.[73] In the event, the Duma on 19 July 2000 adopted the bill allowing the president to dismiss regional leaders and to disband local parliaments.

The law allows Russia's president to dismiss regional leaders, including governors of oblasts and presidents of republics, for violating federal laws. A court ruling that the official has broken the law and a letter from the Prosecutor-General that a case had been opened against a regional leader regarding a serious crime is required to confirm that a regional leader is facing criminal charges. To dissolve a regional legislature, the president has to submit a bill to the State Duma.[74] Nazdratenko was the first victim of the new presidential powers (which came into effect on 1 February 2001), resigning from the post of governor of Primorskii *krai* on 5 February 2001 after nearly a decade of misrule. Although the full power of the new law was not applied against him, the threat (in the form of repeated inspections) apparently was enough for him to step down. On 4 April 2002 the Constitutional Court confirmed the president's right to fire governors and the State Duma's power to disband regional legislatures.

Local self-government

The third measure proposed granting the regional leaders the right to dismiss local authorities subordinate to them. Regional executives have long sought greater control over local self-government, including the power to fire mayors and dissolve legislatures in towns and cities on their territory. Local self-government is not part of the state system, and thus the proposal ran directly contrary to the attempt to democratise local government that had been one of the main aspirations of social movements since the late 1980s, quite apart from violating the principle enshrined by the constitution.[75] It appeared that Putin was willing to contemplate the weakening of local self-government to allow the implementation of his broader reorganisation of regional affairs. The State Duma at its session of 19 July 2000 approved Putin's amendments to the law on local government, allowing regional governors to fire mayors. However, the Federation Council on 26 July rejected the Duma's revised version of the bill that would allow only the president, and not the governors of *oblasts* or presidents of autonomous *okrugs*, to dismiss mayors of major cities and local administration heads in certain circumstances.

Local self-government remained in limbo. In his proposals on how to rebuild a new Russia, Solzhenitsyn argued that the only genuine way for Russia to be reborn was through the development of local self-government and the revival of the Tsarist-era *zemstva*.[76] The actual number of sub-national governments in Russia ranges from 2 to 4, and there remains significant confusion over the budgetary and legitimate legal rights of the various levels. There is no precise correspondence between levels of government and levels of the intra-regional budgetary system.[77] In financial affairs, for example, the situation sharply deteriorated under Putin. If in 2000 revenues between the centre and the regions were being shared 51:49, then today it is 67:33, with Russia's 11,500 municipalities receiving only 14 per cent of the third, even though their budgetary commitments comprise 30 per cent of regional expenditures. Half of them do not even have budgets of their own. In his interview on the anniversary of his first year in power Putin argued that rent support should be more targeted; old Soviet traditions of subsidies for all were to be abolished.[78] The reform of the 'communal-housing complex' (*kommunal'no-zhilishchnoe kompleks*, KZhK) is designed to raise more money locally from consumers, but all such reforms threaten the survival of large numbers of people. Since local government provides a range of welfare goods, the chronic under-funding, exacerbated by Putin's reforms, always threatened to provoke some sort of social crisis. In Voronezh in spring 2002 protests against reform of municipal services provoked protests that culminated in the storming of the local administration building. The governor Vladimir Kulakov, himself a former KGB general, telephoned the Kremlin for help, but once again (as Putin found in the GDR in 1989), 'Moscow was silent'. The foundations of the Russian state still appeared decidedly shaky.

Delineation of powers and functions

In a follow-up measure to earlier reforms of federal relations, on 26 June 2001 Putin established a commission to examine federal relations as a whole, and the role of the treaties in particular, under the leadership of his close colleague and deputy head of the presidential administration, Kozak. The unsatisfactory condition of local government was a strong reason for its creation. The commission sought to develop the legislative basis for the division of power between the federal, regional and local levels of government. The constitution's assignment of a number of responsibilities to joint jurisdiction had proved to be a recipe for confusion, and now the idea was to draw up a list of functions and designate them to specific levels. The role of the bilateral treaties would be reduced (when not abolished in their entirety) and subordinated to the constitution, federal law, presidential decrees and federal government directives. The aim was to establish a common set of rules for all regions and to provide them with equal rights. The 22-member commission included a number of governors, and sought to proceed, in a manner typical of Putin, by consensus. Putin's decree even agreed that some of Shaimiev's ideas on federal reform placed before the State Council in Autumn 2000, that at the time were condemned by Kozak as 'threatening the destruction of the country's legal system', were to be taken into account, and indeed Shaimiev was made a member of the commission. The seven federal districts each established their own mini-commissions, which reported back to the main commission by the end of 2001.

The commission sought to delineate what bodies were responsible for what at each of the three levels (national, regional, municipal) of governance. The issue of resources and division of taxes was central to this. The issue of the accountability of public bodies was also at the centre of the commission's work, with an attempt to clarify lines of financial and public accountability. The fourth sphere focused on the work of local self-government. Russia in 2002 had 153,000 local self-government units (including sub-units within regions and municipalities), with 90,000 comprising fewer than one hundred people and 24,000 with fewer than a thousand. The commission recommended that smaller units should be merged to create some 30,000 bodies, with none with fewer than one thousand people. By contrast, many large towns lacked municipal self-government bodies. A new standardised system able to fulfil its responsibilities and with adequate resources was to be introduced. Each unit of local government would be divided into an executive (*uprava*) and legislative (*munitsipalitet*) branch, with most funding going to the former (typically 90:10). Unfunded mandates would no longer be allowed, raising fears that the reform would lead to sharp cuts in social programmes.[79] The changes would start in 2003 after the adoption of a new law on local self-government in Russia.

Changes in fiscal federalism

The attempt to recreate a national market became one of the central planks of Putin's regional policy. The general weakening of the power of individual regions during his presidency had important economic consequences, in particular aiding the struggle against the 'virtual economy' (the network of barter and non-payments) that was very much regionally-based. At the same time, the federal government began to revoke many of the tax concessions that it had granted under Yeltsin. Income tax revenue at the close of Yeltsin's term was collected 50:50 between the federal government and the regions, but was divided 70:30 in the federal government's favour. On 26 July 2000 the second part of the new tax code was overwhelmingly approved by the Federation Council (128 to 13), even though it caused an immediate fall in regional tax revenue. In the long run, according to the government, there would be an increase. The main features of the tax package were a flat rate 13 per cent income tax, a minimum 5 per cent unified social tax, the raising of some excise taxes, and the amending of the law on value added tax. Instead of the regions keeping 15 per cent of VAT, it was now to be transferred in its entirety to the federal centre. The 4 per cent turnover tax, raised mostly in the regions, was abolished.

The new tax code was designed to be easier to understand, as well as to implement. Above all, there would be greater centralisation of collection and distribution of tax revenues previously left to governors. The reform provided for much greater redistribution of revenues between the regions than had hitherto existed. Not surprisingly, the poorer regions (the great majority) supported the bill, while the richer minority, led by Moscow mayor Luzhkov, argued against it. According to Luzhkov, Moscow stood to lose 30 per cent of its budget.[80] There was considerable controversy over the impact on federal and regional revenues.[81] While most governors believed that the federal government would receive 70 per cent of tax revenue, leaving 30 per cent to the regions, the finance minister, Alexei Kudrin, claimed that the regions would get 52.5 per cent, while the centre's share would be just 47.5 per cent.[82] The government claimed that only 8 to 10 regions would actually have less income as a result of the legislation.[83] What was not in doubt is that the government now intended to pursue an active regional policy: concentrating more resources and redistributing them as part of a conscious strategy of levelling some of the disparities between regions.

Regional governors and legislatures

Although enjoying an autonomous political legitimacy derived from popular election, according to the constitution (Articles 5.3 and 77.2) governors were part of a single vertically-integrated executive structure. In recognition of this, some regional governors themselves called for the abolition of direct elections and the formal re-subordination of regional executives to the federal authorities. Yeltsin's traditional style of managing the regions, where relative independence and selective privileges had been granted in return for support for the Kremlin at the federal level, now gave way to a period of federal activism. This activism, however, was filtered through the seven presidential representatives, but at the regional level life went on much as before.

The election of governors

The vagaries and uncertainties associated with elections encouraged some governors to contemplate giving up whatever legitimacy they may have gained through the electoral process and return to the old system of appointment from the centre. Federal legislation allowed only a maximum of two terms, and thus most of those who favoured the abolition of the post of elected governors were either in their second term or were confident of becoming appointed governors, with no limit to their terms. In return, governors sought greater powers of appointment over mayors of regional centres and heads of districts, thus re-establishing the presidential (or executive) vertical all the way from the Kremlin to the local level. A notable expression of this trend was the letter of three governors to Putin in February 2000 calling for such a reform, with the necessary constitutional amendments to be enacted through a Constitutional Assembly, spiced with the call for the presidential term of office to be extended to seven years.[84] Quite apart from instrumental considerations, as far as they were concerned electoralism fostered regional particularism, something in their view that could only be over-come by recentralisation.[85] For others, like Konstantin Titov of Samara, such a change represented 'a detailed plan for the liquidation of democratic achievements in Russia', undermining the emergent democratic political links in the federal system and once again reasserting administrative ties.[86]

The law allowing governors a maximum of two terms was signed into law on 19 October 1999, coming into effect on 19 October 2001, giving the gov-ernors a two-year grace period.[87] By early 2000 there were 32 governors serving their second terms, with the first of the putative third term governors coming up for election being Shaimiev in Tatarstan. Regional leaders hoped to win a third term before the deadline, forcing some to plan to move up their elections before the fateful date. In the event, on 25 January 2001 the Duma adopted a generous amendment to the law concerning the terms of governors. The amendment counted the first term of the governor as the one starting after 19 October 1999, allowing 69 regional executives to run for a third term, and an additional 17 to serve a fourth. Luzhkov, who was re-elected in December 1999, could stand for one more term, while Shaimiev could seek two more terms. This represented a major capitulation to the regional lobby, although some pressure remained to remove restrictive elect-oral conditions (like that in Tatarstan specifying that a candidate had to speak both Russian and Tatar). The Constitutional Court on 9 July 2002 con-firmed that the 2001 amendment was legal, but specified that subjects of the federation should be divided into two groups: those where charters and con-stitutions specified a two-term limit and those where there was no such stipu-lation. In the first group regional legislatures were allowed to decide term limits, while in the second group all terms in office beginning before October 1999 were to be ignored. Thus 43 governors were allowed to run for a third, and in some cases a fourth, term. The Kremlin had made this conces-sion, expecting in return support for its candidates in the 2003–04 electoral cycle.

In general, the Kremlin appeared successful in getting most of its favoured candidates elected in regional executive elections, with 11 out of the 15 going its way in 2002.[88] In Ingushetia, neighbouring the war-torn Chechen republic and home to tens of thousands of Chechen refugees, the Kremlin forced the resignation of president Ruslan Aushev, who had been extremely critical of Kremlin policies, and in his place managed to engineer the 'election' of FSB general Murat Zyazikov following the disqualification on a minor technicality of the leading (and pro-Aushev) candidate Khamzad Gutseriev. A number of authoritarian presidents were re-elected for a third term.[89]

Despite the obvious concern shown by the Kremlin in regional elections, no consistent pattern emerges either in the manner of Kremlin interference or in the outcomes. Despite the extra powers granted to the presidential administration, it was notable that these were not used in the case of Naz-dratenko in Primorsky *krai*, and instead a deal was struck that allowed him to resign and be rewarded a plum job in Moscow as head of the federal fisheries service (until he disgraced himself there, too, and was relieved of his post by Kasyanov in February 2003, but then popped up in May 2003, as a deputy head of the Security Council, in part to keep him out of the way and to prevent him returning to the *krai*). Putin appeared hesitant to apply the mechanisms that he had created. The Kremlin's role in using the courts to disqualify candidates on the eve of gubernatorial elections (as with Rutskoi in Kursk) is not clear, but as we have noted changes to electoral laws now limit this. As for outcomes, no clear new pattern has emerged here either. For example, despite much talk of a surge of generals coming to power in the regions, this has not been the case in practice. In the 26 gubernatorial elections held in *oblasts* and *krais* between 26 March 2000 and January 2001 candidates from security agencies participated in only four (Kaliningrad, Kamchatka, Voronezh and Ul'yanovsk), and won in only three (Vice-Admiral Valerii Dorogin came a poor fourth in Kamchatka). The election of General Vladimir Shamanov, who had a tough track record in Chechnya, as governor of Ulyanovsk *oblast* seemed to be the most spectacular case of the military coming to power, but once in office his behaviour was indistinguishable from other governors and his team came from all over the country with different interests.[90] Other aspects of his identity (he had been a sociologist by training) came to the fore. It would be an exaggeration to talk of the 'militarisation' of Russian regional politics under Putin, although the presence of *siloviki* undoubtedly increased.

It would also be incorrect to say that Putin was able to transform the set of regional actors. There has been no significant turnover in the gubernatorial corps, with incumbent governors winning in 20 of the 26 cases (73 per cent) noted above. Taken alongside the almost universal re-election of incumbents in the republics and autonomous *okrugs*, we should note the extraordinary stability of elites in Putin's early years. There was little that the Kremlin could do to influence electoral outcomes one way or the other. For example, in the election of 14 January 2001 in Tyumen *oblast* the Kremlin clearly favoured the incumbent (Leonid Roketskii won the coveted accolade of 'governor of the year' in 2000), but he lost badly to the challenger Sergei Sobyanin. Of the 14 elections held in 'red belt' regions, incumbents won in eleven and lost in three: Ulyanovsk, Voronezh (where a candidate from the FSB won), and Kursk (where a candidate – Alexander Mikhailov – from the CPRF won). If Putin was trying to reshape the regional elite, then he did it in a very strange way. Although granted the power to remove elected governors, he was reluctant to use it directly. Putin's reform of the federal system has not significantly weakened traditional elite structures at the regional level.

Regional legislatures

Russia has a rich variety of regional legislatures: some are bicameral while others are unicameral, some deputies are professional and paid, while others are volunteers, and electoral systems also vary. Almost everywhere one thing was common: the weakness of party representation. In 1998 only 635 (18 per cent) of the 3,481 elected deputies had been nominated by political parties, overwhelmingly from the CPRF.[91] Despite Putin's attempt to extend the reach of the national party system to shape regional politics, the trend in the early part of his leadership was if anything in the opposite direction. Fewer governors were elected who had explicitly declared their party affiliation, and ever more declared independents were elected to regional legislatures.[92] The influx of the representatives of big business into regional legislatures sharpened the struggle for the redistribution of resources.[93] The emergence of a dynamic presidency put all parties in the shade, and at the regional level party groups, however active, found it hard to have any effect on governor-business networks.[94] Regional assemblies have traditionally been dominated by executives and powerful business or other local elites, and Putin now sought to break up these local blocs that had together too often in his view conspired to undermine the writ of the constitution.

The reform of the electoral system to regional legislatures, as we saw in Chapter 5, does have the potential to remove one of the props of gubernatorial power and to create an alternative power system in the regions that could challenge the governors. The law on elections of May 2002 stipulates that regional executives have to be elected in at least two rounds, while from July 2003 elections to regional legislatures follow the national pattern: half of their members are elected from party lists proposed by national parties; and the other half are elected from single-mandate districts. The introduction of party-list elections allowed central politicians to exert rather more influence over regional elections, an area where governors had hitherto predominated. However, very few of the fifty-odd parties registered at the national level have vibrant regional networks, and even the active ones are often dominated by the local governor. Putin sought to empower democratic processes to establish a countervailing power in the regions. The effects of this have yet to be seen.

State reconstitution and federalism

Just as Putin sought to distance the oligarchs from the centre of political power so, too, he sought to remove the regional barons from what could be seen as excessive influence over government policy. Putin put an end to Yeltsin's liberalism in this respect, and repudiated sub-national claims to 'sovereignty'. The difference between oligarchs and regional leaders, however, was that the latter were part of the system of the constitutional separation of powers in a federal system. Thus the 'equi-distancing' of regional leaderships from federal power could assume defederalising traits. The transformation of the Federation Council from a club of governors and heads of regional legislatures to one of representatives markedly limited the access of regional leaders to the corridors of central power. In addition, the introduction of new powers allowing the president to dismiss elected regional heads and legislative assemblies demonstrated that a new era in managing federal-regional relations had begun. Yeltsin's traditional style of managing the regions, where relative independence and selective privileges had been granted in return for support for the Kremlin, now gave way to a period of federal activism and attempts to reassert central authority and pre-rogatives. The degree to which this was compatible with the federal separa-tion of powers remained to be seen. While too much ethno-federalism and regional segmentation had undermined the coherence of the state, too much centralism could have a similar result. As one scholar puts it:

> While the constitution stresses the concentration of power in the presi-dency and central legislative supremacy, only the independent constitu-tion-making and the bilateral treaties create preconditions for a federal 'social contract'. Without forms of asymmetry, Russia's political system would be barely more than the substitution of former party centralism with presidentialism, while formally retaining the legacy of Soviet feder-alism.[95]

It was with these issues that the Kozak commission grappled. By mid-2002 he noted that some 6,500 regional normative acts had been brought into con-formity with federal legislation. Rakhimov in Bashkortostan sought to divert pressure to bring his republican constitution into line with federal norms by adopting a new constitution – which violated federal norms as much as the old one, while the revised Tatarstan constitution still used the word 'sover-eignty'. One of his specific proposals was for federal agencies working in the regions to have dual subordination (to the federal and republican authori-ties) like the union-republic agencies that existed in the USSR.[96] Fedorov was scathing in his criticisms of the new system, arguing 'Was it necessary to establish an entire unconstitutional system of presidential envoys in order to bring the laws of Tatarstan into compliance with federal standards?' Tatarstan, moreover, had been prevented from abandoning the Cyrillic alphabet in favour of Latin. Fedorov went on to note the lack of political will reflected in the new institutions, and concluded: 'We are following the usual Russian path: instead of taking out the rubbish, we establish a commission on fighting rubbish.'[97] At the same time, the bilateral treaties were gradually abolished, with the federal government adamant in its view that they had been a very ineffective way of managing federal relations. As far as it was con-cerned, the constitution should be applicable with equal force across the country. If in April 2002 Putin noted (see above) that 28 of the 42 treaties had been repudiated, another four had gone by mid-2002 and negotiations were being conducted over the fate of the remaining ten, of whom Tatarstan and Bashkortostan were the most intractable. The government conceded that treaties could be used in exceptional circumstances, such as if Belarus were to join the Russian Federation of if they dealt with very specific issues like natural resources, but they were inadmissible as an instrument to govern political relations.

The manner in which Putin approached the regions is also noteworthy. As he reminded his audience in his televised address of 17 May 2002, in his inaugural speech of 7 May 'I promised you that there would be open government, with policy aims and specific steps clearly explained to citizens'. The use of direct public addresses sought to ensure a popular base for his reforms, but he avoided populist sloganeering. He sought to forge a reform consensus that would include the governors themselves. Putin tried to avoid alienating the regional leaders, refusing to engage in populist forms of mobilisation and anti-elite rhetoric. In his television broadcast of 17 May Putin was at pains to stress that his recently announced package of draft laws was 'not directed against regional leaders'; on the contrary, he insisted that 'regional leaders are the most important support for the president and will act as such in the strengthening of our state'.[98] As he put it on a later occasion, the 'management reforms' (*'upravlenchenskie reformy'*) are 'not to limit the rights of the regions. Our historical experience proves that super-centralisation and the attempt to manage "all and everything" from Moscow is ineffective ... I am convinced that the real self-dependency (*samostoy-atel'nost'*) of the regions is one of the most important achievements of the last decade.'[99] Putin went out of his way to demonstrate his openness to enter into dialogue with regional elites, conducting an active policy of meeting with regional leaders, although not of the back-slapping sort that Yeltsin enjoyed.[100] He was thus able to forestall concerted opposition from the regions and republics. The response of Tatarstan, with the most to lose from the proposed reforms, can be taken as symptomatic. After meeting with Putin, Shaimiev argued that the majority of regional leaders approved of the laws because they understood that the measures were intended to improve the country's governance.[101]

Although Putin sought to avoid a direct confrontation with regional leaders, the clear effect of the creation of a presidential federal administration was to shift power away from regional elites. As more and more federal agencies shifted their main regional offices to the seven new FD capitals, regional governors lost one of their main sources of local control. As one report put it, they were now reduced to 'ordinary medium-rank officials'.[102] It was not surprising that after an initial calm reaction, there were signs of growing unease in the regions, while the speaker of the Federation Council, Stroev, criticised several features of Putin's reform of the upper chamber.[103] Berezovsky argued that the creation of the seven federal districts would divide regional leaders into first and second classes and could ultimately provoke the disintegration of the country.[104] The attempt to reassert the authority of the centre was seen as a challenge to the rights of the subjects of the federation. As the then president of Ingushetiya, Ruslan Aushev, put it following the Duma's over-ride vote on the president's power to remove regional executives accused of violating the law and to disband regional legislatures: 'What kind of federation is it if the president can remove the popularly elected head of a region or disband the regional legislature?' He insisted that the plan violated 'democracy and parliamentarianism'.[105] Fedorov, president of Chuvashia, noted 'we all aimed for and tried to build a state with the rule of law. But it turns out now that society – or at least the prevailing atmosphere – is such that the will of the emperor, the will of the president, is law'.[106] Fedorov thus acknowledged the high level of popular support for Putin's reforms, something that the regional elites were unable to ignore.

We have already noted Putin's comment in his book *First Person*: 'But from the very beginning, Russia was created as a supercentralized state. That's practically laid down in its genetic code, its traditions, and the mentality of its people.'[107] Were these policies vis-à-vis the regions now a concrete manifestation of these traditions? The question can be considered within the framework of theories of sovereignty and their relationship to Russian practices. For the republics in Russia, sovereignty came to be equated with federal non-interference in their internal affairs and a degree of economic autonomy. As we have seen above, however, instead of developing a sustained legal framework for federalism, under Yeltsin a segmented regionalism had emerged reflecting not so much the spatial separation of powers but the fragmentation of political authority. Sovereignty claims by regional leaders, including in the republics, gained little support among the non-titular peoples, and even titular groups were divided. The fragmentation of citizenship was particularly resented. A survey in Komi revealed that 60 per cent of the ethnic Russians considered themselves primarily citizens of Russia rather than of the republic.[108]

The net effect of these measures was to reduce the influence of regional leaders on federal policy, but in return their control over regional politics was confirmed. Centre-regional conflicts were less politicised and instead the courts, above all the Constitutional Court, played a more active role in managing federal relations. The writ of the constitution now began to run unimpeded throughout the territory of Russia. This legal offensive against segmented regionalism brought regional charters, republican constitutions and all other normative acts more into conformity with the constitution and federal law. However, the move towards legal uniformity was blunted by concessions to the governors as the country entered the 2003–04 electoral cycle.

Changes in budgetary allocations means that today no more than five regions are net donors to the federal budget. In conditions of economic dependency, it is not clear that governors can be independent political actors: they cannot be full subjects in the political sense. According to Nikolai Petrov, the 'logic of Putin's federal reforms is to create a new structure that is completely subordinate to the president next to the old one and transfer power to it over time'. This was very different to what had happened under Yeltsin, which was to destroy the old communist-based system and to try to create a new one.[109] There was considerable scepticism whether the attempt to undermine the boyar-like powers of regional leaders would actually represent an increase in the democratic rights of citizens. For example, Yulia Latynina argued that the changes would do no more than substitute 'the arbitrary rule of the governors' with 'centralized arbitrary rule'[110] In addition, the regional authorities had acted as an important 'check and balance' against the overweening power of the centre; now this federal element in the separation of powers had been undermined.[111] The attempt to ensure legal homogeneity itself can be considered a simplification: in the USA each state has different laws, up to and including different approaches to the death penalty. Putin set his face against an asymmetrical model of state development, but federalism is all about legally-guaranteed heterogeneity – within the limits of the constitution and the normative commitment to democracy.

The era of special privileges for territorial entities was over, although the programme was tempered by the political needs of the Moscow authorities, notably as the country entered the 2003–04 electoral season. A new balance began to emerge. Regional authorities had long been condemned for transforming their territories into separate fiefdoms where they ruled like the boyars of old, apparently insulated from the writ of federal laws and the constitution. The vote for Putin in March 2000 had been, according to one observer, for 'the instilling of order in the country and for strong authority that could defend everyone from the highhandedness of bureaucrats and ensure the supremacy and dictatorship of law at all levels'.[112] Putin's attempts to rein in the regions were not only about the reassertion of federal authority but about the defence of the rights of citizens. Regional leaders were to obey the constiution and share power with the people. The country now was to live according to one constitution and one set of laws regardless of the region where one lived. Whether federalism can survive this onslaught of the homogenising powers of the modern democratic state remains in balance.

*   *   *

What is Russian federalism for? Is it to provide a framework for the national development of ethnic minorities, to act as a bulwark against what Lenin called 'Great Russian chauvinism', to provide decentralised administration and tailored solutions for Russia's huge territory, or to act as fourth pivot to guard against the possibility of the restoration of an authoritarian government in Moscow? We still do not have answers to these questions. Segmented regionalism threatened the rights of minorities and of individuals. It was in response to this that the countervailing universalistic agenda represented by the national state was asserted. This reassertion took two forms: the establishment of a direct presidential supervisory mechanism (the presidential 'vertical'); and a broader strategy of developing robust political institutions, such as regional legislatures and competitive national political parties, that would make regional political elites more accountable to their own constituents as well as to the national political community. Although the success of his attempts to restore the 'vertical of power' remains contested, at the level of political theory Putin's 'new statism' is rooted in the Jacobin republican state building tradition, where citizenship is considered individual, universal and homogeneous. As in other spheres, Putin sought to establish the rules of the political game, and then left the actors involved to play it – although the referee was sometimes not averse to picking up the ball and running! In addition, the assimilationist aspect of French (unitary) nation building threatens the accrued rights of the ethno-federal formations on Russia's territory, and in particular the privileges of the 'ethnocratic' elites based on the titular nationalities at their heart. The tension between the reassertion of the prerogatives of the centre and federalism's promise of shared sovereignty is still not adequately resolved. Klyuchevsky's dictum, cited at the head of this chapter, has not yet been decisively disproved.

7   Reforging the nation

We have been trying to make our choice for a long time – whether to rely on the advice, help and credits of others, or to develop on the basis of our own traditions (*samobytnost'*) and our own strength. Many states in the world were faced with a similar choice. If Russia remains weak, we will indeed have to make this choice. This will be the choice made by a weak state, a weak choice.

(Putin, state-of-the-nation speech, 8 July 2000[1])

Russia emerged blinking and bawling as an independent state in 1991: blinking in surprise, since the unthinkable had happened and the once mighty world power, the USSR, had disintegrated with little warning; bawling to bemoan the loss of imperial territories accumulated over centuries. The independence of the Baltic republics of Estonia, Latvia and Lithuania together with Moldova was one thing, since the territories were only reacquired during the Second World War, but the separation of the Slavic republics of the Ukraine and Belarus was something else. A truncated Russia emerged, with an unclear sense of its own identity and fearful for the future. For all his faults and equivocations, Yeltsin had at least accepted the reality of a smaller Russia. The fourteen other republics once united with Russia in the USSR were in his view unequivocally independent, and for this reason he was condemned by Russian nationalists and the communists for betraying what they perceived to be Russia's national interests. A Yugoslav scenario of endless wars to maintain a 'greater Russia' (such as those fought by Slobodan Milosević under the slogan of a 'greater Serbia') were avoided, but no consensus had been achieved by the end of the 1990s on Russia's proper size and character. National identity is about defined and defensible space; it is also about imbuing that space with a sense of common purpose and destiny. This was the challenge that faced Putin on assuming the presidency.

Images of the nation and symbols of the state

Although an independent Russian state had emerged in 1991, the task now was not only to provide that state with sinews and muscle, a process that we have discussed in earlier chapters, but for that state to create a nation. Charles Tilly and others have long argued that states make war, and wars make states, but another no less important process from the nineteenth century onwards was the way that disparate peoples were forged into nations by states.[2] The failure of the Russian Empire to achieve this is one reason for the collapse in 1917,[3] and in a paradoxical way the Soviet state also failed ultimately in its nation-building efforts.[4] Where autocracy and communism had failed, could a democratic Russia now forge a nation-state out of its over one hundred nationalities, four main traditional religions and enormously diverse climatic conditions in the world's largest territorial agglomeration? As Ernest Renan put it, a nation is constituted by 'the possession in common of a rich legacy of memories' accompanied by 'present-day consent, the desire to live together'. For the past not to become the source of conflict, since the many communities 'each has its own memories' with little in common, Renan argued that a nation is forged as much by what is forgotten as what is remembered. At the same time, he insisted 'a nation's existence is . . . a daily plebiscite'. In other words, the past can be both the basis of unity as well as division; and ultimately the peoples making up a nation must want to live together.[5] As Putin noted in his *Millennium Manifesto*,

> The fruitful and creative work, which our country needs so badly, is impossible in a split and internally disintegrated society, a society where the main social sections and political forces do not share basic values and fundamental ideological orientations. Twice in the outgoing century Russia has found itself in such a state: after October 1917 and in the 1990s.[6]

In previous chapters we have seen how Putin tried to create a political nation in which everyone would be equal as citizens, but the question remained about how this could become a cultural nation that would allow individuals to be different as people and peoples to be different as cultural communities, but all combined within a single political community. Would Putin become a great nation builder on the lines of Kemal Ataturk, who forged the modern Turkish state out of the detritus of the Ottoman empire and defeat in the First World War, or would his legacy be yet another failure to find an adequate political form to reflect Russia's diversity and size?

National values

The traumas and disappointments after 1985 undermined popular respect for the country's institutions. As Kolosov and his colleagues put it, Russian citizens 'had an extremely pessimistic and negative attitude towards their own country and a lack of faith in its future'.[7] They note the identity crisis that struck the country. The bipolar world had collapsed and with it Russia's superpower status, while internally the state lost its commanding position in social life. It was as if Russia and the rest of the developed world lived in different historical time: in the West globalisation and regional integration shaved off layers of sovereignty, whereas in Eurasia the borders between countries were hardening and the Westphalian state system was being recreated. For Kolosov the acute identity crisis could be defined as a period in which 'ethnic or other specific cultural regional or social groups create obstacles to the self-identification of the majority of citizens with the political-territorial community'.[8] It was this terrible and debilitating pessimism, sense of humiliation and identity crisis that Putin began to overcome.

We have argued that at the heart of Putin's attempts to make Russia a 'normal' country was the struggle to overcome the divisions of the past. Already in 1996 Yeltsin had urged his aides to find a 'national idea' around which the country could unite: 'There were various periods in the Russian history of the twentieth century – monarchy, totalitarianism, *perestroika* and, finally, the democratic path of development. Each stage had its own ideology. We do not have it.' He allowed one year for the new idea to emerge.[9] Although in his *Millennium* article Putin insisted that 'I am against the restoration of an official state ideology in Russia in any form',[10] on several occasions he returned to what would constitute the core principles of a revived Russian state. He insisted that the basis of social accord would be based on patriotism: 'Large-scale changes have taken place in an ideological vacuum. One ideology was lost and nothing new was suggested to replace it.' He insisted that 'patriotism in the most positive sense of this word' would be at the core of the new ideology.[11] Soon after the 1999 Duma elections Putin went further in specifying the elements of this ideology: 'It is very difficult to strive for conceptual breakthroughs in the main areas of life if there are no basic values around which the nation could rally. Patriotism, our history and religion can and, of course, should become such basic values.'[12] In his *Millennium* article Putin identified Russia's 'traditional values' as 'patriotism', '*gosudarstvennichestvo*' (statehood) and 'social solidarity'. He defined patriotism as 'a feeling of pride in one's country, its history and accomplishments [and] the striving to make one's country better, richer, stronger and happier'. He insisted that 'When these sentiments are free from the tints of nationalist conceit and imperial ambitions, there is nothing reprehensible or bigoted about them.'[13]

Putin's nation building thus focused on four key elements. At its heart was a patriotism that rejected the exclusivity associated with the concept of nationalism but instead encompassed pride in Russia's diversity, its history and its place in the world. This was to be buttressed by a strong political authority (statehood) that could maintain internal order, the integrity of the country and assert the country's interests abroad. Third, the pragmatic patriotism was to be supra-ethnic and statist, and it was on this basis that segmented regionalism was attacked to create a homogeneous constitutional space in which the ethnocratic rights of titular elites were to be subsumed into a broader political community. As Fish puts it, recentralisation was part of Putin's agenda of 'separating ethnicity from identity'.[14] And finally, the new nation state was to be socially just. In Russia's straitened circumstances the latter was perhaps the most difficult to achieve. Putin's efforts to ensure that wages were paid on time, that the savings deposits that had been rendered worthless by the near hyper-inflation of the early 1990s were compensated, that pensions were increased to at least the level of inflation, and that the costs of utility and other economic reforms did not bear down too hard on the poor all suggest that he took the idea of 'social solidarity' seriously. There was not much here about a rights-based liberalism, yet the lack of emphasis on the need for pluralism and individual human and civic rights was balanced elsewhere by Putin's emphasis on the rule of the law. His ideology, as we have noted before, was liberal conservatism.

Symbols and symbolism

Although material aspects are obviously crucial, a nation exists as much at the level of symbols and images as it does in brute facts. One of the factors that brought down the democratic government in 1917 was its neglect of the symbolic side of state development, and its very designation as a 'Provisional' government could hardly inspire long-term loyalty. This was a mistake that Putin clearly sought to avoid repeating, and he tried to do this by embedding the state in popular legitimacy, and transforming that people into a political and cultural nation.

A nation only exists when it shares a set of symbols and orientations towards its own history. In the 1990s Russia had remained bitterly divided in this respect, with the CPRF insisting that Soviet communism had reflected Russia's national greatness, while liberals pointed out the enormous costs in human lives and ultimately in relative economic backwardness. Now Putin sought to reconcile Russia's various pasts to overcome the divisions between Reds and Whites, Greens and Blacks, and this was most vividly in evidence in the adoption of the country's symbols and anthem.[15] Throughout the 1990s Russia had muddled through with a number of temporary arrangements. The former Tsarist state tricolour (white, blue and red), used by the Provisional Government in 1917, had become the flag of the democratic movement in the late Gorbachev years, and symbolised the defeat of the coup plotters in August 1991. No law, however, had been formally adopted under Yeltsin making this the state flag because of opposition in the Duma. Similarly, the state emblem (the two-headed eagle) had been used, but no law had been adopted. With the fall of communism a new anthem had been devised drawing on the work of Mikhail Glinka, but this wordless melody had never struck a popular response. The governments that ruled for the few months following the fall of Tsarism in February 1917 had also not been able formally to adopt the symbols of the state, and this had been one of the defining aspects of their 'provisional' character. This was one reason why the nationalist opposition in the 1990s considered Yeltsin's government another set of *vremenshchiki* (provisionals), destined to be swept away by the patriotic and nationalist-communist tide.

One of Putin's greatest achievements was to put an end to the provisionality of the post-communist regime. The 'new' national anthem adopted on 25 December 2000 was the old anthem composed in 1943 by Alexander Alexandrov, with new words written by the author of the original lyrics, Sergei Mikhalkov (the father of film director Nikita Mikhalkov).[16] On the same day, the two-headed Tsarist eagle, stripped of the shields denoting Muscovy's victory over the former Russian principalities, but with the addition of two small crowns flanking a large one intended to symbolise the sovereignty of the Russian Federation and its republics, became the state emblem. On 8 December the tricolour was confirmed as the Russian flag. It thus appeared that all three periods of Russian twentieth-century history had been reconciled: the Tsarist, Russia's brief experiment with democracy in 1917, and the Soviet. For many, however, the restoration of a version of the Soviet anthem reflected Putin's neo-Sovietism at its worst.[17] One of the harshest critics was Yeltsin, who implied that the change was symbolic of a broader rejection of post-communist reform. The charge was misjudged and could only be taken seriously if Putin had tried to restore the hammer and sickle.

There were other arenas of symbolic contestation. One of the most controversial was over what to do with Lenin's embalmed remains rotting away slowly in the shrine built on Stalin's orders on Red Square following Lenin's death in January 1924. Putin repeatedly stressed the need to maintain the stability of society and consensus, and he was well aware of just how explosive this issue could become for the country. At his press conference on 18 July 2001 he stated that he opposed the removal of Lenin's body from the mausoleum because many Russians still 'associate the name of Lenin with their own lives'. The reburial of the leader of the Bolsheviks and founder of the Soviet state would send a signal to people that 'they had worshipped false values' and would threaten the existing political and social balance.[18] It need hardly be added that Putin was one of those who had grown up under Lenin's shadow, and an attack on the first Soviet leader would cast a shadow over his own life experience. In addition, up and down the land statues of Lenin still adorned the central squares of countless towns, and the main street almost everywhere was still a Lenin Prospect. An attack on Lenin in Moscow would provoke bitter controversies everywhere else. Putin's policy of acknowledging the sensitivities of the older generation, and letting history lie with the present, gradually took the sting out of the physical presence of the past intruding on the development of the new.

Under Putin the patriotic celebration of victory day (9 May) in the Great Fatherland War was as elaborate as ever, although the anniversary of the October revolution (7 November) continued to be celebrated as a day of accord and reconciliation, a change that Yeltsin had introduced in 1996. Putin's restoration of the Soviet anthem and allowing Lenin to lie undisturbed in the mausoleum were taken by 'democrats' to symbolise his neo-Sovietism. These sentiments were reinforced by Putin's decision to restore the red flag as the symbol of the Russian Army, and then in 2002 restoring the red star as the emblem of Russia's armed forces. Many took this to be a sign of a continuing 'velvet restoration' of the old order in Russia. Putin's selective destalinisation was also in evidence in his refusal to open the Kremlin's Presidential Archive (formerly the Politburo's archive) to scholarly scrutiny. However, as always with Putin, this was balanced by post-Soviet sentiments. An example of this was his intervention in late 2002 in the long drawn out saga of restoring the name of 'Stalingrad' to the city on the Volga that had been the site of one of the world's greatest battles from November 1942 to February 1943, with some two million dead, and which marked the turning point in the Second World War as the German attack was blunted. After Stalin's death Khrushchev had renamed the city Volgograd, and many democrats after 1991 wished to see the pre-revolutionary name of Tsaritsyn restored (derived from a Tatar word and nothing to do with the Tsar), just as Leningrad had become St Petersburg, Kalinin had gone back to Tver, Kuibyshev to Samara, although Lenin's birthplace (officially) remained Ulyanovsk and not Simbirsk. Advocates of honouring the battle noted that there was a Stalingrad Square and metro station by that name in Paris, but none in Russia. However, Putin insisted that Russia was not France, and that 'the return of the name of the city in our country at present would, I am simply convinced of this, generate some sort of suspicions that we are returning to the times of Stalinism'. He insisted that the final decision should lie with the regional legislative body, and whatever was decided at the local level should be ratified by the national parliament.[19]

Patriotism and images of the nation

Putin was clearly imbued with a deep Russian patriotism, but he had absolutely nothing in common with the various trends of Russian nationalist mysticism. The 1990s had spawned hundreds of nationalist movements and trends. One of the most thoughtful, for example, was the 'Spiritual Heritage' (*Dukhovnoe nasledie*) movement led by Alexei Podberezkin. He had formerly been an ally of the communist leader Zyuganov, and had acted as one of the theologians of the peculiar form of national-communism espoused by the CPRF under Zyuganov's leadership, but had separated from the communists before the December 1999 Duma elections. The split was itself an indication of the declining power of the CPRF to bridge the nationalist and communist movements. Podberezkin participated in the March 2000 presidential elections, espousing the idea of a specifically 'Russian way'. His programme sought to modernise the 'Russian idea' for the new period, but as so often with 'national ways', the work was permeated by a strange combination of metaphysical abstraction and ruthless national realism.[20] Podberezkin ended up tenth in a field of eleven (see Table 1.2).

Following the apartment bombings in Moscow and elsewhere, Yeltsin was careful not to identify any national group as responsible: 'This enemy does not have a conscience, shows no sorrow and is without honour. It has no face, nationality or belief. Let me stress – no nationality, no belief,.'[21] Simonsen has argued that Putin was less nuanced and sought to incriminate the Chechens as a nation, allegedly demonising all Chechens as 'terrorists' and 'bandits'. He argues that in the earlier part of his presidency 'Putin was less sensitive to issues of ethnicity than his predecessor, meaning that his statism is not devoid of an ethnic element',[22] a feature that he dubbed 'ethnocentric patriotism'.[23] Putin's alleged willingness to allow racism against Caucasians to grow during the second Chechen war, and his identification of Russia and the Soviet Union primarily with ethnic Russians, as in his Victory Day speech on 9 May 2000: 'The people's pride and Russian [*Russkii*] patriotism are immortal. And therefore no force can triumph over Russian [*Russkii*] arms or defeat the army', appeared evidence of this.[24] However, on innumerable occasions Putin was at pains to ensure that policy was not 'ethnicised', and he sponsored the 2001 law against political extremism. Putin sought to construct an idiom in which patriotism would encompass tolerance and multi-culturalism.

Putin was in the line of the liberal statists (*gosudarstvenniki*), a tendency that had emerged early in the 1990s and whose most coherent exponent was Boris Fedorov, leader of the small liberal party Forward, Russia! Fedorov was a resolute champion of an assertive Russian identity: 'I am personally not willing to abandon a single one of the notions "great Russia", "great power", "introducing order", and "patriotism"', he insisted.[25] The liberal statists were joined by the neo-Eurasianists in asserting Russia's interests, above all in the former Soviet Union. Sergei Stankevich, a political advisor to Yeltsin, was one of the first to try to combine a liberal Russia with the assertion of a great power foreign identity, taking a hard line against Ukraine concerning the Black Sea Fleet stationed in Sevastopol, and indeed suggesting that following a referendum Crimea, in which the majority of the population are ethnic Russians, could become an independent state and later reunite with Russia.[26] Vladimir Lukin, one of the founders of the liberal Yabloko party and in the mid-1990s ambassador to the USA before returning to Moscow and chairing the Duma's foreign affairs committee, was another liberal for whom relations with Ukraine became crucial. He fought long and hard against the signing of a Russo–Ukrainian treaty that would have accepted the existing borders. The mayor of Moscow, Luzhkov, also expressed hard-line views about the status of Sevastopol, insisting that it was a Russian city.[27] The CPRF and a whole raft of nationalist groupings expressed similar sentiments, although in much harsher terms.

Although Putin inherited this strong liberal statist tradition, there are some crucial differences. First, Putin has no time for Eurasianism in any form. As a Petersburger, Putin has been consistently a Westerniser and repudiated any idea of Russia as a balance-holder between East or West, or as a separate civilisation distinct from that found in the West. As far as Putin is concerned, Russia is part of the West, and that is the end of the story. He recognises, of course, that Russia has vital interests in Asia, but these are strategic and economic rather than civilisational. Second, Putin unequivocally accepted the existing post-Soviet territorial settlement, and thus repudiated any hopes that the 'red-brown' nationalists had of Russia becoming a revisionist power seeking to challenge the territorial integrity of neighbouring states. This was seen at its starkest in Putin's relations with Ukraine, where Russian policy now sought active engagement. Third, Putin was unequivocally liberal in his patriotism, accepting the market and rejecting demands for protectionism or any number of models of autarchic development. Fourth, Putin was well aware that in a multiethnic country such as Russia there was a pre-eminent need to preserve interethnic peace and that 'manifestations of xenophobia and crime inspired by interethnic enmity' were 'absolutely inadmissible and the authorities should react to it resolutely'. Anything else could threaten the integrity of the state.[28] Putin was a civic nation builder in which the various ethnic nations – including Russia – would be able to pursue their own cultural identities as long as this did not come into conflict with the provisions of the constitution and the political nation that it represented. Putin, in short, espoused a new type of pragmatic minimal patriotism – shorn of nationalist excesses.

The recognition and acceptance of a smaller Russia was something that Yeltsin had already achieved, but his responsibility for the fall of the USSR introduced an element of equivocation. Putin could come to the question with a clear conscience and unsentimental realism. Putin insisted that 'He who does not regret the break-up of the Soviet Union has no heart; he who wants to revive it in its previous form has no head.'[29] Many in Russia, however, still based their platforms on reunification, if only of the Slavic part of the old Union. This was particularly the case with the leader of the Communists, Zyuganov. During the 2000 presidential elections Gleb Pavlovsky had argued that 'Zyuganov is the leader of an opposition that simply does not want to recognise Russia or live there', with his campaign focused on a non-existent USSR, whereas the majority of the voters 'have moved to a national Russia'.[30] Putin saw the former Soviet states as a reservoir from which Russia could draw people to satisfy its economic needs and to compensate for its demographic problems, with a low birth rate and high mortality rates, especially for men. As Putin noted, 'These are people with our mentality for whom Russian is practically a native language and who have practically the same cultural and, quite often, the same religious background.'[31] He gave no indication, however, of any desire to renew Russian imperial adventures in the region, although he was robust in defending what he perceived to be Russia's interests.

Organised religion and the state

The census of 2002 identified 190 different peoples (nations) living on the territory of Russia. However, the census did not ask a specific question about religious affiliation, and thus we can only guess and use historical data to establish the numbers professing and practising allegiance to any particular faith. Yeltsin personally (as in his second inauguration ceremony in August 1996) and the legislation of September 1997, which sought to regulate the life of organised churches, identified four 'historical' religions in Russia: Orthodoxy, Islam, Buddhism and Judaism. Dozens of others existed, some of which (like various militant Protestant groups funded by fundamentalists in the USA) conducted active proselytising work in Russia, much to the alarm of the official Orthodox hierarchy. Others, notably the Roman Catholic Church, had long existed in Russia with a community numbering over half a million, but Rome and its acolytes were regarded with suspicion verging on paranoia by the leadership of the Russian Orthodox Church (ROC). The creation by the Pope in February 2002 of four new dioceses in Russia enraged Patriarch Aleksii II, who responded by blocking the Pope's visit. Part of this hostility had deep historical roots, reaching back as far as the division in 395 of the Roman Empire into a western part based in Rome and an eastern empire rooted in Constantinople (Istanbul today). The schism between the two faiths, Catholicism and Orthodoxy, was made formal in 1054, and since then very different traditions of religiosity, attitudes towards rationality and faith, had taken root. Orthodox suspicion towards Catholicism is perhaps best reflected in the views of Fedor Dostoevsky who, like the Slavophiles with whom at one period he was associated, argued that Catholicism's acceptance of secular rationality had opened the way to the Reformation and the decline of spirituality in the West.[32]

From the above it is clear that Orthodoxy had a quite exceptional role to play in the development of Russian national identity and the very idea of Russianness. This is not the place to go into the various divisions within Orthodoxy, in particular the struggle within the ROC in the post-communist period between modernisers and hard-line anti-westernists. In some ways the dominance of the ROC was reminiscent of that enjoyed by the Church of England, although the formal separation of church and state stipulated by the 1993 constitution precluded the ROC becoming the established church. Article 14.1 states that 'The Russian Federation is a secular state. No religion may be established as the state religion or a compulsory religion.' While Article 14.2 insists that: 'Religious associations are separated from the state and are equal before the law.' The ROC in the 1990s had retreated from direct participation in political life and sought to present itself as the non-partisan keeper of the nation's spiritual values. In the last years of the Soviet period and in the early post-communist years Aleksii II and other clerics had been elected to the Soviet and Russian parliaments, but by 1993 they had withdrawn from active campaigning and clerics were forbidden from running for office. The church refused to endorse particular candidates or specific party platforms.[33] This withdrawal from partisan activity was one factor allowing the church to retain a high degree of trust as a social institution.[34]

Although not the state religion, Orthodoxy was certainly for Putin the religion of the state. Putin's father had been an active communist, but he had nevertheless turned a blind eye to his wife's religious belief and attendance at services. Putin had imbibed his Orthodox faith from his mother and remains a committed believer, although he strove hard to avoid alienating the many other faiths in the country. In his public activities Putin stressed Russia's religious pluralism, but in his private life he attends Orthodox services and, according to his wife Lyudmila, 'He is a very good man who lives according to Christian principles.'[35] He has a 'spiritual father' (*dukhovnyi otets*), apparently the deputy head of the Sretensky Monastery (just round the corner from the Lubyanka) archimandrite Tikhon.[36] On a visit to the Vaalam monastery in the White Sea Putin remarked that without Orthodoxy there would be no Russia, and this certainly is Tikhon's belief. He is no liberal, insisting that it was a false choice to believe that the only alternatives facing Russia were 'the horrors of Islamic terrorism and the no less terrible power of those who seek to achieve total American hegemony'. Tikhon is a member of the editorial board of the journal *Russkii dom* (*Russian House*), which is associated with a television programme of that name funded by Sergei Pugachev.[37] Putin enjoyed a particularly close relationship with the Patriarch, and on numerous occasions sought his advice. For many Russians the church was the source of values and traditions around which a post-communist national identity could be constructed. This was reflected in Putin's message of congratulation to Aleksii II on the tenth anniversary of his enthronement in 2000: 'The church is recovering its traditional mission as a key force in promoting social stability and moral unity around general priorities of justice, patriotism, good works, constructive labour and family values.'[38] The Orthodox church, moreover, was also a symbol of the unity of the East Slavs, and thus reflected the larger identity of Rus' as the people of Eurasia divided most inconveniently by the borders that had sprung up since 1991. The church helped in part to fill the vacuum left by the demise of the Communist Party and its version of the ideology of Marxism–Leninism, and thus acted as a source of values around which much of the nation could unite. However, the quasi-official role played by the Orthodox Church and its close relationship with the state under Putin suggested to many that it could act as a new instrument of state ideological control.[39]

Chechnya: tombstone or crucible of Russian power?

The year 1991 was for the Soviet Union what Robert Jackson calls 'the Grotian moment', the reshuffling of the title to sovereignty.[40] Bartkus has theorised these liminal periods in the constitution of states as the 'opportune moment' when the weakening of central government (or foreign intervention) raises the prospects for success of a bid for independence.[41] In both the former USSR and Yugoslavia, however, the Grotian moment was limited to existing union republics, and despite repeated wars the new borders have been upheld.

The 1993 Russian constitution does not recognise the right of secession for any of its units. The Chechen secession bid was an attempt to expand the Grotian consensus without a basis in just cause, something that distinguishes this case from that of Kosovo, whose putative secession is clearly grounded in the remedial right to put an end to the persistent violation of human rights.[42] International law and practice does not recognise the unilateral right to secession under whatever conditions and through any procedure, however democratic (like a referendum). International law also stresses that however just a war (*jus ad bellum*) it should be fought in a just way (*jus in bello*). Putin's war in Chechnya may well have been a just war, but it was fought most unjustly.[43]

Putin's war

The Chechen case demonstrated just how high the costs of separatism and partition through wars of secession could be.[44] Ethnic conflicts are seldom resolved by partitioning states.[45] The problem, of course, is one of definition. Is Russia (like France over Algeria) in the position of an imperial state that will sooner or later have to accept the loss of colonial possessions once they realise the unacceptably high cost of attempting to hold on to them? Or is Russia faced with a situation where its very national existence and democratic achievements are under threat by an armed insurgency and, like the Union forces in the American Civil War, cannot but fight the war to a victorious conclusion? Henry E. Hale argued that 'Chechnya is a localized issue focused around the perceived threat of terrorism, not a symptom of naked Russian aggression'.[46] Both wars were relatively insulated from the mainstream of Russian political life and exerted remarkably little influence on it.[47] Rather than Chechnya, in Lieven's words, becoming the tombstone of Russian power,[48] for a time in late 1999 (as we saw in Chapter 1) Chechnya served as the crucible for the restoration of that power. In his *Millennium Manifesto* Putin insisted that Chechnya was 'where the future of Russia is being decided'. In a television statement on 23 January 2000 he noted: 'In my opinion, the active public support for our actions in the Caucasus is due not only to a sense of hurt national identity but also to a vague feeling ... that the state has become weak. And it ought to be strong.'[49] For Putin the war in Chechnya was about preventing the disintegration of Russia, and the associated horrors that would entail.[50]

The fear that the Chechen zone of insecurity would move up the Volga and spread to other republics and result in the Yugoslavisation of Russia had provoked the second war. An 'enclave of banditry', to use Putin's term, was established in Chechnya that threatened not only its immediate neighbours but also the trans-Caspian republics of Kyrgyzstan and Uzbekistan.[51] As far as Putin was concerned,

> the essence of the situation in the Caucasus and Chechnya was a continuation of the collapse of the USSR. It was clear that we had to put an

end to it at some point.... My evaluation of the situation in August [1999] when the bandits attacked Dagestan was that if we don't stop it immediately, Russia as a state in its current form would no longer exist. Then we were talking about stopping the dissolution of the country. I acted assuming it would cost me my political career. This was the minimum price that I was prepared to pay.[52]

The interviewer followed up with the following intriguing question: 'Does the fact that Lenin gave Finland independence many decades ago give you an allergic reaction? Is Chechnya's secession possible in principle?' To which Putin answered:

It is possible, but the issue is not secession.... Chechnya will not stop with its own independence. It will be used as a staging ground for a further attack on Russia.... Why? In order to protect Chechen independence? Of course not. The purpose will be to grab more territory. They would overwhelm Dagestan. Then the whole Caucasus – Dagestan, Ingushetiya, and then up along the Volga – Bashkortostan, Tatarstan, following this direction into the depths of the country.... When I started to compare the scale of the possible tragedy with what we have there now, I had no doubt that we should act as we are acting, maybe even more firmly.[53]

From this it is clear that Putin viewed the Chechen issue in stark terms. However, a policy that in late 1999 served to consolidate the Russian elite within two years looked like the stubborn attempt to achieve a military victory at all costs that ignored the possibility of a political resolution of the war.

The Khasavyurt agreement of 31 August 1996, as we saw in Chapter 1, granted Chechnya de facto independence following the war of 1994–96. The leader of the Chechen insurgents, Aslan Maskhadov, had been elected president for a five-year term in early 1997, and even after his term formally expired in early 2002 he remained the leader of the Chechen national movement. His authority, however, was challenged by militant field commanders, especially those who had assumed militant Islamic identities (like Shamil Basaev and Khattab). Putin was particularly scathing about this period:

During the criminal regime's rule [1996–99], local people, their own fellow citizens, were being shot publicly in squares. Not to mention the atrocities committed against representatives of federal services, servicemen, and so on. It was a criminal regime that was elected when bandits and international terrorists held people at gunpoint. We know full well what followed. The next day they lost control of the republic. Totally different people emerged behind their backs, seeking and trying to use Chechen hands to achieve aims that had nothing to do with the interests of the Chechen people – the creation of the notorious caliphate that we

have already talked about here. Those were the aims set by the
Maskhadov regime. Otherwise, there would have been no attack on
Dagestan.[54]

Putin's thinking remained torn between two concerns: security and sovereignty. Even before the 11 September 2001 attack on the World Trade
Center, security (the defeat of terrorism) tended to predominate over sovereignty issues (the defence of the territorial integrity of the Russian Federation), but the latter concern was never far from the surface. Putin expressed
Moscow's view at the January 2000 CIS summit in Moscow when he defended
the territorial integrity of states, as opposed to the principle of national self-
determination, in the resolution of problems in the Caucasus.[55] Such a
stance suited Georgia, with a challenge to its territorial integrity coming from
Abkhazia and South Ossetia, and also Azerbaijan, in danger of losing control
permanently over Nagorno-Karabakh. However, Moscow's closest strategic
ally in the region was Armenia, a country that could not but be dismayed by
such an inflexible stance as it sought to achieve the reunification of
Nagorno-Karabakh with Armenia. Under Putin it appeared that the Russian
notion advanced between 1996–99 of 'common-states' in the cases of
Georgia-Abkhazia, Azerbaijan-Karabakh and Moldova-Transdniester was to
be shelved. Although Putin later that year in a speech to top military officials
argued that 'Chechnya's formal status is not so important today. What is
important is that this territory should never be used by anybody as a springboard to attack the Russian Federation', it appears clear that Putin himself
did not consider Chechen independence a realistic option.[56]

After the attacks of 11 September 2001 Putin was quick to point out the
alleged connections between Osama bin Laden and the rebels in Chechnya,
identifying a radical Muslim fundamentalism as the core threat to the West.
Putin declared that Russia and the United States now had a 'common foe'
and agreed to assist the US in the campaign. He added the reservation that
the degree of cooperation 'will directly depend on the general level and
quality of our relations with these countries and on mutual understanding in
the sphere of fighting international terrorism', suggesting that co-operation
was dependent on toning down criticism of the conduct of the Russian campaign in Chechnya. After 11 September Russia became part of the international 'coalition against terrorism', and criticism of the way that Russia
conducted the campaign in Chechnya became more muted.

The two Chechen invasions of Dagestan in August 1999 followed by the
spate of apartment bombings, together with sustained hostage taking and the
effective collapse of civil order in Chechnya, provided Russia with the *casus
belli* for a renewed military intervention in September 1999.[57] The enormity
of the perceived threat from Chechen insurgency in part explains the disproportionate use of force in the region. When faced by similarly grave threats
to national security, as after 11 September 2001, the West, too, has resorted
to overwhelming force and the infringement of civil liberties. However the

two Chechen campaigns revealed the essentially Soviet ethos of the Russian armed forces. Despite repeated plans to reform the military in the 1990s, not much had been achieved in the face of determined resistance from large sections of the military establishment. In an attempt to impose his will Putin had appointed his close ally Sergei Ivanov as Russia's first civilian defence minister. The army consisted of some 600,000 conscripts and about 130,000 *kontraktniki*, the core of the professional army of the future to replace the hated conscription system. Putin gave the military considerable leeway in setting the agenda in the Caucasus. The military was thirsting for revenge for the humiliating defeat represented by the Khasavyurt agreement; the armed forces did not consider that they had lost the war militarily. Like the Treaty of Versailles, as far as the military was concerned heroic feats of arms in the field had been betrayed by a 'stab in the back' by politicians. Unlike the German case earlier, there is some evidence to support the assertion that the war was lost in Moscow and not in the Caucasus.

Protracted warfare in Chechnya clearly degraded the quality of Russian political and social life, especially since there was a tendency to dehumanise the Chechen insurgents, the Chechens as a people and Russian servicemen. By February 2000 Russian losses since federal forces entered Chechnya on 1 October 1999 were officially stated to be 1,458 servicemen killed and 4,495 wounded since the start of the North Caucasian military operation on 2 August 1999,[58] a figure that had risen to 4,572 deaths by June 2003.[59] Maskhadov, moreover, had decreed that all those who tried to restore the civil infrastructure and civic administration were to be killed, a position that he later modified when he stated that the insurgents would 'no longer commit terrorist acts against civilians'.[60] At that time Putin distinguished between the first war, which he linked to 'Russia's imperialist ambitions and attempts to rein in the territories it controls' and the second, which he characterised as an 'anti-terrorist operation'.[61] Others, however, like former presidential advisor Emil Pain, characterise Russia's entire policy as 'colonial wars'. Despite certain military successes, the lack of a clear Kremlin strategy in the second war led many to adopt the term 'victorious defeat' to describe the stalemate.[62] As another report put it, noting that 'political regulation of the Chechen problem is impossible': 'Russia has won. The war continues.'[63] The Russian presidential spokesman on the issue, Sergei Yastrzhembsky, argued in May 2001 that the conflict in Chechnya was likely to last for years, noting that there were some thirty low-intensity conflicts in the world, and Chechnya would probably join their number.[64] Few commentators thought that Russia could win the war. The conflict poisoned Russian politics and threatened to inhibit Russia's further development as a democracy. As Furman put it, Moscow's approach to both Chechnya and the Chechens left him unable to 'imagine a peaceful integration of Chechens into Russian society'. His conclusion was that Russian democracy was impossible without Chechen independence.[65]

Russia had a strong case to make in defence of the necessity of the war, in effect dealing with an armed uprising that did not conform to any extant theory of secession and which, for good measure, threatened its neighbours.[66] Public opinion in Russia at first remained supportive of the campaign (rising to an astonishing 70 per cent by early March 2000), realising that the Chechen insurgents had taken over 1,500 individual hostages in their years of effective independence and now tried to take the 146-million strong population of Russia as a collective hostage in the court of world public opinion. Putin represented the threat to Russia from Chechnya as comparable to other times when the very existence of the state was under threat. More than this, the national unity engendered by what was perceived as a just war against nationalist expansionism, terrorism and aggressive fundamentalism for a time forged an unprecedented sense of national unity in the reborn Russian state. This was only part of the story, however, and the tendency to dehumanise all the combatants, Chechen militants, civilians and Russian foot soldiers alike, by 2002 saw public opinion shift towards support for a negotiated settlement.[67]

Squaring the circle

Although Putin's early period in power was accompanied by a general acknowledgement that the Chechen problem required decisive action, the stubborn resistance of the insurgents, the continued evidence of military brutality and corruption, severe abuses of the human rights of Chechen civilians, all fed a growing revulsion against the continuation of the war. Russian casualties in the second war by late 2002 were officially numbered at 4,700, although the true figure was at least double. In the first two years of war some 65,000 Russian soldiers had been turned into cripples, about the same number as in the ten years of the Soviet conflict in Afghanistan.[68] Some 13,500 insurgents were killed in that time according to official sources. Despite the presence of some 80,000 troops in the republic even basic security could not be guaranteed. Terrorist bombs were exploded in Dagestan, Russian military helicopters were downed, police stations bombed, and even the government headquarters in Grozny were attacked by lorries carrying bombs, killing 72 officials on 27 December 2002. No less dreadful was the systematic killing by the rebels of all those trying to re-establish basic services in the republic, with teachers, electricity workers, transport workers and others employed by the local administration in the front line. Moscow's policy of 'Chechenising' local administration only added another layer of hostility and resentment, yet more intrigues between local and federal political actors, but did little to reduce the prevailing anarchy in the region. The conflict took on the bitterest form of all – civil war.

The war at first was marked by a dangerous weakening of traditional civil–military roles, with the command in the field initially granted not only operational but also strategic discretion. The conduct of the war contradicted not only general rules of war but also numerous human rights commitments that Russia had freely entered into. Although the military certainly tried to gain control of the security agenda in the region, Putin fought hard to ensure that presidential policy was not 'captured' by any particular group, and in particular by the security services. In May 2002 the system of rotation of appointments in the interior ministry was re-introduced, designed to ensure that local police chiefs remained independent of regional bosses. The post of commander in chief of the ground forces, abolished in 1998, was now restored and the commanders of the Military Districts were to report to him, while he in turn answered directly to the defence minister rather than to General Staff.[69]

The head of the North Caucasus Military District, General-Colonel Gennady Troshev, was one of the first victims of the policy intended to reassert civilian control over the military, and the powers of the defence ministry over the more conservative General Staff. Troshev had been born in Grozny and represented a rare breed of relatively effective professional and not corrupt soldiers.[70] He was also dedicated to Chechnya in his own way, and when ordered in December 2002 to take up a new appointment as part of the rotation of MD commanders, he refused on the grounds that the Chechen people needed him, and the next day (18 December) he was fired. The incident was only the most spectacular reminder that Russia's Chechnya policy was fragmented between numerous agencies and individuals, both in Moscow and in the republic itself, with military affairs alone handled by some five bodies.[71] The civilian bodies were no less fragmented. Troshev's dismissal was a clear signal that the day of the independent general in Russia was over.

Ground down by the guerrilla war, the army resorted to brutal acts. A confidential report by the Kadyrov adminstration sent to the Kremlin in March 2003 admitted that at least 1,314 civilians had been murdered by the authorities in 2002.[72] In the sea of cruelty the killing of Malika Umazheva, an extraordinarily courageous human rights activist and the former head of Alkhan Kala village, stands out for its blatant contempt of basic norms of human decency. She was abducted by federal forces on 29 November 2002 and was soon found dead. The only trial of a senior Russian officer in either of the Chechen wars was against Colonel Yury Budanov, accused of raping and murdering a Chechen girl, Elza Kungaeva, in 2000. Against all the evidence, he was acquitted on the grounds of diminished mental responsibility on 31 December 2002, but after a retrial was sentenced to 10 years in prison on 27 July 2003. The case is comparable to that of Lieutenant William Calley, whose platoon on 16 March 1968 raped and murdered 400 Vietnamese civilians in My Lai. After a long cover up the case finally came to court, but his sentence of life imprisonment with hard labour was soon commuted to 20 then 10 years, before being released by president Richard Nixon. All other parties to the massacre were acquitted, and most of the 300,000 letters sent to the White House concerning the case supported Calley. Atrocities cannot be justified by the heat of war, although public opinion in both cases sought to licence the events in this way. There were attempts by the Russian government and the commanders in the field to humanise the war. On 27 March 2002, for example, the commander of Russian forces in Chechnya, Colonel General Vladimir Moltenskoi, issued order No. 80 that soldiers involved in operations, especially 'cleansing' ones (*zachistki*) should not wear masks and be able to be held responsible for their actions. All the evidence suggests that the order was ignored.[73] Even the deputy from Chechnya to the State Duma, retired MVD general Aslambek Aslakhanov, and the head of the pro-Moscow Chechen administration Akhmad Kadyrov had difficulty gaining entry to blockaded villages (for example, Mesker-Yurt). Once in, Aslakhanov faced 'a collective moan' about the beatings civilians had endured, and only quick action managed to retrieve young people from an ambulance provided by the military, which in all probability would have ended with their deaths so as to eliminate witnesses. In an interview Aslakhanov was asked:

> How is one to explain the extreme cruelty exhibited by the federal forces towards the Chechen civilians? [He responded] 'Not one of the leaders of the MVD, the FSB, or the Minsitry of Justice has been held responsible for the conducting of cleansing operations in Starye and Novye Atagi, Kurchaloi, Tsatsan-Yurt, Assinskaya, Argun and Chiri-Yurt, where young people disappeared and they later found their mutilated bodies . . . They are lying! They are lying to the president, lying to the State Duma, to the Council of Federation, to the government, and to their ministers. They are lying to the citizens of the Russian Federation, claiming that stabilisation is occurring. The result of so-called cleansing operations is that [Chechen] pupils in schools are now leaving for the forests in order to take revenge for their relatives who suffered during the special operations.'[74]

Despite attempts to restore civilian administration led by Chechens, the heavy-handed *zachistki* alienated even pro-Moscow Chechens, undermining the long-term prospects of ending the conflict on Moscow's terms.

With no acceptable political solution in sight, the war rumbled on throughout Putin's first term, weakening his international stature, dividing society, brutalising domestic policy, and inflaming other conflicts in the Caucasus. There were desultory attempts to find a negotiated settlement, but as far as Moscow was concerned it was not clear with whom to negotiate. In July 2002, as the influence of the 'Arabs' in the Chechen secession struggle weakened, Maskhadov and Basaev reforged their alliance, while at the same time Kazbek Makhashev was named as Maskhadov's representative for discussions with Moscow.[75] Faced by a military leadership that considered the Khasavyurt agreement of 31 August 1996 a betrayal and 'stab in the back', Putin's own room for manoeuvre was severely circumscribed. Although the war slipped far down the list of popular priorities, polls showed growing support for negotiations with the rebels, rising to 60 per cent in January 2003 while only 30 per cent favoured continued military operations.[76] While the pressure for a negotiated settlement was growing, it was not clear whether on this issue Putin would be responsive.

The former speaker of the Russian Supreme Soviet, Ruslan Khasbulatov and an ethnic Chechen himself did try to act as an 'honest broker', meeting with Maskhadov's representative Akhmed Zakaev in Istanbul and came up with a peace plan that would provide a 'special status' for Chechnya. The republic would enjoy a high degree of domestic and foreign autonomy and would not be a subject of Russia, but would come under Russian legislation on a number of questions. Maskhadov approved of the plan, but it would require the support of international organisations like the OSCE to secure its implementation. In the meantime, the pro-Moscow administration headed by Kadyrov pushed ahead with its own plans for a new constitution for the republic. The search for a negotiated solution was imperilled (perhaps deliberately) by the Dubrovka theatre siege of 23–25 October 2002. Over 800 people, watching the popular Nord Ost musical, were taken hostage by 41 Chechen militants (19 of whom were women) headed by the young warlord Movsar Baraev. In the end the security forces forced entry using a gas to incapacitate the terrorists, all of whom were shot, but at the same time 129 hostages also died, all but two from the effects of the gas. Only four days later were medical staff informed that the gas was a fentanyl derivative.

As a result of the siege the Kremlin toughened its stance against negotiations, especially since Maskhadov had been slow to condemn the action publicly. There remains the suspicion that he condoned the attack as a way of bolstering his authority with the warlords, a strategy that had proved tragically futile (because it ultimately provoked the second war) in the interbellum period of 1996–99, and was no more successful now. If he had hoped to use the siege to force Moscow to the negotiating table, then he was no more successful. Moscow instead pushed ahead with the constitutional option that would sideline Maskhadov and create, it was hoped, a new legitimate government for Chechnya. The draft was adopted on 11 December 2002 by a Congress of the Chechen Peoples in Gudermes, and on the following day Putin approved the holding of the referendum and the election laws for the republic's new institutions, including the presidency, later in the year. The October 2002 census had allegedly found a population of over a million in the republic, whereas the true figure was unlikely to be any more than half a million. These widely diverging figures hardly inspired confidence that the referendum would come up with an accurate reflection of popular feelings.

In his question and answer session with the Russian people on 19 December 2002 Putin insisted that 'a bad peace is always better than a good war',[77] but there appeared to be little movement in this direction. Putin nevertheless refused to countenance the imposition of a state of emergency, which would have suspended even the semblance of political normality in the country. Instead, he pushed through the idea of the adoption of a constitution in Chechnya on whose basis new legitimate authorities could be constructed:

To move away from the situation we have today, there is no question that we have to gradually hand over the reins of power completely to the Chechen people. It's not possible to do this without a legal basis, without a constitution. Without this, it would not be possible to elect legitimate bodies of power, a president, a parliament. If we don't do this, we will not be able to get away from what we have today. The process is difficult, but without these political processes, it is just not possible to put the situation in Chechnya on a legitimate footing, and subsequently bring the economic and social situation back to normal.[78]

The draft of the new constitution, proposed by the pro-Moscow administration, was released (in Russian) in January 2003, with the referendum on its adoption to be held in the republic on 23 March. Lord Frank Judd, the chief rapporteur for Chechnya of the Parliamentary Assembly of the Council of Europe (PACE), although initially supporting the text of the document, insisted that no genuine vote could be held in the republic in such violent conditions and when the views of grass-roots Chechens had not been sought. In fact, most Chechens had not even seen the document, and thus Lord Judd argued that 'We don't just want a bit of paper that people say "yes" or "no" to. We want a real political solution rooted in the people and the consensus of the people.'[79] He noted that in the circumstances the Council of Europe would not be sending observers to monitor the referendum, and he insisted, moreover, that Russia should negotiate with Zakaev, a deputy prime minister of the rebel government and by that time in exile in London, threatened with extradition to Russia to face a range of far-fetched claims about involvement in Chechen terrorist acts.

The Russian authorities did everything to stimulate participation in the vote, with Putin on 16 March appealing on television for the population of Chechnya to participate, promising in the event of the document being adopted a special bilateral treaty that would grant Chechnya 'broad autonomy'. The constitution contained many concessions that Putin had repudiated in relations with other regions, also promising 'wide autonomy' and embracing once again the principle of a bilateral treaty. On 23 March voters were presented with three questions: to approve the new constitution; accept a draft law on the election of the president; and a draft law on the election of parliament. An extraordinary 89.48 per cent of the war-torn republic's adult population allegedly took part, with 95.97 per cent approving the constitution, 95.4 per cent backing the presidential election law and 96.05 per cent supporting the draft law on parliamentary elections. In his address to the nation in May, Putin praised the result:

Today I especially thank the Chechen people, for their courage, for the fact that they did not allow themselves to be intimidated and do not allow themselves to be intimidated now, for their wisdom, ever-present in ordinary people who instinctively know what's right and wrong. People in Chechnya had a heartfelt awareness of their responsibility and human interest. Finally, the referendum there showed that the Chechen people legitimately regard themselves as an inseparable part of a unified Russian multinational people.[80]

The road was now open for the election of a new president and parliament on 5 October 2003.

At the same time, PACE finally lost patience with Russian intransigence in putting an end to human rights abuses, and on 2 April 2003 voted to recommend the creation of an international tribunal to try both Russians and Chechens accused of war crimes. The response of the head of the Russian delegation to PACE, Dmitry Rogozin, was typical, trying to tie the vote to Russia's criticisms of American action in Iraq, an interpretation that Lord Judd (who had bent over backwards to be fair to the Russian point of view) characterised as 'absolute nonsense'.[81] Rogozin by a long chalk must take the prize for being the world's worst diplomat. Not surprisingly, he was mooted to become Russia's next foreign minister.

Was there a way of squaring the circle: of accommodating Chechen demands while maintaining the integrity of the Russian state and its nascent democracy? The question of managing sub-national sovereignty claims is growing in importance in the EU, the United States and, of greatest concern to us, in Russia. Do you 'appease', and if so, are you on the 'slippery slope' to independence; or can timely concessions, however lopsided these may render a federal system, avert more radical separatist demands?[82] The experience of the Russian Federation in the 1990s is that flexibility and asymmetry can help preserve the system, however untidy it may look to the constitutional lawyer.

Despite attempts by the authorities to suggest that the war was over, the situation remained far from normal in Chechnya. Only when both sides were thoroughly exhausted could a negotiated settlement be achieved. De Gaulle had come to power in 1958 and pledged to retain Algeria as part of France, but by 1962 granted the former colony independence, despite the murderous onslaught of French settler (*pieds noirs*) organisations. The Russian inhabitants of Chechnya had mostly fled, but independence for Chechnya, after the bitter experience of 1996–99, was not on the cards for a long time to come. Too often Russia is blamed for the failings of the de facto independent state of Chechnya, but such an approach yet again absolves the Chechen elite and society of responsibility for its own fate. Putin repeatedly spoke 'of the need to return the Chechen Republic to the country's political and legal space',[83] and the only serious way forwards is a power-sharing arrangement like the Good Friday agreement in Northern Ireland negotiated in spring 1999. Such an idea was suggested by Primakov, outlining a stage by stage approach to peace: a ceasefire followed by roundtable talks with all parties to find some acceptable solution.[84] Whatever happened, Chechnya would remain part of the Russian Federation, but could be granted significant internal autonomy. Like the Crimea in the Ukraine, the republic could be granted a special constitutional status. The problem of Chechnya ultimately, however, could only be resolved in Chechnya. Only if Maskhadov or some other Chechen leader would be willing to turn his guns against the army of unemployed youthful militants and impose order on the republic would peace be possible. Many noted that if only he had had the courage to do this when Chechnya enjoyed de facto independence between 1996–99, then the second Chechen war could have been avoided. He would certainly face the threat of assassination by disgruntled warlords, but like Michael Collins in Ireland and many others, the transformation of guerrilla leader into statesman offered the country a way out of perpetual war.

*   *   *

Putin sought to restore faith in the symbolical level of governmental action, the belief that the government was acting in the national and popular interest and that this new, smaller, Russian state, was a legitimate successor to the various regimes that had preceded it, and thus was worthy of respect, and indeed, of veneration. As far as Putin was concerned, Russia was not a rump USSR but a country with long traditions of its own. But this new entity had still to become a genuine political nation, sharing not only common rules as defined by the constitution but also enjoying a certain affective cohesion. For Putin the political and the emotional levels of nation building went together, and the fact that he represented a clear vision for both was one of the main sources of his enduring popularity. Putin was able to make Russians feel a bit better about themselves. He also managed to improve Russia's image and perception in the world at large. The process was highly contradictory, and with the continuation of the war in Chechnya elements of crisis remained in the attempt to reforge a coherent national identity.

8 Russian capitalism

> We are a rich country of poor people. And this is an intolerable situation.
>
> (Putin[1])

Earlier we analysed Putin's reform of the federal system designed to ensure the unimpeded application of constitutional norms. No less important was his struggle to modify the close and unhealthy relationship between the state and the economy that had developed under Yeltsin. The privileges of various business and commercial structures had turned into a specific type of 'state within the state', with their own media empires, house politicians, television channels and security services. Hellman described developments under Yeltsin as a 'partial reform equilibrium', with regional bosses and oligarchs taking advantage of an economy stuck midway between the plan and the market.[2] This 'equilibrium' (although the degree to which a balance had been achieved is unclear) was now upset by the emergence of an activist presidency. We have noted that in the struggle against certain oligarchs the principle of 'equidistance' between business interests and the state was advanced. What was the economic legacy that Putin inherited, and how did he plan to move forwards? What was the economic model that he sought to apply? These are the questions that we shall address in this chapter.

Entering the market

In the last years of the Soviet Union its GDP per capita ranked 43rd place in the world; by the time Putin came to power Russia took 135th place, rubbing shoulders with countries such as Costa Rica. Not only was a large proportion of the population impoverished by the shift to the market, inequality had greatly risen. By March 2003 Russia could boast of 17 billionaires, most of whom had made their money in the energy sector,[3] while at that time the average monthly income was 3,868 roubles (about $110) with some 30 million people (22 per cent of the population) gaining less than the minimum living wage of just under 2,000 roubles. As in politics, the political economy of Yeltsinism looked both forwards (towards effective liberalisation, creating a market system and its integration into the global economy) and backwards (towards bureaucratic regulation and arbitrary state interventions). This tension helps in part to explain why regions like Primorsky *krai*, bordering on China, Korea and Japan, failed to take advantage of the opportunities to integrate into the Pacific Rim market but instead focused on sparring with Moscow while ultimately remaining dependent on Moscow.[4] The leadership in this region and many others concentrated on the expanded opportunities for asset-stripping, rent-seeking and other pathologies of a semi-marketised economy to maintain their grip on power. At the same time, the so-called oligarchs had carved up the economy between themselves, and their influence penetrated into the corridors of power. These relations were far from stable, from the point of view of economic competitiveness and from the perspective of the disruptive effect they had on the development of a national market and an effective political system. At some point this regionalised and oligopolistic system would have to give way to a more coherent, although not necessarily more liberal, order.

Yeltsin's legacy

The Russian economic world had changed dramatically from the early 1990s, when each year the economy shrank and price rises approached hyper-inflationary levels. By the time of the rouble crisis of August 1998 Russian GDP had fallen by 42 per cent and poverty had risen from 2 per cent of the population to over 40 per cent. The economy returned to growth in 1997, but the economic crisis of 1998 showed how fragile the recovery had been. The government was unable to collect sufficient taxes to cover its expenditure as the budget deficit rose to about 8 per cent of GDP. The shortfall in tax revenues resulted in part from the enormous subsidies still paid to loss-making enterprises; the government had not been able adequately to cut its expenses, even though it collected (although arbitrarily and incompetently) some one-third of GDP in tax revenues, similar to the US level. The government, headed in the final period by the liberal Kirienko, resorted to issuing a mountain of government bonds (GKOs) at ever-increasing interest rates, until the whole pyramid collapsed in the partial default of 17 August 1998.[5]

The three-fold devaluation of the rouble following this financial crisis, in which numerous banks went under and many foreign financial concerns had their fingers burnt, allowed the economy to enter a period of recovery. It also severely weakened the economic power of the oligarchs. The fall in the value of the rouble after 1998 allowed domestic producers to compete with imports, and demonstrated that the IMF had earlier been wrong in arguing that the absence of domestic productive capacity would fuel inflation if the value of the rouble fell. In fact, there had been excess capacity, and this was now taken up to allow import substitution (especially in consumer goods and foodstuffs), with imports halving in the year after the crisis. Despite growth (see Table 8.1), Russian GDP in 2003 was still 30 per cent below what it had been in 1990. It was clear, as Joseph Stiglitz (chief economist at the World Bank 1997–2000) and others have argued, that the IMF's strategy of artificially maintaining the value of the rouble up to 1998 through loans had not only been mistaken but had saddled Russia with unnecessary debt.[6]

Putin took power at a time when the country was enjoying a mini boom, although poverty was widespread, wage arrears endemic, and the debt crisis permanent. The price of oil rose from its 1998 level of $11 to a peak of $35 in 2000, before falling back to $30 in 2001–03, leading to an enormous balance of trade surplus and a tripling of the country's foreign currency reserves. Energy plays a crucial role in Russia's economic life, with 20 per cent of government revenues coming from oil exports alone. The Organisation of Petroleum Exporting Countries (OPEC) tried to lure Russia into membership to allow it to regulate world oil prices, in particular to balance Iraq's possible departure.[7] The country no longer needed to borrow from the IMF and other bodies, and indeed was able to repay earlier loans as the government's external debt fell to below 40 per cent of GDP. With the economy flush with liquidity there was no longer such pressure to engage in barter, and wages and other social costs could be paid more or less on time. The government in 2003 even planned to reduce the overall tax burden on the economy by two per cent from 35 to 33 per cent of GDP, with the major saving to be made by cutting subsidies to agriculture.[8]

The 1999–2000 electoral cycle was remarkable for how little attention was devoted to the economic problems facing the country. There was some attempt to formulate policies, although debate over different strategies and alternatives was drowned out by the quasi-political manipulations of the regime. Despite the air of almost permanent crisis in Russian politics in the 1990s, considerable evolution had taken place not only in the development of a market economy, but also in the political acceptance of the fact that Russia really did not have a choice except to embrace the market. The only question, which was far from a trivial one, was what sort of market. This was reflected in the programmes advanced by the various electoral associations taking part in the elections, with no serious political actor (except Rogozin's Congress of Russian Communities, KRO) advocating a return to state planning or autarchy, although many proposed a greater role for the state and various levels of protectionism. With capital flight, concentration of ownership, poor corporate governance and widespread poverty, there were plenty of problems, but a fundamental change had taken place. The elections marked a turning point in Russian politics in that for the first time in a decade there appeared to be a near universal consensus in support of the development of capitalism, although some sought to add distinctively Russian features. Again, this was something that Putin could turn to his advantage.

A post-Washington consensus now began to emerge, what we may call the 'Moscow consensus'. The Washington consensus, the term coined by John

Williamson to describe the neo-liberal policies adopted by a number of Latin American states in the mid-1980s, focused on fiscal and monetary discipline, currency convertibility, price and trade liberalisation and the privatisation of state enterprises. These policies were imposed to varying degrees by Russia, India and other countries that had pursued socialist-inclined developmental strategies. Economies were opened up to international influences and domestic monopolies broken up and privatised. In the post-communist countries this was accompanied by falls in economic activity. The Moscow consensus is in some ways reminiscent of the original aims of the IMF as devised by John Maynard Keynes in 1944: 'the promotion and maintenance of high levels of employment and real income and the development of the productive resources of all members as primary objectives of economic policy'.[9] The neo-liberal Washington consensus instead focused on budget cuts, privatisation, deflation, structural adjustment and the like. The new consensus in Moscow sought to combine both the old and neo-liberal approaches, with continued engagement with international economic and financial organisations, regular debt repayments, the maintenance of macroeconomic stability by necessary fiscal measures, the end of threats to renationalise industry, and the gradual modification of protectionism. It no longer mattered how the country's great corporations had moved into private ownership as long as businesses were managed better. The old debate between 'shock therapy' and 'soft landing' gradualist approaches gave way to a recognition that the fundamental condition for economic development was a state strong enough to ensure the rule of law, property rights, transparency in economic transactions such as privatisation, the fostering of improved corporate governance, and the collection of adequate tax revenues to sustain normal functions. More had to be done, as Stanley Fischer put it, to 'enforce the rule of the game for a market economy', including strengthening tax systems, fiscal transparency, government accounting, the legal system and corporate governance.[10] Economic success is most unlikely in conditions of state failure, but the dangers of an over-bearing and intrusive state were equally recognised. The nostrums of the market fundamentalists of the earlier period were rejected in recognition of the fact that market failure is just as bad as state failure. Not everything can be left to Adam Smith's increasingly palsied 'invisible hand'; government has an important part to play in the economy.

Thus, even before Putin came to power the radical rejectionists of market-oriented reform had been marginalised. The Moscow consensus now stretched from the liberals through to the CPRF, whose economic programme for the parliamentary elections was framed by the well-known critic of Yeltsin's economic policies, Sergei Glazyev. The only serious organisations stepping beyond the bounds of this consensus were some nationalists (for example, KRO headed by Rogozin – eccentric in this as in most other things) and the radical left. The consensus broke down when it came to questions such as whether Russia should join the World Trade Organisation (WTO) immediately or after a long transition period, but the desirability of membership was agreed by most. This is a measure of the degree to which the 1990s had been a harsh learning experience for the Russian political elite; the great majority understood that any attempt to achieve quick fixes outside the constraints of the emerging consensus would have unpredictable and probably dire consequences. State reconstitution in the sphere of the economy meant establishing institutions strong enough to prevent state capture by countering the power of the oligarchs. The key, as Hedlund puts it, 'is not the performance indicators as such, but the institutional arrangments that determine performance'.[11] The main modifications of the Washington consensus focus on a more active social policy, a stronger state role in establishing a more friendly investment climate to achieve the recapitalisation of the economy, and less tolerance of official corruption. This was the programme that Putin was to pursue.

Economic performance under Putin

When Putin came to power the rudiments of a market system had been established, painfully and corruptly but nevertheless there. Putin had not personally been involved at the national level in the grimy process of capitalist transformation, above all privatisation, and thus could enter office with relatively clean hands. For Putin the transition was over, although he did not deny that much remained to be changed. The government, led by Kasyanov, did try to deal with some of the profound structural problems of the economy, but with great equivocation and a certain lack of urgency given the safety blanket of high oil prices.[12] Putin's early years were accompanied by extraordinarily favourable circumstances that provided a cushion for the economy. Above all, the price of oil remained high, bringing in enormous revenues and endowing Russia with a large trade surplus. Every dollar rise in the price of oil provides the Russian exchequer with one billion dollars in extra revenue. Russia's oil and gas industries account for 50 per cent of export revenues, 40 per cent of gross fixed investment, and through taxes provide 25 per cent of government revenues.[13] The economy was growing, inflation was down, investment was up, and there was trade and budget surplus (see Table 8.1).

Putin continued Yeltsin's policy of macroeconomic stabilisation, above all of the national currency. Some successes were evident, above all reflected in the fall in inflation (Table 8.1). Thus the thousand-fold price rises that had characterised the early phase of Russian capitalism in the early 1990s now gave way to relative price stability, although the still rather high inflation eroded the cheap rouble advantage. At the same time, indicators for investment growth began to improve, with the figures for 2000 and 2001 looking particularly good (see Table 8.1) when investment in fixed capital exceeded GDP growth. The figures for 2002, however, were more disappointing and reinforced the view that 2002 had been a year of lost opportunities. The benefits of the currency devaluation of 1998 had worn off, and it appeared that the government had not created the conditions for sustained growth. Rising real incomes once again sucked in imports; domestic production once again proved itself to be uncompetitive. Reform of the tax system also appeared to be half-hearted. The introduction of a 13 per cent flat rate on personal incomes had much improved tax collection rates, but while the tax on corporate profits had been reduced from 35 to 24 per cent, the abolition of allowances on investment meant a rise in the effective tax rate from 17 to 24 per cent.[14] With economic reform incomplete, the investment capacity of the economy stagnated, as did its ability to absorb investment.

The privatisation process was now rather more ordered, with the plan for privatisation in 2002 for example comprising 312 limited companies and 141 state enterprises. The biggest sale of all, that of Slavneft in late 2002, however, was accompanied by traditional claims of insider dealing and favouritism. The old director, Mikhail Gutseriev, had been ousted in May 2002 in a boardroom coup instigated by the prime minister Kasyanov, and replaced by a former Sibneft official Yury Sukhanov. Sibneft, under the leadership of the Kremlin 'family' insider and Kasyanov ally Roman Abramovich, then proceeded to buy up shares in alliance with the Tyumen Oil Company (TNK). The ugly scenes in May 2002, when the Slavneft offices in the centre of Moscow were seized by private security guards in an attempt to restore Gutseriev to power, were reminiscent of Yeltsin's 'wild East' days of the 1990s, especially when Kasyanov sent in the police to evict the intruders. In October Kasyanov hastily pushed through the privatisation of Slavneft, with all 75 per cent of the state's stake to be sold as a single block with a reserve price of $1.3 billion (later raised to $1.7 billion). In the days preceding the auction (set for 19 December) the competitors, Lukoil and Surgutneftegaz, were encouraged to withdraw their bids while the Chinese National Petroleum Company (CNPC) was barred on a technicality. Sibneft and TNK went on to win the auction as the sole joint bidders for $1.86 billion. The case recalled the insider dealings of the Yeltsin years, above all the 'loans for shares' scandals from 1995 when major companies were privatised for a song to those with an inside track to the Kremlin.

Under Putin budgets were adopted on time and were balanced. In late 1991 Russian foreign debt was $65.3 billion, but by 1997 had tripled to $110

Table 8.1 Economic indicators

Year	GDP change (%)	Inflation (%)	Investment growth (%)
1999	3.2	36.5	1.0
2000	10.0	20.2	17.2
2001	5.0	18.6	7.5
2002	4.3	14.0	2.5
2003	7.2	12.0	12.0

billion and rose further thereafter. Debt repayment peaked in 2003, when the country was due to pay $17 billion, but even here there were signs of improvement. Because of repayments this was considerably less than had been anticipated earlier. In 1998 debts amounted to 130 per cent of GDP, whereas by late 2002 they reached only 40 per cent of GDP and fell to some 35 per cent in 2003. In comparison, on average in the EU debts represent 60 per cent of GDP. Under Putin there was no default of the sort that had hit Russia in 1998. Now all debts were paid on time and the country's credit rating rose steadily. By late 2003, moreover, the currency reserves held in the Central Bank rose above $50 billion. Although Putin insisted that the country simply could not afford to compensate savers in full for the loss of their savings in the financial crash of 1989–92, the government did apply a rolling policy of repayments, with the ultimate aim of providing recompense in full. Acknowledgement of this problem and Putin's attempts to resolve it earned him considerable popular respect. The year 2003 had also been talked about as one in which Russia's crumbling infrastructure would finally collapse, but although under strain no wholesale cataclysm took place.

In June 2002 the United States officially declared that Russia was a market economy, in November the EU followed suit, while in October the country was removed from the blacklist of the Financial Action Task Force (FATF), a 29-nation agency established by the OECD in 1989 to fight against money laundering. The problem of capital flight continued, however, one that had begun in 1992. Although the flow under Putin decreased, it still represented a significant drain on resources available for investment. At least $45–50 billion left the country annually between 1992–98, with the figure according to the Central Bank falling to $10 billion in 2002, $6 billion less than in 2001 and $14 billion less than in 2000. Not all of this came from criminal activities, with much scared away by high taxation and an insecure investment climate. According to some estimates about 30 per cent of the money illegally expatriated in 1999–2001 returned, and to encourage the process the government considered the reduction of taxes from the usual 13 per cent to an 'amnesty rate' of 5 per cent. Investment however remained far below what was required to allow growth rates to rise above the pedestrian.

Slow progress was made in reform of the energy, transport, banking and utility sectors. Attempts to break up Gazprom into separate production and distribution companies moved extremely slowly. Although Putin was able to change the leadership of the company, the new CEO, Alexei Miller, sought to ensure that the integrated system remained intact. As for the giant electricity company, UES (United Energy Systems) with the architect of privatisation Chubais at its head, reform plans engendered enormous controversy. Chubais sought to break up the monopoly horizontally into generating companies and a state-controlled distribution system, whereas his critics, notably Putin's economic advisor, Andrei Illarionov, sought the vertical division of the company into a number of regionally integrated production and distribution companies. The plan adopted in early 2003 envisaged the creation of a number of competing generating companies, with prices to industrial companies to be deregulated and, ultimately, domestic prices too. The 30 big thermal power generating plants and 72 local generating and power distribution companies were intended to be consolidated into ten large 'wholesale' power generation companies, 30 regional power generation companies, seven distribution companies, and a network of regional suppliers.[15] The various electricity-consuming oligarchs sought to win control of parts of the company to provide cheap electricity for their aluminium smelting and other activities. An amendment to the plan forbids an operator of generating plants acquiring a market share of more than 40 per cent in any region, a measure intended to prevent a factory or region becoming hostage to a local power monopoly. The state was to retain control over the national transmission grid, and the nuclear and hydroelectric power stations that account for a third of Russia's generating capacity. The plan was to come into effect by 2005–06. Chubais himself exercised enormous political leverage at the head of such a strategically central company.

Putin's economic policy sought to apply prudent fiscal policies, to make some amends to the population for earlier losses, to balance the budget, to repay all foreign debts on time while reducing the capital, to build up reserves, and in general to avoid making economic promises that could not be honoured. The early successes of the economy were under-pinned by confidence that under Putin there would be no grand redistribution of property, and therefore owners could now turn to running their businesses for long-run profitability rather than short-term asset-stripping. Despite enormous pressure Putin refused to sponsor particular industries, the selective industrial support policy that has proven to be a failure in many other countries, and instead concentrated on providing an improved general business environment. However, the lag of investment rates behind GDP growth suggested that entrenched problems were not being tackled. There was still far too much government regulation and no effective banking system. The economy was also in danger of being infected with the 'Dutch disease', when energy exports bring in large revenues that raise the value of the currency, pricing domestic goods out of export markets and sucking in imports.

Putin sought to avoid economic populism (in particular in the run-up to the 2003 Duma elections) and tried to restrain the Duma from adopting policies that would undermine the credibility of the country's return to fiscal rectitude. All this, however, concerned the macroeconomic situation. People live, however, in their own micro worlds, and here things for the majority of the population were far from easy. Standards of living for those outside the global cities of Moscow and St Petersburg and some others continued to stagnate. According to some estimates the number of Russians below the poverty line after the 1998 crash was as high as 64 million, but by early 2002 this had fallen to around 35 million and, as we have seen, fell thereafter. This still left about a quarter of the population in poverty. Wage arrears continued in some sectors as companies sought to become more competitive by diverting resources from their wage fund. The World Bank estimated that some 50 per cent of the economy remained in the shadows, trapped between the state and the mafia.

Although Putin sought to encourage the development of small and medium-sized enterprises (SMEs), and had simplified the registration procedures to encourage more start-ups, the sheer weight of the bureaucracy and lack of developed financial services meant that in the first three years of his presidency the numbers employed in SMEs actually fell by some four million. Official figures suggest that SMEs account for only 10 to 15 per cent of Russian GDP compared to the 50 per cent that is typical for more developed transition economies. Russia had fewer than a million SMEs, whereas Poland had four times as many with only a quarter of the population. The crushing weight of start-up registration formalities and for numerous licences and permits, the burden of arbitrary fire and health inspections, and the ever-present fear of the mafia stifled the development of this sphere.

The economic policies of Putin's first term were thus characterised by contradictory processes, and the government under Kasyanov failed to provide adequate economic leadership. The ideology of leaving everything to the market, while probably preferable to old-fashioned state interventionism, was ultimately inadequate. What was required was a robust set of government policies that would stimulate investment, above all in the small and medium business sector. Whether this required a massive cutback in government spending from the current 35 per cent of GDP to around 12 per cent, as advocated by Illarionov, was more controversial. What certainly did not help was the simple exhortation from above, like a Communist Party General Secretary in the old days, that growth rates had to rise from the 4 per cent predicted by the government to 5 to 6 per cent a year, as Putin did in his 2002 state-of-the-nation speech, or demand a doubling of GDP within a decade, as demanded in his speech to the federal assembly the following year. Russian capitalism had arrived, but it was of a peculiar sort.

Models of capitalism – oligarchical democracy?

Putin came to power committed to the liberal development of the Russian economy. He enacted a range of pro-business measures, including a cut in the tax rate on corporate profits from 35 to 24 per cent, a reduction in the compulsory repatriation of export earnings from 75 to 50 per cent and cut the number of business activities requiring government licences from over five hundred to one hundred. However, the system that had emerged out of the conversion of the centralised Soviet economy and the wild privatisation of the 1990s was far from being a classical capitalist economy. The economy was dominated by powerful economic actors, with influential 'oligarchs' at their head.[16] In 1996 the oligarchs had played a crucial role in re-electing Yeltsin, and Berezovsky had bragged about the power of the *'semibankirshchina'* (rule of the seven banks) and their ownership of half of the Russian economy. A study in 2002 found that the eight largest conglomerates controlled 85 per cent of the shares in the country's top 64 firms.[17] Under Yeltsin the oligarchs had become part of the power system, and although Putin tried to maintain 'equidistance' from them, he could not ignore them.[18] The classic question was posed: who rules Russia?[19]

The financial-industrial conglomerates (FICs)

In the 1990s the term 'financial-industrial group' (FIG) had been used to describe two things: officially registered combines, usually based on traditional enterprises; and unregistered conglomerates of banks and enterprises. The former had been sponsored in particular by the deputy prime minister Oleg Soskovets as a model of state-sponsored economic development, but in that predatory and pathologically rent-seeking era they had not been able to provide a coherent model for either economic development or rational state-economy relations, and the idea had fallen out of favour. Instead of state-directed integration, powerful economic players emerged out of the fires of Russia's headlong rush to the market. The sealed bid auctions of 1995 and the subsequent investment auctions signalled the rise of these groups. There is no single term used to describe them. Yakov Pappe, for example, uses the term 'industrial business-groups' (IBGs),[20] while Dynkin and Sokolov talk of 'integrated business-groups' (also IBGs).[21] We shall use the term 'financial-industrial conglomerates' (FICs), used by Sergei Kolmakov and others,[22] as a way of stressing the concentration of capital that they represented while emphasising the ramshackle nature of many of these emergent corporations.

Dynkin and Sokolov note that as a result of historical circumstances there are only two forces capable of acting as agents of modernisation in Russia: the state and big business.[23] The role of the state in industrialisation both in the Tsarist and Soviet periods had been exceptionally great: was the baton now to be passed to big business? Only what they call IBGs enjoyed trained and qualified staff, managerial skills, leading technologies and financial resources. In the absence of an effective banking system and capital markets, FICs drew on internal sources of finance or borrowing on bond markets. They exclude from their analysis companies in which the state has a large stake since they were often forced to act in non market-oriented ways – the natural monopolies like Gazprom and UES in particular were unable to charge market rates for their products and were forced on occasion to act as the source of indirect subsidy for whole economic sectors and communities. With domestic prices fixed by the state, the energy companies sought to increase exports where they could charge market rates – but only after they had supplied the domestic market with government-set quotas. At the same time, the 1,600 defence industry enterprises represented an enormous opportunity, since they remained research-intensive and focused on exports (since there was little money for domestic procurement); in 2002 they exported a record $4.5 billion worth of arms. The defence industries were also a threat, since many required extensive modernisation and in some towns were the only industry. The appointment of Major-General Alexander Burutin to be Putin's adviser on the defence industry and arms procurement in April 2003 was a sign of the need to devise a more coherent policy in this area, as was the appointment of the electronics expert Boris Alyoshin, to the post of deputy prime minister in charge of the defence industry and arms exports a month later.

The top eight independent FICs in 2002 employed 1.76 per cent of Russia's workforce of 64.3 million, yet provided a quarter of the country's exports and a third of the country's tax revenues.[24] Table 8.2 lists the main non-state national FICs. Each of these companies had a core enterprise (typically extractive or processing) around which a constellation of businesses turned, including a bank, insurance company, media holding, distribution networks and transport, with a range of support services including hospitals, security, recreation services and even agricultural enterprises. Lukoil's holdings even included the Tchaikovsky Symphony Orchestra. The FICs thus mimicked the typically Soviet vertically-integrated holding, since external supplies could never be guaranteed. Only Sistema in Moscow (part of Luzhkov's fiefdom) was not based on raw materials but on 'post-modern' science and high-tech industries (see Table 8.3). These ramshackle organisations had been formed as part of an adaptive process to the uncertainty and hazards of the transition to the market, but now took on a stable character. Self-sufficiency is characteristic of enterprises in the early stages of extensive capitalist development, as with American companies in the early decades of the twentieth century (the Ford Motor Company for example had its own rail system and farms, carpentry workshops and newspaper), Western European companies in the 1950s, Japanese *keiretsu* in the 1950s and 1960s, and the South Korean *chaebols* up to the present time.

A distinctive feature of the Russian system is the under-developed nature of the banking system and financial mediation services (insurance companies, pension management, investment and venture capital agencies), all of which made entry into the market particularly difficult for new companies and expansion hard for established businesses. Russian banks are notoriously under-capitalised, with only Sberbank entering the *Financial Times'* 2001 list of top 13 banks in Eastern Europe, compared to seven in Poland. Russian banks simply do not have adequate resources to finance business development, to fund new entrepreneurs or to provide the specialist skills to provide complex financial services for business and product development.[25] In these conditions, only FICs could accumulate resources for development and investment not only in their own businesses but also through acquisitions. Under-investment in the Russian economy in the 1990s would cast a long shadow over the potential for Russian economic development, a historic deficit that was unlikely to be made up by foreign direct investment (FDI) (typically running at under $4 billion annually, less than Portugal attracted). The main investor in the Russian economy therefore could only be the FICs, possibly in partnership with Western companies. However, FDI was deterred

Table 8.2 Russia's leading financial-industrial conglomerates (FICs)

IBG	Output (bn roubles)	Number of staff (annual average, 000s)	Volume of export (bn $)	Volume of investment (bn roubles)
Lukoil	406	191	6	22
Yukos	252	135	5	13
Interros (Norilsk Nickel)	184	274	4	12
Surgutneftegaz	171	79	2	33
Alfa-group-TNK–'Renova'	164	103	5	11
Siberian Aluminium– Russian Aluminium– Sibneft	155	220	4	2
AFK Sistema	147	144	N/A	N/A
Severstal'	79	105	1	2

Source: A. Dynkin and A. Sokolov, 'Integrirovannye biznes-gruppy v rossiiskom ekonomike', *Voprosy ekonomiki*, No. 4, 2002, p. 80.

Table 8.3 Russia's oligarchs

Name of oligarch	Name of business	Main activities of the business
Abramovich, Roman	Former head of Sibneft, governor of Chukotka	Energy, politics
Alekperov, Vagit	Lukoil head	Energy
Aven, Petr	Alfa Bank head	Banking
Berezovsky, Boris	AvtoVaz, Sibneft	Car dealership, energy
Bogdanov, Vladimir	Surgutneftegaz	Energy
Chubais, Anatoly	United Energy Systems (UES)	Electricity monopoly
Deripaska, Oleg	Russian Aluminium	Non-ferrous metals
Fridman, Mikhail	Alfa-Group head	Energy and metals
Gusinsky, Vladimir	Most-group	Media, banking
Khodorkovsky, Mikhail	Yukos-TNK head	Oil, banking, light industry
Mamut, Alexander	MDM Bank, former head	Banking
Mordashev, Alexei	Severstal	Ferrous metals
Nevzlin, Leonid	Yukos	Energy
Potanin, Vladimir	Interros	Metals
Prokhorov, Mikhail	Norilsk Nickel	Metals
Shvidler, Yevgeny	Sibneft	Energy
Vainstok, Semyon	Transneft head	State pipeline monopoly
Vekselberg, Viktor	TNK	Energy
Yevtushenkov, Vladimir	Sistema head	Communications, finance and services

by a sad litany of minority shareholders losing their assets. A $480 million deal whereby BP bought 10 per cent of the shares in Potanin's Sidanko in November 1997 turned very sour when Mikhail Fridman's rival TNK took over one of Sidanko's main producing subsidiaries, while at the same time Sidanko was restructured, further reducing the value of the minority stake. After a long struggle BP's assets were returned in 2001. BP retained a long-term commitment to Russia and returned to the fray. The $6.75 billion deal struck in February 2003 between Lord Browne of BP Amoco and Fridman's TNK was perhaps a harbinger of things to come. Together they established Russia's third largest oil company, TNK-BP, but if the global assets of the two companies are taken together then this was the world's largest, producing 2.57 million barrels per day and with the world's second largest reserves. BP had at last found a new source to replace its ageing fields in Alaska and the North Sea, while TNK, whose corporate governance had greatly improved, was given the seal of Western approval. A spate of mergers in 2003 saw Yukos and Sibneft create a company with a combined market capitalisation of $35 billion – from companies that had been privatised by Mikhail Khodorkovsky and Berezovsky eight years earlier for merely $259 million. The new company had the world's largest reserves of oil and was fourth in production terms.[26] Although the government may well have had a hand in creating the company (to avoid it falling into foreign ownership), the enormous power of the new company will undoubtedly allow it to influence government policy.[27]

The challenge facing the post-communist world is very different to that of developing countries. Instead of the need to build the infrastructure of an industrial society, the aim is to shift towards market forms of operation and to achieve the most efficient use of resources. In Russia's case the legacy of the Soviet era was huge concentration and large plants, and this element of 'path dependency' to a degree predetermined the concentrated structure of Russian business. The FICs were the main elements of the economy that could withstand international competition, and the majority were in favour of entry into the WTO. For most large energy producers, domestic sales were considered little more than a 'charitable contribution', since export prices were considerably higher.[28] At the same time, as the most dynamic and competitive elements of the economy (as outlined in Putin's Candidate dissertation), the state sought to work in partnership with these companies to modernise the economy. The FICs were to act as the locomotives pulling the Russian economy towards modernity. They would have to adapt in response to changes in the world economy and probably needed to focus on core business interests and divest themselves of non-commercial activities. The FICs would also have to conform more to the accounting and other standards of corporate behaviour of the best corporations in the West. This would require the active partnership of the state to ensure property rights and contract, a stable and equitable tax regime, a benign investment climate, the develop-ment of the banking system, less predatory bankruptcy laws and incentives for technological innovation. Other scenarios were also possible, notably destructive predatory rivalries and the break-up of these businesses. Putin certainly sought to realise the first scenario by safeguarding property rights and trying to create a secure climate for investment at home and abroad. As one businessman put it, 'Russian industry is now able to restructure: the age of stealing is over; the age of arrogance is over; the age of instability is over.'[29]

Regional aspects

The FICs gradually extended the scope of regional coverage and penetration. If in 1993 Lukoil operated in 5 regions, by 2000 it was active in 21; over the same period Interros's coverage rose from 1 to 23, and Alfa-group from 2 to 37 regions; while the primordially Moscow-centric Sistema by 2001 operated in 42 regions.[30] While political elites were concerned to diversify the main economic players in their region, they also tended to oppose the intrusion of economic interests that they could not control; that is, whose provenance was not from the region itself.[31] The role of a company like Tatneft in Tatarstan reproduced on a smaller scale that of the FICs on the national scene.

Following the 1998 crisis big business had actively sought to extend their regional influence, complicating the established cosy relationships between governors and regional businesses. Nazdratenko's regime in Primorsky *krai* had been a classic case of a regional political and business elite joining together to exclude outsiders for mutual benefit, leading to the establishment of a corrupt, protectionist and authoritarian system in which the consumers suffered.[32] Putin had forced Nazdratenko to resign, and his successor, Sergei Darkin, opened the region up to Moscow business interests. The *polpredy* also acted against attempts to reassert regional autarchical development models. Nevertheless, they could do little to alter the extraordinary, and rising, level of concentration of economic power in the regions. The average four-firm concentration ratio (the total of the market share of the four top companies) is about 95 per cent.[33] Newcomers found it extremely difficult to break into these markets.[34] A type of corporate regionalism emerged.

Under Putin the FIC's strengthened their hold on the regions, particularly the ones where they had investments and holdings.[35] Gubernatorial elections sometimes became open contests for power between competing oligarchical groups, notably in the Krasnoyarsk election of 22 September 2002 to replace Alexander Lebed, after the latter's death on 28 April 2002. Here Vladimir Potanin's Interros supported the former director of its Norilsk Nickel plant and former governor of Taimyr Autonomous Okrug, Alexander Khloponin, who had begun his career as a financier in Moscow. They were pitted against Alexander Uss, the speaker of the regional legislature supported by Russian Aluminium and the 'family'. The official political parties were hardly to be seen. Khloponin was declared the winner, following the Kremlin's intervention, after desperate attempts by the Uss camp to have the election declared invalid. Komi Republic appeared to have become a satrapy of Lukoil, and while its legislature was dominated by business interests.[36] The election of Roman Abramovich as governor of Chukotka autonomous *okrug* rendered the dominance of Sibneft complete there, complementing its 'ownership' of Omsk. Big business was now certainly making its presence felt at the regional level.

Capitalism with a corporatist face

The oligarchical capitalism that the FICs represented enjoyed its heyday in 1996, following Yeltsin's re-election as president with their help, up to the partial default of August 1998. The FICs under Yeltsin at this time enjoyed direct access to political power, with some of the more notorious oligarchs either joining the government directly (such as Potanin in 1996–97) or enjoying access to the corridors of power, like Berezovsky. However, the appointment of Primakov as prime minister in September 1998 and the pre-electoral divisions within the elite as the end of the Yeltsin era approached placed them on the defensive. Some FICs supported the opposition that appeared set to take power, led above all by Luzhkov and his Fatherland (*Otechestvo*) organisation, which in August 1999 joined forces with the more regionally-based All-Russia (*Vsya Rossiya*) association. It was clear that the Yeltsin system was collapsing, and with it the 'family' regime system that connected the political and business worlds. While some FICs (for example, Lukoil) adopted a cautious wait and see attitude, those most closely associated with the family, such as the Berezovsky empire, Sibneft, Siberian Aluminium, as well as Chubais's electricity giant UES had most to fear from the end of the regime and thus were the most active in devising a 'succession' strategy. The fierceness of the parliamentary electoral campaign (which was also a struggle of oligarchical groupings) from August to December 1999 reflected the high stakes involved. The FICs were by no means the puppet masters behind the political actors, yet their financial support of political associations and individuals was a fundamental element of the political process at this time.[37] In a sense, just as the Kremlin itself acted as a vast pseudo-party, so the oligarchical corporations acted as party substitutes lower down the political hierarchy.

From the early 1990s big business had to a degree usurped the functions of the state, and indeed often rendered politicians little more than their clients, a feature that remains in certain regions, especially those based on extractive industries. This phase then gave way to that of oligarchical capitalism, based on some powerful personalities who tended to see their own businesses as little more than a source of cash flow and whose relationship with the state was neither institutionalised nor structured. The arrival of liberals like Nemtsov and Kirienko into the government in the spring of 1997 signalled an attempt to limit the irresponsibility of the oligarchs and to reform the anarcho-capitalist power system, a programme accelerated spontaneously by the financial crisis of 1998. The outcome, according to Dynkin and

Sokolov, was to reveal that 'the oligarchy was not so much a genuine political force as a phantom of mass consciousness'.[38] That may well be the case, but the combination of FICs and the state bureaucracy was certainly very real. A significant example of this oligarchy-state alliance, within the framework of Putin's new rules of the game, was the involvement of Oleg Deripaska's Russian Aluminium company in the purchase and subsequent restructuring of the Gorky Automotive Works (GAZ). In a globalising world the power of states is reckoned to be eroding while that of transnational corporations is growing, but in Russia under Putin a distinctive system appeared to be emerging where the FICs themselves provided the state with resources for its industrial policy, and in general acted as substitute sinews of the state. The interests of big business and the state did not always coincide, of course, and the peculiar development of the state and Russian capitalism were characterised by numerous political contradictions.

Whether the dominance of these groups was tantamount to corporatism has been the subject of considerable debate.[39] Corporatism refers to a situation where the state grants certain groups a monopoly on representation in return for loyalty and occasional rights over choosing their leaders, with the group concerned then exercising exclusionary rights over demand articulation. We have seen that Putin sought to practice a policy of 'equidistance' from the oligarchs, with some of them (notably Berezovsky and Gusinsky) largely removed from the Russian political arena by going into exile. Others, however, appeared to have become a new type of 'transmission belt' for Kremlin policies. They were allowed to enjoy what they had gained in the heady 1990s as long as they invested in the 'real' economy, such as motor manufacturing (as in the example of GAZ, above), or supported political movements and actions to the Kremlin's liking. Representatives of big business were also important in framing political strategies, particularly in the sphere of industrial policy. Arkady Volsky, the president of the Russian Union of Industrialists and Entrepreneurs (RUIE), was one of the great survivors in Russian politics, having reinvented himself several times since coming to prominence during Andropov's brief leadership from November 1982 to February 1984 and had led the RUIE since 1991. The RUIE itself had evolved considerably. From being a mouthpiece of the 'red directors', addicted to state subsidies and dependent on protectionism, the RUIE had become one of the most coherent and well-organised interest groups. On Putin's accession the ranks of the RUIE were swelled by the new tycoons, oligarchs and other entrepreneurs eager to come under the protection of its corporatist umbrella. Putin's corporatist instincts did not neglect the other side of the equation either, and he met regularly with the leader (Mikhail Shmakov) of the federal trade union organisation, the Federation of Independent Trade Unions of Russia.[40]

Under Putin a new model of business–state relations began to emerge, characterised above all by greater institutionalisation. The role of business associations was greatly increased, particularly that of the RUIE for big business. Putin met regularly with them as he shifted towards the greater institutionalisation of governmental practices. Medium business was represented by Delovaya Rossiya, while small business was served by the Organisation of Entrepreneurs' Organisations of Russia (Ob'edinenie pred-prinimatel'skikh organizatsii Rossii, OPORA). The influence of the RF Chamber of Commerce (Torgovo-promyshlennoi palaty RF) greatly increased with Primakov's appointment as its head in 2001. The old informal relations now gave way to the creation of a new *system* of relations that allowed a certain depoliticisation of state-economy relations and reduced the level of conflicts within the business world itself. This did not however mean that the FICs had withdrawn from politics, and neither did it signal that the old model of oligarchy/bureaucracy had disappeared.

The Russian economy remained fundamentally bureaucratised. This is not just a question of the 10,000-odd state enterprises (*gosudarstvennykh uni-tarnykh predpriyatii*, GUPs, including those in the defence sector) that oper-ated less by the laws of the free market than for corporatist gain, but of the suffocating power of the economic bureaucracy, imbued with a Soviet spirit, that instinctively tried to stifle any non-state economic initiative in a sea of regulation. Under Putin the economic bureaucracy was now joined by various *siloviki* who sought to get their share in the endless churning of the national product by the state. Although three-quarters of the Russian economy had been privatised, bureaucratic pressure in direct or indirect forms (including outright illegal ones) meant that the state still effectively managed at least three-quarters of economic life. It is for this reason that Putin's economic adviser, Illarionov, insisted, as noted, that economic growth could only be increased if state expenditure was sharply reduced. According to him, in 2000–02 expenditure (the combined federal and regional budgets plus off-budget funds) rose by 28 per cent while GDP growth was only 19 per cent. He argued that state expenditure as a propor-tion of GDP rose from 33.8 to 36.5 per cent, and could rise to 39 per cent in 2003.[41] The heavily statised economy was not only the ideal breeding ground for corruption and stagnation, but the struggle of economic clans and inter-ests also subverted democracy.

Oligarchical capitalism and democracy

The 1998 financial crisis had much reduced the ability of FICs to intervene effectively in party politics.[42] The exception to this was Berezovsky's role in the 1999 parliamentary elections, but here he acted less as a representative of big business than as an insider oligarch and member of the 'family'.[43] Gusin-sky also was active in this electoral cycle, but his involvement appears to have been as much an indication of weakness as of strength, seeking to use media leverage on state power to have his debts (to Gazprom and others) written off. In general, structural factors had already weakened the predominance of the oligarchical system of power even before Putin came to power and thus, in this as in other spheres, luck and circumstances were on his side. Once in power Putin moved to re-assert central authority over enterprises in which the state had a large stake. As noted, the Kremlin forced out Rem Vyakhirev from the head of Gazprom, and replaced him with Alexei Miller, a younger government professional.

Big business groups play an important role in party politics. Volsky, for example, had been a member of the central council of the Fatherland party. Top figures of FICs were heavily represented in leading positions in political parties, above all in Our Home is Russia (NDR) and Fatherland – All Russia (OVR). Our Home is Russia had a particularly close relationship with Gazprom. The leader of the party, Chernomyrdin, had been a former head of the gas industry and in 1992 the energy minister before he became prime minister in December of that year. On leaving the premiership in April 1998 he became chairman of the Council of Directors of Gazprom. As OVR looked set to replace NDR as the 'party of power', Gazprom in 1999 delegated one of its vice-presidents, P. Rodionov to a central position in its leadership. Lukoil, a company that preferred to keep out of the political limelight, also sent one of its vice-presidents to OVR. Gazprom, as we have seen, played an important part in the transformation of NTV in 2000, effectively acting as a surrogate for the presidency. The other great natural monopoly, Chubais's UES, was open about its links with SPS. Chubais chaired the SPS founding congress in May 2001 and became one of the party's vice-chairmen and top 3 candidates in the 2003 Duma elections.

Clearly these and other links were more than symbolic and provided the main source of private funding for parties and presidential candidates. This had been particularly strong after 1995, but following the 1998 financial crisis contributions had been drastically reduced, leading to major financial problems for all parties except Unity in the 1999 Duma elections. Gazprom had been the main banker of Our Home is Russia, and no doubt provided generous support for Unity and later United Russia, a group that was also funded by Lukoil, Sibneft and Russian Aluminium. Fatherland had been financed by Moscow financial groups beholden to Luzhkov, while All Russia and the Russia's Regions group of deputies were supported by Lukoil, Interros and the regional oil companies Tatneft and Bashneft. The opposition liberal party Yabloko had been supported by Gusinsky's Most group from its earliest days in 1993, not only with funds but with favourable coverage and access to NTV. Later Yabloko's main sponsor became Yukos, headed by Khodorkovsky (which also supported SPS and the CPRF). The fact that in April 2003 Khodorkovsky made his funding open was something new, and was enthusiastically greeted by Alexander Veshnyakov, the head of the Central Election Commission, as showing 'civilized rules of funding are beginning to be adopted'.[44] In 2003 Yukos increased its support for Yabloko 20-fold, providing them with up to one million Euros a month in the run-up to the December 2003 elections. The Kremlin had clearly given the go-ahead, wanting to ensure Yabloko's presence in the Fourth Duma.

Khodorkovsky did not lack political ambitions of his own, and was sometimes spoken of as a future president after 2008.

The other main liberal grouping, the Union of Right Forces (SPS), was financed by Yukos, Alfa-TNK and Chubais's UES, and in general the party was tainted by its perhaps excessively close oligarchical connections. On the left, the CPRF and the Agrarian Party had been funded by SBS Agro-Bank, through which the government's agricultural subsidies had been channelled, until the collapse of the bank as a result of the 1998 financial crisis. The CPRF was probably also funded by various branches of the military-industrial complex and the engineering industry, in particular Rosagropromstroi headed by the 'red director' Victor Vidamov, who since 1998 has had a seat on the CPRF's presidium. Under Putin some of the main corporations such as Gazprom, Lukoil, Interros and Yukos also supported the CPRF in an attempt to moderate its behaviour, and above all to ensure the victory of candidates sympathetic to their interests in the regions. Apart from funding parties, some of the giant state monopolies such as Gazprom, UES and the railway ministry have been very active in supporting candidates in single-mandate constituencies. In the 1999 elections Gazprom supported some 130 candidates and provided them with specialist electoral advice from one of the leading political consultancy firms, Niccolo-M.[45] Putin's reform of the electoral system stipulates that at least half of the seats in regional legislatures have to be contested by party lists (with only national parties allowed) and the other half by individuals in single-member constituencies, a measure intended to reduce not only the influence of regional barons but also that of oligarchs as well.

The question remains as to why Russian business has played such an active part in funding political life. Clearly, some businesses, especially those in which the state had a large stake (Gazprom, UES) acted as financial surrogates to advance the Kremlin's 'parties of power' and the election of presidents, and this in turn was seen as a way of protecting their gains and interests. Given the close relationship between business and the state under Yeltsin, contributions were a way of opening channels directly into the decision-making process. In addition, the weakness of institutionalised and open forms of lobbying means that indirect and often nefarious forms predominate. Another facet of this is that business lobbies on occasion dispensed with the intermediary services of parties altogether and set up their own factions in parliament. The best-known case of this is the establishment of the seventy-strong *Energiya* Duma faction in 2000.[46] This trend was reinforced by the attempts of many parties, notably Yabloko and the CPRF, to keep their sponsors at arms length, while the strong and eccentric leadership of Zhirinovsky over the LDPR meant that no oligarchical group was able to dictate terms to his party.

Putin as we have seen insisted on the 'equidistant' policy concerning business interests, but he was not interested in a mass revision of the anarchic privatisation exercise of the 1990s. However, he did seek to have some of the property, worth about \$15 to \$20 billion, stolen by Gazprom insiders restored to the company. The struggle for control over the state-owned Slavneft in early 2002, however, showed that politics had not entirely left the sphere of business, but in certain respects this was perhaps the last of the old-style oligarchical struggles where ownership issues were resolved in behind-the-scenes struggles in the corridors of power.[47] On Putin's accession many spoke in favour of some sort of 'controlled democracy' to accompany economic development based on giant corporations, like the *chaebols* in South Korea or the *keiretsu* earlier in Japan. Andrei Piontovsky notes that those who argue in favour of some sort of 'controlled democracy' to accompany economic development based on giant corporations, like the *chaebols*, were once again imposing on Russia an already anachronistic model, one that would be inappropriate for a post-industrial society.[48] What remains indisputable is that big business interests remain central players in the Russian political scene, sponsoring parties and acting directly to influence political outcomes. In this context Putin's attempt to establish a rather more robust national party system can be interpreted as part of a strategy to establish a countervailing power to the oligarchs, one more institutionalised and with independent political resources.

State, economy and society

Do Putin's policies in the economic sphere add up to much more than a shift towards 'a more pro-state, socially oriented model of mutant capitalism'.[49] The shape of Putin's economic programme emerged only gradually, suggesting great difficulties in combining what might appear at first sight to be its contradictory commitment to greater liberalisation and increased state oversight. Was the state to remain a central player *in* the economy, or would it restrict itself to ensuring a benign economic and regulatory framework *over* the economy? On a visit to Ivanovo on 7 March 2000 Putin called for greater economic freedom, arguing that 'The higher the degree of freedom of economic entities, the higher the development of the state.'[50] He suggested that the state should lower interest rates to make it easier for enterprises to borrow, and he insisted that the state would protect domestic producers. On many occasions Putin condemned the prevalence of bureaucracy and insisted that 'Administrative bodies should be transparent, clear, comprehensible and employ technology. We should do everything to rid ourselves of superfluous bureaucracy in the economy.'[51]

Programmes and reality

The economic programme outlined by German Gref on 28 June 2000 was permeated by a liberal spirit and openness to the world economy. The aim was to establish the conditions for stable economic growth to restore Russia to the ranks of the world's major industrialised nations. How this could be achieved remained unclear. The plan firmly sought Russia's admission into the WTO. The attempt to protect domestic producers by high import tariffs was recognised to be pernicious, encouraging smuggling, protecting inefficient domestic producers and inhibiting the technological modernisation of Russian industry. The tax system was to be overhauled, changing the basis of the division of tax revenues between the centre and the regions. As we saw in Chapter 6, budgetary revenues were now centralised, with a far higher proportion of VAT and other revenues going to the centre, a move supported by the majority of governors who sought more generous subsidies while of course opposed by donor regions.[52] At the same time, ideas were advanced for reducing budget expenditures. In the year 2000 state spending commitments amounted to around 60 per cent of GDP, while commitments actually fulfilled was far lower. Gref's plan sought to reduce fulfilled commitments to around 32.5 per cent of GDP, most of which was to be at the expense of regional budgets and social spending.[53] In the social sphere resources were to be more targeted on need, with benefits cut except only to those families with incomes under the living minimum. For the others, private healthcare and education was to be introduced.

Although Russia had seen many economic programmes since independence, all had been implemented half-heartedly and often pursued incompatible goals at the same time. The draft economic programme prepared by Gref was different for several reasons: it was coherent, taking a holistic approach to Russia's economic problems and suggesting an integrated solution. However, the government under Kasyanov put forward its own plans, and although elements of Gref's plan were implemented, overall coherence was lost. Although the position of liberal pro-market economists in Putin's government was strong, they were not agreed among themselves about the optimal economic strategy.

The debate over WTO membership divided the Russian business community. Putin was unambiguously of the view that only through membership could Russian industry be modernised, yet certain sectors stood to lose. WTO entry could make it harder for the government to take into account the specific needs of the regions, possibly leading to the closure of plants and greater unemployment. Membership would also force energy price rises for residential and industrial consumers. Cheap energy, reflecting Russia's abundant resources, was a way of compensating for low wages and standards of living, and thus WTO membership could exacerbate social tensions. In the industrial sphere, cheap energy acted as a subsidy to other industries and allowed Russian goods to maintain a competitive edge. WTO membership would force manufacturing quality to rise if these goods were to find international markets, and even the domestic market would become more competitive as foreign goods gained greater access. WTO membership would affect certain sectors particularly hard, like the aluminium producers enjoying cheap electricity from the massive hydroelectric schemes in Irkutsk *oblast* (Bratsk). However, even within sectors there were divisions, as in the motor industry. Car manufacturing represents 9 per cent of national industrial output and employs 10 per cent of the working population. Some companies feared the influx of foreign competitors, whereas others argued that Russia's bad roads and severe climatic conditions would allow the robust domestic product to keep its market share. The cheapness of the cars, above all Ladas produced by the giant AvtoVAZ works in Togliatti, would secure them a substantial market share come what may. As noted, oil and natural gas companies favoured WTO entry since it would open up Western markets for them, as it would for the timber industry, occupying fifth place in the country's GDP. Timber processing was highly concentrated with 10 plants accounting for 85 per cent of output. The industry was ripe for the predatory attack of FICs, and the state stood by helplessly as the oligarchs (such as Deripaska's Siberian Aluminium) sought to bring some of the major plants under its control. As Yulia Latynina noted, only within the framework of 'vertically integrated fiefdoms' would businessmen be protected from the attacks of other oligarchs.[54] It was assumed that WTO membership would force Russian business to become more transparent and prevent certain companies from enjoying an 'exclusive' relationship with the state – and as a result enjoying preferential tax breaks and other privileges that would be illegal under WTO rules and would render Russia liable to large fines. Putin pushed ahead with WTO membership against the advice of some of the oligarchs, illustrating the increasing autonomy that the state enjoyed during his presidency, but at the same time his ambitious entry date of 2003 proved unfeasible and only after the elections would it come back to the top of the agenda. The WTO itself was wracked by disputes over farm trade and pharmaceuticals, and many in Russia felt that it would be best to stay on the sidelines.

The fundamental problem facing the Putin government was that real relations in the law and economy in the 1990s had developed in parallel with the formal development of institutions, the bi-legalism that we noted in Chapter 4. For the legal scholar Vladimir Pastukhov, for example, the problem was not so much that Russian legislation was violated but that it did not work, and hence legal arbitrariness and corruption as such were not adequate categories through which Russian conditions could be analysed. As Skyner puts the argument, 'Russian laws exist, but they do not regulate real relations of subjects of the law, one of the main reasons for this situation being that real relations between subjects of law in Russia are established in a dimension that is parallel to the one at which formal legal regulation is aimed.' These are not so much Western-style 'grey zones' formed in parallel with state administration and in opposition to it, but are established within the machinery of the state and sustained by its resources. The existence of these non-formal spheres are increasingly recognised, and that is perhaps one of the first steps towards overcoming them. In this context any administrative reform would entail a thorough-going cultural revolution that would require changes to the role and functioning of the state and its relationship with society. Societal demands, fuelled by contemporary needs of a market economy, for constitutionalism and secure property rights come into contradiction with the attempts of the state to preserve and reproduce its own expanded functions, based on traditional Soviet-type relations, in which property rights remain ill-defined and rhetorically subject to popular control.[55] These contradictions help explain the many tensions in the development of Russia's market economy and require a socio-legal rather than linear institutional explanation.

Economy and environment

Nowhere was Putin's post-Sovietism stronger than in his attempt to create a benign business climate. Putin's pro-market instincts, however, appeared at times to reproduce some of the excesses of Western capitalism at its most environmentally hostile. Encouragement of rapid resource development appeared to be at the expense of ecological balance. In other words, Putin's post-Sovietism was imbued with a neo-Soviet approach that regarded nature no more as the field for human exploitation, irrespective of the consequences. This was in evidence in one of Putin's first acts on coming to power; the abolition of the State Committee for Environmental Protection, dissolved on 17 May 2000. The environmental protection agency had been created as a ministry in 1991 under Gorbachev, but had been downgraded to a state committee in 1996 following Yeltsin's re-election. In his drive for administrative rationalisation the job of environmental protection was transferred to the Ministry of Natural Resources, a move that many considered akin to placing the fox in charge of the hencoop. The old Committee had been criticised for its intrusive (some argued exploitative, and indeed corrupt) interference in business, but its abolition represented a drastic reduction in the state's capacity for environmental regulation and monitoring. At the same time, the State Committee on Forestry was also eliminated. The appointment of Alexander Gavrin, who had close links with Lukoil, the country's biggest oil producer, as energy minister added further to the impression that business had captured government in this sphere.

The need for an environmental protection agency would appear to be indisputable. According to Viktor Danilov-Danilyan, who headed the committee when it was abolished, some 61 million Russians live in environmentally dangerous conditions. In 120 cities air pollution is five times higher than established standards. Every month about a million tons of oil spills out of pipelines and into Russia's ground soil and water. At least 30 per cent of Chechnya was an ecological disaster zone as a result of the 26 oil wells that burned for months during the second Chechen war.[56] Above all, the weakness of regulatory oversight over Russia's nuclear industry was notorious. None of Russia's 29 nuclear power plants has a full safety certificate, yet the minister for economic energy, Yevgeny Adamov, planned to build another 23 nuclear power stations, as well as 40 advanced 'fast breeder' reactors. While the Chernobyl nuclear catastrophe of 26 April 1986 was well-known, the contamination by three disasters in 1946, 1957 and 1967 caused by the nuclear waste produced by the Mayak plant 50 miles north of Chelyabinsk, the centre of the Soviet nuclear weapons production system, was if anything worse than that caused by Chernobyl. The Soviet Northern fleet based on the Kola peninsula, near the border with Norway, dumped submarine reactors, spent fuel and other nuclear waste into the sea.

It was in connection with this that Alexander Nikitin, the former naval captain mentioned in Chapter 4, produced a report for the Norwegian environmental group, Bellona. As a result he was arrested by the FSB in 1996, and Putin, at the head of the FSB in 1998 and 1999, defended the action on the grounds that environmental groups provided a cover for foreign spies. Nikitin was cleared by the Supreme Court in April 2000, but the result could hardly be claimed as a resounding victory for freedom of speech. Indeed, the FSB refused to let the case die and through the Prosecutor's office filed an appeal with the Supreme Court's Appeals Collegium. The Nikitin case appeared to be symptomatic of the way that environmentalists, human rights activists and others were treated under Putin. In addition, the government in 2001 forced through legislation allowing the importation of nuclear waste for reprocessing, although public opinion was solidly against.

In all fields Putin's presidency adopted strongly pro-market policies. In agriculture the new land code adopted in 2001 allowed the private sale and purchase of commercial and residential land in cities and villages. Only about 2 per cent of the country's land area came under the provisions of this law, but it opened up the prospect for the development of a mortgage industry to provide the funds for investment. Later, the code was amended to allow the sale of agricultural land. Some 22 per cent of the world's forests are in Russia, and the natural resources agency, with the encouragement of the World Bank, sought to improve the investment climate for logging in Russia. Russia's natural resources were now ruthlessly exploited, regardless of sustainability or the environmental consequences. If the environment was to suffer as a result of Russia's modernisation, so was labour. The new labour code adopted on 30 December 2001 restricted collective bargaining to the unions representing a majority of the workers in an enterprise. Employers had more scope to agree fixed-price labour contracts, and the hiring and firing of workers was made easier. The minimum wage was set at the subsistence level. The greatest criticism of the new code was directed against its regulations concerning the role of trade unions in labour relations. As in other countries, the drive for labour market flexibility eroded workers' rights. The corporatist note sounded here, too, with malleable trade unions being favoured over those that took a more militant approach to defending the interests of their members. It appeared that some of the worst aspects of predatory capitalism now came to replace oppressive communism.

*   *   *

A significant cultural shift was achieved during Putin's leadership. Endless talk about Russia's civilisational destiny now gave way to a pragmatic recognition that in the modern world, as Weimar Germany had earlier recognised, 'economics had become destiny'.[57] On coming to power Putin enjoyed a benign economic environment, with high prices for oil and the benefits of the threefold devaluation of the rouble in August 1998 stimulating domestic production through import substitution. Putin built on this by ensuring greater political stability and transparency in government-business relations, new tax, labour and land codes, a new criminal code, and attempts to de-bureaucratise the environment for small businesses. Building on the 'Moscow consensus', he eschewed the excesses of shock therapy while not reverting back to Soviet-style autarchy. His model was a controlled extension of market relations. However, the failure to tackle the bureaucratisation of the economy meant that there would be no economic miracle. The dynamic capitalism that characterised Moscow and St Petersburg was little in evidence outside these and some other cities. Putin's model of capitalism was a central issue. He sought to finesse the fundamental contradiction that faced Russia as it moved to the market; the giant and monopolistic *structure* of economic forces inherited from the Soviet Union and the new type of economic *relations*. The encouragement of concentration in financial-industrial conglomerates tried to take advantage of these giant concerns by turning them into capitalist multinationals. Putin's policies were pro-big business, but the development of small and medium enterprises was relatively neglected. At the same time Putin established a more structured relationship with the business community that could be seen as an attempt to create a 'managed market economy'.[58] Putin was unequivocally in favour of Russia's economic integration into the international economic system, as the only way of pulling the country out of relative economic backwardness, but the strategy for domestic economic reform was rather more hesitantly implemented.

9   Putin and the world

The only realistic choice for Russia is the choice to be a strong country, strong and confident in its strength, strong not in spite of the world community, not against other strong states, but together with them.

(Putin, state-of-the-nation speech, 8 July 2000[1])

Throughout the 1990s all sides of the political spectrum had insisted that 'Russia is a great power'. Although they may have meant different things by this, such a rare display of unanimity suggested a profound consensus that Russia was not just an ordinary country but had a unique role to play in the Eurasian region and in the world at large. One of the five permanent members of the UN Security Council, a nuclear power, enjoying huge technological and cultural achievements, sitting atop enormous reserves of hydrocarbons and other natural resources, and with a history as an ally of Britain in the defeat of continental dictators, Russia felt itself different from other medium-ranking powers because it *was* different. Although in the 1990s it may have found itself trapped in poverty amidst a sea of plenty, even its location at the Eastern end of the European sphere of prosperity suggested that sooner rather than later its fortunes would improve. How to convert potential into reality? Would Russia become one of those countries of which it is said that they will always have a great future? Putin clearly was aware of the great gulf between rhetoric and reality, and sought to tailor Russia's ambitions to feasibility while not losing sight of what made Russia distinctive.

The normalisation of foreign policy

Putin's over-riding purpose from the very first days of his presidency was the normalisation of Russian foreign policy. Russia was to be treated as neither supplicant nor potential disruptor, but as just one more 'normal' great power. Through a combination of luck, skill and circumstances Putin achieved this remarkably quickly and effectively. By the time of the second Iraq war of 2003 Russia was treated no differently than any other country.

That is to say, the harsh realities of the post-post-cold war world hit Russia just as hard as any other country. The shedding of exaggerated illusions about Russia's status in the world did not mean that the country could avoid making hard choices and assuming responsibility for some of the world's problems.

Towards a new realism

Throughout the 1990s, although with varying intensity, Russia under Yeltsin had been committed to integration with the West. It had joined the IMF and had been willing to subordinate elements of economic policy to that agency's advice. With the fall of communism the old East–West bipolar world had given way to a more concentric version with a number of core states enjoying the 'democratic peace'[2] while the periphery remained a zone of conflict and economic hardship.[3] Russia sought to move from the periphery to the core and this had been welcomed by the West, although in practice some core countries, above all the United States, maintained obstacles to entry, particularly in the economic sphere. Russia's own problems, above all economic weakness, criminality, corruption and political divisions, made integration more difficult. Russia under Yeltsin appeared to enter a twilight zone of semi-acceptance. The main point, however, was that strategic direction had been established, and it was on this that Putin could build.[4] The desire to join the West was if anything even stronger in the rest of post-communist Eastern Europe, and represented a yearning to overcome the divisions that were particularly intense and bitter during the communist era but which predated it. Thus the different speeds of moving into the core created tensions. Poland, Hungary and the Czech Republic, for example, joined Nato in 1999, while Russia was at best ambivalent about the enlargement of cold war institutions to the East.

It has often been noted that in the 1990s Russian no longer had any enemies, as the structural features of the cold war were transcended, but neither did it have any real friends. The legacy of cold war suspicion only slowly dissipated, and indeed was occasionally replenished by Russia's halting acceptance of the sovereignty of former Soviet states, heavy handed 'peace keeping' operations in the breakaway Transdniestria territory in Moldova and Abkhazia in Georgia, brutal war in Chechnya, unsophisticated rhetorical support for the Serbian strongman, Slobodan Milosevič until his overthrow in October 2000, and crude attempts to play the Chinese 'card' against the West. Russian foreign policy under the stewardship of Primakov can be characterised as 'pragmatism', although of a relatively unrealistic sort, underscored by a heavy dose of anti-Western realism and by calls for 'multi-polarity'.

Primakov's so-called 'pragmatism' in foreign policy had not achieved positive results for Russia, alienating its friends and confirming the hostility of those traditionally suspicious of Russian intentions. Russian foreign policy in the late 1990s was built on fake history and mythopoeic representations of traditional alliances. Putin found himself in a position remarkably reminiscent to that facing Gorbachev when he came to power in 1985: surrounded by sullen neighbours and increasingly robust foes. If nothing else, Putin had to launch a charm offensive, and this he did with considerable verve and skill. Although Putin's policy was certainly characterised by pragmatism, this was of a different character to that pursued by Primakov. The latter could be dubbed 'competitive pragmatism', assuming that at root the interests of Russia and the West were divergent and thus every agreement and even the very idea of alliance was temporary and instrumental. Under Putin the underlying competitive edge now gave way to what could be called 'cooperative pragmatism', based on a sense of shared destiny and an awareness of mutual threats and opportunities. It is this fundamental shift that allowed such warm relations to be built between Putin and a number of world leaders, above all with Tony Blair, Gerhard Schroeder and, after an initial period of hesitation, with George Bush Jr, who came into office in January 2001.[5] At their summit in Ljubljana, Slovenia, on 16 June 2001 Bush and Putin established a remarkable personal rapport. Although the Bush camp had earlier repudiated Clinton's politics of charm, Bush now outdid his predecessor: 'I looked into that man's eyes and saw that he is direct and trustworthy. We had a very good dialogue. And I saw his soul.'[6]

The dual and contradictory position of Russia on the world stage on Putin's accession has been characterised as follows:

> On the one hand, it has many of the attributes of a world power – in the club of nuclear powers, a permanent seat in the UN Security Council, participates (although not always on an equal footing) in summits of world leaders. On the other hand, its present economic capacities clearly do not correspond to its still surviving nominal military power and political influence. In many respects Russia has declined to the level of a less developed country.[7]

With an economy the size of Holland's (around $400 billion), Russia tried to maintain a space programme, advanced strategic rocket development, over a million men in uniform, an extended welfare system and a bureaucracy that was bigger than the Soviet Union's. This mismatch between ambition and capacity had imbued Russian foreign policy in the 1990s with a bombastic and ineffectual edge.[8] There was clearly a gulf between the way that the outside world saw Russia and the pretensions of its elites and many of its citizens. This was an explosive situation, with an aggrieved Russia potentially becoming a disruptive force in the world community. A number of theories were applied to prop up Russia's exaggerated idea of its role in the world, notably various strains of neo-Eurasian thinking drawing on the ideas of the 1920s and 1930s. This was based on the belief that Russia's geopolitical position imbued it with unique geopolitical advantages that effectively forced it to be a great power and to make a bid for world leadership in opposition to the West. Time had moved on, however, and this was something that Putin recognised. There is little trace of Eurasianism in his thinking, but much about Russia's position in Eurasia. New strains of geopolitical thinking had emerged, for example the school of critical geopolitics that questioned the imperatives of space and geography. Putin appeared remarkably free of the traditionally static, monolithic and zero sum representation of Russia's role in the world. In short, Putin normalised the debate on Russian foreign policy, stripping it of its neo-Eurasianism.

Under Putin a 'new realism' rapidly emerged. Most of the elements were already visible under Primakov and even earlier, in particular his predecessor, Andrei Kozyrev, who had shaped Russia's foreign policies as it emerged as an independent state from 1990 until his resignation in January 1996. In the 'new realism' there was a much sharper recognition of the limits of Russian power, grounded above all in economic weakness. This did not mean giving up aspirations to global influence, but it did mean the pursuit of a far more conscious attempt to match ambitions to resources. The style and priorities of policy were also to change. According to the foreign minister, Igor Ivanov, 'Russian foreign policy will be independent, predictable and transparent.'[9] A number of commentators have noted the *economisation* of Russian foreign policy, and in numerous public statements Putin insisted that the country's foreign policy had to be subordinated to domestic economic interests.[10] In a keynote speech at the foreign ministry on 26 January 2001 Putin stressed that Russia's strategic aim was 'integrating into the world community', and for this the priority task of Russian diplomacy was the promotion of Russia's economic interests abroad. In the same speech he stressed another important aspect of his foreign policy: its *Europeanisation*. He stressed that the 'European direction is traditionally the most important for us'.[11] In the same vein, addressing a conference of Russia's ambassadors on 12 July 2002 he argued that economic ties with the EU, especially in the energy sphere, remained the top priority. He did not ignore Russia's other concerns, including accession to the WTO, without which he insisted Russia could not realise its potential. Economic relations with China, he argued, should be raised to the same level as bilateral political and military co-operation.[12] Some commentators have identified a third leg to Putin's policy, namely its *securitisation*.[13] For authors in the tradition of the Copenhagen school of international relations, security in the post-cold war era is less about direct threats than about the perception of risk, with the concept of risk defined rather more strongly than general threats or problems.[14]

Putin immediately sought to devise policies to overcome Russia's isolation and to establish good relations with the West, China and the world. Russia would do this, moreover, by finding a 'third way' between what many had seen as humiliating subservience to the West that characterised Russian policy from the late 1980s and the bombastic great powerism that predominated in the late 1990s. This new way would be based on overcoming Russia's traditional idealised view of the world and recognising a few hard realities: Russia's economy could no longer maintain aspirations to superpower status; Nato was here to stay and increasing numbers of Russia's neighbours wanted to join it, including (perhaps most humiliatingly for 'pragmatists' of Primakov's ilk), the Ukraine; and the Commonwealth of Independent States (CIS) could not be used as an instrument for Russian aggrandisement policy but would have to be based on genuine partnerships or it would wither away. At the same time, as Ivanov stressed, Russia would defend the idea of 'a democratic, multi-polar system of international relations', although stressing that 'Russia is by no means looking for a pretext for rivalry'.[15]

In the first period of his presidency there appeared to be a shift from an American-centred foreign policy towards a greater European orientation. This was in part because Clinton was in the last year of his presidency in 2000, and in early 2001 the Bush newcomers reassessed policy towards Russia, which in the first period meant pointedly avoiding Clinton's back-slapping style. Blair was the first to congratulate Putin when he became president, and Putin's first foreign visit as elected president was to London, suggesting that if there were to be a strategic partnership with anyone, it would be with Britain. The close relationship between Blair and Putin was sealed by over a dozen meetings in the first 30 months of Putin's presidency. In his speech to the Bundestag in 2002 Putin insisted that Russia's destiny is a European one, and this was borne out later when a fundamental choice had to be made between the European and the American versions of the West during the Iraq crisis of 2003.

Even when Russo-American relations improved, Putin clearly remained committed to close links with the EU. The EU was Russia's main economic partner, representing 40 per cent of Russian trade, although Russia represented only 3.3 per cent of EU-15 trade. Russia has the world's largest gas reserves, mostly found in Siberia, and became a major supplier to Western Europe and the primary supplier to Turkey. With a developed network of supply pipelines to Europe, Russia supplies 20 per cent of gas consumption (40 per cent of imports), making it the primary gas supplier. Russia also supplied the EU-15 with 16 per cent of its oil requirements.[16] The Partnership and Cooperation Agreement of 1994, that came into force in December 1997, provided the framework for bilateral relations (including biannual EU–Russia summits) and sought to develop common policies in the four fields of trade and economic co-operation; science and technology; political dialogue on issues of mutual concern, including democracy and human rights; and justice and home affairs issues, such as drug trafficking, money laundering and organised crime. The EU's Common Strategy on Russia of June 1999, valid for four years, sought to provide greater coherence in its relations with Russia, dealing with such areas as the consolidation of democracy, the integration of Russia into a common European economic and social space, stability and security in Europe and beyond, and coordinated approaches to common challenges such as environment and migration.[17]

The EU summits were used by Putin to reaffirm his belief that Russia was part of Europe. However, the enlargement to the East in 2004 (Estonia, Latvia, Lithuania, Poland, the Czech Republic, Slovakia, Hungary and Slovenia, together with Cyprus and Malta, with Romania and Bulgaria to join a few years later) brought the EU to the borders of Russia and raised new problems in its wake. Enlargement raised major problems over access, the visa regime and other issues concerning the Kaliningrad exclave, separated from Russia by Lithuania and Belarus. In Helsinki in October 1999 Putin had suggested that Kaliningrad could become a 'pilot region' for EU–Russian relations, and in a sense it did. The conflict over the status of the region came to a head at the EU–Russia summit on 29 May 2002, when the EU sharply rejected all Russian proposals to deal with the problems arising from the imposition of the Schengen regime on the EU's new members. Later in the year (11 November) an agreement allowed the use of a Facilitated Transport Document (FTD) system from 1 July 2003 for Russian citizens travelling between Kaliningrad and other parts of Russia.

Although Putin sought to normalise Russia's relations with the rest of the world, he remained loyal to a vision of international relations consisting of a world of sovereign nation states. Speaking at a conference on the Middle East in Moscow on 1 February 2000 Putin argued that 'It is unacceptable to cancel such basic principles of international law as national sovereignty and territorial integrity under the slogan of so-called humanitarian intervention.'[18] Russia appeared now to stand as the champion of an anti-universalistic agenda. Opposition to the idea that the international community had a right to intervene when governments were guilty of abusing their own population entailed a repudiation of much of the drift in international politics since the Second World War, but it also represented a stand in favour of international law. On this and other occasions Putin insisted that the principles of territorial integrity and national sovereignty should take priority over humanitarian intervention. It appeared that although rhetorically Russia favoured good relations with the West, it would insist on remaining part of an alternative pole of world politics and advance an alternative ideology of international affairs. It was for this reason that so much of Russian policy since the early 1990s had had a dual character, with Russia becoming both an insider and an outsider.[19] The tension in Russian policy was one that was to divide the West itself during the second Iraq war of 2003.

In all spheres there could be no direct return to 'normalcy', that is, to some sort of *status quo ante*. Russian imperial foreign policy had been marked by a striving for territorial gain (as was the policy of all the other great powers at the time), while Soviet foreign policy tried both to be a reliable partner in the existing international order while at the same time espousing a revisionist rhetoric based on communist internationalism. Elements of this tension between Russia as a status quo and a revisionist power remained in the 1990s. Russia became a vigorous joiner of the international political and economic order, yet talk of 'multi-polarism', strategic partnership with China and India, and Pan-Slavic mythologising in the Balkans revealed a latent vision of Russia as the anchor of an alternative pole to that of the West. It was this second multi-polar strand that propelled Russia into the camp of 'old Europe' and the 'axis of peace' during the Iraq crisis of 2003, no longer intended to create an anti-Western front but as one of the West's factions. Long-standing divisions within the West now burst into the open, with on the one hand a Gaullist version headed by France arrayed against what it condemned as American hyper-power based on unilateralism and the flaunting of international law. President Jacques Chirac's neo-Gaullism was not based on the EU as an altern-ative normative model of international politics (although the Germans prob-ably thought that it did), since France as much as America shares the same ruthless view of international organisations as little more than instruments for the pursuit of their own perceived self-interest. Chirac's derisive and insulting dismissal of the concerns of the accession countries was vivid testimony of this.[20] Russia could not return to a version of its own normality since it was unclear when and where this normality had existed, while in the world at large the normality that had prevailed since 1945 disintegrated.

Self-definition and doctrine

Before Putin's new realism could come into effect, however, policy had to come to terms with the doctrinal legacy of the past. In foreign policy the traditional centre of the Russian national security debate in the 1990s had been occupied by the 'statist' views reflected in the concept of 'Eurasianism'. The National Security Concept of December 1997 had insisted that the great-est threats to Russia's security came not from the international system but from various internal threats. This liberalism, however, was tempered by the continuing insistence that Russia was not a subordinate member of the inter-national community but a major player without whose active participation no political, economic or security problem could be resolved. The document acknowledged the threat posed by Nato enlargement but insisted that effect-ive multilateral means for co-operation remained, like the Organisation for Security and Co-operation in Europe (OSCE), in which Russia remained central as the only truly Eurasian power.[21]

In Putin's first year three major documents were adopted, each designed to clarify the risks and opportunities faced by Russia and ways of dealing with them. The first to be adopted was a new National Security Concept, to replace the 1997 version, signed into law on 10 January 2000.[22] The docu-ment was less sanguine about the external environment. The use of Nato with an unclear UN mandate to enforce attempts to stop Serbia's violation of Kosovan human and political rights, together with Nato enlargement, the aftershock of the August 1998 economic meltdown that revealed Russia's vul-nerability to speculative international financial markets, strategic arms control tensions and renewed war in Chechnya all combined to provoke a rethinking of the international environment. The new document expanded the list of external threats to Russia's security, noting in particular the weakening of the OSCE, the UN and the CIS. The tension between the emergence of a multipolar world, in which relations are based on international law and an acceptance of a significant role for Russia, and the attempt by the US and its allies to carve out a unipolar world outside of international law was stressed. There was no longer talk of 'partnership' with the West and instead more emphasis placed on more limited 'co-operation'.[23] To complement the above, a new Military Doctrine (replacing the 2 November 1993 version) was ratified by presidential decree on 21 April 2000. The 'no first use' of nuclear weapons was dropped, and as part of the reassessment of the risks facing the country the document called for the forward deployment of troops outside Russian territory.

The new Foreign Policy Concept of 28 June 2000, replacing Yeltsin's 29 April 1993 document, stressed that Russia's policy should be rational and realistic and designed to serve Russian economic and political interests.[24] The link between domestic and foreign policy was stressed. The Concept insisted that the 'relationship with European states is a traditional priority of Russian foreign policy'. As with all these documents, contradictory perceptions jostled cheek by jowl, with Russia defined as a great power in one paragraph and as fundamentally pragmatic in the next. The tone however was a realistic one, stressing the need to find a 'reasonable balance between its objectives and possibilities for attaining these objectives'. The document called for Russia to lead the development of a multipolar world, a policy explicitly designed to counter the threat of US global domination under the guise of 'humanitarian intervention' and 'limited sovereignty'. The emphasis in relations with the CIS shifted from multilateralism to bilateralism, a change that Putin adhered to throughout his leadership, above all with Belarus, while at the same time the need to protect Russian ethnic minorities in the former Soviet states was stressed. Good relations with Europe, the US and Asia were stressed, in that order, although the openly anti-American tone did not help. In the wake of the Kosovo intervention the tone was bitter; nevertheless the concept stated that Russia was interested in constructive co-operation with Nato 'in the interests of maintaining security and stability in the continent and is open to constructive interaction'.[25] Commenting on the Concept on 25 April 2002 in a speech devoted to the two-hundredth anniversary of the Russian foreign ministry, Ivanov stressed that 'Russia has consciously given up the global Messianic ideology that had been intrinsic to the former USSR and at the end of its existence had come into insurmountable contradiction with the national interests of the country.'[26] The concept broadly set the parameters for policy, but as so often with these documents real life quickly passed it by.

These documents reflected a traditional concept of power where the ultimate sanction was coercion and war. In the post-cold war era such traditional 'hard power' began to give way to 'soft power' where the emphasis shifts to 'the ability to set the political agenda in a way that shapes the preferences of others'.[27] Putin no doubt appreciated the value of soft power in proportion to the absence of effective instruments of hard power.

Doctrinal evolution was accompanied by more coherent management of the country's international relations. Foreign policy is dominated by the head of the executive and is highly personalised: rather than reflecting Russia's primordial peasant traditions, it is characteristic of many advanced societies. Putin drew effectively on the professionalism of the Russian foreign ministry and overall there appeared to be a greater institutionalisation of the making and conduct of foreign policy. There was an underlying normalisation both in the goals of foreign policy and in the manner in which it was conducted. Economic concerns came to the fore, but security issues were never far from the surface. In his state-of-the-nation addresses Putin repeatedly condemned the sluggish pace of military reform, even though the military budget rose significantly,[28] although not as much as the military had wanted. Reform of the armed services remained locked in controversy, but at least a certain strategy was now apparent, above all in reducing numbers and shifting to a fully professional army. It seemed at this time that Putin was traditional in seeking to restore 'Russia's "greatness" through building up its "power" in the most traditional geopolitical sense'.[29] This judgement was to be placed in question by the events of September 2001.

Putin's choice

From the first days of his leadership Putin pursued an active and personalised foreign policy. In his first year he visited some two dozen countries, and when representing Russia at various summits and meetings such as the 'Group of Eight', insisted that Russia be treated as an equal, expecting neither privileges nor aid, but respect. Russian foreign policy indeed became 'normal', neither supplicant nor bully and inspired by nothing more – and nothing less – than the principle that foreign policy should serve the country's internal, above all economic, development. To achieve this strategic goal, Putin's choice clearly lay along the path of integration into the world capitalist market and the community of Western democratic nations. Putin did not turn Russia's back on the East, but the emphasis had clearly moved away from Primakovian ideas of a 'strategic partnership' with China and India or the attempt to develop a 'multipolar' system of international relations. Russia was no longer even implicitly a 'revisionist' power in foreign affairs but sought to exploit the *status quo* for the pursuit of its own, rather more modest, national interests. The only attempt at a 'third way' here was that the fundamental civilisational choice in favour of the West should be practised on terms that suited Russia. Russia's dramatic choice to join the 'coalition against terror' after the events of 11 September 2001, therefore, built on earlier developments. This is not to deny, however, the courage of Putin's radical choice at that time unequivocally to join the Western alliance, despite the grumbling of the military and the uncertainty of public opinion.

Responses to 9/11

Putin was the first to telephone Bush after the al-Qaeda attack on the twin towers of the World Trade Center and the Pentagon on 11 September 2001. He offered not only sympathy but stressed that Russia would stand full-square with the United States in the struggle against international terrorism. In a special meeting with security and military chiefs on 22 September in Sochi Putin discussed Russia's specific actions, and on his return to Moscow on 24 September he held further meetings with all major party leaders and Duma factions. Despite some stiff opposition among the elite, Putin gave concrete form to the new alliance in a television broadcast that day in which he outlined five areas of co-operation with the West. Russia would provide all the information at its disposal about terrorist bases and its secret services would co-operate fully with the West; Russia would open its airspace to planes carrying humanitarian goods to regions where anti-terrorist operations took place; air bases in Central Asia would be made available to Western planes; Russia in case of necessity would participate in search and rescue operations; and Russia would support the internationally-recognised government in Afghanistan with military and other supplies.[30] This policy of close co-operation was the logical conclusion of Putin's earlier approach.

Although there has been much commentary about the strength of popular anti-American feeling, a number of commentators after 9/11 noted, in the light of the outpouring of genuine popular sympathy for those who had suffered, that this had probably always been exaggerated.[31] Although at times of international tension, as during the Nato campaign in 1999 over Kosovo, the number of Russian citizens who considered America a potential enemy peaked at 48 per cent, by 2001 this had fallen to 13 per cent.[32] For most citizens of St Petersburg, Russia's European identity is not a matter in question. Putin, too, has no doubts about the matter. After 11 September Putin made a calculated decision (although this choice was in keeping with his intuition and Yeltsin's precedent) that Russia's security and broader interests lay in alliance with the West. At a stroke, Russian ambiguities and doubts about its civilisational identity, whether it was part of the West or an alternative to it, found a framework in which to be resolved and to provide Russia with a place at the centre of global processes and leadership. We should however keep this in perspective and reject some of the overblown rhetoric prompted by Putin's actions at this time. Putin's courageous stance following 11 September did not mark a fundamental repudiation of long-standing Russian concerns or interests. Putin's choice in favour of normalising relations with the West had been taken long before, and afterwards, as seen by his principled stance during the second Iraq war, it was clear that good relations with the West did not mean becoming America's junior partner.

In the months that followed the Kremlin cooperated with the United States on a number of key issues: the Afghan war; the deployment of US forces in Central Asia and, later, in Georgia; arms control and the American unilateral abrogation of the 1972 Anti-Ballistic Missile (ABM) treaty. Tony Blair noted,

> In respect of Russia, common commitment to tackle terrorism after September 11 demonstrated a new partnership between Russia and the West. Central to that new relationship should be a step change in Russia–Nato relations. We also need a fresh economic approach, with the aim of creating in Europe a single economic space in which lasting prosperity and peace can flourish. We will all benefit from a thriving Russia. We want a successful, prosperous Russia with which we can work in partnership.[33]

Not much of this came to pass, although Russia's concessions aligned the country as part of the 'coalition against terrorism' but there appeared to be little tangible benefit. Putin had joined the coalition as a matter of principle, so discussion of tangible benefits may be misplaced. Russia did however gain two immediate advantages: a muting of Western criticism of its behaviour in Chechnya (and indeed, a partial reclassification of the war there as part of the international struggle against terrorism); and the overthrow of the hated Taliban regime in Afghanistan (that had long threatened Russia's ally Tajikistan) by the Russian-backed Northern Alliance forces.

Despite a strong personal relationship between Bush and Putin, Moscow's trust in Washington's good faith was threatened by America's heavy-handedness. Although no formal deal was struck in return for Russia's support for the allied intervention in Afghanistan in late 2001, Russia made no fuss about the placing of US troops in Central Asia but expected US–Russia trade restrictions to be lifted. They were still there long after 9/11, and other possible benefits for Russia were also slow to materialise. Already in February 2002 Russian public opinion was incensed at what Putin called 'non-objective judges' at the Winter Olympic Games in Salt Lake City, and soon afterwards the bitter trade war over punitive American tariffs on Russian steel imports and Russia's reciprocal ban on 'Bush chicken legs' revealed how fragile (or perhaps just how 'normal') the relationship between the two countries was. The question of the repeal of the Jackson–Vanik amendment of 1975, which tied trade relations between the two countries to the emigration of 60,000 Jews a year from the Soviet Union, dragged on for years despite repeated promises to repeal the act. The Soviet Union had long disappeared, exit visas were granted freely, and yet the amendment remained. As Alex Pravda notes, Putin's 'policy of active cooperation appears fragile on two main fronts: domestic criticism and inadequate Western reciprocity'.[34] In his survey of 'The world after 11 September', Primakov insisted that not much had changed except America's improved geopolitical position in Central Asia and the Caucasus and the increased dangers of American unilateralism.[35] This was a view shared by much of Russia's political elite including the foreign minister, Ivanov, who insisted on an appropriate role for the United Nations.[36] In this context Russia's stance during the Iraq crisis should not have come as a surprise.

Under Putin Russia's 'great retreat' continued. The 25-year lease on the former American base at Cam Ranh Bay was due to end in 2004, and in the negotiations for its renewal in 2001 the Vietnamese insisted on raising the rent. However, Putin's decision to withdraw was not primarily motivated by economic factors (especially since the Vietnamese debt to Russia was some $17 billion), but was a recognition that over-extended ambitions undermined the possibility of real achievements in military reform and in general, economic development. Similarly, the Lourdes listening post on Cuba, at $200 million a year, was relatively cheap for the enormous role it played in intelligence gathering. The decision to close the post (it ended its work in January 2002), which had monitored US communications, reflected a deeper choice that the cold war had really ended.

During Bush's visit to Moscow on 24 May 2002 he and Putin signed the Strategic Offensive Reduction Treaty, pledging each side to reduce their stockpile to no more than 2,200 warheads by 31 December 2012. Much to Russia's displeasure, the treaty allowed warheads to be dismantled rather than destroyed and there was no verification procedure. Nevertheless, the Duma ratified what became known as the Moscow Treaty on 14 May 2003, and thus divisions that had opened up in Russo–American relations over Iraq appeared healed. At that time the US still had 7,500 nuclear warheads, while Russia had 7,300. According to the Start treaty, these arsenals were each to be cut to about 1,700 to 2,200, allowing plenty of scope for the two countries to destroy each other and much of the rest of the world. Russia apparently had 1,249 identified targets in America. Since 1945 around 128,000 nuclear warheads have been produced, 70,000 by the US and 55,000 by the USSR (Russia), and as the number fell stockpiles of plutonium would allow 85,000 nuclear warheads to be produced.[37] The protection of these stockpiles in Russia was notoriously lax. In addition, nuclear power stations had stockpiles of fissionable materials that could become the object of terrorist attack. A report in July 2002 noted that radioactive metals, possibly including plutonium, had been stolen by Chechen rebels from the newly opened Volgodonskaya nuclear plant.[38]

Nato and its enlargement

If in 1952 the Nato Secretary-General Lord Ismay had defined Nato's purpose as to 'keep the Americans in, the Russians out and the Germans down', in the succeeding years Nato adapted to changing circumstances. With the fall of communism it faced perhaps the greatest challenge of all to its survival: to generate a new sense of purpose in conditions of peace rather than forging an alliance in preparation of war. In the absence of an immediate and over-riding threat in the form of Warsaw Pact armies looming over the horizon in the East, Nato was no longer so focused on collective defence. The question then became ever more pressing: could it transform itself into an instrument of collective security? The scope of Nato functions also expanded, above all to 'out of area' activities, suggesting a global rather than merely a regional role. With continuing tensions in the Gulf, regional conflicts in the Balkans, the persistent threat of international terrorism, and fears about nuclear proliferation it appeared that there was no shortage of work for Nato to do. However, while Article 5 of the Nato Charter, declaring that an attack on one state represented an attack on them all, was invoked for the first time following the attack on the World Trade Center, the war in Afghanistan in late 2001 was not conducted under the aegis of Nato. The tensions within the organisation were vividly manifested during the Iraq crisis, when a profound division occurred between what the Americans dubbed 'old Europe' (France, Germany and Belgium) and the American-oriented countries of Britain, Spain and most of the enlargement countries to the East, the 'new Europe' comprising the former communist countries that now wished to join Nato. Paradoxically, just as it became possible for them to join Nato, it appeared no longer necessary. In the age of American military predominance and reluctance to subordinate itself to multilateral bodies, Nato appeared increasingly redundant.

The debate over Nato's role in the post-cold war world was accompanied by controversy over enlargement. Russia's elites were particularly exercised over the latter, although polls suggested that public opinion was also opposed to the organisation's extension to the East, a view that was reinforced by Nato's bombing of Serbia during the Kosovo conflict between March and June 1999.[39] Conflicts in the Balkans demonstrated that only Nato had the capacity to intervene decisively within a multilateral framework, whereas the EU had shown itself paralysed and divided. It was for this reason that in 1999 the EU sought to provide muscle to its diplomatic activity by building on what had earlier been called its Common Foreign and Security Policy (CFSP) to develop a European Security and Defence Policy (ESDP). On this basis there were plans to create a 60,000 strong joint combat force. Nato's first enlargement, bringing in Poland, Hungary and the Czech Republic in March 1999, coincided with the beginning of the Kosovo campaign and provoked much anger in Russia, yet later events were to demonstrate that their membership of Nato posed no threat to Russia and in fact enhanced the security of all.

On coming to power Putin signalled an open mind on the question of Nato enlargement. On a visit to Britain in spring 2000, asked by David Frost about Russia's membership of Nato Putin answered: 'Why not?' The answer was not so much a serious bid for membership, but a signal (as Putin put it in the same interview) that 'Russia is part of European culture and I can't imagine my country cut off from Europe or from what we often refer to as the "civilized world" ... seeing Nato as an enemy is destructive for Russia.'[40] At the Genoa G7 summit in July 2001 premier Silvio Berlusconi of Italy worked hard to promote his strategy of opening Nato to closer Russian engagement. Russian representatives, withdrawn at the time of the Kosovo crisis, returned to Nato headquarters, and in February 2001 Nato's information office in Moscow was reopened. Although intent on enlarging, Nato worked hard to ensure that this was not at the price of excluding Russia. The basic strategy of integrating Russia into the larger security community, in creative and tailor-made ways, continued.

The events of 11 September changed the framework in which relations between Russia and Nato were conducted. Blair in particular sought to bring Russia into an enlarged security community, although stopping short of actually inviting it to join the organisation. The establishment in June 2002 of a reconstituted Nato–Russia Council built on the 1997 Russia–Nato Founding Act, but instead of the model being 19 Nato members relating to Russia singly, the new 'Nato at 20' elevated Russia symbolically to equal rank with all the others and thus represented yet another step in the transcendence of the cold war. The issues to be dealt with by the new body included the struggle against terrorism, proliferation of weapons of mass destruction, management of regional crises and peacekeeping, anti-ballistic missile defence and search-and-rescue operations. Even though the cold war had once again ended, Russia was still treated as a special case and the unwieldy character of the new body reduced its ability to deal effectively with complex issues, once again dividing Russia from its 19 (and more) new allies. Equally, if Russia were able to win over any significant number of Council members to its side in any dispute with the United States, the latter, in keeping with its unilateralist inclinations, would no doubt seek to move on.

Eleven September changed the parameters of discussions over Nato enlargement. Rather than the anticipated and rather limited Slo-Slo (Slovenia and Slovakia) expansion, the scope was broadened to encompass seven countries. After 11 September Russian resistance to the inclusion of the three Baltic states weakened, and the membership of Bulgaria and Romania seemed likely. Even the Ukraine on 23 May 2002 announced that it would seek membership of Nato, although its leadership admitted that it would take at least eight to ten years for this to be achieved.[41] The Nato summit in Prague on 21–22 November 2002 went for the 'big bang' approach and invited almost all the former communist states to join, with the exception of those in the Balkans. The three Baltic republics (Estonia, Latvia and Lithuania) were invited to join along with Slovakia, Slovenia, Romania and Bulgaria. The door was left open for a further enlargement that would include at the minimum Croatia, and possibly Albania and Macedonia. It would be a long time before the union of Serbia and Montenegro (as the former was renamed in February 2003) or Bosnia would be able to join. As for the Ukraine's aspirations, these were demonstratively shunned by a boycott of contacts with the Ukrainian president, Leonid Kuchma, at the Prague summit because of the anti-democratic trends in his country. Belarus was not even in the running because of the authoritarianism of president Alexander

Lukashenko's rule in that country. Nato's enlargement paradoxically took place at a time when its role was undermined by the creation of ad hoc coalitions of the willing, as in the Iraq war of 2003.

At the same time, the swift defeat of the Iraqis in that war (equipped by the Soviet Union and using Soviet tactics) demonstrated to Russia that its military forces, made up of raw conscripts and with an old-fashioned war fighting posture (massed artillery, static positions and the like), would be no match for the modern equipment and tactics of the Western powers. This was a lesson of the 1982 Lebanon war, when the American-equipped Israeli air force downed dozens of Soviet-supplied Syrian jets with no losses to itself, and it had still not fully sunk into the Soviet-Russian military mind. We have noted the new appointments at the head of the defence industries in Chapter 6 that followed the second Iraq war. At the same time a detailed strategy for military reform was finally adopted, at a time when the contrast between the rapid success of coalition forces in Iraq and the stalemate in Chechnya could hardly be starker. The defence ministry's plan for reform, rather than the speedier and cheaper version proposed by SPS,[42] was finally adopted by the government in April 2003. There was to be an incremental expansion of volunteer service that would replace all conscripts with professional soldiers, at so-called permanent readiness units in the armed services proper and other forces, by 2008. Only after these 209 combat units, ranging in size from airborne divisions to border guard forces, were fully staffed with 170,000 professional sergeants and soldiers would compulsory military service be cut from two years to one. There were to be fewer exemptions from conscription, but those called up would spend half the year gaining military skills in educational units and would then have the choice of serving in non-combat units or to enter contract-based professional service. Plenty of sceptical voices remained, above all because of the lack of adequate funding for the changes. Given the low pay, the armed forces sought to attract professional soldiers from the CIS by offering them Russian citizenship after three years of unblemished service.

Practising normality

Even though Putin's European orientation came naturally to him, there was no evidence that he sought to resurrect Soviet-style attempts to drive a wedge between the American and European wings of the Western alliance. In part this may have been a recognition that, despite many points of conflict and tensions, the alliance was built on solid foundations of mutual interest and that any attempt to exploit divisions would be counter-productive. This self-denying ordinance was particularly impressive as the US under Bush entered a period of international activism. Paradoxically, as we have seen, the divisions within the West became most apparent just at the time when Russia renounced attempts to exploit them. In the Iraq crisis Russia sought to ensure its role as mediator between Europe and America, a role Britain had traditionally tried to play.

The bifurcation of the West

The American insistence on 'regime change' in Iraq threatened the $8 billion owed as sovereign debt by the Iraqi regime to Russia, and jeopardised the lucrative contracts (worth some $30 billion) that Russian oil companies (headed by Lukoil) had signed in 1997 with the Iraqi government for the exploitation of the West Qurna oilfield. Although later repudiated by Saddam Hussein, the Russian side insisted that the deal still held. A later agreement between Zarubezhneft (a company that had been working in Iraq since 1967) to exploit the Bin Umar oilfield was potentially even more valuable: the concession was estimated to be worth $90 billion. It was clear that growing American doubts about the reliability of Saudi Arabia as the main source of its energy supplies led it to seek alternatives, and Iraq, with the world's second largest oil reserves, was an obvious candidate.[43] American dominance of Iraq would help ensure uninterrupted supplies, undermine the oil-pricing cartel OPEC, and allow the US to dictate prices for decades. This would not be good news for Russia or its oil companies, since relatively high prices for energy exports (as we have seen) played a large part in funding the Russian exchequer. Both France and Russia had long-standing economic interests in Iraq, and these were now threatened.

It was not surprising in this context that Russia, like France, insisted that any war against Iraq should be conducted under the aegis of the UN, and that the legitimate interests of Russia (and France) in the country should be respected in a post-Saddam Iraq. Russia reluctantly agreed to a tougher sanctions regime imposed on Iraq by the UN on 14 May 2002, and again for the 8 November resolution 1441 that threatened Iraq with 'serious consequences' if it impeded the work of UN weapons inspectors. As the Anglo-American forces built up in Kuwait ready to overthrow Saddam Hussein, on 20 March 2003 Putin issued a harsh statement aligning Russia with the Franco-German refusal to support a second UN resolution that would implicitly authorise the use of force to overthrow the dictator, even though no weapons of mass destruction had been found by the UN inspections team headed by Hans Blix. Putin warned that the coalition was committing 'a grave political error' that could destroy 'the established system of international security':

> If we allow international law to be replaced by 'the law of the fist' whereby the strong is always right and has the right to do anything and in choosing methods to achieve his goals is not constrained by anything, then one of the basic principles of international law will be put into question, and that is the principle of immutable sovereignty of a state. And then no one, not a single country in the world will feel secure. And the vast area of instability that has arisen will grow and cause negative consequences in other regions of the world.

The harsh tone of Putin's statement caught many by surprise, but it reflected long-standing Russian views on the role of international law and organisations. Russia's support for the war against terrorism would not preclude criticism, especially since America since September 2001 had too often given the appearance of not engaging with Russian concerns. Putin signalled that Russia would remain an ally but on particular questions its support should not be taken for granted. Classic balance of power theories suggest that when one power is predominant the others ally to counter-balance it, and this appeared to be occurring – no longer restricted to Europe as in the late nineteenth century but now on a global scale.

Russia found itself torn between the two faces of the West: the interventionist Anglo-American bloc and the Franco-German 'axis of peace' alliance.[44] Many in Washington had anticipated that Putin would support American policy in Iraq, especially given the need to secure its economic interests in the post-Saddam order. Why did Putin join the 'old Europeans'? According to Alexander Vershbow, the American ambassador to Russia, one of the reasons is that Russia did not receive enough in exchange for its support after 9/11. The US presence in Central Asia and the Caucasus, Nato enlargement, and missile defence plans had been perceived by Russia's security establishment not only as long-term but also as immediate threats to Russian security.[45] The Jackson–Vanik amendment had not been repealed, a trade war over steel and chicken legs, small US investment in Russia compared to the Europeans, and strong public sentiments against the forcible overthrow of Saddam Hussein were all factors in Putin's calculation. In April 2003 only 17 per cent of respondents said they disliked Saddam, down from 22 per cent a year earlier, whereas Bush's popularity had nose-dived: 76 per cent said they disliked Bush, up from 45 per cent in May 2002. Another poll found that 59 per cent called the US an unfriendly nation, 71 per cent considered the US played a negative role in the world, and 91 per cent opposed the US-led war in Iraq.[46] Putin had also gone far with reform to the agricultural and communal services sector, and with elections imminent he needed to bolster support. All these were undoubtedly factors, together with the economic interests discussed above, but ultimately decisive was Putin's instinctive Europeanism and his commitment to agreed multilateral approaches to conflict resolution. In speech after speech he had stressed the need to abide by international law, and now he did no more than what he had been preaching.

Putin's performance in the Iraq crisis was much criticised, but in the event he played a very difficult hand well. He had clearly been misled by his intelligence services, who had predicted a long-drawn out conflict. There was also much evidence of lack of coordination in Russia's policy making, probably reflecting the absence of an over-riding strategic goal. It was not clear which was the most important for Russia: protecting its economic interests in Iraq; defending the international legal order and the UN; or remaining on good terms with the United States. A group in the Kremlin (apparently consisting of Voloshin, Putin's foreign policy aide Sergei Prikhodko, and Federation Council foreign affairs committee chairman Mikhail Margelov) fought hard to maintain a pro-American stance, but the 'anti-American elite ... managed to regain control of decision-making'.[47] One thing was clear, however, as the crisis came to an end; as Karaganov put it, 'It is counter-productive at the UN – even for tactical purposes – to attempt to play against its most powerful member.' As he noted: 'September 11, 2001, did not give birth to a new reality, but simply opened people's eyes to the existing state of affairs. The Iraqi crisis likewise has not begotten a new reality, but now it will be harder to ignore things that we chose to ignore previously.' He had in mind America's attempts 'to proactively impose order and modernization' on troubled regions of the world, an approach that could end up by treating Russia's direct interests with little ceremony.[48] A commentary at the time drew the broader lesson:

> If followed through consistently, this new policy line will destroy the political concept of the West and create a new bipolar world of political and military rivalry between the United States and Europe (more precisely, the European Union) ... the world of politics may be deprived of a point of reference that has been called 'western democracy' with all its standards and institutions.[49]

Russia under Putin sought to become the new Britain, mediating between America and Europe. Instead, as the crisis over the second Iraq war deepened, Russia was in danger of becoming the new France, part of an 'anti-hegemonic' implicitly anti-American 'multipolar' bloc. The 'peace camp' alliance of Russia with France and Germany did not outlast the war, and talk of a new Moscow–Berlin–Paris axis was exaggerated. America's reliance on 'coalitions of the willing' rendered new allies, such as Russia, Bulgaria, Uzbekistan and Pakistan no less important than its traditional allies in Nato. Putin, moreover, understood that nothing would be gained by trying to drive a wedge between Europe and America (and in this respect he was genuinely post-Soviet) or by permanently alienating America. He swiftly mended his fences with the victors over Baghdad. The split however suggested the onset of the post-post-cold war era, where Russia's former communism was no longer a relevant factor in international relations. All countries were faced by the challenge of the new 'normality': voluntary acceptance of US hegemony or pariah status. The seismic shift in the international order at this time seemed to threaten the whole system of international organisations (UN, Nato, OSCE and even the EU – the only serious challenger in the long run to American dominance) that had taken shape since 1945, and signalled the end of the long post-(Second World) War period. A new, more critical, self confident and independent Russia emerged out of the crisis, and that perhaps was no bad thing.

Beyond East and West

The debate over Russian foreign policy in the 1990s tended to focus on a single stark polarity: Atlanticism versus Eurasianism. This in turn was a debate over the attitude towards and meaning of 'West' and 'East'. The West was susceptible to a number of geographical and ideological interpretations. Geographically, there was a tension between the American and the European versions, while Japan represented a world of its own. The ideological ambiguity of the West was reflected above all in the tension between perceptions of the West as a security (primarily Nato) identity, as a zone of capitalist prosperity (in particular the EU), or as the core of a set of universal values based on human rights and a set of international ethical norms (represented, for example, by the Council of Europe). Gref, the head as we have seen of the Centre for Strategic Development whose task it was to devise a medium-term plan for Russia's development, argued that ' "the West" as some sort of definition does not mean much in particular'.[50] It was not 'the West' as such that would do this or the other, but concrete investors. Thus Gref reflected one of the characteristic features of the new conception of geopolitical space: the deconstruction of the West as a monolithic unitary actor into a more dynamic conception of the West as the site of conflicts, divergent interests and economic dynamism. It was this more subtle understanding of the West that allowed the transcendence of traditional 'Russia versus the West' discourses.

The identity and perception of the East was no less multilayered. At least three 'Easts' can be identified.[51] The first saw the East as a zone of geopolitical contestation and affirmation. While the West may have been dominated by America, in the East Russia could reaffirm itself as a great power. The main actor here was China, and the rhetoric of a Sino-Russian 'strategic partnership' was an attempt to establish a counter-balance to what by the late 1990s had become an increasingly fraught relationship with the West. A second interpretation of the East focused more on geo-economics, with a recognition that the Pacific rim had overtaken the Atlantic basin as the centre of global economic activity and increasing prosperity. Despite the economic crisis in the region in the late 1990s, the economic success of the 'Asian tigers' stood in stark contrast with Russia's continued struggle to come to terms with modernity and modernisation. The chronic underdevelopment of the Russian Far East would require investment from Asian countries, above all Japan, as would the effective exploitation of the energy reserves on Sakhalin. There is also a third East, a geo-ideological one in which the East represented not only a spiritual alternative to Western materialism but a broader alternative to the West in general. Although India would play a role in such a version of the East, it was Russia itself that sought to become emblematic of this tendency.

Putin's accession to the presidency led to a rapid reconceptualisation of both East and West. The end of the cold war had been followed by the unalloyed supremacy, indeed triumphalism, of 'the West'. Repeated Russian and Chinese calls for the restoration of a multipolar world reflected concern about the unbalanced world system that had emerged as a result of the disintegration of the USSR and the end of bipolarity and superpower balance. In the event, in the post-cold war world the Eastern pole could find no satisfactory political form or ideological rationale. There would be no distinctive third way between, on the one hand, the traditional cold war confrontation between East and West, and on the other hand, the unabashed reduction of modernisation into Westernisation. Under Putin the geopolitical element, and in particular the idea of a 'strategic partnership' with China, was swiftly de-emphasised.[52]

For most of the late 1990s Russian diplomacy sought to forge an Indian–Chinese–Russian triangle as a counterbalance to the US and Nato. The Indian link in this chain was always the weakest, but even the Chinese one was beset with contradictions. The success of China's 'four modernisations', launched by Deng Xiaoping in 1979, especially in contrast with Russia's travails in the 1990s, meant that the Chinese path of authoritarian modernisation (in which the Communist Party acted as the instrument of capitalist restoration) appeared attractive to many in Russia.[53] With both Russia and China emphasising the need for a 'multipolar' world and the 'territorial integrity' of states (that is, Chinese support for Russia's war in Chechnya and Russia's support for the 'one China' policy that claims Chinese sovereignty over Taiwan), there were plenty of points in common in the Russian and Chinese view of the world.[54] The Russo-Chinese link was built on a number of shared concerns: the struggle against 'unipolar' hegemonism; against 'humanitarian' interventionism (the principle of noninterference in internal affairs);[55] Islamic secessionism (Chechnya, Kosova, Xinxiang); arms sales; opposition to Nato enlargement; developing economic links; and some mutual acceptance of Russia's hegemony as a guarantor of order in Eurasia. There would be no strategic alliance with China, however, since China has historically avoided multilateral alliances. In addition, despite a long shared border trade between Russia and China for long remained low, totalling only $6 billion in 1999. Russia was in ninth place as a trading partner, far below the $66 billion between China and Japan and the $62 billion between China and the US. From 2002, however, there was a rapid growth in Sino-Russian trade. Fear over the fate of the underpopulated, under-developed and isolated Eastern regions of the country, sharing a 4,300 kilometre-long border with China, remained a top concern. The population of the Russian Far East is eight million and that of Siberia 25 million, and both are decreasing, whereas Northeast China's population is approaching 300 million. The population of the three provinces closest to Russia (Heilongjiang, Jilin and Liaoning) have a combined population of eighty million, provoking Russian concern about inflows of people from China. Estimates suggest that there are some two million illegal Chinese immigrants in Russia's eastern territories. In contrast to the rapid development of the Pacific region as a whole, the Russian Far East remains backward and under-developed.

In his 26 January 2001 speech at the foreign ministry Putin had insisted that 'The Asian direction is gaining increasing significance.... I believe that it would be wrong to measure where we have more priorities, in Europe or Asia. There must not be a Western or an Eastern preference. The reality is that a power with such a geopolitical position as Russia has national interests everywhere.'[56] Deputy foreign minister Grigory Karasin outlined Russia's three strategic objectives vis-à-vis the Far East. First, Moscow sought 'maximum participation in [international] security structures' to help ensure 'stability and predictability' in that region. Second, it aims to ensure the security of its borders and the implementation of long-term confidence building measures. And third, it sought to establish political and economic relations with countries in the region that could help the development of Russia's Far East, above all dealing with the energy, transport and high technology sectors.[57] Russia repeatedly stated the view that its presence in Asia was a 'factor for regional stability'. Meeting with the Chinese foreign minister, Tang Jiaxuan, in Moscow on 1 March 2000, Putin declared that relations between Moscow and Beijing 'resolves the problem of stability in the world on a global scale as much as they do in bilateral relations'.[58] The establishment of the Shanghai Co-operation Organisation (SCO) at a summit in Shanghai on 14–15 June 2001 as a regional mechanism for security and co-operation, comprising Russia, China, Kazakhstan, Kyrgyzstan and Uzbekistan, brought China into Central Asian politics and under-scored the shift away from a 'strategic partnership' between Russia and China towards a more pragmatic relationship based on shared interests and concerns.

China became one of Russia's main markets for arms sales. Military-technical co-operation had deepened significantly following the war in Kosovo, with up to 2,000 Russian specialists working in Chinese laboratories on advanced weapons projects.[59] However, there were points of tension in the relationship. Sections of the Russian military and political elite harboured concern over a potential military threat from China. The transfer of sensitive military technology and know-how to China alarmed many Russian strategists, fearing China's rise to great power status. Moscow was concerned that China was buying Russian military technology and know-how while avoiding the purchase of large ready-made stocks of military hardware.[60] Already one of the world's most advanced fighter planes, the SU-27, was being assembled in China. In other words, the perception in Moscow that China sought to achieve technology transfer to develop its own defence production capabilities while lessening its dependence on Moscow was partially true. Putin's attempts to mend relations with Nato provoked concern in China, especially since China had earlier enthusiastically joined with Russia in condemning Nato, above all intervention in the Balkans.

From the beginning of Putin's presidency there had been a noticeable shift in the rhetoric away from overblown Primakovian talk of a 'strategic partnership' between Moscow and Beijing towards a more modest and in fact far more realistic emphasis on technical and economic ties between the two countries.[61] The shift in rhetoric marked a change in Russia's foreign policy priorities vis-à-vis China. American plans for a Missile Defence (MD) scheme to protect the US from missile attacks together with plans for the deployment of theatre missile defences (TMD) in the Western Pacific provoked China into adopting a $10 billion package for strengthening its nuclear capabilities. Moscow had long supported China's opposition to the proposed US–Japanese theatre missile defence system in Asia, while Beijing supported Moscow's opposition to any weakening of the ABM treaty (until its abrogation in December 2001). At present China has only some two dozen strategic missiles capable of hitting the North American mainland, making them vulnerable to even a limited MD system. The Chinese build-up affects not only the US but also Russia. China's predominance in conventional weaponry today is offset by Russia's nuclear strength, but this could now be eroded. Fears about the vulnerability of Russia's vast but under-populated Russian Far East neighbouring China's land-hungry population endowed the psychological climate with anxiety. Russia's membership of G8, moreover, while China continued to be excluded could not but add a hint of bitterness in the relationship.

Russia and Japan were unable to sign the much-awaited bilateral treaty by the end of 2000, as promised by Yeltsin and then Japanese prime minister Ryutaro Hashimoto at the 'no-neckties' summit in Krasnoyarsk in November 1997. The problem remained active into the Putin era. The fundamental obstacle to the improvement of bilateral ties remained: the conflict over the Kurile Islands, called by Japan the Northern Territories (Habomai Islands, Iturup (Etorofu), Kunashiri and Shikotan Islands), occupied by the USSR since 1945. For Japan the question was motivated primarily neither by economic nor security concerns but by the very principle of territorial integrity; similar feelings informed Russia's refusal to give up territory.

Russia's turn to the West and multi-layered relationship with the East reflected a more profound turning away from the South. The former USSR had posed as champion of the third world, and however ambivalently it reflected aspirations for global social justice and a more equitable world order. The collapse of the Eastern pole of the bipolar left the South without a powerful champion. From being the core of the East, Russia now became a rather isolated North.

Post-cold war geopolitics

Under Putin Russia turned decisively to the West while at the same time recasting its eastern policy. This was no longer an Easternism provoked by failure to become Western, but an attempt to forge a realistic and mutually beneficial relationship. It also represented a move beyond the Eurasian 'bridge' metaphor of Russia linking East and West and an affirmation that Russia was a destination in itself. For Putin the Eurasianist notion of Russia between East and West was a bridge leading nowhere. Dmitry Trenin argued that China's growing strength in the East and the instability of the Islamic south, meant that Russia's only geopolitical future lay with the West. This would mean accelerated integration with the EU and solid relations with the United States.[62] It was clear that Eurasianism had died, both intellectually and geopolitically. It was unable to sustain a coherent foreign policy.

However, just at the time that Russia began to reject the logic of geopolitics, the US advanced it with renewed vigour. While Russia had become a partisan of geopolitical pluralism, the United States developed ever more layers to its hegemonic predominance.[63] The post-cold war world has been unable to sustain the Helsinki approach to international order. Helsinki represented the repudiation of Yalta and the assertion that the international system is made up of a community of states, however small. Instead, international affairs appear to be heading back towards a return to the politics of Yalta: small countries perhaps do not matter. This is the great failure of the post-cold war world, and the marginalisation of the OSCE and the UN in the post-cold war era reflects a larger failure to sustain the politics of Helsinki.

One test whether Russian foreign policy has become 'normal' is the country's ability to establish balanced relations with countries that had once been in its orbit. This concerned not only the former Soviet states, but also the countries of Central and Eastern Europe. These issues were highlighted during Putin's visit to Poland in January 2002. The Polish president, Alexander Kwasnieski, was a former communist and fluent Russian speaker, and the visit was full of the rhetoric of an 'equal partnership'. However, relations were soured by energy issues, in particular the 1993 agreement that committed Poland to buying gas from Russia in excess of its requirement, leading to a $3.7 billion trade deficit. Poland was unhappy with the low level of transit fees it could charge on the Yamal pipeline that ran across its territory taking gas to Germany. Discussions in Poland at this time centred on whether Russia had indeed become a 'normal' country with which Poland could enjoy normal relations, or whether Russia continued to use trade and other economic issues as instruments to exert geopolitical power.[64] If the latter, then no long-term viable relations could be established; if the former, then Poland's accession to the EU would provide enormous opportunities for the development of diversified economic relations with Russia, formerly its largest trading partner; while Poland for Russia would be a door to the larger European market.

The end of CIS resurrectionism

The CIS never lived up to the aspirations of some of its founders. It proved unable to regulate disputes between its own members, covering not only conflicts over borders, support for insurgency in other member states, economic relations, and on occasion open war, between Armenia and Azerbaijan over the disputed territory of Nagorno-Karabakh. Fear of Russian domination from the very beginning prompted countries like the Ukraine to impede the institutional and political development of the CIS, while all (with the exception of Belarus) actively diversified traditional links away from Russia towards the West and regional powers. In security affairs membership of Nato had become the open aspiration of countries ranging from the Ukraine to Azerbaijan, Uzbekistan and Kazakhstan. The establishment of an American security presence in Central Asia and Georgia after 11 September was vivid manifestation that old patterns and regional alliances had given way to a far more fluid global geo-political situation.

Although Putin may have had a sentimental regard for the recreation of some sort of post-Soviet integrated space, his approach in practice was ruthlessly realistic. It was clear that he recognised that the CIS would not be able to act as the focus for integration. For him, the CIS had no interests of its own but was instead the immediate sphere for the pursuit of Russian interests and concerns. The adoption of a new citizenship law in July 2002 revealed the new unsentimental approach, with the CIS states seen as the source of labour while at the same time cutting off all those who had failed to claim Russian citizenship by then. The new law finally drew a line between who was and who was not a Russian citizen and thus was designed to play its part in reinforcing Russia's national identity. The term *sootechestvennik* (compatriot) was to be used henceforth strictly to describe Russian citizens living abroad, and not to the great mass of ethnic Russians living in the former Soviet republics.[65]

Surrounded by relatively weak states and with powerful security threats emanating from the South, Russia had little choice but to reassert some sort of hegemony over the region. But there were different ways in which this could be achieved, above all either coercive or co-operative, and Russia appeared to pursue them all simultaneously.[66] Popular opinion strongly favoured the reintegration of the post-Soviet space, although links with Belarus, the Ukraine, Kazakhstan and Moldova came top of the list.[67] The great strategic problem facing Russia was the challenge of foreign policy diversification by its former brother Soviet states. It was clear that the CIS had failed to become the great counter-European institutions that some in Moscow had anticipated.

The most vivid evidence of the decline of the CIS was the creation in 1998 of the GUUAM group of states (Georgia, Ukraine, Uzbekistan – which joined in April 1999 – Azerbaijan and Moldova). The aim was to stay outside Russia's orbit and Russian-dominated bodies like the CIS Collective Security Treaty (CST) and the Eurasian Economic Community. GUUAM clearly was an implicitly anti-Russian alliance, and at one time it looked as if, with American support, it would be able to push back Russian influence in the region. However, the relative failure of GUUAM, with almost no achievements to its credit other than resisting Moscow's attempts to revise the Treaty on Conventional Forces in Europe, showed in fact how central Moscow was to the region. Uzbekistan by early 2000 had clearly cooled towards the body, wanting Russian assistance in its struggle against 'Islamic extremism', while Moldova feared antagonising Russia and, now led by a neo-communist government, suffered from multiple vulnerabilities. At a summit meeting of its leaders in Yalta in July 2001 GUUAM became an organisation with its own secretariat and headquarters, but already by the time of another summit exactly a year later (19–20 July 2002), again in Yalta, the Uzbekistan leader, Islam Karimov, stayed away. The meeting went ahead and agreed to rename the organisation the Black Sea–Caspian Initiative, and took further plans to establish a free trade area, now comprising only the four countries. Discussions also centred on the development of oil pipelines bypassing Russia, one of the main *raisons d'être* of GU(U)AM.[68] A rump GAU (Georgia, Azerbaijan and Ukraine) would probably provoke more problems than it would be able to resolve.

The US had strongly supported the GUUAM initiative as part of its two-prong strategy of supporting Moscow verbally at the state level while doing all in its power politically to isolate Russia and to push it out of its traditional sphere of influence in the Caucasus and Central Asia.[69] A type of neo-containment policy was pursued in the former Soviet South while the integration of Moscow into Western institutions was proceeding in the North. The Ukraine was a willing accomplice, and indeed instrument, of this strategy. Some went so far to suggest that American policy had given hope to the secessionists in Chechnya, and hence had to bear some of the responsibility for the tragic outcome. It is unclear whether the United States favoured the disintegration of Russia or not; an ambiguity that in the Byzantine politics of the Caucasus would not remain unexploited for long. Just as Russia had anti-Western hard liners, the West had many (possibly among the neo-conservatives prominent in Bush's entourage) who insisted that Russia remained a real threat and all should be done to ensure that it never rose to great power status again.

Putin maintained Yeltsin's policy of support for the various de facto states left behind in the detritus of the break-up of the USSR. One way or another Russia continued to support Abkhazia's struggle for autonomy from Georgia. Russia's support for the intransigent and corrupt regime headed by Igor Smirnov at the head of the breakaway Transdniester region of Moldova, however, was liable to cause Putin considerable embarrassment. Russia had agreed at the OSCE summit in November 1999 to withdraw its forces from the region by December 2002, and failure to do so undermined international trust in his leadership. Russia was reluctant to fulfil its pledge made at the OSCE summit in late 1999 to close down its Gudauta base in Georgia by July 2001, and to negotiate the closure of the Batumi and Akhalkalaki bases.

Putin sought to find effective instruments to institutionalise links with willing CIS partners. Russia tried to reinvigorate the Eurasian Economic Community and the Collective Security Treaty. The latter had been established in Tashkent in 1992 and represented one of the very few successful attempts to build a broad multilateral body within the framework of the CIS, with eight countries having joined by 1994.[70] But it also reflected the weakness of such bodies, and Azerbaijan, Georgia and Uzbekistan never took part in any of its activities and abandoned it altogether in 1999. The remaining countries divided into three operational groups; Russia and Belarus in the West, Russia and Armenia in the Caucasus, and Russia, Kazakhstan, Kyrgyzstan and Tajikistan in Central Asia. On the very day in June 2002 that the new partnership council was established with Nato, Putin signed the papers that transformed the CST into a Collective Security Treaty Organisation (CSTO). The tripartite regional structure was preserved, but now the aim was to pour some operational content into what had been a largely political organisation. A rapid reaction force was created, with Russia deploying aircraft to the Kant airbase near Bishkek in Kyrgyzstan. While the anti-Western Lukashenko greeted the creation of the CSTO as a counter-weight to Nato, few really believed that a new geopolitical force was emerging in the East as the successor to the Warsaw Pact.

Unification with Belarus

These regional alliances however were not able to substitute for bilateral links, the most intense of which was with Belarus. There was strong and consistent public support for unification with Belarus, with 62 per cent in support in 1997 and 72 per cent in November 2000, while on average only 15 per cent were opposed.[71] Russia's link with 'Europe's last dictator',[72] Lukashenko, was understandable in purely *Realpolitik* terms but did little to enhance Russia's reputation as a supporter of human rights. Putin rejected Lukashenko's plan of 10 June 2002 for unification, insisting that unification should not be at the 'expense of Russia's economic interests'. He refused to countenance Lukashenko's demands that Belarus, whose economy was only 3 per cent of Russia's, would have 'rights of veto, sovereignty and territorial integrity' unless Russia had them too, and spoke against creating 'a supranational organ with undefined functions'.[73] The speech much displeased Yeltsin, since Lukashenko's plan had been endorsed by him. Putin later, however, insisted that 'the Belarusian and Russian peoples are brotherly people in the full sense of this word', and stressed the close economic links between the two countries and that Russia could be strengthened by unification with Belarus as part of the 'movement of the Russian Federation – both territorial and demographic – in the direction of Europe'. The main thing, however, he insisted was that 'the form and methods of the unification should be beneficial for both the Belarusian and Russian peoples'.[74]

*   *   *

Russian policy under Putin entered a period of co-operative pragmatism, but the West did not always reciprocate. Close relations with the United States did not lead to the lifting of the Jackson–Vanik amendment on emigration policy, although in 2002 the US did recognise Russia as a market economy.

Indeed, it appeared that Russian policy had entered a period of unilateral concessions. Nato enlargement to include the Baltic republics, the stationing of American troops in Central Asia and even in Georgia was considered by Putin as 'no tragedy', while Putin considered America's unilateral withdrawal from the ABM treaty 'no threat to Russian security'. The old Soviet and Primakovian politics of linkage in negotiations and symmetry in concessions gave way to a thoroughly new understanding of diplomacy that some saw as a new version of Gorbachevian capitulationism. Putin's approach, however, differed radically from Gorbachev's since as far as he was concerned the very language of 'concessions' was redolent of the old competitive ideological logic between two systems or the geopolitical competition between two states. Competitive pragmatism gave way to a co-operative form. Although he had spent his first career in the security services, Putin was well aware of the limits of military power. He had witnessed the impotence of the Red Army as the communist order crumbled in the GDR ('Moscow is silent'). Putin's understanding of the importance of what Joseph Nye and others have called 'soft power' was very much his own, since it was a view that was certainly not shared by most of the military, the diplomatic service, politicians (even liberal ones), let alone the public, yet gradually most of these groups came to understand that a genuine post-cold war approach to international relations could pay greater dividends than traditional 'realist' attitudes.

10 Conclusion

> Russia should be and will be a country with a developed civil society and stable democracy. Russia will guarantee full human rights, civil liberties and political freedom. Russia should be and will be a country with a competitive market economy, a country where property rights are reliably protected and where economic freedom makes it possible for people to work honestly and to earn without fear or restriction. Russia will be a strong country with modern, well-equipped and mobile armed forces, with an army ready to defend Russia and its allies and the national interests of the country and of its citizens. All this will and should create worthy living conditions for people and will make it possible to be an equal in the society of the most developed states. And people can not only be proud of such a country – they will multiply its wealth, will remember and respect our great history. This is our strategic goal.
>
> (Putin, state-of-the-nation address, 16 May 2003[1])

In his work on political leadership Machiavelli applied the classic distinction between *fortuna*, or random luck, and *virtù*, success emanating from the intrinsic qualities of the person. Putin's meteoric rise to become president of Russia was certainly characterised by an awesome degree of luck, but without his extraordinary *virtù* this luck would have probably availed him nothing. Periods of war and dislocation, moreover, often allow outsiders to come to power, but in Putin's case leadership succession took place in peacetime, although of course in far from settled circumstances. Similarly, the banal adage that a leader was 'the right man at the right time' is in this case not far off the mark, although more often than not it is the wrong person for any time who comes to power. Putin's rise reflected the structural conditions of a society desperate to put an end to utopian experimentation and to overcome the bitter divisions that this experimentation provoked. His own background, as a child of the 1970s, loyal to the old regime yet sceptical about it, deeply patriotic yet having internalised the multiculturalism that the communist regime proclaimed (although did not always practice), and a natural European for whom the question of Russia's civilisational identity was not a problem, meant that he reflected the aspirations of society for resolution and closure. Perhaps above all, it was clear that for Putin power was not an end in itself, to

achieve self-aggrandisement and to enjoy the trappings of pomp and ceremony, but to achieve goals to serve what he considered the country's needs.

We have argued that drawing a simple dichotomy between Putin's neo-
Soviet and post-Soviet faces is inadequate, although not untrue. These two
faces undoubtedly existed in uncomfortable tension, but the fundamental
dynamic of Putin's leadership, and what prevented either one or the other
face enjoying predominance, was the development of a 'third path' that
began to transcend the sterile divisions of the past. However, it would be a
hard job convincing the people that the promised land of democratic capitalist modernity was attainable and actually an improvement over the years of
Soviet captivity; and like the Israelites of old, Russians cast many a wistful
glance back to comforts and security of Egyptian (read Soviet) enslavement.
As Glinski puts it, 'For the overwhelming majority of Russians . . . the costs of
transition to normalcy still clearly outweigh the benefits. . . .'[2] There is clearly
something of the prophet about Putin's dogged insistence that Russia's
future lies with Europe, the West and democratic capitalist modernity, while
insisting at the same time that this did not mean that Russia had to repress its
own identity or give up the pursuit of its national interests. Let us try below
to sum up some of the themes explored in this book and to explore how we
can move beyond a straightforward dichotomous view of Putin's presidency.

The rules of the game

There is a large degree of continuity between Yeltsin's aims and the policies
pursued by Putin. Economic modernisation, the creation of a democratic
state and international integration are all policies begun by Russia's first
president. However, Putin's leadership style differs substantially from that of
his predecessor. Revolutions are characterised by chaos, the weakening of
the state and illegality, but there then follows a phase of post-revolutionary
stabilisation. Putin's leadership represented such a period. Putin rejected
revolution as a method and sought to build a law-governed state based on
stable institutions and predictable rules. On gaining popular legitimacy
through the ballot box, Putin wasted no time in beginning to reform the way
that the country was governed. At the centre of this was a new relationship
with the regional governors and with the oligarchs. A flurry of initiatives
changed the way that the regime related to other centres of power: seven
federal districts were established; regional governors were removed from the
Federation Council; finance and law enforcement agencies were removed
from regional subordination and 'refederalised'; some of the most odious
oligarchs were exiled; the liberalisation of the economy continued and new
incentives for development put in place; and in foreign policy Russia
unequivocally turned to the West, but on its own terms. The aim was to make
the federal system more structured, impartial, coherent and efficient.
Regional leaders, legislatures and local government were to abide by uniform
rules. The oligarchs were evicted from the corridors of powers, and the

policy of 'equidistance' meant that the relationship was now structured through such bodies as the RUIE. As long as the oligarchs did not flaunt their power and wealth, they were allowed to get on with their business – which was now to be business and not politics. Even the insider oligarchs understood that new patterns of behaviour were required. Many were able to clean up their acts and to transform themselves from 'oligarchs' into businesspeople. In foreign policy Russia was no longer a supplicant nor outcast but just another 'normal' great power.

Putin's presidency represented the attempt to establish a set of rules that could sustain and guide the revival of the state, in both its domestic and foreign aspects. These rules could be summarised as follows: regional leaders as a group were not to make claims on national power; business leaders were to be kept at a distance from the management of the state; and foreign powers could no longer expect to discipline and punish Russia. While at the margins there were authoritarian elements to his leadership, perhaps far more importantly is the fact that it was authoritative. We have suggested above that Putin represented a 'revolt of the masses' against the venality and greed of the Yeltsin years. This revolt gained not only popular but also widespread elite support. It allowed the institutions of the Russian state, born in the trauma of the dissolution of communism in August 1991, the disintegration of the USSR in December of that year, and the birth of the new constitutional order in the bloodshed of October 1993, to gain a deeper legitimacy that had been so singularly lacking in the Yeltsin years. Although a majority had voted for the new constitution on 12 December 1993, the vote had always been tainted by accusations of fraud and was certainly stained by the polarised circumstances in which it was adopted. Putin now sought to ground the constitutional order in a set of political practices that would give it a new lease of legitimacy. Putin inherited an unstable political order, but gradually imbued it with a greater sense of permanence. The 'provisionality' of post-communist Russian governance did not entirely disappear, and could not do so until the structural gulf between regime, state and society had been transcended, but the ground rules of the new order at home and abroad were now more firmly established.

State reconstitution or reconcentration

Putin's programme of state reassertion is capable of at least two broad and very different interpretations: reconstitution is a pluralistic law-based model; whereas reconcentration is a more authoritarian attempt to impose authority over recalcitrant social actors in which it is the regime that is consolidated rather than the constitutional state. In the first version the aim is to achieve the supremacy of the constitution and to ensure the development of what Robert Dahl calls polyarchy in society, the institutionalised basis for a pluralistic politics.[3] However, the dangers of the very uncivil society that Putin inherited, where the major independent actors in society were the oligarchs, regional bosses and criminal elements, encouraged the state to concentrate power in itself to counter-balance these overweening social interests. It is the 'contradictions' between these models and approaches that dominated politics in the Putin era.

Putin's policies can only be understood in the context of the time, coming after Yeltsin's ten years at the helm when social and political relations had been degraded, although certain freedoms had become established. As the public relations expert and Kremlin election adviser Gleb Pavlovsky put it, 'Yeltsin did not build a state. He led a revolution for ten years. . . .'[4] It fell to Putin to become the consolidator of the tenuous democratic freedoms that had emerged out of Yeltsin's permanent revolution. Putin's task was to start building an effective state, freed from the corruption, clientelism and dependency of the Yeltsin years. However, if during the first two years of his rule Putin concentrated on building the presidential 'vertical', thereafter his main concern appeared to be re-election. Putin had been able to stem the disintegration of the state, but he had not been able to build a state strong enough to prosecute organised crime and stamp out corruption. More than that, while in his early years Putin had been able to impose a sense of purpose and unity to the very concept of 'the state', towards the end of his first term it appeared once again to be disintegrating into the struggle of clans and factions. The Yeltsinite 'conglomerate state' began to reappear. From this perspective it could well be argued (as Zinoviev does) that Putin's historical 'mission' was no more than to consolidate and legalise the results of the social revolution that had taken place in the Gorbachev–Yeltsin years, but at the same time to strip them of the defects of the Yeltsin period.[5] Having done that, it was not clear whether the Putin presidency could retain its dynamism.

We have identified a darker neo-Soviet face to Putin's rule. The veteran human rights activist, Sergei Kovalev, argued that 'it was not accidental that KGB Lieutenant-Colonel Putin became president of Russia'.[6] Schooled in the worst traditions of the Soviet Union, it was argued that Putin's liberal veneer could not hide his authoritarian centralisation of power. Freedom of the press appeared an early victim, while the development of Russia as a unitary state in practice, despite formal commitments to the development of federalism, was reminiscent of the worst Soviet days. Once again a climate of fear pervaded social relations, with contacts with outsiders frowned upon and a number of people gaoled for 'anti-state' activities. The secret police intercepted email and telephone traffic, but proved unable to root out corruption. Putin, some argued, turned out to be little more than a more active version of Brezhnev. His assertions about the need for a 'dictatorship of law' revealed perhaps more than he intended, showing his lack of understanding of the need for an independent judiciary and a proper legal system to regulate a genuinely free market.[7]

Undoubtedly characterised by contradictory social processes, we argue that Putin sought to achieve the necessary reconstitution of the state through largely democratic means. He remained committed to the 1993 constitutional settlement and sought to work through legal means to rebuild the state and social order. Putin can be seen as a representative of the type that has a long pedigree in Russian history, the decisive leader who forges the nation's consolidation in a time of crisis. This usually took place at a time of a foreign threat, accompanied sometimes by internal disintegration. In Putin's case, the main threats were domestic. In his reform of the federal system Putin sought to bring some order and justice into a society where the arbitrariness of the regional barons was plain for all to see. He pushed through over 200 major pieces of legislation that affected most aspects of government and society. In addition, the struggle for 'social justice' entailed an assault on the extra-democratic privileges of the oligarchs while trying to ensure basic standards of living for the population. Another facet of Russia's reforming leaders is also apparent: early activism is ground down by the bureaucracy and energy dissipated in court intrigues. Putin's consensual approach could be seen as excessive caution that allowed the corrupt oligarchs and bureaucracy to blunt the reforming impulse. The revenge of the bureaucracy, as Gorbachev discovered, is a terrible thing. Rather than achieving the 'normality' prevalent in Western democracies, a deeper Russian 'normality', many have argued, began to reassert itself.

Beyond segmented regionalism

Segmented regionalism was characterised by the erosion of constitutional principles of a single legal and economic space. Regional authorities took advantage of the weakness of the Russian state under Yeltsin to develop a highly variegated set of policies and political regimes. The concept of asymmetrical federalism disguised the way that national norms guaranteeing individual rights, legal standards and the development of a national market were undermined by strong regional executives, often little constrained by their own representative assemblies. It was this segmented regionalism that Putin sought to reverse, but his attempt to reconstitute the state was torn between compacted and more pluralistic forms of statism. The struggle against segmented regionalism could easily undermine the development of federalism, and in taking the form of traditional centralism threatened the development of Russian democracy. Caught between segmented regionalism and the Putinite normative reconstitution of the state, federalism itself as the legal separation of powers in the spatial context appeared under threat. The methods and principles that appeared to work so well in France could not automatically be applied to Russia. While France is a unitary state, Russia is a federal system in which sovereignty as a matter of principle is to be shared between the federal government and sub-national federal units.

The effect of Putin's reforms of the federal system were mixed. The old segmentation has been decreased, with regional laws and republican constitutions beginning to converge with federal constitutional and legal norms, the state's own agencies in the regions brought back under central control, and some of the more egregious centrifugal tendencies checked. However, regional reforms have not entirely been able to overcome institutional confusion, and in some cases instead of being resolved these contradictions have intensified. For example, the reform of the Federation Council has only raised in sharper form the idea that it should be formed through direct elections. New tensions have emerged, as between the presidential envoys and the government: the envoys have been urged to ensure federal control over ministerial branches in the regions but the representatives themselves do not sit in the cabinet. Relations with the presidential administration are not always smooth, while relations with the governors are structurally unstable. While regionalisation may be a response to globalisation, Russia's confused federalism means that this response is equally confused. Putin's reforms are centralising insofar as they seek to fulfil the liberal republican ideal of equality of law across the whole territory, but in practice they have managed to reproduce new forms of segmentation, but at a higher level. Institutional fragmentation continues, and instead of a power 'vertical' being established, we have instead a power 'triangle', intensifying bureaucratic conflicts and complicating public administration. At the same time the interests of regime perpetuation have undermined state reconstitution. It has been argued that the 9 July 2002 Constitutional Court ruling allowing governors to seek a third term marks a symbolic dividing line between the era of strengthening state authority (*vertikal vlasti*) and a 'post-vertical' period: 'Hoping to avoid a conflict with the powerful regional elite on the eve of the 2003–04 electoral cycle, Putin demonstrated that his own conflict-free re-election was his top priority, while reforming Russian federalism had lower standing.'[8]

All federations are designed to constrain central political power, but not all do so with equal effect. In Russia, whatever the nature of the local regimes themselves, regions acted as a check on the central authorities; a type of horizontal separation of powers emerged that to a degree compensated for the inadequacy of the vertical separation of powers in the constitutional order established in December 1993. Russian regionalism emerged as a more effective check, if not democratic balance, on executive authority than the relatively weak legislature and judiciary. Thus, although Putin may well have sought the democratic reconstitution of the state, the weakening of the regional 'fourth pivot' acting as a check on the central authorities undermined the democratic separation of powers. The reconstitution of the state, although a laudable aim in itself, could also be dangerous in the regional context for the development of a democratic and federal pluralism.

Reconstitution and universal citizenship

State consolidation can act as both the facilitator of democratisation and as its gravedigger, and elements of both were visible under Putin. Putin was both a centraliser of state power, but at the same time it was argued that this centralisation served to equalise the rights of citizens across Russia. The declared aim was to ensure that citizenship became universal across the country, not impeded by the emergence of various neo-feudal localistic patrimonial or ethnocratic regimes. Thus it could be argued that Putin was an equaliser rather than a centraliser, but the fundamental question is whether the basis of this equalisation would be full civil and democratic rights, or an equality in subordination.

Putin's reassertion of central authority in defence of the writ of the constitution represented the defence of a particular vision of democracy. Although there were undoubtedly elements of reconcentration at work (the 'normalisation' factor that accompanies the striving for normality), the overall thrust of Putin's reforms was an attempt, literally, to *reconstitute* the state, to place the constitution at the centre of regional relations. For some this was no more than a new form of Russia's traditional tendency towards centralisation; but the case could be made with equal plausibility that it offered an opportunity to move away from asymmetrical federalism and asymmetrical power relations in general towards a more balanced form. Asymmetrical federalism not only granted differential rights to regional leaderships, but effectively established different gradations of democratic citizenship to those living in different parts of the country. Asymmetrical power relations meant that the citizen had few recourses against the rich and powerful through the courts, or against wilful bureaucrats in day to day dealings with the state administration. The attempt to achieve a universal and homogeneous type of citizenship lay at the heart of Putin's attempt to reconstitute the state.

Citizenship was now to be equal across the whole country and rather less 'lumpy'. No longer was the exercise of citizenship to vary between republics and regions, and indeed between classes. That at least was the idea, but soon Putin was forced to recognise that the enormous asymmetries in power and wealth across the country could not so easily be reduced, and even he was forced to engage in bargaining and compromises that left the country far short of the universal model that he had initially announced. Putin announced the new rules of the game, with an end to the bilateral treaties with the regions and with the oligarchs kept at an equal distance from power, but the regime was both a player and the referee. The regime's own interests in survival came into contradiction with the ideals that it proclaimed.

Beyond transition

Under Putin the notion of a post-communist *transition* was abandoned in favour of a more systematic attempt to build consensus for the continued transformation of the country into a democratic market system. The ideology of transition gave way to one of consolidation. Although the changes launched by Yeltsin have been continued, and in many respects deepened, the way that change is managed has changed dramatically. The changes are no longer couched in revolutionary terms, although their outcome in the long term will be no less revolutionary than Yeltsin's. Putin's rejection of the revolutionary method was accompanied by the development of a politics of normality in which procedure and institutions begin to take priority over revolutionary expediency and personalistic leadership. The intention now was to 'live in the present' by putting an end to revolutionary leaps of faith into the future. This 'present', moreover, was to be defined within a politics of the possible, a pragmatic acceptance of the 'normality' of the West.

Putin inherited a country that had the full gamut of democratic institutions, but it was not a fully-fledged or 'consolidated' democracy. One of the reasons for this, quite apart from Yeltsin's personal eccentricities, was that the state itself lacked a firm institutional base. As Linz and Stepan have stressed, 'democracy is a form of governance of a modern state', and therefore 'without a state, no modern democracy is possible'.[9] Was Putin able to transform Russia's imperfect democracy into something better? By putting a conclusive end to the border question (unless negotiated and agreed with all parties), he at least ensured that the vessel in which a putative democracy could develop was assured. The *boundary* question was effectively resolved, although at some point Belarus or some other region could possibly join. He also insisted that the fledgling political institutions created in the 1990s and formalised by the 1993 constitution should be given a chance to work, and thus he consolidated the *polity*, the formal institutions of the state. As we have seen Putin established a new set of rules in relations between state and society, oligarchs and government, regions and the centre. Finally, his policies, above all regional and judicial reforms, were designed to ensure that the question of *regime type* was closed: as far as he was concerned, Russia would be a democracy or it would be nothing.

The power of contradiction

In discussing contradictions classic Marxism distinguishes between those that are solvable (non-antagonistic) or antinomies (antagonistic contradictions that cannot be resolved). There were plenty of contradictions of both sorts in Putin's leadership, but ultimately he was able for a time to finesse some of the most glaring antinomies while seeking to resolve some of the non-antagonistic contradictions. The contradictory nature of Putin's policies and approach, paradoxically, became the source of his power. By adopting elements of both reconstituted and reconcentrated statism, of neo-Soviet and post-Soviet identities, of continuity with the whole long history of Russian development while at the same time repudiating the most egregious negative pathologies of each of Russia's stages of historical evolution (above all, the imperial, the Soviet and the 'democratic'), Putin achieved a historical reconciliation of the many threads of Russian identity and the many layers of Russian society.

Putin was a child of the 'family' while at the same time an independent politician. There is, moreover, a contradiction between Putin's reliance on liberals from St Petersburg while drawing on security personnel from the former KGB; a tension that is reflected in his own career path. A liberal security officer may, to paraphrase Kolakowski in his comments on liberal communism, be like warm ice, yet there are clear limits to the influence of the security establishment on policy formation in Putin's Russia. This is clearly a non-antagonistic contradiction. Putin may well have been a *chekist*, but *chekism* has not come to power with him. The contradictory nature of his past, however, is a significant power resource to Putin in developing his personnel policy and in appealing to mutually exclusive popular constituencies. Equally, the lack of an independent base meant that Putin was ready to work with some of the oligarchs, and it would be simplistic to see the model of oligarchical capitalism that has emerged in Russia as a wholly negative phenomenon since it has the potential to evolve towards a more transparent market-based long-term profit-seeking business sector. The outlines of a modern corporate capitalism are emerging, with some of the oligarchs ready to ally with the reforming Kremlin.

The contradiction in personnel policy is reflected more broadly in policy: the tough language of state reassertion is balanced by a consistent commitment to a liberal economic policy, and more broadly, by looking for the support of the main constituency of liberalism in Russia, the intelligentsia. When seeking class or group alliances the choices for Putin were limited, above all because of the absence of a substantive and legitimate property-based conservative middle class. The traditional conservative classes had long ago been swept away and the 'new Russians' who have emerged since the fall of communism have not yet become a 'bourgeoisie' of the sort that Barrington Moore insisted were necessary for democracy to survive.[10] As for interests, Putin tried to ensure the broad support of security apparatus and its personnel in all of their multifarious manifestations; of officialdom in all of its hydra-headed forms; of key segments in society like pensioners and peasants; and of big business, both organised and oligarchical. He avoided appealing directly to the working class out of fear that this could lead to demagogic populism. The *siloviki* have resolutely been excluded from influencing certain public policy spheres, above all in economic and informational matters (other than when directly connected to the Chechen war). In addition, although Putin is clearly something of a statist and patriot himself, he has to a remarkable extent been able to marginalise strident Russophilic nationalist statism. Their influence on the policy process is probably even less than ever it was under Yeltsin, while the ideology of statism or Russian great power thinking (the *derzhavniki*) has probably not been weaker in the last decade and a half. The only coherent policy-forming ideology today in Russia is pro-Western liberalism, however fragmented its political representation may be. Once again there is no antagonistic contradiction here, but the very existence of a contradiction is a source of power to Putin's regime.

Putin persecuted the oligarchs on a selective and partial, although not arbitrary, basis. With the others he struck a bargain: invest your ill-gotten gains in the manufacturing ('real') part of the Russian economy or else face the consequences. Putin thereby hoped to see filched assets return from off-shore haunts and invested to revive the economy. The obvious contradiction inherent in such a policy is that companies forged in the corrupt world of the epoch of *prikhvatizatsiya* ('grabbing') will find it difficult to become good capitalists based on transparent accounting standards and responsibility to shareholders (including minority ones) and legally-accountable directors. While Putin's policy is logical from a short-term perspective, this model of economic development effectively represents the state-sanctioned laundering of resources. In addition, there is much speculation about how close this monopolistic model comes to the South Korean *chaebol* or Japanese *keiretsu*. The fundamental question is whether the development of a healthy market economy can be achieved by increasing state regulation. With the East Asian financial crises of 1997–98 in mind, provoked in part by 'croney capitalism', there is a danger that Russian *nomenklatura* capitalism could evolve into something equally unstable. The jury remains out over whether this is an antagonistic contradiction.

There is another contradiction characteristic of all 'third way' approaches. The attempt to pursue a radical politics of the centre (in both Britain and Russia) can generate new forms of non-ideological extremism. While centrist politics assumes a politics based on consensus and the rational generation of policy, in practice a paradoxical *extremism of the centre* may emerge. The policies pursued are centrist, that is, not sustained by extreme class, national, religious or other ideological presumptions. However, their implementation and the fervour with which they are pursued undermines consensus: form comes into contradiction with content. In Britain the third way by the time of New Labour's second term was marred by what some characterised as a fanatical commitment to 'modernisation' and a target-oriented mechanical managerialism designed to reshape the labour process in a narrow and alienating manner. In Russia the communists and others argued that Putin's radical modernising agenda failed to rebuild social solidarity, subordinated Russia to the power of the economic magnates and to foreign powers. The basic criticism is that Russia could not be rebuilt from the centre. Putin drew back from this extremism of the centre to pursue a more consensual centrism. Nevertheless, the combination of attempts to push through liberal modernising reforms while trying to avoid alienating significant political actors threatened either to lead to extremism (if the modernising agenda was pushed through vigorously) or stagnation (if it was not). It appeared almost that the only thing worse than extremism of the centre was stagnation of the centre.

There is clearly a tension between liberal democracy and liberal statism. Reliance on a liberal elite inevitably raises the question of the degree to which this brings Putin into contradiction with 'the masses'. Is the liberal Westernising elite confined to little more than the academies, institutes and talking shops of the big cities, while the people move to a different rhythm? Although Putin may have enjoyed popularity, his continued pursuit of Yeltsin's agenda, in some ways even more vigorously and certainly more efficaciously, could ultimately lead to his political isolation and possible downfall. Putin's early attempts to build consensus with the CPRF in the Duma, revealed in the division of committee chairmanships in January 2000, had never been accompanied by concessions in the economic sphere. The deal with the CPRF was later repudiated. Putin had clearly made the political calculation that the CPRF no longer mattered that much. But what about the 30 per cent of the population who have traditionally voted for the CPRF? Will reliance on a relatively narrow liberal elite and the pursuit of a pro-Western foreign policy ultimately bring the regime into contradiction with the people?

Liberal patriotism

State reconstitution under Putin was conducted in a non-ideological, technocratic, spirit. Nevertheless, it was conducted under the banner of a 'common sense' state patriotism. There may well be a fundamental contradiction between Putin's attempts to 'nativise' modern liberal democracy while at the same time repudiating 'Eurasianist' alternatives to Western capitalist democracy. Putin's rise can be seen as the triumph of a nativist strand of liberal patriotism. It was nativist because it sought to do what Dostoevsky had tried in the 1840s by developing the 'native soil' (*pochvennik*) idea; between backward-looking Slavophilism and impressionable Westernisers there lay a way of reconciling the imperatives of both. The greatest modern exponent of *pochvennichestvo* is Solzhenitsyn, and thus it is perhaps not surprising that Putin actively sought contact with him in the first period of his leadership. The very term 'liberal patriotism' may appear at first sight to be an oxymoron, but it has a long tradition in Russia. Stolypin, clearly one of Putin's heroes, could be considered the greatest of its practitioners, seeking to modernise Russia while appealing to national pride, trying to achieve liberal reforms with an iron hand. In the realm of philosophy the idea was investigated and to a degree espoused by the likes of Semyon Frank and Peter Struve. The aim was to combine a liberal view of the political and ethical worth of the individual with a strong sense of the collective values represented by the community and its highest expression, the state. Many doubted whether such a combination is viable. The lesson of the national liberals in late nineteenth-century Germany appeared to show the dangers of such a synthesis: in the first years of the twentieth century they ended up by stressing rather more the 'national' than the 'liberal' side of their thinking. The social and international context has changed radically, but history continues to provide warnings – if not lessons.

This ambiguity is reflected in Putin's well-known statement, that we have cited before, that: 'It will not happen soon, if it ever happens at all, that

Russia will become a second edition of, say, the US or Britain in which liberal values have deep historical traditions.' While some critics have taken this to mean that Russia will not become a liberal state, Putin is clearly saying the opposite: that Russia will become a liberal state, but in its own way. There appears to be a contradiction: has Russia given up exceptionalist *Sonderweg* aspirations or not? The old messianism has undoubtedly been jettisoned, of both the Slavophile populist and Marxist statist forms, together with Russian nationalist and neo-imperialist Eurasianism, but the basis of Putin's nativisation is both insubstantive and contradictory.

Normality or 'normalisation'?

Putin's presidency was polymorphic, capable of varying interpretations and driving simultaneously in different directions. It is for this reason that his leadership was capable of such dramatically divergent evaluations. His attempt to reconcile the various Soviet and Russian generations glossed over the substantial differences that they represented. For example, although Putin condemned the 'excessively politicised and bureaucratised' nature of the former Communist Youth League (Komsomol) and Young Pioneers, he insisted that 'there was a meaning in all of this. Along with these purely political ideas, people would receive many useful, general things – the new generation was raised in the spirit of love of the homeland, of their fatherland. There was a great deal of good in that system'.[11]

Putin's reforms were imbued with numerous paradoxes. Perhaps the most notable was the belief that the enhancement of the powers of the state would enable that same strengthened state to defend individual rights. Putin's reforms sought to remake the state; but they may also represent yet another radical shift, so common in Russia, from a period of anarchy and ungovernability to the birth of a new Leviathan. Putin's reforms may provoke precisely the result that they were designed to avert, the erosion of democratic freedoms and the establishment of new forms of exclusive elite rule. In the event, fears on the latter score were mostly exaggerated. Instead, Putin's presidency was increasingly condemned as 'a time of lost and wasted opportunities'.[12]

From regime to governance, from stability to order

It is at this point one of the starkest contradictions creeps in. Have we seen mainly the consolidation of *regime* rule rather than the state, let alone democracy? We defined the regime system as one in which an autonomous power centre becomes established in the interstices between the constitutional state and popular accountability. Under Putin the structure and operation of the regime system undoubtedly changed. There were major shifts in the balance of power between the components constituting the regime, above all between the presidency, elements of the state administration (for example the security services) and societal inputs (above all, the direct access of oligarchs and other 'family' members to the corridors of power was closed), and a more ordered and institutionalised system of governance was established. The presidency, indeed, allied with the constitutional resources of the state to secure greater autonomy from the regime that it nominally led. The problem was that doubts remained whether the constitutional state was being used to strengthen the presidency or whether it would be able to regain its own autonomy, where all parts of the regime (including the presidency) were equally subordinate to the rule of the law.

The full panoply of the Soviet repressive apparatus was not restored, but not enough was done to ensure the impartial operation of law and the solid defence of human and civil rights. Putin's Russia was not a more modern version of Brezhnev's Soviet Union, but neither was it a fully functioning liberal democracy. The tension between efficacy and democracy was not overcome. A gulf remained between the autonomy of the regime and its subordination to the constitutional principles that it espoused. The regime sought to strengthen the state, but the regime itself remained outside the constitutionality represented by the state. There was a danger that improving the performance of the state would simply strengthen the regime rather than reinforce the rule of law and the constitutional state. However, one of Putin's themes was that a state built on authoritarian foundations, as Russian history has repeatedly demonstrated, would be neither strong nor durable. His aim was to establish a system based on a self-sustaining order, but the inability of the regime to relax its grip on the management of democracy reintroduced elements of the 'manual' system of stability.

There is a contradiction between the regime's encouragement of civic activism and attempts to control this activism. It remains unclear whether the concept of 'managed democracy' described by Putin's advisors is a danger to be avoided or a programme to be implemented. The Putin regime is part of a much broader process of constitutive politics in the post-communist states, where the regime becomes constitutive not only of its own preservation but of the foundations of the socio-political order in its entirety. Rather than operating as a delimited sub-system of governance reproducing itself within the norms of the system itself, the regime inevitably becomes more expansive. The government merges into the regime, which itself at times is indistinguishable from the state. If for Carl Schmitt the tragedy of the Weimar republic was that the political was swallowed up by the social, with social interests and movements able to exert direct and unmediated authority over the state, in Russia it is the political that is in danger of swallowing the social. Schmitt in 1927 defined the political as the ability to choose between friend and foe, and to act accordingly, then Putin's regime represents the substantive reassertion of the political.

The constitution grants the presidency enormous powers, and under Yeltsin it emerged as a relatively independent political resource but over time was undermined by his physical debilitation and preference for personalised relations. Under Putin the presidency as an institution revived and became the core of a 'state gathering' project: the presidency became the key instrument of policy innovation and state development. The presidency remained relatively independent both from the normative and constitutional constraints governing the state (the political system), and relatively immune from oversight and accountability to social forces, above all those exercised by parliament. Under Putin the reconstitution of the state was a genuine attempt to enhance the rule of law and the constitution, and to that degree there was a shift from regime relations to governance. However, only when the regime was subordinate to the rule of law and placed itself at the mercy of the vagaries of the democratic process could we say that the shift was complete. As long as a force remained outside the political process the system would be based more on an attempt to maintain artificial stability rather than reflecting an organic order.

The world and Russia

To what degree were Putin's choices constrained by the international system? We have seen that Putin sought to redefine the terms of Russia's relations with the rest of the world. Dealings with the West were now to be practical and goal-oriented, and no longer so intensively filtered through visions of geopolitical competition or the chatter of 'the clash of civilisations'. Putin's own personality, as a target-oriented pragmatist, was now applied to the conduct of foreign policy. Russian foreign policy became 'normal' to the extent that the logic of primordial struggle for pre-eminence (xenophobia) was abandoned together with its accompanying opposite extreme, the slavish copying of Western models (xenomania). Instead, as demonstrated over Chechnya and some other issues, Russia under Putin pursued what it perceived to be its own interests. The same applies to the question of democratisation. Putin's attempts to modernise Russia's political institutions were driven by domestic imperatives rather than by external pressures. The development of a distinctive regime system, in which democratic legitimation is accompanied by the relative independence of the power system from popular control, and the emergence of oligarchical capitalism and bureaucratic neo-patrimonialism, were products of Russian circumstances, although of course shaped by interactions with the global economy and political society.

Normality and universality

Putin's attempt to modernise Russia is undoubtedly an attempt to Westernise it, but it is more than that. Liberal, democratic and market values historically arose in the West, but since at least the Second World War they have taken on a universal quality, as formulated for example in the UN's Universal Charter of Human Rights. It is to this universalism that Putin appealed, while accepting that in the contemporary world the dominance of the West means that the international legal order and other elements of universalism are distorted by the hegemonic powers. At the same time, Putin's strategic choice towards the Western model of universalism would be achieved largely by Russia's own efforts; the decade of Western 'aid' in the 1990s was at best marginally helpful, in ensuring a commitment to marketisation, but possibly harmful in distorting economic policy formation. We should all be grateful for at least one thing arising out of Putin's presidency: an end to chatter about 'who lost Russia?'. Russia's destiny would be forged in Russia, and nowhere else. At the same time, as Rose points out,

> Russians aspire to live in a normal society, and their ideas of normality are much the same as those of people anywhere else – a society where people are safe from crime, where money does not lose its value from inflation, where welfare services help if things go wrong, and where children have opportunities.[13]

Putin sought to craft a model of normality that combined Westernisation with something broader, taking into account Russia's particular history, traditions and place in the world. It is only by combining the universal and the particular that a country can find what is normal for itself. Too far in one direction or another leads to abnormality.

Destiny and decision

There were numerous constraints on Putin's leadership, above all on his ability to create his own leadership team to implement the policies that he espoused. To a remarkable extent, however, Putin forged an administration that could transcend these contradictions and constraints. A relatively coherent and apparently durable new political order began to emerge. Whether this was little more than the temporary consolidation of a regime based on the personality of the president or a more permanent rearrangement of relations between the state, governing regime and society to create a new political order that would outlast Putin's presidency remains to be seen. The outcome of his choices at this stage cannot be predicted.

The legitimacy of Putin's presidency was formally based on democratic and legal procedures, but his leadership also contained a charismatic element that transcended the legal-rational political order that was struggling to be born in post-communist Russia. As Weber noted,

> Charisma knows only inner determination and inner restraint. The holder of charisma seizes the task that is adequate for him and demands obedience and a following by virtue of his mission. His success determines whether he finds them. His charismatic claim

breaks down if his mission is not recognized by those to whom he feels he has been sent'.[14]

In a paradoxical way, Putin's charisma (defined here as leadership qualities that had an appeal beyond the constraints of the formal authority endowed to him by the constitution) was intended to serve precisely the consolidation of constitutional authority. As so often in politics, the most effective route between intention and outcome is not always the shortest. Charismatic leadership is a powerful political resource, especially in a country such as Russia where the post-communist political terrain was bleak, with no long established parties and few civic associations with the power, resources or willingness to build a dynamic, pluralistic, socially fair and democratic society. In this context there is inevitably a tension between preserving and transforming the system.

Given the highly concentrated nature of Russian politics and the weakness of checks and balances, much depended on Putin's personal choices. His power was certainly constrained by the inherited structure of power and elite relations, but his leadership consisted of far more than simply balancing the interests of Kremlin factions. Putin's mini cult of the personality, although clearly offensive to many and retrograde in inhibiting the institutionalisation of authority and the maturing of civic democracy, was perhaps the price to pay to allow the presidency to retain its political autonomy. Putin was a pragmatic politician committed not only to the concentration of his own authority but also driven by a commitment to modernise Russia, with modernisation defined as the adoption of the norms prevalent in mature capitalist democracies, but with a Russian face. Although elements of both neo-Soviet and post-Soviet were in evidence throughout his rule, it is clear that Putin was the first genuine post-Soviet leader in Russian politics. Although Yeltsin may have become a democrat by necessity, his instincts remained steeped in Soviet practices. Putin was more of a democrat by conviction, but remained torn between neo- and post-Soviet impulses, imbuing his policies with contradictory qualities that added to the enigmatic and contradictory character of his rule. The approach was pragmatic, but in this case pragmatism did not mean that the end justified the means. Instead, in a manner reminiscent of Eduard Bernstein's insistence that the *movement* meant everything to him and the *final aim* of socialism nothing,[15] as a matter of principle he rejected revolutionary methods to reunify ends and means. While there may well have been dangers attendant upon Putin succeeding in establishing his authority, there were even greater dangers if he failed.

Putin's victory in 2000 reflected more than a successful manoeuvre by the Kremlin in the succession struggle. Putin's victory, in a strange and distorted way, reflected the victory of the people against the oligarchs, over-powerful regional bosses and corrupt bureaucrats. As an ordinary Soviet person, Putin's life reflected the lives of millions of his fellow citizens. In Putin, the people could see themselves. Putin, in short, reflected a mass revolt against the corruption of the Yeltsin years and the humiliation of Gorbachev's final period in office. If we understand Yeltsin's rule as a period of 'permanent revolution', then Putin becomes the consolidator, the Napoleon (not necessarily on horseback) who rebuilds the state and incorporates into the new order the progressive elements of the revolutionary epoch that are necessary for social development, but discards the excesses and the revolutionary froth. Putin consigned the revolutionary period of Yeltsin's leadership to history. The fundamental question ultimately is not so much which of the paths predominated, but that in the system managed by Putin all roads led back to him. Only when Putin's choices were part of a larger chorus and no longer so decisive could we say that Russia unequivocally was a democracy. The best way to demonstrate that would be to lose an election and to hand power over to the leader of an opposition as part of the change of government and not of regime. We have argued in this book that many of Putin's choices led in this direction, but the final proof of his commitment to them would be if he followed his own path.

Appendix

Russia at the turn of the millennium

Vladimir Putin, 29 December 1999
(translated by the author)

The contemporary world lives under the sign of two global events: the new millennium and the two thousandth anniversary of Christianity. In my view the enormous interest in these two events represents something greater and deeper than just the tradition of celebrating significant dates.

New possibilities, new problems

It may or may not be a coincidence, but the onset of the new millennium coincides with a dramatic turn in global developments in the past 20–30 years. *I mean the rapid and profound changes in the life of humanity associated with the development of what we call the post-industrial society.* [Italics throughout in the original.] Its main features include:

- Changes in the economic structure of society, with the decreasing weight of material production and the growing share of secondary and tertiary sectors.
- The continuous renewal and rapid introduction of advanced technologies and the growing output of science-based commodities.
- The tempestuous development of information technologies and telecommunications.
- Priority attention to management and the modification of organisational and managerial systems in all spheres of social activity.
- And finally, human leadership. High levels of the education, professional training, entrepreneurial and social activity of the individual are becoming the main dynamic forces of progress today.

The development of a new type of society is a drawn-out enough process for attentive politicians, statesmen, scientists and all those who use their minds to observe *two elements of concern in this process.* The first is that changes bring not only new possibilities to improve life, but also new problems and dangers. These were first most clearly revealed in the ecological sphere, but other acute problems soon became apparent in all other spheres of social life. Even the most economically advanced states are not free from organised crime, growing cruelty and violence, alcoholism and drug addiction, and the weakening cohesion and educational role of the family, and the like.

The second alarming factor is that not all countries can take advantage of the benefits of modern economies and their associated standards of prosperity. The rapid progress of science, technology and advanced economy is underway in only a small number of states, populated by the so-called 'golden billion'. Quite a few other countries achieved much economic and social development in the outgoing century, but they were unable to enter the process of creating a post-industrial society. Most of them are still far from it, and there is much evidence to suggest that this gap will persist for quite some time yet. This is probably why humanity is looking into the future with both hope and trepidation at the turn of the new millennium.

The contemporary situation in Russia

It would be no exaggeration to say that this combination of hope and fear is particularly strong in Russia. There are few countries in the world that have faced so many trials as Russia in the twentieth century.

First, Russia is not among those states with the highest levels of economic and social development. And second, it is facing economic and social difficulties. Russia's GDP nearly halved in the 1990s, and its GNP is ten times smaller than that of the USA and five times smaller than that of China. After the 1998 crisis, per capita GDP dropped to roughly \$3,500, which is roughly five times smaller than the average level for G7 states.

The structure of the Russian economy has changed. The economy is now dominated by the energy sector, power engineering, and ferrous and non-ferrous metallurgy. These spheres account for some 15 per cent of GDP, 50 per cent of overall industrial output, and over 70 per cent of exports.

Labour productivity in the real economy is extremely low. In the raw materials and electricity sectors it has risen to comparable world levels, but in other fields it is 20–24 per cent of, for example, the US average. The technical and technological standards of manufactured commodities are largely dependent on the proportion of equipment that is less than five years old. This proportion fell from 29 per cent in 1990 to 4.5 per cent in 1998. Over 70 per cent of our machinery and equipment is over ten years old, which is more than double the figure in economically developed countries.

This is the result of consistently falling national investment, above all in the real economy. Foreign investors moreover are not rushing to contribute to the development of Russian industry. The overall volume of foreign direct investment in Russia amounts to barely \$11.5 billion. China has received as much as \$43 billion in foreign investment. Russia has been reducing allocations to research and development, while the 300 largest transnational companies invested \$216 billion in research and development in 1997, and some

$240 billion in 1998. Only 5 per cent of Russian enterprises are engaged in innovative production, and output of this type remains very low.

The lack of capital investment and insufficient attention to innovation resulted in a dramatic fall in the production of commodities that are competitive in world markets in terms of price-quality ratio. Foreign competitors have pushed Russia especially far back in the market for science-intensive civilian commodities. Russia accounts for less than 1 per cent of such commodities on the world market, while the USA provides 36 per cent and Japan 30 per cent.

The population's real income has been falling since the beginning of the reforms. The deepest fall was registered after the August 1998 crisis, and it will be impossible to restore the pre-crisis living standards this year. The overall monetary incomes of the population, calculated by the UN methods, comprise less than 10 per cent of the US figure. Health and average life expectancy, the indicators that determine the quality of life, have also deteriorated.

The current difficult economic and social situation in the country is the price that we have to pay for the economy we inherited from the Soviet Union. But then, what else could we have inherited? We had to introduce market mechanisms into a system based on completely different standards, with a gigantic and distorted structure. This was bound to affect the progress of the reforms.

We had to pay for the excessive focus of the Soviet economy on the development of the raw materials sector and defence industries, which negatively affected the development of consumer production and services. We are paying for the Soviet neglect of such key sectors as information science, electronics and communications. We are paying for the absence of competition between producers and industries, which inhibited scientific and technological progress and rendered the Russian economy non-competitive in world markets. This is the price to pay for the impediments and bans on initiative and entrepreneurship of companies and workers. Today we are reaping the bitter fruit, both material and intellectual, of past decades.

On the other hand, we could have avoided some of the problems in the renewal process. They are the result of our own mistakes, miscalculation and lack of experience. *And yet, we could not have avoided the main problems facing Russian society.* The road to the market and democracy was difficult for all states that entered it in the 1990s. They all broadly encountered the same problems, although to varying degrees.

Russia is completing the first, transition stage of economic and political reforms. Despite problems and mistakes, we have entered the main highway of human development. World experience convincingly shows that only this path offers the possibility of dynamic economic growth and higher living standards. There is no alternative.

The question for Russia today is what to do next. How can we make the new market mechanisms work to full capacity? How can we overcome the still deep ideological and political divisions in society? What strategic goals can

consolidate Russian society? What place can Russia occupy in the international community in the twenty-first century? What economic, social and
cultural frontiers do we want to attain in 10–15 years? What are our strong
and weak points? And what material and spiritual resources do we have now?

These are the questions posed by life itself. Unless we find clear answers
comprehensible to the people we will be unable to move forwards quickly to
the goals that are worthy of our great country.

The lessons for Russia

Our future depends on the answers to these questions and the lessons we
draw from our past and present. This is a long-term task for society as a
whole, but some of these lessons are already clear.

1   For three-quarters of the twentieth century Russia was dominated by the
    attempt to implement communist doctrine. It would be a mistake not to
    recognise, and even more to deny, the unquestionable achievements of
    those times. But it would be an even bigger mistake not to realise the
    outrageous price our country and its people had to pay for that social
    experiment. What is more, it would be an even bigger mistake not to
    understand its historic futility. *Communism and Soviet power did not make
    Russia a prosperous country with a dynamically developing society and free
    people.* Communism vividly demonstrated its inability to promote sound
    self-development, dooming our country to persistently lagging behind
    economically advanced countries. However bitter it may now be to admit
    it, but for nearly seven decades we were moving along a blind alley, far
    from the mainstream of civilisation.

2   *Russia has reached its limit for political and socio-economic upheavals, cataclysms
    and radical reforms.* Only fanatics or political forces that have absolutely
    no concern for Russia and are indifferent to its people can make calls for
    a new revolution. Be it under communist, national-patriotic or radical-
    liberal slogans, our country, our people cannot endure another new
    radical upheaval. The nation's patience and its ability to survive as well as
    its capacity to work creatively have reached their limits. Society will
    simply collapse economically, politically, psychologically and morally.

    *Responsible socio-political forces should offer the country a strategy for Russia's
    revival and prosperity based on the positive experience that has been gained
    during the period of market and democratic reforms and implemented only by evo-
    lutionary, gradual and prudent methods.* This strategy should be carried out
    on the basis of political stability and should not lead to the deterioration
    in the lives of any section or groups of the Russian people. This indis-
    putable condition arises from the present situation of our country.

3   The experience of the 1990s vividly demonstrates that our country's
    genuine renewal without excessive costs cannot be achieved by merely
    experimenting with abstract models and schemes taken from foreign

textbooks. The mechanical copying of other nations' experience will not guarantee success, either.

Every country, Russia included, has to find its own path of renewal. We have so far not been very successful in this respect. Only in the past year or two have we started groping for our own road and our model of transformation. *Our future depends on combining the universal principles of the market economy and democracy with Russian realities.* Our scholars, analysts, experts, public servants at all levels and political and public organisations should work with this aim in mind.

A chance for a worthy future

Such are the main lessons of the outgoing century. They make it possible to outline the contours of a long-term strategy which will enable us, within a comparatively short time, to overcome the present protracted crisis and create conditions for the country's rapid and stable economic and social improvement. I stress the need for speed; we have no time to dawdle.

Let me quote the calculations of experts. It will take us approximately 15 years and annual GDP growth of 8 per cent to reach the per capita GDP level of present-day Portugal or Spain, which are not among the world's industrial leaders. If during the same 15 years we manage annually to increase our GDP by 10 per cent, we will then catch up with Britain or France.

Even if we suppose that these calculations are not quite accurate and our current economic backwardness is not that serious and we can overcome it faster, it will still require many years of work. That is why we should formulate our long-term strategy and start fulfilling it as soon as possible.

We have already taken the first step in this direction. In late December the Centre for Strategic Research, created on the initiative and with the active support of the government, began its work. This Centre will bring together the best minds of our country to draft recommendations and proposals for the government for both theoretical and applied projects. It will help devise the strategy and seek effective ways of implementing it. *I am convinced that ensuring the necessary growth dynamics is not only an economic problem. It is also a political and, in a certain sense, – and I am not afraid to use this word – an ideological problem.* To be more precise, it is an ideological, spiritual and moral problem. It seems to me that the latter is of particular importance in our current efforts to ensure the unity of Russian society.

(A) The Russian idea

The fruitful and creative work, which our country needs so badly, is impossible in a divided and internally atomised society, a society where the main social groups and political forces do not share basic values and fundamental ideological orientations.

Twice in the outgoing century has Russia found itself in such a state: after October 1917 and in the 1990s. In the first case, civil accord and social unity were achieved not so much by what was then called 'ideological-educational work' as by coercion. Those who disagreed with the ideology and policy of the regime were subjected to persecution and repression. That is why I think that the term 'state ideology', advocated by some politicians, publicists and scholars, is not quite appropriate. It creates certain associations with our recent Soviet past. Where there is a state ideology approved and supported by the state, there is practically no room for intellectual and spiritual freedom, ideological pluralism and freedom of the press. In other words, there is no political freedom.

I am against the restoration of an official state ideology in Russia in any guise. There should be no forced civil accord in a democratic Russia. Social accord can only be voluntary. That is why it is so important to achieve civic consensus on such basic issues as the aims, values and direction of development, which would be desirable for and attractive to the overwhelming majority of Russians. The absence of civil accord and unity is one of the reasons why our reforms are so slow and painful. Too much energy is spent on political squabbling instead of dealing with the concrete tasks of Russia's renewal. Nonetheless, some positive changes have appeared in this sphere in the past year and a half. Most Russians demonstrate greater wisdom and responsibility than many politicians. Russians want stability, confidence in the future and the ability to plan ahead for themselves and their children, not just for a month but for years and even decades. They want to work in peace, security and in a sound law-based order. They want to take advantage of the opportunities and prospects opened up by the diversity in the forms of ownership, free enterprise and market relations.

It is on this basis that our people have begun to understand and accept supra-national universal values, which are above social, group or ethnic interests. Our people have accepted such values as freedom of expression, freedom to travel abroad and other fundamental political rights and human liberties. People value the fact that they can own property, engage in free enterprise, build up their own wealth, and so on and so forth.

Another foundation for the consolidation of Russian society is what can be called the primordial, traditional values of Russians. These values are clearly seen today.

Patriotism

This term is sometimes used ironically and even derogatively. However, for the majority of Russians it retains its original and positive meaning. Patriotism is a feeling of pride in one's country, its history and accomplishments. It is the striving to make one's country better, richer, stronger and happier. When these sentiments are free from the taint of nationalist conceit and imperial ambitions, there is nothing reprehensible or bigoted about them. Patriotism is the source of the courage, staunchness and strength of our people. If we lose patriotism and the national pride and dignity that are connected with it, we will lose ourselves as a people capable of great achievements.

*The greatness of Russia (***Derzhavnost***)*

Russia was and will remain a great power. It is preconditioned by the inseparable characteristics of its geopolitical, economic and cultural existence. They determined the mentality of Russians and the policy of the government throughout the history of Russia and they cannot but do so now. This Russian mentality however should incorporate new ideas. In today's world the might of a country is measured more by its ability to develop and use advanced technologies, a high level of popular wellbeing, the reliable protection of its security and the upholding of its national interests in the international arena than in its military strength.

Statism

It will not happen soon, if ever, that Russia will become the second edition of, say, the US or Britain in which liberal values have deep historic roots. Our state and its institutions and structures have always played an exceptionally important role in the life of the country and its people. For Russians a strong state is not an anomaly to be discarded. Quite the contrary, they see it as the source and guarantee of order, and the initiator and the main driving force of change.

Contemporary Russian society does not identify a strong and effective state with a totalitarian state. We have come to value the benefits of democracy, a law-based state, and personal and political freedom. At the same time, people are concerned by the obvious weakening of state power. The public wishes to see the appropriate restoration of the guiding and regulating role of the state, proceeding from the traditions and present state of the country.

Social solidarity

A striving for collective forms of social activity has always predominated over individualism. Paternalistic sentiments have struck deep roots in Russian society. The majority of Russians are used to depending more on the state and society for improvements in their conditions than on their own efforts, initiative and entrepreneurial abilities. It will take a long time for this habit to die out. We will not dwell on whether this is good or bad. The important thing is that such sentiments exist and, indeed, predominate. That is why they cannot be ignored. They must be taken into consideration first and foremost in social policy.

I suppose that the new Russian idea will come about as a mixture or as an organic combination of universal general humanitarian values with the traditional Russian values that have stood the test of time, including the turbulent twentieth century. *This vitally important process must not be accelerated, discontinued nor destroyed.* It is important to prevent the first shoots of civil accord from being crushed underfoot in the heat of political campaigns or elections. The results of the recent elections to the State Duma inspire great optimism in this respect. They reflect a turn in our society towards greater stability and civil consensus. The overwhelming majority of Russians rejected radicalism, extremism and revolutionary opposition. For probably the first time since the reforms began favourable conditions have been created for constructive co-operation between the executive and legislative branches of power.

Serious politicians, whose parties and movements are represented in the new State Duma, are advised to draw conclusions from this fact. I am sure that their sense of responsibility for the destiny of the nation will prevail and Russia's parties, organisations and movements and their leaders will not sacrifice Russia's common interests and prospects, requiring the consolidation of all healthy forces, to narrow partisan or opportunistic considerations.

(B) Strong state

We live in a time when even the most correct economic and social policies go awry during implementation because of the weakness of the state and managerial bodies. *The key to Russia's recovery and growth today lies in the state–political sphere. Russia needs strong state power and must have it.* I am not calling for totalitarianism. History proves all dictatorships, all authoritarian forms of government are transient. Only democratic systems are lasting. Whatever the shortcomings, humanity has not devised anything superior. *Strong state power in Russia is a democratic, law-based, workable federal state.*

I see the following aspects in its formation:

- a streamlined structure for bodies of state authority and governance; improved professionalism, discipline and responsibility of civil servants; intensification of the struggle against corruption
- a restructuring of state personnel policy to select the best people
- creating conditions that will foster the development in the country of a full-blooded civil society to balance and monitor the authorities
- a larger role for and greater authority of the judiciary
- improved federal relations, including budgetary and financial matters
- an active offensive on crime.

Amending the constitution does not seem to be an urgent, priority task. We have a good constitution. Its provisions concerning individual rights and freedoms are considered among the best constitutional arrangements of the kind in the world. Rather than draft a new basic law for the country the most serious task is to render the current constitution and the laws drafted on its basis the norms of the life of the state, society and each individual. A major problem is the constitutionality of adopted laws. Russia currently has over a thousand federal laws and several thousand laws of the republics, territories, regions and autonomous areas. Not all of them correspond to the above criterion. If the justice ministry, the prosecutor's office and the judiciary continue to be as slow in dealing with this matter as they are today, the mass of questionable or simply unconstitutional laws may become critical legally and politically. The constitutional security of the state, the federal centre's capabilities, the country's manageability and Russia's integrity would then be in jeopardy.

Another serious problem is inherent in government authority. International experience suggests that the main threat to human rights and freedoms, to democracy as such, arises from the executive authority. Of course, a legislature that makes bad laws also contributes, but the main threat emanates from executive authority. It organises the country's life, applies laws and can objectively quite substantively distort, although not always maliciously, these laws through executive orders. The global trend is towards stronger executive authority. Not surprisingly, society seeks to strengthen its control over the executive to preclude arbitrariness and the abuse of office. This is why I, personally, give priority attention to building partner relations between the executive authorities and civil society, to developing the institutions and structures of the latter, and to waging an active and merciless struggle against corruption.

(C) Efficient economy

I have already said that the reform years have generated many problems in the economy and social sphere. The situation is indeed complex, but, to put it mildly, *it is too early to bury Russia as a great power.* All troubles notwithstanding, we have preserved our intellectual potential and human resources. A number of research and development achievements and advanced technologies have not been wasted. We still have our natural resources. *The country has a worthy future in store for it.*

At the same time, we must learn the lessons of the 1990s and examine the experience of market transformations.

1   One of the main lessons is that throughout these years we were groping in the dark without a clear understanding of national objectives and advances that would ensure Russia's standing as a developed, prosperous and great country of the world. The lack of a long-range development strategy for the next 15–20 and more years has damaged the economy.

   The government firmly intends to structure its work on the basis of the principle of the unity of the strategy and tactics. Without it, we are doomed to patching up holes and operating in the fire-fighting mode. Serious politics and big business are not conducted like that. *The country needs a long-term national strategy of development.* I have already said that the government has started devising it.

2   *Another important lesson of the 1990s is the conclusion that Russia needs to form a coherent system of state regulation of the economy and social sphere.* I do not mean to return to a system of planning and managing the economy by fiat, where the all-pervasive state regulated all aspects of an enterprise's work from top to bottom. I mean to make the Russian state an efficient co-ordinator of the country's economic and social forces that balances their interests, optimises the aims and parameters of social development and creates the conditions and mechanisms for their attainment.

   The above clearly goes beyond the standard formula that limits the state's role in the economy to devising rules of the game and ensuring their observance. With time, we are likely to evolve to this formula. But today's situation necessitates deeper state involvement in social and economic processes. While setting the parameters and mechanisms for state regulation we should be guided by the following principle: the state must act where and when it is needed; freedom must exist where and when it is required.

3   *The third lesson is to adopt a reform strategy that is best suited to our circumstances.* It should consist of the following elements.

3.1 *To encourage dynamic economic growth*
Primary here is the encouragement of investment. We have not yet resolved this problem. Investment in the real economy sector fell five-fold in the 1990s, including by 3.5 times in fixed assets. The material foundations of the Russian economy are being undermined. *We call for the pursuit of an investment policy that combines purely market mechanisms with state guidance.* At the same time, we will continue to create an investment climate attractive to foreign investors. Frankly speaking, without foreign investment our country's recovery will be long and hard. We do not have the time for slow growth. Consequently, we must do all in our power to attract foreign capital to the country.

3.2 *To pursue an energetic industrial policy*
The future of the country and the quality of the Russian economy in the twenty-first century will depend above all on progress in the high technology and science-intensive sectors. Ninety per cent of economic growth today depends on the introduction of new knowledge and technologies. *The government is prepared to pursue an economic policy of priority development of leading industries in the sphere of research and technological progress.* The requisite measures include:

- assisting the development of extra-budgetary internal demand for advanced technologies and science-intensive production, and supporting export-oriented high-tech production
- supporting non-raw materials industries working mostly to satisfy internal demand
- reinforcing the export possibilities of the fuel and energy and raw-materials complexes.

We should use the mechanisms that have long been applied in the world to mobilise the funds necessary for pursuing this policy. The most important of them are target-oriented loan and tax instruments and the provision of privileges against state guarantees.

3.3 *To carry out a rational structural policy*

The government thinks that, as in other industrialised countries, there is a place in the Russian economy for financial-industrial groups, corporations, small and medium businesses. Any attempt to slow down the development of some, and artificially encourage the development of other, economic forms will only hinder the development of the economy. The government will create a structure that can ensure the optimal balance between all forms of economic activity.

Another major issue is the rational regulation of the natural monopolies. This is a key question, as monopolies largely determine the structure of production and consumer prices. They therefore influence both economic and financial processes, as well as people's incomes.

3.4 *To create an effective financial system*

This is a challenging task, which includes the following aspects:

- to improve the effectiveness of the budget as a major instrument of the state's economic policy
- to carry out a tax reform
- to put an end to non-payments, barter and other pseudo-monetary forms of settlement
- to maintain a low inflation rate and stability of the rouble
- to create civilised financial and stock markets, and to turn them into an instrument to accumulate investment resources
- to restructure the bank system.

3.5 *To combat the shadow economy and organised crime in the economic and financial-credit sphere*

All countries have shadow economies, but in industrialised countries their share of GDP does not exceed 15–20 per cent, while the figure for Russia is 40 per cent. To resolve this painful problem we should not just raise the effectiveness of the law-enforcement agencies but also strengthen licence, tax, hard currency and export controls.

3.6 *To integrate consistently the Russian economy into world economic structures*

If we do not do this we will not be able to rise to the high level of economic and social progress attained in the industrialised countries. The main directions of this work are:

- to ensure the state's active support of the foreign economic operations of Russian enterprises, companies and corporations. In particular, it is time to create a federal agency to support exports, which would guarantee the export contracts of Russian producers

- to combat resolutely discrimination against Russia in world commodity, services and investment markets, and to approve and apply national anti-dumping legislation
- to incorporate Russia into the international system of regulating foreign economic operation, above all the WTO.

3.7 *To pursue a modern agrarian policy*

The revival of Russia will be impossible without the revival of the countryside and agriculture. We need a farm policy that can organically combine measures of state assistance and state regulation with market reforms in the countryside and in land ownership relations.

4   We must recognise that virtually all changes and measures that entail a fall in the living conditions of the people are inadmissible in Russia. We have reached a point beyond which we must not go. *Poverty has reached an awesome scale in Russia.* In early 1998, the average weighted world per capita income amounted to some $5,000 a year, but in Russia it was only $2,200. It dropped still lower after the August 1998 crisis. Since the beginning of reforms the share of wages in GDP has dropped from 50 per cent to 30 per cent.

This is the most acute social problem. The government is elaborating a new incomes policy designed to ensure stable growth in the real disposable incomes of the people. Despite these difficulties, the government is resolved to take new measures to support science, education, culture and health care. A country in which the people are not healthy physically and psychologically, are poorly educated and illiterate, will never rise to the peaks of world civilisation.

Russia is in the midst of one of the most difficult periods in its history. For the first time in the past 200–300 years, it is facing the real threat of slipping down to the second, and possibly even third, rank of world states. We are running out of time to avoid this. We must apply all the intellectual, physical and moral forces of the nation. We need co-ordinated creative work. Nobody will do it for us. Everything depends on us, and us alone, on our ability to recognise the scale of the threat, to unite and apply ourselves to lengthy and hard work.

This article first appeared on 28 December 1999 on the government of the Russian Federation's website (http://pravitelstvo.gov.ru/), and in *Nezavisimaya gazeta* and *Rossiiskaya gazeta*, 30 December 1999.

Notes

1 The unlikely path to power

1 Plato, *The Republic*, 'The Philosopher Ruler', Part Seven, Book Seven, translated by H. D. P. Lee (Harmondsworth, Penguin Books, 1955), p. 285.
2 Oleg Blotskii, *Vladimir Putin: istoriya zhizni*, Book 1 (Moscow, Mezhdunarodnye otnosheniya, 2002), p. 87.
3 Ibid., p. 25.
4 A. A. Mukhin, *Kto est' mister Putin i kto s nim prishel? Dos'e na Prezidenta Rossii i ego spetssluzhby* (Moscow, Centre for Political Information, 2002), p. 9.
5 Bortsov, Yu. S., *Vladimir Putin* (Moscow and Rostov, Feniks, 2001), p. 28.
6 Blotskii, *Vladimir Putin*, Book 1, p. 211.
7 Ibid., p. 25.
8 Bortsov, *Vladimir Putin*, p. 32.
9 Vera Gurevich, *Vospominaniya o budushchem prezidente* (Moscow, Mezhdunarodnye otnosheniya, 2001), p. 25.
10 Vladimir Putin, *First Person: An Astonishingly Frank Self-Portrait by Russia's President Vladimir Putin*, with Nataliya Gevorkyan, Natalya Timakova, and Andrei Kolesnikov, translated by Catherine A. Fitzpatrick (London, Hutchinson, 2000), p. 12.
11 This period is described in detail by Blotskii, *Vladimir Putin*, Book 1, Chapters 6–8.
12 Ibid., p. 68.
13 Gurevich, *Vospominaniya o budushchem prezidente*, p. 10.
14 Ibid., p. 31; Blotskii, *Vladimir Putin*, Book 1, p. 110.
15 Blotskii, *Vladimir Putin*, Book 1, p. 163.
16 Ibid., p. 147.
17 *Komsomol'skaya pravda*, 12 January 2000.
18 Putin, *First Person*, p. 19.
19 Mukhin, *Kto est' mister Putin i kto s nim prishel?*, p. 19.
20 Putin, *Ot pervogo litsa*, pp. 20–1; Putin, *First Person*, p. 19.
21 Blotskii, *Vladimir Putin*, Book 1, p. 163.
22 Ibid., p. 91.
23 *Rossiiskaya gazeta*, 16 February 2001.
24 Putin, *First Person*, p. 42.
25 Oleg Blotskii, *Vladimir Putin: doroga k vlasti*, Book 2 (Moscow, Mezhdunarodnye otnosheniya, 2002), p. 114.
26 For example, Gurevich, *Vospominaniya o budushchem prezidente*, p. 47.
27 Aleksandr Rar, *Vladimir Putin: 'Nemets' v Kremle* (Moscow, Olma-Press, 2001), p. 28.
28 Mukhin, *Kto est' mister Putin i kto s nim prishel?*, p. 20.

29 Putin, *First Person*, p. 22.
30 Ibid., p. 49.
31 *Kommersant-Daily*, 10 March 2000; Putin, *First Person*, p. 23.
32 Blotskii, *Vladimir Putin*, Book 1, pp. 173, 195–6, 283.
33 Gurevich, *Vospominaniya o budushchem prezidente*, p. 54.
34 Blotskii, *Vladimir Putin*, Book 1, p. 221.
35 Putin, *First Person*, p. 29.
36 Bortsov, *Vladimir Putin*, p. 59; Rar, *Vladimir Putin*, p. 34.
37 Mukhin, *Kto est' mister Putin i kto s nim prishel?*, p. 27.
38 Putin, *First Person*, p. 38.
39 Mukhin, *Kto est' mister Putin i kto s nim prishel?*, p. 12.
40 Bortsov, *Vladimir Putin*, p. 402.
41 Putin, *First Person*, pp. 41–2.
42 At that time only 4,783 out of the KGB's 296,591 staff were in the first depart-
    ment, Blotskii, *Vladimir Putin*, Book 2, p. 95.
43 Aleksandr Elisov, 'Prezident Putin v proshlom byl maoirom Platovym',
    Moskovskii komsomolets, 25 April 2003, p. 4; Blotskii, *Vladimir Putin*, Book 2,
    p. 175.
44 Putin, *First Person*, p. 77.
45 Bortsov, *Vladimir Putin*, p. 96.
46 Blotskii, *Vladimir Putin*, Book 2, p. 229.
47 Mukhin, *Kto est' mister Putin i kto s nim prishel?*, p. 31.
48 Described in the book by Irene Pietsch, translated from German as Iren Pitch,
    Pikantnaya druzhba: moya podruga Lyudmila Putina, ee sem'ya i drugie tovarishchi
    (Moscow, Zakharov, 2002).
49 Mukhin, *Kto est' mister Putin i kto s nim prishel?*, p. 32.
50 Putin, *First Person*, p. 76.
51 Bortsov, *Vladimir Putin*, p. 89.
52 Putin, *First Person*, p. 79.
53 Ibid., p. 80.
54 Blotskii, *Vladimir Putin*, Book 2, p. 259.
55 Putin, *First Person*, p. 80.
56 Bortsov, *Vladimir Putin*, pp. 98, 100.
57 Blotskii, *Vladimir Putin*, Book 2, pp. 273, 280–6.
58 Putin, *First Person*, p. 85.
59 Blotskii, *Vladimir Putin*, Book 2, p. 301; V. Lupan, *Russkii vyzov* (Moscow, Terra,
    2001), p. 58.
60 Blotskii, *Vladimir Putin*, Book 2, pp. 290–1.
61 Putin, *Ot pervogo litsa*, p. 84.
62 Ibid., p. 85.
63 Full details are in Mukhin, *Kto est' mister Putin i kto s nim prishel?*, pp. 37–45.
64 For example, O. Lur'e, 'Kak V. Putin pytalsya spasti svoi gorod ot goloda',
    Novaya gazeta, 13–19 March 2000. The city council set up a committee headed by
    Marina Salie to investigate the charges, but no evidence of Putin's complicity in
    wrong-doing was found.
65 'Putin's Shadowy Past', *Newsday*, 30 January 2000; in *Johnson's Russia List* (hence-
    forth *JRL*), 4079/4.
66 Lupan, *Russkii vyzov*, p. 66.
67 Putin, *First Person*, p. 113.
68 Bortsov, *Vladimir Putin*, p. 340.
69 Ibid., pp. 388–90.
70 Ibid., p. 138.
71 Leonid Mlechin, *KGB predsedateli organov gosbezopasnosti: rassekrechennye sud'by*
    (Moscow, Tsentrpoligraf, 2002), p. 836.

72 Putin, *First Person*, p. 129.

73 Bortsov, *Vladimir Putin*, pp. 140–1; Blotskii, *Vladimir Putin*, Book 2, p. 409.

74 Putin, *First Person*, p. 130.

75 Ibid., p. 133.

76 Mlechin, *KGB predsedateli organov gosbezopasnosti*, p. 838.

77 Putin did not, however, reject his KGB past. For example, on the occasion of the 85th anniversary of Andropov's birth in December 1999 Putin, as prime minister, unveiled a plaque and placed a wreath to his memory and addressed the FSB Collegium with the following words: 'Let me report that the FSB staff sent to work in the government are satisfactorily fulfilling their duties', Mlechin, *KGB predsedateli organov gosbezopasnosti*, p. 816.

78 Mukhin, *Kto est' mister Putin i kto s nim prishel?*, p. 52.

79 In spring 1998 'three out of five Russians did not routinely receive the wages or pensions to which they were entitled', Richard Rose, 'Living in an Antimodern Society', *East European Constitutional Review*, Vol. 8, No. 1/2, Winter/Spring 1999, p. 71.

80 In the same way, as he moved up the career ladder he retained close links, as far as possible, with his earlier friends, Blotskii, *Vladimir Putin*, Book 2, pp. 344–5.

81 Putin participated in a book where the philosophy of judo, based on self-discipline, ceremony and the ability to turn your opponent's strength against him, is described: Vladimir Putin, Vasilii Shestakov and Aleksei Levitskii, *Uchimsya dzyudo s Vladirom Putinym* (Moscow, Olma-Press, 2002).

82 Mukhin, *Kto est' mister Putin i kto s nim prishel?*, p. 21.

83 Bortsov, *Vladimir Putin*, p. 393.

84 For examples, see Yurii Drozdov and Vasilii Fartyshev, *Yurii Andropov i Vladimir Putin: na puti k vozrozhdeniyu* (Moscow, Olma-Press, 2001), p. 106; Bortsov, *Vladimir Putin*, p. 398.

85 Viktor Talanov, *Psikhologicheskii portret Vladimira Putina* (St Petersburg, B & K, 2000), p. 16.

86 R. F. Avramchenko, *Pokhoronit li Putin Rossiyu? Idei i kontsepsii preobrazovaniya Rossii* (Moscow, Editorial URSS, 2001), pp. 17, 24. Avramchenko had earlier sent the new president a draft plan to save Russia, (*Put' Putina: do prezidenta ili reformatora? Novaya kontseptsiya razvitiya Rossii* (Moscow, self-published, 2000), and was most upset that Putin had not answered him personally.

87 Mukhin, *Kto est' mister Putin i kto s nim prishel?*, p. 24.

88 On a lighter note, the alternation between bald and hairy Russian and Soviet leaders has often been noted: Lenin's baldness gave way to a hairy Stalin, followed by a bald Khrushchev and a hairy Brezhnev, a bald Andropov and a hairy Chernenko, a bald Gorbachev and a hairy Yeltsin. Putin's receding hairline suggests a characteristically third way approach to the question. Others, however, have suggested that the suffix -in may be more significant. Built up by the -ins (Len and Stal), the Soviet Union was brought down by the -evs and their ilk: Brezhn, Androp, Chernenk and Gorbach. To become a success, Vladimir Ilyich Ulyanov had to drop his -ev to become an -in. Boris Nikolaevich Yeltsin demonstrated that to lead Russia you have to be a bisyllabic -in. In this context, Putin was a shoo-in. Letter from John Yates, Exeter, in *The Guardian*, 10 March 2000, p. 25.

89 Joseph A. Schumpeter, *Capitalism, Socialism and Democracy*, fifth edition (London, George Allen & Unwin, 1976), p. 269.

90 Ibid., p. 272.

91 Every twist and turn is described by Leonid Mlechin, *Kreml' prezidenty Rossii: strategiya vlasti ot B. N. El'tsina do V. V. Putina* (Moscow, Tsentrpoligraf, 2002).

92 Boris Yeltsin, *Midnight Diaries* (London, Weidenfeld & Nicolson, 2000), p. 29.

93 Ibid., p. 103.

94 Mlechin, *KGB predsedateli organov gosbezopasnosti*, p. 843.
95 Yeltsin, *Midnight Diaries*, pp. 283–7.
96 Ibid., p. 326.
97 Ibid., p. 327.
98 Ibid., p. 329.
99 Ibid., p. 330.
100 Putin, *First Person*, p. 137.
101 Mlechin, *KGB predsedateli organov gosbezopasnosti*, p. 845.
102 Reported later in *Kommersant vlast'*, 28 March 2000, p. 16.
103 Putin, *First Person*, p. 204.
104 Putin's ability to deflect hostility and sense of humour was in evidence on this occasion. Both Yavlinsky and Zyuganov pretended that they had forgotten Putin's name, so in thanking deputies for their support he noted that he was especially grateful to 'Grigory Alekseevich Zyuganov', a mix of the two names, in Roi Medvedev, *Vremya Putina? Rossiya na rubezhe vekov* (Moscow, Prava Cheloveka, 2001), p. 165.
105 Medvedev, *Vremya Putina?*, p. 19.
106 Stepashin in *Nezavisimaya gazeta*, 14 January 2000. Lupan lists 26 atrocities committed in the region between September 1998 and October 1999, *Russkii vyzov*, pp. 117–20.
107 Peter Rutland, 'Putin's Path to Power', *Post-Soviet Affairs*, Vol. 16, No. 4, 2000, p. 323, fn 24.
108 Amy Knight, 'The Enduring Legacy of the KGB in Russian Politics', *Problems of Post-Communism*, Vol. 47, No. 4, July/August 2000, p. 10.
109 The explosive used was hexogen, which had allegedly been manufactured in a bomb-making factory in Chechnya. Among the many versions explaining the bombings is the one actively propagated by Berezovsky later, namely that the FSB either deliberately or by omission was responsible for the bombings. The events, soon after the four actual bombings, in Ryazan where a 'dummy' bomb, explained as a test exercise by the FSB, was found in an apartment block primed and ready to explode, still requires full explanation. The 'Public Commission to Investigate the 1999 Explosions in Moscow and Volgodonsk and the Ryazan Exercises', chaired by State Duma deputy Sergei Kovalev, the former Russian human rights commissioner, was an independent attempt to get to the bottom of the tragedy. The Commission in effect took the place of what should have been a parliamentary commission, but the Duma had refused to set one up. A film sponsored by Berezovsky (*Attack on Russia*), released in March 2002, accused the government headed by Putin of being guilty of the crime, but the evidence was at best circumstantial. The report on the atrocities issued by the RF Prosecutor General's office in April 2003 concluded that the 'foreign citizens Khattab and Amu Umar' were the organisers of the attacks with the involvement of Khakim Abayev, Denis Saitakov, the brothers Zaur and Timur Batchaev, Yusif Krymshamkhalov and Alam Dekkushiyev. Some of these had already been killed in fighting in Chechnya, and the trials of Krymshamkhalov and Dekkushiyev were to follow. The jury remains out on who was responsible for the atrocities.
110 Putin, *First Person*, p. 139.
111 Yeltsin, *Midnight Diaries*, p. 335.
112 Ibid., p. 337.
113 Ibid., p. 338.
114 Medvedev, *Vremya Putina?*, p. 23.
115 R. Kolchanov, 'Kremlevskii syurpriz', *Trud*, 5 January 2000; in Bortsov, *Vladimir Putin*, pp. 381–2.
116 Sergei Kovalev, 'Putin's War', *New York Review of Books*, 10 February 2000, p. 8.
117 Nikolai Petrov, 'Introduction: What Choice Faces Us?', in Michael McFaul,

Nikolai Petrov and Andrei Ryabov (eds), *Rossiya nakanune dumskikh vyborov 1999 goda*, Moscow, Moscow Carnegie Center (Moscow, Gendal'f, 1999), p. 6.

118 Igor Klyamkin and Lilia Shevtsova, *Vnesistemnyi rezhim Boris II: nekotorye osobennosti politicheskogo razvitiya postsovetskoi Rossii* (Moscow, Moscow Carnegie Center, 1999), p. 10.

119 Ibid., p. 11.

120 Lilia Shevtsova, *Putin's Russia* (Washington, DC, Carnegie Endowment for International Peace, 2003), p. 46.

121 For details, see Richard Sakwa, 'Russia's "Permanent" (Uninterrupted) Elections of 1999–2000', *Journal of Communist Studies and Transition Politics*, Vol. 16, No. 3, September 2000, pp. 85–112.

122 *Itogi*, 23 December 1999, p. 7.

123 Yeltsin, *Midnight Diaries*, p. 4.

124 Putin recounts his own doubts in *First Person*, pp. 204–5: "You know, Boris Nikolayevich, to be honest, I don't know if I'm ready for this or whether I want it, because it's a rather difficult fate", p. 204.

125 Yeltsin, *Midnight Diaries*, p. 6.

126 Ibid., p. 7.

127 Ibid., p. 14.

128 Bortsov, *Vladimir Putin*, p. 170. The text of the decree is in Dale R. Herspring (ed.), *Putin's Russia: Past Imperfect, Future Uncertain* (Oxford, Rowman & Littlefield, 2003), pp. 100–2.

129 A. Zinoviev in Lupan, *Russkii vyzov*, pp. 12–13.

130 Yulia Latynina, 'Weary Nation Lurks Behind Duma Results', *Moscow Times*, 22 December 1999, p. 8.

131 Quoted by John Thornhill, 'Paradoxes in the Wild East: After Six Years in Moscow', *Financial Times*, 8 July 2000.

132 Medvedev insists that those who argue that 'Putin's authority was built on the Chechen campaign are mistaken', Medvedev, *Vremya Putina?*, p. 185.

133 In a survey of the most important events over the past decade, respondents in 2002 reacted most positively to Yeltsin's resignation (viewed positively by 86 per cent), *Russian Political Weekly*, 18 March 2002.

134 Alexander Prokhanov in *Zavtra*, 29 February 2000, cited by Roi Medvedev, *Zagadka Putina* (Moscow, Prava cheloveka, 2000), p. 11; Medvedev, *Vremya Putina?*, p. 36.

135 Medvedev, *Zagadka Putina*, p. 18.

136 Ibid., p. 56.

137 ORT, *Vremya*, 5 March 2000.

138 This at least was the the view of Gleb Musikhin, 'Yavlinskii prav, no istina dorozhe', *Nezavisimaya gazeta*, 2 March 2000, p. 3.

139 Those who supported Putin in the election included Boris Nemtsov's Young Russia (*Rossiya Molodaya*), Sergei Kirienko's New Power (*Novaya Sila*) and Nikolai Brusnikin's New Generation (*Novoe Pokolenie*), together with a personal endorsement by Chubais.

140 RFE/RL, *Newsline*, 7 March 2000.

141 *Izvestiya*, 9 February 2000.

142 Vladimir Putin, 'Otkrytoe pis'mo Vladimira Putina k Rossiiskim izbiratelyam', *Izvestiya*, 25 February 2000, p. 5; www.putin2000.ru

143 Published in Russian as Vladimir Putin, *Ot pervogo litsa: razgovory s Vladimirom Putinym*, with Nataliya Gevorkyan, Natalya Timakova and Andrei Kolesnikov (Moscow, Vagrius, 2000). The book was published in English as Putin, *First Person*, op cit. The '*Millennium Manifesto*' is published as an appendix, pp. 209–19, and in this book, pp. 251–62.

144 *Moscow Times*, 9 September 2000; more details can be found at *The Moscow*

Times.Com Special Report/Election Fraud; for associated material see http://www.moscowtimes.ru

145 Aleksei Zudin, 'Soyuz pravykh sil', Moskovskii tsentr Karnegi, *Parlamentskie vybory 1999 goda v Rossii*, Byulleten', No. 2, December 1999, p. 18.

146 The point is made by Laura Belin, 'Commission Releases Final Results', RFE/RL, *Russian Election Report*, No. 5 (13), 7 April 2000.

147 Medvedev, *Vremya Putina?*, p. 69.

148 Nikolai Vavilov, '"Putin – absolyuten". Tak schitayut rossiyane, zhivushchie v stranakh SNG, i lidery gosudarstv Sodruzhestva', *Sodruzhestvo NG*, No. 3 (26), 29 March 2000, pp. 9, 12.

149 A study of 2000 respondents in Samara found that Putin 'was backed by 58 per cent of students and 20–25 year olds, compared to only 40 per cent of those over 55. He was also preferred by 50 per cent of women compared to 46.5 per cent of men. Sixty per cent of those whose living standard had improved over the past year backed Putin, compared to 40 per cent of those who said it had worsened'. The study also found that Putin drew his support from right across the political spectrum. Three quarters of those who voted for Unity in the December Duma election backed Putin for president, as did 61 per cent of SPS supporters and 49 per cent of those who backed Fatherland – All Russia (OVR). Putin even beat Yavlinsky among Yabloko voters, by 37 to 36 per cent. More remarkable, 10 per cent of CPRF voters backed Putin. Putin was also the favourite of those who had abstained in the December 1999 poll, and of those who had voted 'against all', Jamestown Foundation, *Monitor*, 8 March 2000.

150 Henry E. Hale, 'Is Russian Nationalism on the Rise?', Program on New Approaches to Russian Security, Davis Center for Russian Studies, Harvard University, *Policy Memo Series*, No. 110, February 2000, p. 1.

151 For the tension between order and democracy in these elections, see Richard Rose and Neil Munro, *Elections without Order: Russia's Challenge to Vladimir Putin* (Cambridge, Cambridge University Press, 2002).

152 See Yitzhak M. Brudny, 'In Pursuit of the Russian Presidency: Why and How Yeltsin Won the 1996 Presidential Election', *Communist and Post-Communist Studies*, Vol. 30, No. 3 1997, p. 273.

153 Press conference televised at 1.30 am on 27 March 2000. See also Laura Belin, 'How State Television Aided Putin's Campaign', RFE/RL, *Russian Election Report*, No. 5 (13), 7 April 2000.

154 Sergei Mitrokhin, 'Put', kotoryi my vybiraem', *Nezavisimaya gazeta*, 3 March 2000, p. 3.

155 The terms are used by Ian Traynor, 'Weary Nation Turns to Putin', *The Guardian*, 16 March 2000, p. 20.

156 Mlechin, *Kreml' prezidenty Rossii*, p. 611.

2 The ideas behind the choice

1 Friedrich Nietzsche, *Thus Spoke Zarathustra*.

2 For example, *Al'ternativa: vybor puti. Perestroika upravleniya i gorizonty rynka* (Moscow, Mysl', 1990).

3 Yurii N. Afanas'ev (ed.), *Inogo ne dano* (Moscow, Progress, 1988).

4 The question was asked at the Davos economic forum in late January 2000. Mukhin took up the theme in his *Kto est' mister Putin i kto s nim prishel?* In Russian the word *zagadka* (a puzzle or a mystery) was often used, for example Medvedev, *Zagadka Putina*.

5 Alexander Zinoviev, 30 January 2000, Itar-Tass; in *JRL* 4080/11.

6 Zinoviev in Lupan, *Russkii vyzov*, p. 5.

7 Interview with Alexander Solzhenitsyn, first published in *Der Spiegel*, by Fritjof

Meyer, Jorg R. Mettke and Martin Derry, reprinted as 'Russia's Darkest Night of the Soul', *The Guardian*, 18 March 2000, p. 2.

8 'Mr Putin's Two Faces', *The Guardian*, 12 July 2000, p. 21.

9 *Nezavisimaya gazeta*, 2 November 2000.

10 Margarita Mommsen, 'The Sphinx in the Kremlin', *Internationale Politik: Transatlantic Edition*, Vol. 1, No. 3, 2000, pp. 21–2.

11 Andrei Kozyrev, 'Russia: A Chance for Survival', *Foreign Affairs*, Vol. 71, No. 2, Spring 1992, pp. 8–9.

12 Leszek Balcerowicz, *Common Fallacies in the Debate on the Economic Transition in Central and Eastern Europe* (London, EBRD Working Paper 11, 1993).

13 For details about the October 1993 crisis and the institutional arrangements of the constitutional system introduced in December 1993, see Richard Sakwa, *Russian Politics and Society*, third edition (London and New York, Routledge, 2002).

14 Peter Reddaway and Dmitri Glinski, *The Tragedy of Russia's Reforms: Market Bolshevism against Democracy* (Washington, DC, The United States Institute of Peace Press, 2001).

15 Gordon M. Hahn, *Russia's Revolution from Above, 1985–2000: Reform, Transition, and Revolution in the Fall of the Soviet Communist Regime* (New Brunswick, NJ, Transaction Publishers, 2002), p. xii.

16 Ibid., p. 2.

17 Ibid., p. 9.

18 For a discussion of the concept of electoral democracy, see Larry Diamond, *Developing Democracy: Towards Consolidation* (Baltimore, Johns Hopkins University Press, 1999).

19 Michael McFaul, *Russia's Unfinished Revolution: Political Change from Gorbachev to Putin* (Ithaca and London, Cornell University Press, 2001), p. 29.

20 Ralf Dahrendorf, *Society and Democracy in Germany* (London, Weidenfeld & Nicolson, 1968).

21 Matvei Maly, *Kak sdelat' Rossiyu normal'noi stranoi?* (St Petersburg, Dmitrii Bulanin, 2003), p. 7.

22 Ralf Dahrendorf, *Reflections on the Revolution in Europe* (London, Chatto & Windus, 1990), pp. 92–3.

23 Ibid., pp. 60, 85 and *passim*.

24 Schumpeter, *Capitalism, Socialism and Democracy*, second edition (New York, Harper, 1947), p. 269.

25 G. O'Donnell, P. Schmitter and L. Whitehead (eds), *Transitions from Authoritarian Rule*, Vol. 4, *Tentative Conclusions about Uncertain Democracies* (Baltimore, MD, Johns Hopkins University Press, 1986), p. 65.

26 S. I. Kaspe, 'Tsentr i vertikal': politicheskaya priroda putinskogo prezidentstva', *Politiya*, No. 4 (22), Winter 2001–2002, p. 5.

27 See Sheila Fitzpatrick, 'Postwar Soviet Society: The Return to Normalcy, 1945–1953', in Susan J. Linz (ed.), *The Impact of World War II on the Soviet Union* (Totowa, NJ, Rowman and Allanheld, 1985), pp. 129–56.

28 Guillermo O'Donnell, 'Delegative Democracy', *Journal of Democracy*, Vol. 5, No. 1, January 1994, pp. 55–69.

29 Fareed Zakaria, 'The Rise of Illiberal Democracy', *Foreign Affairs*, Vol. 76, No. 6, November/December 1997, pp. 22–43.

30 Bortsov, *Vladimir Putin*, pp. 211–15.

31 The comparison is made at length by Drozdov and Fartyshev, *Yurii Andropov i Vladimir Putin*, in particular pp. 133–47.

32 Vadim Pechenov, *Vladimir Putin – poslednii shans Rossii?* (Moscow, Infra-M, 2001), p. vii. Pechenev worked periodically as part of an analytical group with Andropov for some eight years, and thus is in a position to know.

33 The document appeared on 28 December on the Russian Federation government web site: http://www.gov.ru/ministry/isp-vlast47.html; also on www.pravitelstvo. gov.ru. Published in Russian in Vladimir Putin, 'Rossiya na rubezhe tysyacheletii', *Nezavisimaya gazeta*, 30 December 1999, p. 4. An English version can be found in Putin, *First Person*, pp. 209–19, and at the end of this book.

34 Pechenev, *Vladimir Putin*, p. 45.

35 Putin, *First Person*, p. 210; Sakwa, *Putin*, p. 252.

36 Putin, *First Person*, p. 211; Sakwa, *Putin*, p. 253.

37 Putin, *First Person*, p. 212; Sakwa, *Putin*, p. 254.

38 Putin, *First Person*, p. 212; Sakwa, *Putin*, p. 254.

39 Putin, *First Person*, p. 212; Sakwa, *Putin*, p. 255.

40 Putin, *First Person*, p. 213; Sakwa, *Putin*, p. 256.

41 Putin, *First Person*, p. 215; Sakwa, *Putin*, p. 257.

42 Putin, *First Person*, p. 214; Sakwa, *Putin*, p. 257.

43 Putin, *First Person*, p. 215; Sakwa, *Putin*, p. 258.

44 Full details about the Centre can be found in *Moskovskie novosti*, No. 6, 15–21 February 2000, p. 11.

45 Sergei Parkhomenko, 'Sostavitel's kontrakta', *Itogi*, 8 February 2000, pp. 21–4.

46 Lidiya Andrusenko, 'Oligarkhi sovetuyut', *Nezavisimaya gazeta*, 1 April 2000, p. 3.

47 http://www.kommersant.ru/Docs/reforma.htm, 'Reforming the Structure of the Presidential Administration', Gref Centre document, excerpts from Book No. 2, 'Introduction'.

48 S. A. Karaganov (ed.), *Strategiya dlya Rossii: povestka dnya dlya prezidenta-2000* (Moscow, Vagrius/SVOP, 2000), abstract.

49 Karaganov (ed.), *Strategiya dlya Rossii*, p. 6.

50 Ibid., p. 8.

51 Ibid., pp. 14–15.

52 Ibid., p. 17.

53 Ibid., p. 19.

54 Ibid., p. 21.

55 Ibid., p. 24.

56 Data based on VTsIOM polls, in Karaganov (ed.), *Strategiya dlya Rossii*, p. 28.

57 Timothy J. Colton and Michael McFaul, *Are Russians Undemocratic?* (Carnegie Endowment for International Peace, Russian Domestics Politics Project, Russian and Eurasian Program, Working Paper No. 20, June 2001); republished in *Post-Soviet Affairs*, Vol. 18, No. 2, 2002, pp. 91–121; and a version called 'Putin and Democratization' in Herspring (ed.), *Putin's Russia*, Chapter 2, pp. 13–38.

58 Karaganov (ed.), *Strategiya dlya Rossii*, pp. 80–1.

59 Ibid., p. 96.

60 I. Ya. Bogdanov and A. P. Kalinin, *Korruptsiya v Rossii: Sotsial'no-ekonomicheskie i pravovye aspekty* (Moscow, Institute of Socio-Political research, RAS, 2001), p. 67.

61 One of the best analyses is A. A. Mukhin, *Rossiiskaya organizovannaya prestupnost' i vlast': Istoriya vzaimootnoshenii* (Moscow, Tsentr politicheskoi informatsii, 2003).

62 Pavel Khlebnikov, *Krestnyi otets Kremlya Boris Berezovskii ili Istoriya razgrableniya Rossii* (Moscow, Detektiv-Press, 2001), pp. 188–93.

63 Mukhin, *Rossiiskaya organizovannaya prestupnost' i vlast'*, p. 5.

64 Bogdanov and Kalinin, *Korruptsiya v Rossii*, p. 149.

65 Karaganov (ed.), *Strategiya dlya Rossii*, pp. 197–8.

66 Ibid., pp. 209–10.

67 Ibid., p. 211.

68 Ibid., p. 213.

69 'Vystuplenie pri predstavlenii ezhegodnogo Poslaniya Prezidenta Rossiiskoi Feder-atsii Federal'nomu Sobraniyu Rossiiskoi Federatsii', http://www.president. kremlin.ru/events/42.html.

70 RIA Novosti, 4 April 2001.

71 http://www.president.kremlin.ru/events/510/html.

72 'Ustalost' reform', *Izvestiya*, 24 April 2003, p. 1.

73 BBC Monitoring, 16 May 2003; in *JRL* 7186/1. http://www.president.kremlin.ru/text/appears/2003/05/44623.shtml.

74 An earlier version of this section was published as 'Regime Change from Yeltsin to Putin', in Cameron Ross (ed.), *Russian Politics under Putin* (Manchester, Manchester University Press, 2003).

75 V. T. Tret'yakov, *Russkaya politika i politiki v norme i v patologii: Vzglyad na sobytiya rossiiskoi zhizni 1990–2000* (Moscow, Ladomir, 2001), p. 769.

76 Roi Medvedev, *Vladimir Putin – deistvuyushchii prezident* (Moscow, Vremya, 2002), p. 410.

77 For the development of this argument, see Richard Sakwa, 'The Age of Paradox: The Anti-revolutionary Revolutions of 1989–91', in Moira Donald and Tim Rees (eds), *Reinterpreting Revolution in Twentieth-Century Europe* (London, Macmillan, 2001), pp. 159–76.

78 Yeltsin, *Midnight Diaries*, p. 197.

79 In *First Person* (p. 21) Putin recounts an intriguing moment when one of his school teachers set the topic 'A revolution has a beginning, a revolution has no end'. Clearly this struck an echo in Putin's thinking, hence its appearance in his book.

80 RIA Novosti, 4 April 2001.

81 'Stenogramma "Pryamoi linii" Prezidenta Rossiiskoi Federatsii V. V. Putina', 24 December 2001, http://www.president.kremlin.ru/events/423.html.

82 Interview in a TV film made by Igor Shadkhan called 'Vladimir Putin: A Conversation in the Evening', BBC Monitoring; in *JRL* 6483/6.

83 Samuel P. Huntington, *Political Order in Changing Societies* (New Haven, CT, Yale University Press, 1968).

84 V. V. Putin, *Razgovor s Rossiei: Stenogramma 'Pryamoi linii s Prezidentom Rossiiskoi Federatsii V. V. Putinym'*, 19 December 2002 (Moscow, Olma-Politizdat, 2003), p. 14.

85 Russia is not the only country where democratic consolidation has lacked depth. András Bozóki notes how the coalition government of Victor Orban between 1998 and 2002 saw electoral victory as an opportunity to achieve a fundamental cultural change. The programme of 'more than government change' saw one vision of Hungary being imposed on the rest. Bozóki notes that this sort of *Kulturkampf* politics has emerged in a mature democracy such as Italy, 'where the former power of multiple parties has disappeared and the only frontline of political struggle lies between pro-Berlusconi and anti-Berlusconi people'. András Bozóki, 'Hungary's Social-Democratic Turn', *East European Constitutional Review*, Vol. 11, No. 3, Summer 2002, pp. 80–6, at p. 85.

86 Tret'yakov, *Russkaya politika i politiki v norme i v patologii*, p. 771.

87 http://www.president.kremlin.ru/events/131.html.

88 *Moskovskii komsomolets*, 30 December 2000; *Monitor*, 2 January 2001.

89 The 'contradiction' between Russia and Western-generated models of development was symbolised by the shift of the capital from Russia's Muscovite heartland to St Petersburg as a 'window to the West'; and it perhaps was not accidental that a citizen of St Petersburg sought to resolve this contradiction.

90 One of the most eloquent exponents of the alternativity thesis for Russia are the many works by Akhiezer. See, for example, A. S. Akhiezer, *Rossiiya: kritika istoricheskogo opyta*, Vol. 1, *Ot proshlogo k budushchemu*, second edition, reworked and extended (Novosibirsk, Sibirskii khronograf, 1997).

91 'V Kreml' "cherez postel'" ne popadesh', *Argumenty i fakty*, No. 12, 2000, p. 9.

3 The Putin way

1 Cited in T. Wright, *Socialisms Old and New*, 2nd Edition (London, Routledge, 1996), p. 123.

2 Bortsov, *Vladimir Putin*, pp. 19–20.

3 Medvedev, *Vremya Putina?*, p. 9.

4 Samuel P. Huntington, *The Third Wave: Democratization in the Late Twentieth Century* (Norman, University of Oklahoma Press, 1991), pp. 144ff.

5 See Peter Reddaway, 'Will Putin be Able to Consolidate Power?', *Post-Soviet Affairs*, Vol. 17, No. 1, 2001, pp. 23–44; see also his 'Is Putin's Power More Formal Than Real?', *Post-Soviet Affairs*, Vol. 18, No. 1, 2002, pp. 31–40.

6 Hahn, *Russia's Revolution from Above*, pp. 520–1.

7 For a detailed analysis of the various groups, see Peter Rutland, 'Putin and the Oligarchs', in Herspring (ed.), *Putin's Russia*, Chapter 7, in particular pp. 138–9.

8 Paul Goble, 'Does Putin have Plans for St Petersburg', *Newsline*, 15 March 2000.

9 Cited by Elena Dikun, *Prism*, Vol. VI, Issue 6, Part 1, June 2000.

10 Igor Kharichev, 'Politseiskoe gosudarstvo grozit stat' nashim budushchim', *Nezavisimaya gazeta*, 8 February 2000.

11 *Financial Times*, 18 July 2000.

12 Yeltsin's daughter commented on Voloshin as follows: 'At work he is like some complex well-maintained machine that does not know tiredness. I sometimes don't know how he can stand it.' Mlechin, *KGB predsedateli organov gosbezopasnosti*, p. 844.

13 They bought large stakes from the London-based Trans-World Group (headed by Lev Chernoi) in the Krasnoyarsk (KrAZ) and Bratsk (BrAZ) aluminium plants and the Achinsk alumina enterprise. The head of the Anti-Monopoly Committee, Anatoly Yuzhanov, ruled that no anti-trust laws had been violated since none of the stakes sold were larger than 20 per cent (ignoring the role of various front companies), a finding that suggested that Putin would not challenge the power of the oligarchs and that he would implement his plan for the creation of large vertically integrated companies.

14 To ensure that his consulting services remained necessary for Putin, Pavlovsky allegedly set about discrediting Gref's Centre for Strategic Studies, something that he did successfully, Mukhin, *Kto est' mister Putin i kto s nim prishel?*, pp. 62–3.

15 *Russian Regional Report*, Vol. 7, No. 20, 17 June 2002.

16 Elena Dikun, *Prism*, Vol. VI, Issue 6, Part 1, June 2000.

17 *Segodnya*, 17 June 2000; *Monitor*, 19 June 2000.

18 *Moscow Times*, 22 June 2000.

19 Andrei Ryabov interviewed by Avtandil Tsuladze, 'Putin Must Become the "Father of the Nation" – To Maintain his Rating', *Segodnya*, 8 July 2000.

20 http://www.president.kremlin.ru/text/APPTemplAppearId16748.shtml.

21 *Komsomolskaya Pravda*, 26 January 2000; *Washington Times*, 7 February 2000.

22 Interview with Vladimir Kosarev and Yurii Gladkevich, *Profil*, No. 25, 2000; in *JRL* 4394/10.

23 Sophie Lambroschini, 'KGB Veterans Head has High Hopes of Putin', *Newsline*, 30 June 2000.

24 Findings of Olga Kryshtanovskaya, reported in *Russian Political Weekly*, 17 January 2003.

25 In socio-occupational terms 21.9 per cent of all Russian households considered themselves middle class; in terms of material position 21.2 per cent; and in terms of self-identification 39.5 per cent, Tatyana Maleva, *The Middle Class: Here and Now*, Moscow, Moscow Carnegie Center, *Briefing Papers*, Vol. 4, Issue 12, December 2002.

26 See, for example, A. Tsuladze, *Bol'shaya manipulativnaya igra: tekhnologii politicheskikh manipulyatsii v period vyborov 1999–2000* (Moscow, Algoritm, 2000).

27 Stephen White, 'Ten Years On: What do the Russians Think?', in Rick Fawn and Stephen White (eds), *Russia After Communism* (London, Frank Cass, 2002), p. 41.

28 Ibid., p. 42.

29 Ibid., p. 42.

30 Gleb Pavlovsky, 'Russia Can be Easily Provoked into Revolution', *Kommersant-Vlast'*, No. 26, 4 July 2000.

31 Michael McFaul, *Generational Change in Russia*, PONARS Working Paper Series No. 21 (Washington, DC, CSIS, 2002).

32 Yury Chernega, 'Putin Our Teflon President', *Kommersant*, 7 July 2000; in *JRL* 4396/5.

33 http://www/riisnp.ru/contents.htm; in *Russian Political Weekly*, 18 March 2002.

34 Richard Rose, *A Bottom Up Evaluation of Enlargement Countries: New Europe Barometer 1* (University of Strathclyde, Centre for the Study of Public Policy, Studies in Public Policy No. 364, 2002), p. 8.

35 Ibid., p. 13.

36 Ibid., p. 24.

37 Public Opinion Foundation (FOM), http://english.fom.ru/reports/frames/ed030908.html

38 *Atgumenty i fakty*, No. 16, April 2003, p. 1.

39 http://english.fom.ru/reports/frames/ed031004.html.

40 Ibid.

41 Richard Rose, Neil Munro, and Stephen White, 'How Strong is Vladimir Putin's Support?', *Post-Soviet Affairs*, Vol. 16, No. 4, 2000, pp. 287–312.

42 Dmitri K. Simes, 'With Friends Like These, Putin Needs a Smarter Strategy', *Washington Post*, 16 July 2000.

43 http://english.fom.ru/reports/frames/ed030107.html.

44 Rose and Munro, *Elections without Order*, pp. 189–95.

45 The changes can be tracked on the basis of VTsIOM data, posted at www.russia-votes.org.

46 http://english.fom.ru/reports/frames/ed030921.html.

47 Nikolai Petrov notes 'the calculated way in which the political arena has been cleared of any real heroes other than the president himself', *Russia and Eurasia Review*, Vol. 2, Issue 8, 15 April 2003.

48 http://english.fom.ru/reports/frames/eof023806.html.

49 Elena Shestopal, 'Popular Perceptions of Vladimir Putin', paper presented to the BASEES conference, Cambridge, 29–31 March 2003.

50 In March 2003 47 per cent of respondents were ready to vote for Putin, http://www.fom.ru/surveys/dominant/152/368/1367.html.

51 Robert Moore, *A Time to Die: The Kursk Disaster* (New York, Doubleday, 2002).

52 Medvedev, *Vremya Putina?*, pp. 113–33 covers the tragedy in detail.

53 Viktor Stepankov, *Bitva za "Nord-Ost"* (Moscow, Yauza/Eksmo, 2003), p. 59.

54 *Gazeta.ru*, 29 January 2003.

55 Figure cited by Andrei Ryabov interviewed by Avtandil Tsuladze, 'Putin Must Become the "Father of the Nation" – To Maintain his Rating', *Segodnya*, 8 July 2000.

56 Schumpeter, *Capitalism, Socialism and Democracy*, p. 270.

57 'The Rebirth of Right-Wing Charisma? The Cases of Jean-Marie Le Pen and Vladimir Zhirinovsky', *Totalitarian Movements and Political Religions*, Vol. 3, No. 3, Winter 2002, pp. 1–23.

58 This issue is explored by Colin Lawson and Howard White, 'Images of Leadership in Ukraine and Russia: Preliminary Findings', paper presented to the BASEES conference, Cambridge, 6–8 April 2002.

59 Archie Brown, 'Introduction', in Archie Brown and Lilia Shevtsova (eds), *Gorbachev, Yeltsin, and Putin: Political Leadership in Russia's Transition* (Washington, DC, Carnegie Endowment for International Peace, 2001), pp. 6–8.

60 Sophie Lambroschini, 'Russia: Analysts Say Putin May Be Overreaching', *Newsline*, 11 July 2000.
61 *Monitor*, 19 July 2001.
62 For example, Aleksandr Ushakov, *Fenomenon Atatyurka: Turetskii pravitel', tvorets i diktator* (Moscow, Tsentropoligraf, 2002).
63 See, for example, Alexander Chubarov, *The Fragile Empire: A History of Imperial Russia* (London, Continuum, 1999). See also his *Russia's Bitter Path to Modernity: A History of the Soviet and Post-Soviet Eras* (London, Continuum, 2001).
64 See George W. Breslauer, *Gorbachev and Yeltsin as Leaders* (Cambridge, Cambridge University Press, 2002).
65 See Yevgenia Albats, 'Power Play: Two Evils Once Again on Our Plate', *Moscow Times*, 22 June 2000.
66 Interview with Primakov, *Parlamentskaya gazeta*, 8 June 2000. Other cases are recounted in Medvedev, *Vremya Putina?*, p. 166.
67 Asked which political leaders he found most interesting, Putin answered De Gaulle and Erhard, *First Person*, p. 194. It may also be noted that Putin was only 47 years old on assuming the presidency; at that age De Gaulle was no more than a tank commander.
68 *Argumenty i fakty*, No. 12, 2000, p. 3.
69 V. A. Mironov, 'The December Prologue to the June Elections', *Prism*, No. 20, Part 2, December 1999.
70 Viktor Sheinis, 'Posle bitvy: itogi parlamentskikh vyborov i novaya Gosudarstvennaya Duma', *Nezavisimaya gazeta*, 29 December 1999, p. 8.
71 Anthony Giddens, *The Third Way: The Renewal of Social Democracy* (Cambridge, Polity Press, 1998). See also Anthony Giddens, *The Third Way and Its Critics* (Cambridge, Polity Press, 2000); Anthony Giddens (ed.), *The Global Third Way Debate* (Cambridge, Polity Press, 2001).
72 For a comparable discussion of radical centrism, see Michael Lind and Ted Halstead, *The Radical Center: The Future of American Politics* (New York, Doubleday, 2001). Note also the problems with the approach put forward by these two authors, trying to take the best from left and right and instead creating a mix of often incoherent and incompatible policies (quasi-centrism). It appears that in the American context, probably as much as in the Russian, the attempt to generate a non-ideological radical politics of the center falls prey to anti-democratic technocratism (as in Britain under New labour).
73 Kaspe, 'Tsentr i vertikal', pp. 11–12.
74 Kenneth Jowitt, *New World Disorder: The Leninist Extinction* (Berkeley, University of California Press, 1992).
75 Huntington, *Political Order in Changing Societies*.
76 Alexander Yanov, 'Open Letter to Colleagues in the West'; in *JRL* 3410, 26 July 1999.
77 Polly Toynbee, 'Let's Hope Gore Wins', *The Guardian*, 10 March 2000, p. 23.

4 State and society

1 Putin, *First Person*, p. 179.
2 Thomas M. Nichols, *The Russian Presidency: Society and Politics in the Second Russian Republic* (Basingstoke, Macmillan, 2000), p. 2.
3 For the development of the Russian presidency, see Eugene Huskey, *Presidential Power in Russia* (Armonk, NY, M. E. Sharpe, 1999).
4 Igor Klyamkin and Lilia Shevtsova, *This Omnipotent and Impotent Government: The Evolution of the Political System in Post-Communist Russia* (Washington, DC, Carnegie Endowment for International Peace, 1999).

5 S. Holmes, 'Cultural Legacies or State Collapse? Probing the Post-Communist Dilemma', in M. Mandelbaum (ed.), *Post-Communism: Four Views* (New York, Council for Foreign Relations, 1996), p. 50.

6 Ralph Miliband, 'State Power and Class Interests', *New Left Review*, No. 138, 1983, pp. 57–68.

7 Robert Fatton, 'Bringing the Ruling Class Back In', *Comparative Politics*, Vol. 20, No. 3, 1988, p. 254.

8 *Newsline*, 25 February 2000.

9 *Nezavisimaya gazeta*, 24 February 2000.

10 *World Development Report 1997: The State in a Changing World* (Washington, DC, World Bank, 1997), p. 15.

11 The definition is from Alexander Lukin, 'Putin's Regime: Restoration or Revolution?', *Problems of Post-Communism*, Vol. 48, No. 4, July/August 2000, p. 47.

12 Andrei Medushevskii, 'Bonapartistskaya model' vlasti dlya Rossii?', *Konstitutsionnoe pravo: vostochnoevropeiskoe obozrenie*, No. 4 (33)/No. 1 (34), 2001, p. 28.

13 Lukin, 'Putin's Regime', p. 47.

14 Sakwa, *Russian Politics and Society*, third edition, pp. 454–8; see also 'The Regime System in Russia', *Contemporary Politics*, Vol. 3, No. 1, 1997, pp. 7–25.

15 Michael McFaul, 'Indifferent to Democracy', *The Washington Post*, 3 March 2000, p. A29.

16 Douglass North, *Institutions, Institutional Change, and Economic Performance* (Cambridge, Cambridge University Press, 1991).

17 Speaking to a meeting of workers of the Soviet procuracy Gorbachev warned that there could be no return to the past, but equally ultra-radical positions were inadmissible, especially those that could lead to the disintegration of the country or the creation of parallel centres of power: 'there should be only one dictatorship for all – the dictatorship of law'. Mikhail Gorbachev, *Zhizn' i reformy*, Book 2 (Moscow, Novosti, 1995), p. 516.

18 Interfax, 31 January 2000.

19 *Izvestiya*, 14 July 2000.

20 See M. N. Afanas'ev, *Klientizm i Rossiisskaya gosudarstvennost'*, second edition (Moscow, MONF, 1997/2000), pp. 206–22.

21 Sidney Tarrow, *Between Center and Periphery: Grassroots Politicians in Italy and France* (New Haven/London, Yale University Press, 1977), in particular p. 195.

22 For a typical representation of such a polarised approach, see Paul Goble, 'Strong and Weak', *Newsline*, 10 March 2000, pp. 13–15.

23 Lilia Shevtsova, 'Power and Leadership in Putin's Russia', in Andrew Kuchins (ed.), *Russia After the Fall* (Washington, DC, Carnegie Endowment for International Peace, 2002).

24 BBC Monitoring, text of NTV International television, 8 July; in *JRL* 4392/3.

25 Thomas Graham, 'Tackling Tycoons: Revenge, or Rule of Law?', *Wall Street Journal*, 20 July 2000.

26 Dmitri K. Simes, 'With Friends Like These, Putin Needs a Smarter Strategy', *Washington Post*, 16 July 2000.

27 Bortsov, *Vladimir Putin*, p. 236.

28 'Razgovor Goliafa s Leviafanom', *Nezavisimaya gazeta*, 11 July 2000.

29 *Kommersant*, 14 April 2003.

30 BBC Monitoring, 16 May 2003; in *JRL* 7186/1.

31 Thomas Graham, 'Tackling Tycoons: Revenge, or Rule of Law?', *Wall Street Journal*, 20 July 2000.

32 18 March 2000 interview on Radio Mayak, reported by Reddaway, 'Will Putin Be Able to Consolidate Power?', p. 27, fn. 5.

33 See Paul Klebnikov, *Godfather of the Kremlin: Boris Berezovsky and the Looting of Russia* (New York, Harcourt, 2000).

34 Cited in Dale R. Herspring and Jacob Kipp, 'Understanding the Elusive Mr. Putin', *Problems of Post-Communism*, Vol. 48, No. 5, September/October 2001, p. 9.

35 For his analysis of the anti-oligarch investigations and his dismissal, see Yurii Skuratov, *Variant drakona* (Moscow, Detektiv-Press, 2000).

36 *The Guardian*, 18 July 2000, p. 12.

37 *Financial Times*, 18 July 2000.

38 *Segodnya*, 18 July 2000.

39 *The Guardian*, 18 July 2000, p. 12.

40 *Moscow Times*, 18 July 2000.

41 'Russia's President Bares his Teeth', *The Economist*, 15–21 July 2000. The governor of Novgorod, Mikhail Prusak, argued that 'Trying to create a party of governors is like trying to build a bridge of ice in the summer', *Business Week*, 24 July 2000; in *JRL* 4402/7.

42 *Kommersant-Daily*, 8 July 2000; *Newsline*, 10 July 2000.

43 *Business Week*, 24 July 2000; in *JRL* 4402/7.

44 Ibid.

45 *Izvestiya*, 18 July 2000.

46 The new media concern would include ORT, TV6, *Kommersant, Nezavisimaya gazeta, Novye izvestiya, Ogonëk* and *Nashe Radio, Nezavisimaya gazeta*, 18 July 2000.

47 *Newsline*, 3 August 2000.

48 Amelia Gentleman, 'Putin Picks Off Opponents Who Matter Most', *The Guardian*, 14 July 2000, p. 20.

49 For a good study of the background to these events, see Laura Belin, 'The Russian Media in the 1990s', in Rick Fawn and Stephen White (eds), *Russia After Communism* (London, Frank Cass, 2002), pp. 139–60.

50 Amelia Gentleman, 'Putin Picks Off Opponents Who Matter Most', *The Guardian*, 14 July 2000, p. 20.

51 *Izvestiya*, 14 July 2000.

52 For an analysis of this, see A. A. Mukhin, *Novye pravila igry dlya bol'shogo biznesa, prodiktovannye logikoi pravleniya V. V. Putina* (Moscow, Tsentr politicheskoi informatsii, 2002).

53 Among those attending were Vagit Alekperov, head of Lukoil, at the time being investigated for alleged large-scale tax evasion; Vladimir Potanin, head of the Interros financial–industrial group, whom prosecutors accused of conspiring to defraud the state of $140 million in connection with the 1995 privatization of Norilsk Nickel; Rem Vyakhirev, head of Gazprom, Russia's natural gas monopoly, whose offices were raided in connection with the criminal case against Media-Most chief Vladimir Gusinsky; Alfa Group co-founder Mikhail Fridman; Russian Aluminium co-founder Oleg Deripaska; Yevgeny Shvidler, the president of the Sibneft oil company; and United Energy Systems (UES) chief Anatoly Chubais, whose company, state auditors charged, may have been partially sold to foreigners in violation of Russian law. Leading absentees were Media-Most's Gusinsky; Berezovsky, the archetypal insider who at this time declared himself in 'constructive opposition' before later that year moving into 'unconstructive' opposition; Roman Abramovich, formally a State Duma deputy but the brains behind Sibneft and Oleg Deripaska's partner in Russian Aluminium; and Moscow banker Alexander Mamut, who was close to Abramovich and who remains a key Kremlin insider, *Monitor*, 27 July 2000. Although Berezovsky was not physically present, his interests were considered to be represented by Sibneft chief Yevgeny Shvidler and Deripaska, the head of Russian Aluminium, two companies partially owned by Berezovsky, Gregory Feifer, 'Oligarchs Hope for Agreement with Putin', *The St Petersburg Times*, 28 July 2000, p. 3.

54 Arkady Ostrovsky, 'Oligarchs to Seek Peace Deal with Putin', *Financial Times*, 24 July 2000.

55 The points were outlined by Nemtsov, in Arkady Ostrovsky, 'Oligarchs to Seek Peace Deal with Putin', *Financial Times*, 24 July 2000.

56 Reported in *El Mundo* and Russian agencies, in Jamestown Foundation, *Monitor*, 14 July 2000.

57 Vitaly Tretyakov, Editorial, *Nezavisimaya gazeta*, 22 June 2000.

58 Ibid.

59 *Moscow Times*, 14 July 2000.

60 Putin, *First Person*, p. 197.

61 'Diktatura razrushit stranu', *Obshchaya gaezeta*, 13–20 May 2000.

62 'Vystuplenie', http://www.president.kremlin.ru/events/42.html.

63 *Izvestiya*, 14 July 2000.

64 Kiselev in the *Itogi* programme on NTV on 9 July 2000, who also asserted that when Putin referred to some of the media that 'carry out anti-state activity', he had above all NTV in mind.

65 For a discussion of these events and a biographical note on Kiselev, see *Russian Political Weekly*, 2 April 2002.

66 Cited in Julie A. Corwin, 'The New Centralizer', *Newsline*, 21 June 2000.

67 Andrei Zolotov, 'Press Ministry Demands Licencing for Print Media', *Moscow Times*, 10 June 2000.

68 'Doktrina informatsionnoi bezopasnosti Rossiiskoi Federatsii', Drozdov and Fartyshev, *Yurii Andropov i Vladimir Putin*, pp. 268–324; http://www.scrf.gov.ru/Documents/decree/2000/09–09.html.

69 Interview with Vladimir Kosarev and Yurii Gladkevich, in *Profil*, No. 25, 2000; in *JRL* 4394/10.

70 *Izvestiya*, 14 July 2000.

71 *Pravda.ru*, 26 March 2003.

72 Robert Sharlet, 'Putin and the Politics of Law in Russia', *Post-Soviet Affairs*, Vol. 17, No. 3, 2001, p. 196.

73 In Harry G. Broadman (ed.), *Unleashing Russia's Business Potential: Lessons from the Regions for Building Market Institutions* (Washington, DC, World Bank Discussion Paper No. 434, 2002).

74 *The Guardian*, 21 June 2002, p. 18.

75 Vladimir Pastukhov, 'Pravo pod administrativnym pressom v postsovetskoi Rossii', *Konstitutsionnnoe pravo: vostochnoevropeiskoe obozrenie*, No. 2 (39), pp. 105–12.

76 For a negative evaluation, see Sarah E. Mendelson, 'The Putin Path: Civil Liberties and Human Rights in Retreat', *Problems of Post-Communism*, Vol. 47, No. 5, September/October 2000, pp. 3–12.

77 *Newsline*, 12 July 2002.

78 *Moskovskie novosti*, 5 September 2002.

79 *Chechnya Weekly*, 24 July 2002.

5 Restructuring political space

1 Putin, *First Person*, p. 215.

2 V. A. Kolosov (ed.), *Mir glazami rossiyan: mify i vneshnyaya politika* (Moscow, Institut fonda 'Obshchestvennoe mnenie', 2003,) p. 10.

3 See Stephen White, Richard Rose and Ian McAllister, *How Russia Votes* (Chatham, NJ, Chatham House Publishers, 1997).

4 Richard Rose, Neil Munro and Stephen White, 'Voting in a Floating Party System: the 1999 Duma Election', *Europe-Asia Studies*, Vol. 53, No. 3, May 2001, pp. 419–43.

5 For a discussion of the factors inhibiting party development, see Sakwa, *Russian Politics and Society*, third edition, Chapter 8.

6　Scott P. Mainwaring, *Rethinking Party Systems in the Third Wave of Transition: The Case of Brazil* (Stanford, Stanford University Press, 1999), p. 11.
7　Indem study cited by Alexander Domrin, 'The Sin of Party-Building in Russia', *Russia Watch*, No. 9, January 2003, p. 15.
8　*Value Change and the Survival of Democracy in Russia,1995–2000* (Moscow, ROMIR, 2001).
9　Mukhin, *Kto est' mister Putin i kto s nim prishel?*, p. 4.
10　*Newsline*, 10 July 2000.
11　Federal'nyi zakon 'O politicheskikh partiyakh', proekt No. 43556–3 v tret'em chtenii.
12　Keston Institute, Oxford, *Keston News Service*, 3 July 2002.
13　BBC Monitoring, 16 May 2003; in *JRL* 7186/1.
14　Those in favour of the so-called 'project of the parliamentary majority' were allegedly the representatives of the 'family': Voloshin and his deputy Vladislav Surkov, backed by the oligarch Khodorkovsky, who may well have had ambitions to take on the premiership himself. Pavel Ivanov, 'Putin's Sad Anniversary', *Asia Times*, 16 May 2003; in *JRL*, 7184/7. There is of course the possibility that after the end of the two terms as president allowed by the constitution, Putin could himself seek to use the enhanced powers of the premiership to continue his leadership.
15　Joel M. Ostrow, *Comparing Post-Soviet Legislatures: A Theory of Institutional Design and Political Conflict* (Columbus, Ohio State University Press, 2000). See also Joel M. Ostrow, 'Procedural Breakdown and Deadlock in the Russian State Duma: The Problems of an Unlinked Dual-channel Institutional Design', *Europe-Asia Studies*, Vol. 50, No. 5, 1998, pp. 793–816; and Joel M. Ostrow, 'Conflict-Management in Russia's Federal Institutions', *Post-Soviet Affairs*, Vol. 18, No. 1, 2002, pp. 49–70.
16　Thomas F. Remington, *The Russian Parliament: Institutional Evolution in a Transitional Regime* (New Haven, CT, Yale University Press, 2001). See also Thomas F. Remington, Steven S. Smith and Moshe Haspel, 'Decrees, Laws and Inter-Branch Relations in the Russian Federation', *Post-Soviet Affairs*, Vol. 14, No. 4, 1998, pp. 287–322.
17　Thomas F. Remington, 'Putin and the Duma', *Post-Soviet Affairs*, Vol. 17, No. 4, 2001, p. 288.
18　Federico Varese, *The Russian Mafia: Private Protection in a New Market Economy* (Oxford, Oxford University Press, 2001), p. 184.
19　For an examination of the question of measuring significance, and a discussion of the contradiction between the actual productivity of the Duma and its poor image, see Paul Chaisty and Petra Schleiter, 'Productive but Not Valued: The Russia State Duma, 1994–2001', *Europe-Asia Studies*, Vol. 54, No. 5, 2002, pp. 701–24.
20　Sergei Reshul'skii, 'Nizhnyaya palata prevratilas' v filial pravitel'stva', *Nezavisimaya gazeta*, 27 December 2001, p. 2.
21　Chaisty and Schleiter, 'Productive but Not Valued', p. 715.
22　The Jamestown Foundation, *Monitor*, 19 July 2001.
23　The argument is made by Nikolas K. Gvosdev, 'Managed Pluralism and Political Parties in Russia', *Analysis of Current Events*, Vol. 14, No. 3, October 2002, pp. 15–17.
24　*Segodnya*, 29 December 2000.
25　Medvedev, *Vremya Putina?*, p. 89.
26　Grigory Yavlinsky, 'Going Backwards', *Journal of Democracy*, Vol. 12, No. 4, October 2001, pp. 79–86, at pp. 79, 80.
27　*Segodnya*, 6 July 2000.
28　Speech reported at the World Economic Forum Central and Eastern European Economic Summit in Salzburg, Austria, Paul Hofheinz, 'Putin's Critics Fear Russia Resembles Pinochet's Chile', *Wall Street Journal*, 5 July 2000.

29 Grigory Yavlinsky, 'Un-Managing Democracy', *Russia Watch*, No. 9, January 2003, pp. 12–13.
30 Shevtsova, *Putin's Russia*, p. 51.
31 *Gazeta*, 2 July 2002; in *JRL* 6325/8.
32 Polit.ru, 30 May 2002, in an interview with Mikhail Fishman; reported in *Monitor*, 31 May 2002.
33 Yelena Yakovleva, 'Gleb Pavlovsky on the Prospects for Civil Society in Russia', *Izvestiya*, 3 July 2002.
34 These issues are explored in Sudipta Kaviraj and Sunil Khilnani (eds), *Civil Society: History and Possibilities* (Cambridge, Cambridge University Press, 2001).
35 Lilia Shevtsova, *Elective Monarchy Under Putin: Perspectives on the Evolution of the Political Regime and Its Problems* (Moscow, Moscow Carnegie Center, 2001); available in Russian at http://pubs.carnegie.ru/briefings/2001/issue01–01.asp.
36 'O tselyakh i zadachakh Grazhdanskogo foruma', *Prezident*, No. 17 (226), 28 November–12 December 2001, p. 1.
37 Vladimir Putin, 'Grazhdanskoe obshchestvo nel'zya sozdat' po ukaske', *Prezident*, No. 17 (226), 28 November–12 December 2001, p. 1; *Grazhdanskii forum*, 22 November 2001, p. 2; www.civilforum.ru.
38 BBC Monitoring, 16 May 2003; in *JRL* 7186/1.
39 *Vremya novostei*, No. 64, April 2003.

6 Putin and the regions

1 See Cameron Ross (ed.), *Regional Politics in Russia* (Manchester, Manchester University Press, 2002); and his *Federalism and Democratisation in Russia* (Manchester, Manchester University Press, 2002).
2 Kathryn Stoner-Weiss, 'Central Weakness and Provincial Autonomy: Observations on the Devolution Process in Russia', *Post-Soviet Affairs*, Vol. 15, No. 1, 1999, pp. 87–106.
3 For a useful discussion, see S. D. Valentei, *Federalizm: Rossiiskaya istoriya i Rossiiskaya real'nost'* (Moscow, Institute of the Economy, Centre for the Socio-Economic Problems of Federalism, RAS, 1998).
4 For a development of this argument, see Richard Sakwa, 'Russian Regionalism, Policy-Making and State Development', in Stefanie Harter and Gerald Easter (eds), *Shaping the Economic Space in Russia: Decision Making Processes, Institutions and Adjustment to Change in the El'tsin Era* (Aldershot, Ashgate, 2000), Chapter 1, pp. 11–34.
5 Some of the arguments of this section were outlined in Richard Sakwa, 'Putin's New Federalism', *Russian Regional Report*, Vol. 5, No. 21, 31 May 2000, pp. 12–17.
6 For a critique of this, see Grigory Yavlinsky, 'The Last Phase of Agony', *Obshchaya gazeta*, 10–16 June 1999.
7 Mikhail A. Alexseev, 'Introduction: Challenges to the Russian Federation', in Mikhail A. Alexseev (ed.), *Center-Periphery Conflict in Post-Soviet Russia: A Federation Imperiled* (Basingstoke, Macmillan, 1999), p. 1.
8 Leonid Smirnyagin, 'The Great Seven', *Russian Regional Report*, Vol. 5, No. 20, 24 May 2000.
9 Sophie Lambroschini, 'KGB Veterans Head has High Hopes of Putin', *Newsline*, 30 June 2000.
10 A theme explored by Kathryn Stoner-Weiss, *Local Heroes: The Political Economy of Russian Regional Governance* (Princeton, NJ, Princeton University Press, 1997).
11 James Hughes, 'Moscow's Bilateral Treaties Add to Confusion', *Transition*, 20 September 1996, p. 43.

12 *Izvestiya*, 4 November 1997; *Russian Regional Report*, Vol. 2, No. 38, 6 November 1997.

13 *Rossiiskaya gazeta*, 30 June 1999.

14 The issue is examined in A. Lavrov (ed.), *Federal'nyi byudzhet i regiony: opyt analiza finansovykh potokov* (Moscow, Dialog-MGU, 1999). See also S. D. Valentei (ed.), *Ekonomicheskie problemy stanovleniya Rossiiskogo federalizma* (Moscow, Nauka, 1999).

15 Aleksei Salmin notes that the margin of error in the calculation of transfers in some cases reached 100 per cent, allowing great scope for bureaucratic arbitrariness and encouraging corruption. Press conference with Sergei Karaganov and other Foreign and Defence Policy Council officials, 14 April 2000; in *JRL*, 4255.

16 *Russian Regional Report*, Vol. 4, No. 20, 27 May 1999.

17 For example, in Pskov, see Darrell Slider, 'Pskov Under the LDPR: Elections and Dysfunctional Federalism in One Region', *Europe-Asia Studies*, Vol. 51, No. 5, 1999, p. 764.

18 Daniel Treisman, 'The Politics of Intergovernmental Transfers in Post-Soviet Russia', *British Journal of Political Science*, Vol. 26, No. 3, July 1996, pp. 299–335. See also his 'Deciphering Russia's Federal Finance: Fiscal Appeasement in 1995 and 1996', *Europe-Asia Studies*, Vol. 50, No. 5, July 1998, pp. 893–906; Daniel Treisman, *After the Deluge: Regional Crises and Political Consolidation in Russia* (Ann Arbor, MI, The University of Michigan Press, 1999).

19 Alistair McAuley, 'The Determinants of Russian Federal-Regional Fiscal Relations: Equity or Political Influence', *Europe-Asia Studies*, Vol. 49, No. 3, May 1997, pp. 431–44.

20 See Neil Robinson, 'The Global Economy, Reform and Crisis in Russia', *Review of International Political Economy*, Vol. 6, No. 4, Winter 1999, pp. 531–64.

21 *Kommersant-Daily*, 31 October 1997.

22 For example, in the case of Gorno-Altai, discussed below, *Rossiiskaya gazeta*, 21 June 2000, pp. 5–6.

23 Peter Kirkow, *Russia's Provinces: Authoritarian Transformation versus Local Autonomy?* (Basingstoke, Macmillan, 1998), p. 125.

24 This is argued, for example, by Andreas Heinemann-Grüder, 'Asymmetry and Federal Integration in Russia', in Vladimir Tikhomirov (ed.), *Anatomy of the 1998 Russian Crisis* (University of Melbourne, Contemporary Europe Research Centre, 1999), Chapter 4, pp. 79–107.

25 The argument is developed in Richard Sakwa, 'The Republicanisation of Russia: Federalism and Democratization in Transition I', in Chris Pierson and Simon Tormey (eds), *Politics at the Edge*, The PSA Yearbook 1999 (Basingstoke, Macmillan, 1999), Chapter 16, pp. 215–26. See also the chapter by Cameron Ross in the same volume, Chapter 17, pp. 227–40.

26 Pechenev notes that as early as April–May 1994 a report commissioned by the then head of the presidential administration, Sergei Filatov, had identified and condemned the divergences in constitutional norms between those expounded in the RF constitition and the constitutions in republics such as Tatarstan, Bashkortostan, Tuva and Ingushetiya, *Vladimir Putin*, p. 56.

27 Darrell Slider, Vladimir Gimpel'son and Sergei Chugrov, 'Political Tendencies in Russia's Regions: Evidence from the 1993 Parliamentary Elections', *Slavic Review*, Vol. 53, No. 3, Fall 1994, pp. 711–32, at pp. 726, 730–1.

28 For example in Tatarstan, as reported by Robert Orttung and Peter Reddaway, *Russian Regional Report*, Vol. 5, No. 25, 28 June 2000.

29 *Zvezda Povolzhia*, 20–26 January 2000, in Midkhat Faroukshin, 'Tatarstan Opposition Seeks Putin's Help', *Russian Regional Report*, Vol. 5, No. 4, 2 February 2000. A detailed description of how the electoral system was manipulated can be found in *Osobaya zona: vybory v Tatarstane* (Ul'yanovsk, Kazan Branch of the International Human Rights Assembly, 2000).

30 Putin, *First Person*, pp. 182–3.
31 Interview with *Welt am Sontag*, June 2000, http://www.president.kremlin.ru/events/38.html.
32 'Vystuplenie na vstreche s liderami delovogo mira Italii', 6 June 2000, http://www.president.kremlin.ru/events/37.html.
33 The announcement was made after a meeting with Putin on 16 March 2000.
34 http:/www.president.kremlin.ru/events/34.html.
35 *Rossiiskaya gazeta*, 13 May 2000.
36 *Russian Regional Report*, Vol. 5, No. 19, 17 May 2000.
37 *Izvestiya*, 12 May 2000; *Nezavisimaya gazeta*, 12 May 2000; http://press.main dir.gov.ru.
38 'Postanovlenie Konstitutsionnogo Suda Rossiiskoi Federatsii po delu o proverke konstitutsionnosti otdel'nykh polozhenii Konstitutsii Respubliki Altai i Federal'nogo zakona "Ob obshchikh printsipakh organizatsii zakonodatel'nykh (predstavitel'nykh) i ispolnitel'nykh organov gosudarstvennoi vlasti sub" ektov Rossiiskoi Federatsii', *Rossiiskaya gazeta*, 21 June 2000, pp. 5–6.
39 The ruling is discussed in *Russian Regional Report*, Vol. 5, No. 25, 28 June 2000.
40 Aleksandr Shipkin, 'Altai perebral. Suvereniteta', *Rossiiskaya gazeta*, 10 June 2000, p. 3.
41 *Russian Regional Report*, Vol. 5, No. 25, 28 June 2000.
42 This at least was the view of Zufar Yenikeev, a deputy to the Bashkortostan State Assembly and Russia's representative to the European Chamber of the Regions, *Russian Regional Report*, Vol. 5, No. 25, 28 June 2000.
43 *Rossiiskaya gazeta*, 16 May 2000.
44 *Nezavisimaya gazeta*, 16 May 2000.
45 *Rossiiskaya gazeta*, 17 July 1997.
46 Petr Akopov and Svetlana Babaeva, *Izvestiya*, 15 May 2000.
47 The seven capitals of the new Federal Districts (FD) are: Moscow for the Central FD, St Petersburg for the Northwest FD, Rostov-na-Donu for the North Caucasus (later renamed South Russia) FD, Nizhny Novgorod for the Volga FD, Ekaterinburg for the Urals FD, Novosibirsk for the Siberian FD and Khabarovsk for the Far East FD. The later merger of the Volga and Urals military districts accentuated the mismatch between the borders of the seven FDs and what had now become six military districts.
48 The full list is as follows: Sergei Kirienko, the former prime minister and one of the leaders of the Union of Rightist Forces (SPS) headed the Volga FD; CIS Affairs Minister and former Russian ambassador to Poland, Leonid Drachevsky, headed the Siberian FD; Victor Cherkesov, the First Deputy Director of the FSB, headed the Northwest FD (until replaced in March 2003 by Valentina Matvienko); General Viktor Kazantsev, who had directed the latest onslaught against Chechnya, the North Caucasus (South Russia) FD; First Deputy Interior Minister Petr Latyshev, the Urals FD; former presidential representative to Leningrad *oblast* (and before that with years of service in the KGB), Georgy Poltavchenko, headed the Central FD; and Lieutenant-General Konstantin Pulikovsky, who had been a commander in the Chechen war of 1994–96, headed the Far East FD.
49 RIA Novosti 9 March 2000.
50 V. V. Cherkesov (ed.), *Institut general-guvernatorstva i namestnichestva v rossiiskoi imperii* (St Petersburg, Yuridicheskii Tsentr Press, 2003).
51 Interfax, 31 July 2000; RFE/RL *Newsline*, 1 August 2000.
52 *Russian Regional Report*, Vol. 5, No. 28, 19 July 2000.
53 Ibid., No. 29, 26 July 2000.
54 Luzhkov continued to remain obdurate, however, insisting on 23 July 2000 that the city had no intention of dropping registration requirements, arguing that

they were necessary 'protective measures' for the capital, *Moscow Times*, 25 July 2000. Not only was it unclear how Luzhkov could be forced to comply with the law, Moscow *oblast* also intended to introduce a similar registration system.

55 See Jeffrey Kahn, *Federalism, Democratization, and the Rule of Law in Russia* (Oxford, Oxford University Press, 2002).
56 Olivier Blanchard and Andrei Shleifer, 'Federalism With and Without Political Centralisation: China Versus Russia', *IMF Staff Papers*, Vol. 48, Special Issue, 2001, p. 176.
57 *Russian Regional Report*, Vol. 5, No. 29, 26 July 2000; *Nezavisimaya gazeta*, 26 July 2000.
58 *Russian Regional Report*, Vol. 8, No. 5, 8 April 2003.
59 http://www.president.kremlin.ru/events/510/html.
60 D. V. Badovskii, 'Sistema federal'nykh okrugov i institut polnomnykh predstavitelei prezidenta RF: sovremennoe sostoyanie i problemy razvitiya', in *Polpredy Prezidenta: problemy stanovleniya novogo instituta* (MGU, Nauchnye doklady, No. 3, January 2001), p. 5.
61 Nikolai Petrov, 'Federal Reform, Two and a Half Years On', *Russia and Eurasia Review*, Vol. 2, No. 1, 7 January 2003.
62 http://www.president.kremlin.ru/events/34.html.
63 Sarah Karush and Catherine Belton, 'Putin to Tighten Grip on Regions', *Moscow Times*, 18 May 2000.
64 *Newsline*, 18 May 2000.
65 The Federal Law No. 113–F3 of 5 August 2000, 'O poryadke formirovaniya Soveta Federatsiya Federal'nogo Sobraniya Rossiiskoi Federatsii', adopted by the State Duma on 19 July and ratified by the Federation Council on 26 July 2000, *Rossiiskaya gazeta*, 5 August 2000.
66 Sarah Karush, 'Governors Give Up Federation Fight', *The St. Petersburg Times*, 28 July 2000, p. 2.
67 Ibid.
68 *Russian Regional Report*, Vol. 5, No. 29, 26 July 2000.
69 The head of the Northwest Federal District, Cherkesov (a close Putin ally), on 21 July 2000 did in fact suggest that in future the upper house could be elected, *Russian Regional Report*, Vol. 5, No. 29, 26 July 2000.
70 Sergei Sarychev, 'Stroev Deems Attempts to Reform Legislature Absurd', *Russian Regional Report*, Vol. 5, No. 28, 19 July 2000.
71 *Nezavisimaya gazeta*, 3 August 2000.
72 Ibid.
73 Julie A. Corwin, 'The New Centralizer', *Newsline*, 21 June 2000.
74 'On Removing from Office the Regional Leaders of Legislative and Executive Bodies', *Izvestiya*, 20 July 2000; *Newsline*, 19 July 2000.
75 *Nezavisimaya gazeta*, 19 May 2000.
76 Alexander Solzhenitsyn, *Rebuilding Russia* (London, Harvill, 1991), pp. 71–8.
77 For a discussion of these issues, see Galina Kurlyandskaya, *Budgetary Pluralism of Russian Authorities*, Open Society Institute, Local Government and Public Service Reform Initiative, Discussion Papers, No. 17, Budapest, 2001.
78 'Intervyu s prezidentom Rossii', *Komsomol'skaya pravda*, 22 March 2001, p. 3.
79 Kozak denied that this would be an outcome of the changes, 'Reforma vlasti: kak podelit' na troikh?', *Argumenty i fakty*, No. 16, April 2003, p. 6.
80 *Russian Regional Report*, Vol. 5, No. 29, 26 July 2000.
81 Regional tax revenues fell by 0.2 per cent of GDP, whereas the wages of state-sector employees (for which the regions were responsible) rose by 70 per cent in 2001–02. The number of 'deficit' regions rose from 42 in 2001 to 63 in 2002. The consolidated budget of the 89 federal regions at that time showed a deficit of 0.4 per cent of GDP, *Russian Political Weekly*, Vol. 3, No. 6, 5 February 2003.

82 www.polit.ru, 26 July.
83 According to First Deputy Finance Minister, Sergei Shatalov, *Russian Regional Report*, Vol. 5, No. 29, 26 July 2000.
84 The driving force behind the letter was governor Mikhail Prusak of Novgorod, and it was signed by Belgorod governor Yevgeny Savchenko and Kurgan governor Oleg Bogomolov, 'I vlast', i ekonomika, i prezident na 7 let', *Nezavisimaya gazeta*, 25 February 2000, pp. 1, 4.
85 For an instructive comparative discussion of particularism, see Stein Rokkan, 'The Survival of Peripheral Identity', in *State Formation, Nation Building, and Mass Politics in Europe: The Theory of Stein Rokkan*, edited by Peter Flora with Stein Kuhle and Derek Urwin (Oxford, Oxford University Press, 1999), pp. 191–208.
86 'Titov protiv naznacheniya gubernatorov', *Nezavisimaya gazeta*, 3 March 2000; see also *Moscow Times*, 3 March 2000; and *Russian Regional Report*, Vol. 5, No. 9, 9 March 2000.
87 'Ob obshchikh printsipakh organizatsii zokonodatel'nykh (predstavitel'nykh) i ispolnitel'nykh organov gosudarstvennoi vlasti sub'ektov Rossiiskoi Federatsii', *Rossiiskaya gazeta*, 19 October 1999, pp. 4–5.
88 *Russian Regional Report*, Vol. 8, No. 2, 3 February 2003. Julia Corwin reckons the Kremlin's success rate in gubernatorial elections as follows: 7 out of 44 in 2000, 7 out of 14 in 2001 and 10 out of 14 in 2002, *Russian Political Weekly*, Vol. 3, No. 1, January 2003.
89 Valery Kokov in Kabardino-Balkaria, Sherig-ool Oorzhak in Tyva, Magomedali Magomedov in Dagestan and Kirsan Ilyumzhinov in Kalmykia.
90 Derek S. Hutcheson, *Political Parties in the Russian Regions* (London, Routledge-Curzon, 2003), p. 45.
91 A. S. Avtonomov, A. A. Zakharov and Ye. M. Orlova, *Regional'nye parlamenty v sovremennoi Rossii*, Nauchnye doklady No. 118 (Moscow, MONF, 2000).
92 See Alexander Kynev, 'The Role of Political Parties in Russia's 2002 Regional Elections', *Russia and Eurasia Review*, Vol. 2, Issue 8, 15 April 2003.
93 For example, in Rostov, *Russian Regional Report*, 23 April 2003; Primorsky *krai*, *Russian Regional Report*, 7 May 2003.
94 For details, see Hutcheson, *Political Parties in the Russian Regions*.
95 Heinemann-Grüder, 'Asymmetry and Federal Integration in Russia', p. 80.
96 *Russian Regional Report*, Vol. 6, No. 12, 2 April 2001.
97 *Izvestiya*, 21 March 2001.
98 ORT, 17 May 2000, 1700 gmt; http:/www.president.kremlin.ru/events/ 34.html
99 Interview with *Welt am Sontag*, June 2000, http://www.president.kremlin.ru/events/38.html
100 President Murtaza Rakhimov of Bashkortostan was less satisfied with the level of personal relations with Putin, noting that the federal government is 'drifting away from the regions' and was 'becoming unapproachable'; ministers were no longer quite so easily available: 'Whenever you call a ministry, some secretary gets the call and starts asking you all sorts of questions – who is calling, what for, and so on. But the ministers themselves should be calling the regions and asking how things are', he complained. As for the federal districts, he argued that the presidential envoys were 'just another layer of government, and we are not rich enough to feed and maintain it'. *Vremya novostei*, 23 March 2001, cited in *Russian Federation Report*, Vol. 3, No. 12, 4 April 2001.
101 Sarah Karush and Catherine Belton, 'Putin to Tighten Grip on Regions', *Moscow Times*, 18 May 2000.
102 *Moskovskii komsomolets*, 24 May 2000.
103 *Nezavisimaya gazeta*, 6 May 2000.
104 *Kommersant Daily*, 31 May 2000.
105 *Russian Regional Report*, Vol. 5, No. 29, 26 July 2000.

106 Cited by Sophie Lambroschini, 'Federation Council Approves Putin-Led Reforms', *Newsline*, 27 July 2000.
107 Putin, *First Person*, p. 186.
108 *Russian Regional Report*, Vol. 5, No. 21, 31 May 2000.
109 Ibid., Vol. 7, No. 20, 17 June 2002.
110 *Moscow Times*, 24 May 2000.
111 As *Obshchaya gazeta* put it on 25 May 2000, Putin's measures were 'a series of blows against the independence . . . of the regional leaders, who under the conditions of the extreme weakness of the legislative and judicial branches are the single real counterweight to the authoritarianism of the Centre'. Cited in *Monitor*, 25 May 2000.
112 Mikhail Kushtapin, 'The Long Expected. And the Unexpected', *Rossiiskaya gazeta*, 16 May 2000.

7 Reforging the nation

1 http://www.president.kremlin.ru/events/42.html.
2 For a recent analysis of the question, see Philip Bobbitt, *The Shield of Achilles* (London, Allen Lane, 2002).
3 Cf. Geoffrey Hosking, *Russia: People and Empire 1552–1917* (London, Harper-Collins, 1997).
4 See Mark Beissinger, *Nationalist Mobilization and the Collapse of the Soviet State* (Cambridge, Cambridge University Press, 2002) for a particularly illuminating discussion of the nature of the Soviet 'empire'.
5 Ernest Renan, 'What is a Nation?', in Homi K. Bhabha (ed.), *Nation and Narration* (London, Routledge, 1990), pp. 19, 11.
6 Putin, *First Person*, p. 213; Sakwa, *Putin*, p. 256.
7 Kolosov (ed.), *Mir glazami rossiyan*, p. 57.
8 Ibid., p. 58.
9 'Yeltsin Call for "Unifying National Idea"', ITAR-Tass 12 July 1996. For a discussion of this, see Michael Urban, 'Remythologising the Russian State', *Europe-Asia Studies*, Vol. 50, No. 6, 1998, pp. 969–92.
10 Putin, *First Person*, p. 213; Sakwa, *Putin*, p. 256.
11 Interfax, 3 November 1999.
12 ITAR-Tass, 22 December 1999.
13 Putin, *First Person*, p. 214; Sakwa, *Putin*, p. 256.
14 M. Steven Fish, 'Putin's Path', *Journal of Democracy*, Vol. 12, No. 4, October 2001, p. 73.
15 Putin's defended his synthetic approach in *Komsomol'skaya pravda*, 6 December 2000.
16 The history of the flag, emblem and anthem are described in B. A. Anikin (ed.), *Natsional'naya ideya Rossii* (Moscow, State Management University, 2002), with the words of the new anthem on p. 44, of earlier versions pp. 45–7.
17 Mlechin, for example, argues that because so many people would be upset by hauling Lenin's body out of the mausoleum, it was best to leave it there for the time being. Similarly, for many the old Soviet anthem represented not wartime victories or Yury Gagarin's space flight, but the Gulag and repression. However, 'Putin decided that the Soviet hymn should be restored. And he got his way. That is a trait of his character', Mlechin, *Kreml' prezidenty Rossii*, p. 695.
18 *Monitor*, 19 July 2001; *Moscow Times*, 19 July 2001.
19 Putin, *Razgovor s Rossiei*, pp. 86–7.
20 A. I. Podberezkin and V. V. Makarov, *Strategiya dlya budushchego prezidenta Rossii: Russkii put'* (Moscow, RAU-Universitet, 2000).
21 Televised address by Boris Yeltsin, 13 September 1999.

22 Sven Gunnar Simonsen, 'Nationalism and the Russian Political Spectrum: Locating and Evaluating the Extremes', *Journal of Political Ideologies*, Vol. 6, No. 3, October 2001; in his *Pains of Partition: Nationalism, National Identity, and the Military in Post-Soviet Russia*, Department of Political Science, Faculty of Social Sciences, University of Oslo, 2001, p. 90.

23 Sven Gunnar Simonsen, 'Putin's Leadership Style: Ethnocentric Patriotism', *Security Dialogue*, Vol. 31, No. 3, 2000, pp. 377–80.

24 Vladimir Putin, 'Vystuplenie na torzhestvennom prieme v oznamenovanie 55–y godovshchinu pobedy v Velikoi Otechestvennoi voyne 1941–1945 godov', http://president.kremlin.ru/events/32.html.

25 Simonsen, 'Nationalism and the Russian Political Spectrum', p. 96.

26 Sergei Stankevich, 'Dlya chego perevozit chto-to iz Rossii v Rossiyu?', *Nezavisimaya gazeta*, 7 April 1992.

27 In December 1996 the Federation Council adopted a resolution moved by Luzhkov declaring Sevastopol a Russian city, RFE/RL, *Daily Brief*, 6 December 1996.

28 Putin, *Razgovor s Rossiei*, 19 December 2002, p. 54.

29 *Komsomol'skaya pravda*, 11 February 2000.

30 'V Kreml' "cherez postel'" ne popadesh', *Argumenty i fakty*, No. 12, 2000, p. 9.

31 Putin, *Razgovor s Rossiei*, p. 52.

32 For an excellent analysis of Dostoevsky's relationship with the Slavophiles and other nativist traditions, see Sarah Hudsmith, *Dostoevsky and the Idea of Russianness: A New Perspective on Unity and Brotherhood* (London, RoutledgeCurzon, 2003).

33 Nicholas K. Gvosdev, 'The New Party Card: Orthodoxy and the Search for Post-Soviet Identity', *Problems of Post-Communism*, Vol. 47, No. 6, November–December 2000, pp. 29–38.

34 See Edwin Bacon, 'Church and State in Contemporary Russia: Conflicting Discourses', in Rick Fawn and Stephen White (eds), *Russia After Communism* (London, Frank Cass, 2002), pp. 97–116.

35 Blotskii, *Vladimir Putin*, Book 2, p. 21.

36 Mlechin, *Kreml' prezidenty Rossii*, p. 691.

37 Ibid., p. 692.

38 Reuters, 9 June 2000.

39 This is the implication of Gvosdev's notion of 'the new party card', 'The New Party Card'.

40 Robert Jackson, 'Sovereignty in World Politics: a Glance at the Conceptual and Historical Landscape', *Political Studies*, Vol. XLVII, Special Issue 1999, *Sovereignty at the Millennium*, p. 434.

41 Viva Ona Bartkus, *The Dynamics of Secession* (Cambridge, Cambridge University Press, 1999), Chapter 8, '"Opportune Moments": a Reduction in the Costs of Secession', pp. 145–66.

42 UN Resolution 1244 recognised the 'sovereignty and territorial integrity of the Federal Republic of Yugoslavia', but by autumn 2000 the United States began to envisage an independent Kosovo.

43 See Richard Sakwa, 'Chechnya: A Just War Fought Unjustly?', in Bruno Coppieters and Richard Sakwa (eds), *Contextualizing Secession: Normative Studies in Comparative Perspective* (Oxford, Oxford University Press, 2003), Chapter 8, pp. 156–86.

44 Metta Spencer (ed.), *Separatism: Democracy and Disintegration* (Lanham, MD, Rowman & Littlefield, 1998).

45 Robert K. Schaeffer, *Severed States: Dilemmas of Democracy in a Divided World* (Lanham, MD, Rowman & Littlefield, 1999).

46 Henry E. Hale, 'Is Russian Nationalism on the Rise?', Program on New

Approaches to Russian Security (PONARS), Davis Center for Russian Studies, Harvard University, *Policy Memo Series*, No. 110, February 2000, p. 1.

47 There were popular protests in the first war and a degree of elite mobilisation to oppose it, and the financial and budgetary implications of both wars were far from negligible, but for most of the population the Chechen wars were perceived as being somehow 'foreign': even though they were fought precisely to ensure that Chechnya remained 'domestic'.

48 Anatol Lieven, *Chechnya: Tombstone of Russian Power* (New Haven and London, Yale University Press, 1998).

49 Quoted by Rutland, 'Putin's Path to Power', p. 324.

50 Henry E. Hale and Rein Taagepera, 'Russia: Consolidation or Collapse?', *Europe-Asia Studies*, Vol. 54, No. 7, 2002, pp. 1101–25 analyse the degree to which Russia's disintegration really is a serious possibility.

51 Interview with Vladimir Putin by Mikhail Leont'ev, Vremya, ORT, 7 February 2000.

52 Putin, *First Person*, pp. 133–4.

53 Putin, *Ot pervogo litsa*, p. 135; *First Person*, pp. 141–2.

54 Putin, *Razgovor s Rossiei*, 19 December 2002, pp. 47–8.

55 *Monitor*, 1 February 2000.

56 Speech of 20 November 2000, *Newsline*, 21 November 2000. He was supported in his view by the Russian elite: a poll conducted by ROMIR-Gallup International in December 2000 found that the overwhelming majority, 92.1 per cent, felt that Chechnya should remain part of the Russian Federation, reported in *JRL* 4675/6.

57 These events are surrounded by controversy. There is an argument, hinted at for example by Vitalii Tret'yakov in *Nezavisimaya gazeta* on 12 October 1999, that the Chechens had been drawn into invading Dagestan to provide Russia with an excuse to avenge the humiliation of the first war. The apartment bombings themselves remain shrouded in mystery, above all the discovery of similar explosives primed to explode in Ryazan, allegedly planted by the FSB to test the vigilance of the local authorities and people (see Chapter 1).

58 *Nezavisimaya gazeta*, 12 February 2000. By April the figure had risen to 1,839 killed and 5,266 wounded, according to Valerii Manilov, First Deputy Chief of the Russian Armed Forces' General Staff. He noted that if the losses incurred in the Dagestani campaign that preceded the second Chechen war are included, then the figures rose to 2,119 killed and 6,253 wounded, Itar-Tass, 13 April 2000; in *JRL* 4248/14.

59 *Novaya gazeta*, 9–15 June 2003. In addition to the 4,572 deaths, 15,549 had been wounded, an average of 117 soldiers dying a month and 399 being wounded.

60 *Moskovskie novosti*, No. 46, November 2000.

61 *Newsline*, 27 October 2000.

62 Otto Latsis, 'Ups and Downs of Political Will', *The Russia Journal*, 7–13 October 2000.

63 Zakhar Vinogradov, 'Vtoraya chechenskaya kampaniya: pobednyi god', *Nezavisimaya gazeta*, 6 October 2000, p. 4.

64 *Chechnya Weekly*, 30 May 2001.

65 Cited by Paul Goble, 'On Equal Terms', *Newsline*, 14 March 2000.

66 For a discussion of theories of secession, see Bruno Coppieters, 'Introduction', in Coppieters and Sakwa (eds), *Contextualizing Secession*.

67 According to VTsIOM in December 2002 56 per cent favoured negotiations with the separatists, while 36 per cent favoured continued military action against them, *Chechnya Weekly*, 22 January 2003.

68 *Nezavisimaya gazeta*, 9 July 2002.

69 Nikolai Petrov, 'Troshev Ouster and the Chechnya Policy', *Russia and Eurasia Review*, Vol. 2, No. 3, 4 February 2003.

70 For his own view of the conflict in Chechnya, see Gennadii Troshev, *Moya voina: Chechenskii dnevnik okopnogo generala* (Moscow, Vagrius, 2001).
71 In October 2002 Putin decreed that the Military Commandant in the republic would coordinate the work of the others, including the North Caucasus MD, the Combined Federal Forces Group in the North Caucasus, the Regional Operations Staff for Control of Counter-terrorist Operations in the North Caucasus Region, and the commander of the defence ministry forces in the republic.
72 *Le Monde*, 12 April 2003; a report issued by Human Rights Watch on 7 April 2003 noted that the violation of humanitarian laws had not decreased, http://www.hrw.org/.
73 Plenty of evidence is adduced in The Jamestown Foundation's *Chechnya Weekly*, for example, 16 July 2002.
74 Interview by Said Bitsoev, *Novye Izvestia*, 19 July 2002; *Chechnya Weekly*, 24 July 2002.
75 *Nezavisimaya gazeta*, 23 July 2002; *Chechnya Weekly*, 29 July 2002.
76 VTsIOM poll, reported in *Chechnya Weekly*, 6 February 2003.
77 Putin, *Razgovor s Rossiei*, p. 41.
78 Ibid., p. 48.
79 *Chechnya Weekly*, 30 January 2003.
80 BBC Monitoring, 16 May 2003; in *JRL* 7186/1.
81 *Chechnya Weekly*, 10 April 2003.
82 The question of why the extension of autonomy in some circumstances blunts the drive for secession while in others only whets the appetite of secessionist movements is at the core of Bartkus's conceptual model in her *The Dynamics of Secession*.
83 BBC Monitoring, 16 May 2003; in *JRL* 7186/1.
84 Primakov, *Rossiiskaya gazeta*, 10 September 2002.

8 Russian capitalism

1 Itar-Tass, 28 February 2000.
2 Joel S. Hellman, 'Winners Take All: The Politics of Partial Reform in Postcommunist Transitions', *World Politics*, Vol. 50, 1998, pp. 203–34.
3 *Forbes Magazine*, 17 March 2003.
4 Mikhail S. Alexseev and Tamara Troyakova, 'A Mirage of the "Amur California": Regional Identity and Economic Incentives for Political Separatism and Primorskiy Kray', in Alexseev (ed.), *Center-Periphery Conflict in Post-Soviet Russia*, Chapter 6, pp. 205–46.
5 Vladimir Tikhomirov (ed.), *Anatomy of the 1998 Russian Crisis* (University of Melbourne, Contemporary Europe Research Centre, 1999).
6 Joseph Stiglitz, *Globalization and its Discontents* (London, Allan Lane The Penguin Press, 2002), Chapter 5.
7 *Moscow News*, No. 14, 16–22 April 2003, p. 7.
8 Ibid. There are other estimates. For example, the finance ministry suggested that the country's 2003 tax burden stood at 30.7 per cent of GDP, *The Moscow Times*, 24 April 2003, p. 5.
9 Larry Elliott, 'World Groups' Reputations Sinking', *The Russia Journal*, 20–26 March 2000, p. iv.
10 Stanley Fischer, 'Ten Years of Transition', *IMF Staff Papers*, Vol. 48, Special Issue, 2001, p. 7.
11 Stefan Hedlund, 'Will the Russian Economy Revive Under Putin?', *Problems of Post-Communism*, March/April 2001, p. 59.
12 For an evaluation, see William Tompson, 'Putin's Challenge: The Politics of Structural Reform in Russia', *Europe-Asia Studies*, Vol. 54, No. 6, September 2002, pp. 933–58.

13 *Financial Times*, 1 April 2003, p. ii.
14 Elena Chinyaeva, 'The Russian Economy, Lost in the Dark', *Russia and Eurasia Review*, Vol. 2, No. 3, 4 February 2003.
15 *Financial Times*, 1 April 2003, p. iv.
16 A. Zudin, 'Oligarkhiya kak politicheskaya problema rossiiskogo postkommunizma', *Obshchestvennie nauki i sovremennost'*, No. 1, 1999, pp. 45–65.
17 *Moscow Times*, 23 August 2002.
18 See Peter Rutland (ed.), *Business and State in Contemporary Russia* (Boulder, CO, Westview, 2001).
19 A. A. Mukhin, *Biznes-elita i gosudarstvennaya vlast': Kto vladeet Rossiei na rubezhe vekov?* (Moscow, Tsentr politicheskoi informatsii, 2001).
20 Ya. Sh. Pappe, *'oligarkhi': ekonomicheska khronika, 1992–2000*, second edition (Moscow, Gosudarstvennyi universitet Vysshaya shkola ekonomiki, 2000).
21 A. Dynkin and A. Sokolov, 'Integrirovannye biznes-gruppy v rossiiskom ekonomike', *Voprosy ekonomiki*, No. 4, 2002, pp. 78–95.
22 Sergei Kolmakov, 'The Role of Financial Industrial Conglomerates in Russian Political Parties', *Russia Watch*, No. 9, January 2003, pp. 15–17.
23 Dynkin and Sokolov, 'Integrirovannye biznes-gruppy v rossiiskom ekonomike', p. 78.
24 Ibid., p. 90.
25 These issues are explored in the chapter by Stijn Claessens and Esen Ulgenerk in Harry G. Broadman (ed.), *Unleashing Russia's Business Potential: Lessons from the Regions for Building Market Institutions*, Discussion Paper No. 434 (Washington, DC, World Bank, 2002).
26 'Nefteglobalizatsiya', *Nezavisimaya gazeta*, 23 April 2003, pp. 1, 3.
27 *Moscow Times*, 23 April 2003, pp. 1–2.
28 *Russian Regional Report*, Vol. 7, No. 23, July 2002.
29 'Putin's Choice: a Survey of Russia', *The Economist*, 21 July 2001, p. 6.
30 Dynkin and Sokolov, 'Integrirovannye biznes-gruppy v rossiiskom ekonomike', pp. 87–8.
31 For analysis of regional-business relations, see Rostislav Turovsky (ed.), *Politika v regionakh: gubernatory i gruppy vliyanie* (Moscow, Tsentr Politicheskikh Tekhnologii, 2002); S. Peregudov, N. Lapina and I. Semenenko, *Gruppy interesov i rossiiskoe gosudarstvo* (Moscow, editorial URSS, 1999), Chapter 5.
32 See Peter Kirkow, 'Regional Warlordism in Russia: The Case of Primorskii *Krai*', *Europe-Asia Studies*, Vol. 47, No. 6 (September 1995), pp. 923–47; also Kirkow, *Russia's Provinces*, op cit.
33 *Russian Regional Report*, Vol. 7, No. 23, 22 July 2002.
34 A well-known case was the dominance of the Tyumen Oil Company (TNK) in the petrol retail market in Kursk *oblast*. Attempts by Yukos to break into the market failed, and entry costs became even higher once the Kursk governor Alexander Mikhailov established friendly relations with TNK president Semen Kukes.
35 Andrew Yorke, 'Business and Politics in Krasnoyarsk *Krai*', *Europe-Asia Studies*, Vol. 55, No. 2, 2003, pp. 241–62.
36 *Russian Regional Report*, 14 March 2003.
37 For details of media holdings, for example, see Pappe, *'Oligarkhi'*, Tables 1 and 5.
38 Dynkin and Sokolov, 'Integrirovannye biznes-gruppy v rossiiskom ekonomike', p. 92.
39 Mukhin, *Biznes-elita i gosudarstvennaya vlast'*.
40 Bortsov, *Vladimir Putin*, p. 257.
41 'Ustalost' reform', *Izvestiya*, 24 April 2003, p. 3.
42 Pappe, *'oligarkhi'*, p. 46.
43 Peregudov, 'Krupnaya rossiiskaya korporatsii v sisteme vlasti', p. 18.
44 *Moscow News*, No. 14, 16–22 April 2003, p. 3.

45 Kolmakov, 'The Role of Financial Industrial Conglomerates', p. 16.
46 Sergei Peregudov, 'Krupnaya rossiiskaya korporatsii v sisteme vlasti', *Polis*, No. 2, 2001, pp. 21–2.
47 *Moskovskii komsomolets*, 13 July 2002.
48 Andrei Piontovski, 'Russia's Misguided Democracy', *The Russian Journal*, 8–14 July 2000.
49 The phrase is from Aleksandr Buzgalin, '1999 Russian Presidential Elections: Just Begun or Already Over?', *Prism*, No. 20, Part 1, December 1999.
50 *Monitor*, 9 March 2000.
51 Putin, *Razgovor s Rossiei*, 19 December 2002, p. 84.
52 Vladimir Kucherenko, *Rossiiskaya gazeta*, 22 June 2000.
53 Mikhail Delyagin, 'Driving Russia to Oblivion', *The Russia Journal*, 15–21 July 2000.
54 Yulia Latynina, 'Forestry Industry: Ripe for Carving Up', *Moscow Times*, 17 July 2002.
55 Vladimir Pastukhov, 'Law Under Administrative Pressure in Post-Soviet Russia', in Louis Skyner (ed.), *Property, the Past and Present: Legal Reform and Political Culture in Contemporary Russia* (London, RoutledgeCurzon, forthcoming).
56 Mark Hertsgaard, 'Russia is an Eco-Disaster, and It Just Got Worse', *Washington Post*, 9 July 2000.
57 Richard Wolin, *Heidegger's Children* (Princeton, NJ, Princeton University Press, 2001), p. 195.
58 Medvedev, *Vremya Putina?*, p. 213.

9 Putin and the world

1 http://www.president.kremlin.ru/events/42.html.
2 For a discussion of the 'democratic peace' idea, see Michael Brown, Sean Lynn-Jones and Steven Miller (eds), *Debating the Democratic Peace* (Cambridge, MA, MIT Press, 1996); and Michael W. Doyle, *Ways of War and Peace* (New York, W. W. Norton, 1997). For an early discussion of the idea of core and periphery, see Barry Buzan, 'New Patterns of Global Security in the Twenty-first Century', *International Affairs*, Vol. 67, No. 3, 1991, pp. 431–51.
3 This model is developed by James M. Goldgeier and Michael McFaul, 'Russians as Joiners: Realist and Liberal Conceptions of Post-Communist Europe', in Kathryn Stoner-Weiss and Michael McFaul (eds), *After the Collapse: Comparative Effects of Post-Communist Transitions* (forthcoming), Chapter 7.
4 The strategy of integration was outlined by Yeltsin's last foreign minister and Putin's first, Igor Ivanov, 'Russia, Europe at the Turn of the Century', *International Affairs* (Moscow), Vol. 46, No. 2, 2000, pp. 1–11.
5 See James Goldgeier and Michael McFaul, 'George W. Bush and Russia', *Current History*, October 2002.
6 Shevtsova, *Putin's Russia*, p. 203.
7 Kolosov (ed.), *Mir glazami rossiyan*, p. 11.
8 For the gulf between rhetoric and reality in the 1990s, see Sherman Garnett, 'Russia's Illusory Ambitions', *Foreign Affairs*, Vol. 72, No. 2, 1997, pp. 61–76.
9 I. Ivanov, 'The New Russian Identity: Innovation and Continuity in Russian Foreign Policy', *The Washington Quarterly*, Vol. 24, No. 3, Summer 2001, p. 3.
10 Bobo Lo, *Vladimir Putin and the Evolution of Russian Foreign Policy* (Oxford, Blackwell and Royal Institute for International Affairs, 2003), Chapter 4.
11 http://www.president.kremlin.ru/events/145.html; strana.ru, 26 January 2001.
12 *Newsline*, 12 July 2002.
13 Bobo Lo stresses the interplay between economisation and securitisation in Putin's foreign policy, 'The Securitization of Russian Foreign Policy Under Putin', in Gabriel Gorodetsky (ed.), *Russia Between East and West: Russian Foreign Policy on*

the Threshold of the Twenty-First Century (London, Frank Cass Publishers, 2003), Chapter 2, pp. 12–32.

14 See for example Barry Buzan, *People, States, Fear: An Agenda for International Security Studies in the Post-Cold War Era* (Hertfordshire, HarvesterWheatsheaf, 1991); Barry Buzan, Ole Waever and J. de Wilde, *Security: A New Framework for Analysis* (Boulder, CO and London, Lynne Rienner, 1998).

15 'New Priorities in Russian Foreign Policy', *Internationale Politik: Translatlantic Edition*, Vol. 1, No. 3, 2000, pp. 2, 3.

16 *Budapest Analysis*, No. 13, 2 March 2003.

17 The House of Lords' Select Committee on the European Union produced a detailed report, *EU Russia Relations* (Session 2002–03, 3rd Report, HL Paper 29, The Stationary Office, 2003), which provides a balanced and informative overview of the key issues. Details of the PCA and Common Strategy are on p. 8.

18 *Newsline*, 2 February 2000; *Monitor*, 2 February 2000.

19 This is explored by Vladimir Baranovsky, 'Russia: Insider or Outsider?', *International Affairs (Moscow)*, Vol. 46, No. 3, July 2000, pp. 443–59.

20 At the conclusion of the EU summit on 17 February 2003 Chirac commented that the accession countries had 'missed a good opportunity to remain silent'. Perhaps no one had told him that these countries were now free, independent and sovereign states.

21 Celeste A. Wallander, *Russian National Security Policy in 2000*, Davis Center for Russian Studies, Harvard University, Program on New Approaches to Russian Security, Policy Memo Series No. 102, January 2000, p. 1.

22 http://www.scrf.gov.ru/Documents.Decree/2002/24–1.html; *Nezavisimoe voennoe obozrenie*, 14 January 2000.

23 See Jakub M. Godzimirski, 'Russian National Security Concepts 1997 and 2000: A Comparative Analysis', *European Security*, Vol. 9, No. 4, Winter 2000, pp. 73–91.

24 *Nezavisimaya gazeta*, 11 July 2000, pp. 1 and 6.

25 'The Foreign Policy Concept of the Russian Federation', http://www.mid.ru/mid/eng/econcept.htm.

26 Russian embassy London press release, 17 May 2002.

27 Joseph Nye, 'Hard and Soft Power in a Global Information Age', in Mark Leonard (ed.), *Re-Ordering the World* (London, The Foreign Policy Centre, 2002), pp. 2–10, at p. 5. For a more extended discussion of the various cultural and other ways in which 'soft power' is exercised by the United States, see Joseph S. Nye Jr, *Bound to Lead: The Changing Nature of American Power* (New York, Basic Books, 1990), Chapter 2.

28 Dale R. Herspring, 'Putin and the Armed Forces', in Herspring, *Putin's Russia*, pp. 170–1.

29 Pavel Baev, cited in S. Neil MacFarlane, 'Nato in Russia's Relations with the West', *Security Dialogue*, Vol. 32, No. 3, September 2001, p. 283.

30 Roi Medvedev, *Vladimir Putin – Deistvuyushchii Prezident* (Moscow, Vremya, 2002), p. 345.

31 G. G. Diligenskii, '"Zapad" i rossiiskoe obshchestvo', (Moscow, FOM, 2001), pp. 205–14; http://usa.fom.ru/razdel/mbi/382/936/3090.html

32 Kolosov (ed.), *Mir glazami rossiyan*, p. 243.

33 Tony Blair, 'The Power of World Community', in Mark Leonard (ed.), *Re-Ordering the World* (London, The Foreign Policy Centre, 2002), pp. 119–24, at p. 123.

34 Alex Pravda, 'Putin's Foreign Policy After 11 September', in Gorodetsky (ed.), *Russia Between East and West*, p. 50.

35 Yevgeny Primakov, *Mir posle 11 sentyabrya* (Moscow, Mysl', 2002).

36 Igor' Ivanov, *Vneshnyaya politika rossii v epokhu globalizatsii* (Moscow, Olma-Press, 2002).

37 *Nezavisimoe voennoe obozrenie*, No. 23, 12–18 July 2002, p. 1.

38 *The Guardian*, 19 July 2002, p. 19.
39 For discussion of polling data on this issue, see Margot Light, Stephen White and John Löwenhardt, 'A Wider Europe: The View from Moscow and Kyiv', *International Affairs*, Vol. 76, No. 1, January 2000, pp. 77–88.
40 'Intervyu V. Putina Devidu Frostu', *Kommersant*, No. 39, 7 March 2000, p. 2; Alexander Golts, 'Putin Could Aim for Europe Alliance', *The Russia Journal*, 20–26 March 2000, p. 8.
41 Oleg Varfolomeyev, 'Is Ukraine Ready to Join Nato?', *Russia and Eurasia Review*, Vol. 1, Issue 4, 16 July 2002.
42 Boris Nemtsov outlined the plan in 'Armeiskaya reforma: sabotazh prodolzhaetsya', *Izvestiya*, 22 April 2003, p. 3.
43 This was the conclusion of the *US National Energy Report* of 2001, also known as the 'Cheney Report' after its author, Vice President Dick Cheney.
44 On the long-standing concerns of the Europeans, see Evgenii Grigor'ev, ' "Bunt" evropeitsev: Politiki starogo kontinenta ne khotyat igrat' role' satellitov SShA', *Nezavisimaya gazeta*, 15 February 2002, p. 6.
45 *Financial Times*, 1 April 2001, p. i.
46 http://english.fom.ru.virtual.body/.
47 Pavel Felgenhauer, 'Kremlin Taking Bad Advice', *The Moscow Times*, 24 April 2003, p. 9.
48 Sergei Karaganov, 'Some Lessons from the Iraqi Crisis', *The Moscow Times*, 25 April 2003, p. 8.
49 *Budapest Analyses*, No. 16, 7 May 2003.
50 Interview with Sergei Parkhomenko, 'Sostavitel's kontrakta', *Itogi*, 8 February 2000, p. 24.
51 Richard Sakwa, 'Putin's Foreign Policy: Transforming "the East" ', in Gorodetsky (ed.), *Russia Between East and West*, pp. 174–94.
52 *Monitor*, 11 April 2000.
53 One of the most detailed and balanced Russian analyses was published to commemorate the fiftieth anniversary of the establishment of the People's Republic of China, M. L. Titarenko (ed.), *Kitai na puti modernizatsii i reform: 1949–1999* (Moscow, Vostochnaya Literatura, 1999).
54 See Sherman Garnett, *Rapprochement or Rivalry: Russia–China Relations in a Changing Asia* (Washington, DC, Carnegie Endowment for International Peace, 2000).
55 See, for example, Andrei Komarov, 'Rossiya i kitai kritikuyut gumanitarnoe vmeshatel'stvo', *Nezavisimaya gazeta*, 16 March 2000, p. 6. The interview reported here was with Oleg Mironov, the Russian Human Rights Commissioner, on a visit to China where he shared Russian experience with the post of Commissioner. He noted that China had signed up to no fewer than 17 international conventions and protocols on human rights.
56 http://www.president.kremlin.ru/events/145.html; strana.ru, 26 January 2001.
57 *Newsline*, 8 February 2000.
58 'Il'ya Kedrov, Dmitrii Kosyrev, 'Pervyi vizit Putina – v Kitai?', *Nezavisimaya gazeta*, 2 March 2000, p. 1.
59 *Monitor*, 14 March 2000.
60 *The Times of India*, 13 March 2000, in *Monitor*, 14 March 2000.
61 *Segodnya*, 2 March 2000.
62 Dmitri Trenin, *The End of Eurasia: Russia on the Border Between Geopolitics and Globalization* (Moscow, Carnegie Moscow Center, 2001).
63 The leading exponent of such an approach was Zbigniew Brzezinski, *The Grand Chessboard: American Primacy and its Geostrategic Imperatives* (New York, Basic Books, 1997). See also his *The Geostrategic Triad* (Washington, DC, Center for Strategic and International Studies, 2001).
64 *Monitor*, 21 January 2002.

65 *Rossiiskaya gazeta*, 20 April 2002.
66 MacFarlane, 'Nato in Russia's Relations with the West', p. 284.
67 Kolosov (ed.), *Mir glazami rossiyan*, pp. 266–7.
68 Vladimir Socor, 'GUUAM Summit: A New Lease on Life', *Russia and Eurasia Review*, Vol. 1, Issue 5, 30 July 2002.
69 For an early exposition of elements of this strategy, see his Zbigniew Brzezinski 'The Premature Partnership', *Foreign Affairs*, Vol. 73, No. 2, 1994, pp. 67–82.
70 Armenia, Kazakhstan, Kyrgyzstan, Tajikistan and Uzbekistan in 1992, and Azerbaijan, Belarus and Georgia in 1993–94.
71 Kolosov (ed.), *Mir glazami rossiyan*, p. 159.
72 David Marples, 'The Isolation of Europe's Last Dictator', *Russia and Eurasia Review*, 17 December 2002.
73 *Newsline*, 14 June 2002.
74 Putin, *Razgovor s Rossiei*, 19 December 2002, p. 108.

10 Conclusion

1 BBC Monitoring, 16 May 2003; in *JRL* 7186/1.
2 Dmitri Glinksi, 'Waiting for a Democratic Left', PONARS Policy Memo No. 257, October 2002, p. 51.
3 Robert Dahl, *Polyarchy: Participation and Opposition* (New Haven, CT, Yale University Press, 1971).
4 Gleb Pavlovsky, 'Russia Can Be Easily Provoked into Revolution', *Kommersant-Vlast'*, No. 26, 2000.
5 *Nezavisimaya gazeta*, 15 November 2000, p. 5.
6 Interview with Sergei Kovalev by Thomas Lubeck, in VI ICCEES World Congress News, 1 August 2000, p. 4.
7 For an account of Putin as an unmitigated centraliser, see Julie A. Corwin, 'The New Centralizer', *Newsline*, 21 June 2000. She notes his typical tactics: 'unleashing federal bureaucrats, via a reorganised or somehow empowered federal organ, and letting loose law enforcement officials and making a few high level arrests – or at the very least, threatening to'.
8 *Russian Regional Report*, 7 May 2003.
9 Juan J. Linz and Alfred Stepan, 'Toward Consolidated Democracies', *Journal of Democracy*, Vol. 7, April 1996, p. 17.
10 As he put it, 'No bourgeois, no democracy'. Barrington Moore, Jr, *Social Origins of Dictatorship and Democracy: Lord and Peasant in the Making of the Modern World* (Harmondsworth, Peregrine, 1967), p. 418.
11 Putin, *Razgovor s Rossiei*, p. 56.
12 Vladimir Pribylovsky, head of the Panorama Information-Research Centre, May 2003; in *JRL* 7193/13.
13 Survey material drawn from Rose and Munro, *Elections Without Order*; quotation from http://www.tol.cz/look, accessed 31 August 2002.
14 *Max Weber on Charisma and Institution Building*, Selected Papers, edited and with an Introduction by S. N. Eisenstadt (Chicago and London, University of Chicago Press, 1968), p. 20.
15 Eduard Bernstein, *Evolutionary Socialism: The Classic Statement of Democratic Socialism* (New York, Schocken Books, 1961).

Select bibliography

Autobiography and speeches

Putin, Vladimir, *First Person: An Astonishingly Frank Self-Portrait by Russia's President Vladimir Putin*, with Nataliya Gevorkyan, Natalya Timakova and Andrei Kolesnikov, translated by Catherine A. Fitzpatrick (London, Hutchinson, 2000).

Putin, Vladimir, *Ot pervogo litsa: Razgovory s Vladimirom Putinym*, with Nataliya Gevorkyan, Natal'ya Timakova and Andrei Kolesnikov (Moscow, Vagrius, 2000).

Putin, V. V., *Razgovor s Rossiei: Stenogramma 'Pryamoi linii s Prezidentom Rossiiskoi Federatsii V. V. Putinym'*, 19 December 2002 (Moscow, Olma-Politizdat, 2003).

Biography

Blotskii, Oleg, *Vladimir Putin: istoriya zhizni*, Book 1 (Moscow, Mezhdunarodnye otnosheniya, 2002).

Blotskii, Oleg, *Vladimir Putin: doroga k vlasti*, Book 2 (Moscow, Mezhdunarodnye otnosheniya, 2002).

Bortsov, Yu. S., *Vladimir Putin* (Moscow and Rostov, Feniks, 2001).

Drozdov, Yurii and Vasilii Fartyshev, *Yurii Andropov i Vladimir Putin: na puti k vozrozhdeniyu* (Moscow, Olma-Press, 2001).

Medvedev, Roi, *Zagadka Putina* (Moscow, Prava cheloveka, 2000).

Medvedev, Roi, *Vremya Putina? Rossiya na rubezhe vekov* (Moscow, Prava Cheloveka, 2001).

Medvedev, Roi, *Vladimir Putin – Deistvuyushchii Prezident* (Moscow, Vremya, 2002).

Mukhin, A. A., *Kto est' mister Putin i kto s nim prishel? Dos'e na Prezidenta Rossii i ego spetssluzhby* (Moscow, Centre for Political Information, 2002).

Pitch, Iren, *Pikantnaya druzhba: moya podruga Lyudmila Putina, ee sem'ya i drugie tovarishchi* (Moscow, Zakharov, 2002); from the German, Irene Pietsch, *Heikle Freundschaften* (Vienna, Molden Verlag, 2001).

Rar, Aleksandr, *Vladimir Putin: 'Nemets' v Kremle*, translated from the German by I. Rozanov (Moscow, Olma-Press, 2001); Alexander Rahr, *Wladimir Putin: Der 'Deutsche' im Kreml*, second edition (Munich, Universitas Publishing House, 2000).

Seiffert, Wolfgang, *Wladimir W. Putin: Wiedergeburt einer Weltmacht?* (Munich, Langen Müller, 2000).

Shevtsova, Lilia, *Putin's Russia* (Washington, DC, Carnegie Endowment for International Peace, 2003).

Talanov, Viktor, *Psikhologicheskii portret Vladimira Putina* (St Petersburg, B & K, 2000).

General analysis

Avramchenko, R. F., *Put' Putina: do prezidenta ili reformatora? Novaya kontseptsiya razvitiya Rossii* (Moscow, self-published, 2000).

Avramchenko, R. F., *Pokhoronit li Putin Rossiyu? Ideii i kontsepsii preobrazovaniya Rossii* (Moscow, Editorial URSS, 2001).

Brown, Archie, 'From Democratization to "Guided Democracy"', *Journal of Democracy*, Vol. 12, No. 4, October 2001, pp. 35–41.

Brown, Archie and Lilia Shevtsova (eds), *Gorbachev, Yeltsin, and Putin: Political Leadership in Russia's Transition* (Washington, DC, Carnegie Endowment for International Peace, 2001).

Colton, Timothy J. and Michael McFaul, *Are Russians Undemocratic?* (Carnegie Endowment for International Peace, Russian Domestics Politics Project, Russian and Eurasian Program, Working Paper No. 20, June 2001); republished in *Post-Soviet Affairs*, Vol. 18, No. 2, 2002, pp. 91–121.

Fish, M. Steven, 'Putin's Path', *Journal of Democracy*, Vol. 12, No. 4, October 2001, pp. 71–8.

Gorodetsky, Gabriel (ed.), *Russia Between East and West: Russian Foreign Policy on the Threshold of the Twenty-First Century* (London, Frank Cass Publishers, 2003).

Graham, Thomas, *Russia's Decline and Uncertain Recovery* (Washington, DC, Carnegie Endowment for International Peace, 2002).

Hedlund, Stefan, 'Will the Russian Economy Revive Under Putin?', *Problems of Post-Communism*, Vol. 48, No. 2, March/April 2001, pp. 54–62.

Herspring, Dale R. and Jacob Kipp, 'Understanding the Elusive Mr. Putin', *Problems of Post-Communism*, Vol. 48, No. 5, September/October 2001, pp. 3–17.

Herspring, Dale R. (ed.), *Putin's Russia: Past Imperfect, Future Uncertain* (Oxford, Rowman & Littlefield, 2003).

Hoffman, David E., *The Oligarchs: Wealth and Power in the New Russia* (New York, Public Affairs, 2002).

Hyde, Matthew, 'Putin's Federal Reforms and their Implications for Presidential Power in Russia', *Europe-Asia Studies*, Vol. 53, No. 5, 2001, pp. 719–43.

Karaganov, S. A. *et al.*, *Strategiya dlya Rossii: povestka dnya dlya prezidenta – 2000* (Moscow, Vagrius, 2000).

Kaspe, S. I., 'Tsentr i vertikal': politicheskaya priroda putinskogo prezidentstva', *Politiya*, No. 4 (22), Winter 2001–2, pp. 5–24.

Klebnikov, Paul, *Godfather of the Kremlin: Boris Berezovsky and the Looting of Russia* (New York, Harcourt Brace, 2000); translated into Russian as Pavel Khlebnikov, *Krestnyi otets Kremlya Boris Berezovskii ili Istoriya razgrableniya Rossii* (Moscow, Detektiv-Press, 2001).

Knight, Amy, 'The Enduring Legacy of the KGB in Russian Politics', *Problems of Post-Communism*, Vol. 47, No. 4, July/August 2000, pp. 3–15.

Kolosov, V. A. (ed.), *Mir glazami rossiyan: mify i vneshnyaya politika* (Moscow, Institut fonda 'Obshchestvennoe mnenie', 2003).

Kovalev, Sergei, 'Putin's War', *New York Review of Books*, Vol. 47, No. 2, 10 February 2000, pp. 6–8.

Kuchins, Andrew, *Russia After the Fall* (Washington, DC, Carnegie Endowment for International Peace, 2002).

Lo, Bobo, *Vladimir Putin and the Evolution of Russian Foreign Policy* (Oxford, Blackwell Publishing, and the Royal Institute of International Affairs, 2003).

Lupan, V., *Russkii vyzov*, translated and with an introduction by A. Zinoviev (Moscow, Terra, 2001); Victor Loupan, *Le défi Russe* (Paris, Editions des Syrtes, 2001).

Lukin, Alexander, 'Putin's Regime: Restoration or Revolution?', *Problems of Post-Communism*, Vol. 48, No. 4, July/August 2000, pp. 38–48.

McFaul, Michael, 'Putin in Power', *Current History*, No. 99, October 2000, pp. 307–14.

Maly, Matvei, *Kak sdelat' Rossiyu normal'noi stranoi?* (St Petersburg, Dmitrii Bulanin, 2003).

Mendelson, Sarah E., 'The Putin Path: Civil Liberties and Human Rights in Retreat', *Problems of Post-Communism*, Vol. 47, No. 5, September/October 2000, pp. 3–12.

Mlechin, Leonid, *Kreml' prezidenty Rossii: strategiya vlasti ot B. N. El'tsina do V. V. Putina* (Moscow, Tsentrpoligraf, 2002).

Mlechin, Leonid, *KGB predsedateli organov gosbezopasnosti: rassekrechennye sud'by* (Moscow, Tsentrpoligraf, 2002).

Moore, Robert, *A Time to Die: The Kursk Disaster* (New York, Doubleday, 2002).

Mukhin, A. A., *Novye pravila igry dlya bol'shogo biznesa, prodiktovannye logikoi pravleniya V. V. Putina* (Moscow, Tsentr politicheskoi informatsii, 2002).

Mukhin, A. A., *Rossiiskaya organizovannaya prestupnost' i vlast': Istoriya vzaimootnoshenii* (Moscow, Tsentr politicheskoi informatsii, 2003).

Pechenov, Vadim, *Vladimir Putin – poslednii shans Rossii?* (Moscow, Infra-M, 2001).

Reddaway, Peter, 'Will Putin Be Able to Consolidate Power?', *Post-Soviet Affairs*, Vol. 17, No. 1, 2001, pp. 23–44.

Reddaway, Peter, 'Is Putin's Power More Formal Than Real?, *Post-Soviet Affairs*, Vol. 18, No. 1, 2002, pp. 31–40.

Remington, Thomas F., 'Putin and the Duma', *Post-Soviet Affairs*, Vol. 17, No. 4, 2001, pp. 285–308.

Rose, Richard and Neil Munro, *Elections Without Order: Russia's Challenge to Vladimir Putin* (Cambridge, Cambridge University Press, 2002).

Rose, Richard, Neil Munro and Stephen White, 'How Strong is Vladimir Putin's Support?', *Post-Soviet Affairs*, Vol. 16, No. 4, 2000, pp. 287–312.

Rutland, Peter, 'Putin's Path to Power', *Post-Soviet Affairs*, Vol. 16, No. 4, 2000, pp. 313–54.

Sakwa, Richard, *Russian Politics and Society*, third edition (London and New York, Routledge, 2002).

Sharlet, Robert, 'Putin and the Politics of Law in Russia', *Post-Soviet Affairs*, Vol. 17, No. 3, 2001, pp. 195–234.

Shlyapentokh, V., 'Putin's First Year in Office: The New Regime's Uniqueness in Russian History', *Communist and Post-Communist Studies*, Vol. 34, No. 4, December 2001, pp. 371–99.

Simonsen, Sven Gunnar, 'Putin's Leadership Style: Ethnocentric Patriotism', *Security Dialogue*, Vol. 31, No. 3, 2000, pp. 377–80.

Stepankov, Viktor, *Bitva za 'Nord-Ost'* (Moscow, Yauza/Eksmo, 2003).

Tikhomirov, Vladimir (ed.), *Russia After Yeltsin* (Aldershot, Ashgate, 2001).

Tompson, William, 'Putin's Challenge: The Politics of Structural Reform in Russia', *Europe-Asia Studies*, Vol. 54, No. 6, September 2002, pp. 933–58.

Troshev, Gennadii, *Moya voina: Chechenskii dnevnik okopnogo generala* (Moscow, Vagrius, 2001).

Index

Page references for tables are in *italics*; those for notes are followed by n

Abkhazia 173, 208, 231
Abramov, Alexander 26
Abramovich, Roman 18, 64, 99, 100, 187, *193*, 196, 272n
Adamov, Yevgeny 204
Administrative Code 122
administrative reforms 52, 53, 95
Administrative Violations Code 109
Adygeia 30
Aeroflot 97
Afghanistan 33, 216, 217, 219
Agrarian Party 121, 200
agriculture 205
Aksyonenko, Nikolai 16, 18
Albania 220
Albats, Yevgeniya 65
Alekperov, Vagit 99, *193*
Aleksii II, Patriarch 169, 170
Alexander I viii
Alexander II 42
Alexander III 42
Alexandrov, Alexander 165
Alexseev, Mikhail 131
Alfa-group *193*, 195, 200
Algeria 180
All Russia 21, 196, 199; *see also* Fatherland – All Russia
Altai 30
alternative civilian service (ACS) 110
aluminium industry 64, 99, 202
Alyoshin, Boris 192
Amur 139
Andropov, Vladimir 7, 13, 37, 43, 265n; authoritarian modernisation 66, 67, 76, 93
anthem 164, 165, 284n
Anti-Ballistic Missile (ABM) treaty 217, 228, 233

Arkhangel 135
armed services *see* military
Armenia 229, 232
Aslakhanov, Aslambek 177
Astrakhan *oblast* 50
asymmetrical federalism 131, 132–4, 135, 137, 143, 159, 240
Ataturk, Kemal 76, 162
Atlanticism 225
Audit Chamber 102, 111
Aushev, Ruslan 153, 157–8
authoritarian modernisation 66, 67, 76, 93
authoritarianism 37, 43, 74, 80, 93, 135, 246
Aven, Petr *193*
Avramchenko, R. F. 15
Avtovaz 97, 99
Azerbaijan 173, 229, 230–1, 232

Babitsky, Andrei 103
Balcerowicz, Leszek 38
banks 86, 192
Baraev, Movsar 178
Bartkus, Viva Ona 170
Basaev, Shamil 19, 171, 177
Bashkortostan 131, 133, 139, 140, 156
Bashneft 199
Bear *see* Unity
Belarus 161, 212, 214, 220–1, 230; authoritarian populism 68, 74; union with Russia 55, 232, 241
Bellona 110, 205
Bem, Horst 9
Berdyaev, Nikolai 36
Berezovsky, Boris 50, *193*, 194, 272n; money-laundering allegations 61; party system 115; political influence 18, 21,

64, 101, 196, 198; Putin's struggle
   against 75, 97–9, 100, 197; regional
   reforms 157; *semibankirshchina* 190–1;
   state reconstitution 85
Berlusconi, Silvio 219–20
Bernstein, Eduard 249
Bespalov, Alexander 121
Bevan, Aneurin 60
bin Laden, Osama 173
Black Sea–Caspian Initiative 231
Blair, Tony 29, 82, 209, 211, 217, 220
Blotskii, Oleg 4, 5
Bogdanov, Vladimir *193*
Bolshoi Ural 142–3
Bordyuzha, Nikolai 16
Borodin, Pavel 12, 24, 64, 103
Bortsov, Yu. S. 15
Bosnia 220
BP 194
Brecht, Bertold 128
Brezhnev, Leonid 43, 57, 265n
Britain 243
Brown, Archie 74
Browne, Lord 194
Brudny, Yitzhak M. 32
Bryansk 30
Budanov, Yury 176
Buddhism 169
budget 133–4, 158, 202
Bulgaria 212, 220, 224
bureaucracy 128, 238; and economy 198,
   201, 206; reforms 52, 53, 95
Burutin, Major-General Alexander 192
Bush, George Jr 209, 211, 217, 218, 223

Calley, Lieutenant William 176
Cam Ranh Bay 218
capitalism 77, 206; oligarchical 190–2,
   193, 194–201, 242–3
Central Electoral Commission (CEC) *22*,
   26, 115, 118
centralisation 240
Centre for Strategic Development 28, 43,
   47–8, 225
centrism 58, 78–80, 82, 243, 274n
charisma 73–4, 248–9
Chechnya 53, 131, 133, 170–1, 247; 2000
   presidential election 30; environment
   204; human rights 110, 111; media 75,
   103, 104; and terrorism 167; and US
   231; war 18–19, 25, 31, 66, 171–81,
   208, 213, 286n; Western criticism 217
chekisty 62, 66, 67, 242
Cheremushkin, Vladimir 7

Cherkesov, Victor 14, 66, 143, 144
Chernenko, Konstantin 265n
Chernomyrdin, Victor 11, 16, 199
Chile 86
China 144, 208, 229; modernisation 42, 67;
   relations with 134, 210, 212, 215, 225–8
Chinese National Petroleum Company
   (CNPC) 187
Chirac, Jacques 213
Chita 142
Chizhova, Tamara 2
Christian Democratic Union 116
Chubais, Anatoly 12, 31, 188, 189, *193*,
   199; privatisations 11, 102
Chuev, Alexander 116
Chutotka autonomous *okrug* 196
Chuvashia 156
citizenship 230, 239–40
Civil Forum 127–8
civil society 110–11, 113, 125–9; regions
   131, 132
Clinton, Bill 29, 82, 209, 211
co-operative pragmatism 233
coalition-building 63
coercion 42
Collective Security Treaty (CST) 230,
   231–2
Collective Security Treaty Organisation
   (CSTO) 232
Collins, Michael 181
Committee for State Security *see* KGB
Commonwealth of Independent States
   (CIS) 55, 211, 214, 229–32
communal-housing complex (KZhK) 150
communism 37–8, 44–5
Communist Party 8, 114
Communist Party of the Russian
   Federation 21, 67; 1999 Duma election
   22; in Duma 120, 121, 122; economy
   185; funding 199, 200; and Putin 123,
   244; regional legislatures 155; Russia
   164; and Spiritual Heritage 166;
   Ukraine 167; and Zyuganov 26, 30, 46
Communist Youth League 4, 245
compacted statism 89–90, 94, 136
competitive pragmatism 208–9, 211, 233
Congress of Russian Communities
   (KRO) 184, 185
consensus-making 63
consent 42
constitution 21, 38, 54–5, 76, 94, 236,
   238; CFDP report 50–1; judicial system
   108; and regions 158; religion 169;
   secession 171

Constitutional Court 139–40, 144, 148, 149, 153, 158, 239
constitutional federalism 137
constitutionalism 88
consumerism 42
controlled democracy 201
cooperative pragmatism 209
corporatism 196–8, 242
corruption 11, 24, 27, 50, 55, 108; *see also* oligarchs
coterie charisma 73
Council of Europe 225
Council for Foreign and Defence Policy (CFDP) 48–51
CPRF *see* Communist Party of the Russian Federation
crime 109
Crimea 167, 180–1
Criminal Procedure Code (UPK) 108–9, 120, 122
Croatia 220
Cuba 218
Cyprus 212
Czech Republic 208, 212, 219
Czechoslovakia 7, 34, 42

Dagestan 30, 132, 135, 172, 173, 175
Dahl, Robert 236
Dahrendorf, Ralf 40, 41
Danilov-Danilyan, Viktor 204
Darkin, Sergei 195
De Gaulle, Charles 27, 40, 42, 180
death penalty 109
debt 187–8
Decembrist Russia 81
decommunisation 94–5
defederalisation 130
delegative democracy 42
democracy 15, 49, 241, 247; and civil society 125–9; and efficacy 246; leadership 73; and oligarchical capitalism 198–201; and order 79; regions 135, 137
Democratic Party of Russia 122
Democratic Russia 78
Deng Xiaoping 42, 226
Deripaska, Oleg 99, *193*, 197
Diamond, Larry 42
dictatorship of law 90, 91, 138, 140, 237, 275n
Dorenko, Sergei 104
Dorogin, Vice-Admiral Valerii 154
Dostoevsky, Fedor 169, 244
Drachevsky, Leonid 142

Dubrovka theatre siege 72, 105, 178
Dugin, Alexander 128
Dukhovnoe nasledie 27, 166
Duma 51, 67, 120–2, 124; Berezovsky 98; economy 189; *Energiya* faction 200; federal reforms 146–7, 149; human rights 110–11; regional governors 153
Duma elections 53; 1993 114; 1999 20–2, *22*, 23, 24, 27, 30, 78–9, 80, 113, 120, 198; legislation 118–19; turnout 69
Durkheim, Emile 41
Dyachenko, Tatyana 18, 64
Dynkin, A. 191, 196–7
Dzhabrailov, Umar 27, *29*

East Germany 1, 9–10
Eatwell, Roger 73–4
economy 44, 52, 53, 182–3, 206, 235; and environment 204–5; FICs 190–2, *193*, 194–6; and foreign policy 210, 211; programmes and reality 201–4; under Putin 186–90, *187*; Yeltsin's legacy 183–6
Edinaya Rossiya see United Russia
Edinstvo see Unity
Effective Policy Foundation 58
Ekho Moskvy 105
elections: legislation 118–19, 155; *see also* Duma elections; presidential elections
electoral democracy 40, 42
Emergency Situations Ministry 71
Energiya faction 200
environment 204–5
equidistance 182, 197, 235–6
Erhard, Ludwig 77
Estonia 161, 212, 220
ethnicity 167, 168
Eurasian Economic Community 230, 231
Eurasianism 167–8, 210, 213, 225, 228–9, 244, 245
European Convention on Human Rights 41
European Security and Defence Policy (ESDP) 219
European Union (EU) 210, 211–12, 213, 219, 224, 225, 229
Europeanisation 210, 211
extraordinary politics 55
extremism of the centre 243

family 18, 55, 64–5, 84, 97; collapse 196; as Putin's power base 62, 68, 76–7, 87, 102, 125

Fatherland 21, 27–8, 75, 196, 199; *see also* United Russia
Fatherland – All Russia 21, *22*, 121, 199; *see also* All Russia
Fatton, Robert 84
Federal Assembly 51; *see also* Duma; Federation Council
federal districts (FDs) 54, 141–6, 281n
Federal Security Service *see* FSB
federalism 54, 91–2, 130, 159–60; segmented regionalism 132; and state reconstitution 89, 136–40, 155–9, 238–9; *see also* regions
Federation Council (FC) 51, 120, 121, 155; local self-government 149; reforming 146–8; and regions 235, 239; tax code 151
Federation of Independent Trade Unions of Russia 197
Fedorov, Anton 141
Fedorov, Boris 167
Fedorov, Nikolai 94, 148, 156, 158
Financial Action Task Force (FATF) 188
financial-industrial conglomerates (FICs) 103, 191–2, *193*, 194–5, 206, 242–3; corporatism 196–201; regional aspects 195–6; timber processing 203
First Person (Putin) 137–8, 158
Fischer, Stanley 185
Fish, M. Steven 163–4
flag 164, 165
floating party system 114
Ford Motor Company 192
foreign direct investment (FDI) 44, 192, 194
foreign policy 52, 55, 76, 207, 215, 235, 236, 247; Belarus 232; beyond East and West 225–8; CIS 229–32; economisation 58; Nato 218–21; normalisation 207–15; post-cold war geopolitics 228–9; regions 134–5; responses to 9/11 216–18; self-definition and doctrine 213–15; Western divisions 221–4
Foreign Policy Concept 214
fortuna 234
Forward, Russia! 167
Foundation for Effective Politics 26
France 40, 42, 213, 222, 224, 238
Frank, Semyon 81, 244
freedom of speech 103–7, 205, 237
Fridman, Mikhail 100, *193*, 194
FSB 1, 13–14, 17, 66; human rights 111;

and Nikitin 205; and oligarchs 102; and regions 132, 143, 146; *see also* KGB
Furman, Dmitry 99, 174

G8 50, 55, 215, 228
Gaidar, Yegor 21, *22*, 38, 78
gas 211, 229
GAU 231
Gavrin, Alexander 65, 204
Gazprom 86, 97, 99, 188, 191, 199, 200–1
Gazprom Media 105
GDP 44, 53, 182, 183, 184, *187*, 190, 198
Georgia 173, 208, 217, 230–1, 232
German Democratic Republic (GDR) 1, 9–10
Germany 14, 40, 44, 224, 244
Gevorkyan, Nataliya 29
Giddens, Anthony 79, 80
GKOs 84, 183
GKU 12–13
Glazyev, Sergei 123, 185
Glinka, Mikhail 164
Glinski, Dmitri 39, 235
Gorbachev, Mikhail 5, 6, 56–7, 265n; bureaucracy 238; dictatorship of law 91, 275n; East Germany 10; foreign policy 233; law degree 7; *perestroika* 9, 34, 38; and Putin 68
Gorky Automotive Works (GAZ) 197
Gorno-Altai 139
gosudarstvenniki 167
governance 247
Govorukhin, Stanislav 27, *29*
Graham, Thomas 94, 96
Great Urals 142–3
Great Volga 142
Gref, German 28, 43, 47–8, 122, 201–2, 225
Grotian moment 170–1
Group of Eight 50, 55, 215, 228
Gryzlov, Boris 121
Guardian, The 36
guberniyas 143
guided democracy 42, 80
Gurevich, Vera 2–3
Gusinsky, Vladimir 99, 100, *193*, 197; Media-Most 18, 97, 101–2, 104; political involvement 198, 199
Gutseriev, Khamzad 153
Gutseriev, Mikhail 187
GUUAM 230–1

Hahn, Gordon 39, 61, 87

Hale, Henry E. 31, 171
hard power 214–15
Hashimoto, Ryutaro 228
Hedlund, Stefan 186
Hellman, Joel S. 182
Hendley, Kathryn 109
Holmes, Stephen 83–4, 93
human rights 89, 110–11, 205, 225, 237, 246; Belarus 232; Chechnya 175–6, 180
Human Rights Ombudsman 111
Hungary 208, 212, 219, 271n
Huntington, Samuel 57, 61, 80
Husak, Gustav 42

Illarionov, Andrei 47, 188, 190
illiberal democracy 42
Ilyumzhinov, Kirsan 135
IMF 183, 184, 185, 208
India 185, 212, 215, 225, 226
industrial-business groups (IBGs) *see* financial-industrial conglomerates
inflation 186, *187*
Information Security Doctrine 106, 107, 111
Ingushetia 139, 153
institutional charisma 74
integrated business-groups (IBGs) *see* financial-industrial conglomerates
intelligentsia 242
Interior Ministry (MVD) 102, 131–2, 142, 143, 146, 176
Interros 99, *193*, 195, 199, 200
investment 186, *187*, 188, 189, 192, 195; *see also* foreign direct investment
Iraq 134–5, 207, 212, 213, 216, 218, 219, 221–4
Islam 134–5, 169, 226
Ismay, Lord 218
Italy 92, 114
Itogi 105
Ivanov, Igor 72, 210, 211, 214, 218
Ivanov, Sergei 14, 66, 67, 106, 174
Ivanov, Victor 62
Ivashov, Leonid 66
Izvestiya 99

Jackson, Robert 170
Jackson–Vanik amendment 217, 223, 232
Japan 48, 114, 192, 201, 225, 228, 243
Jordan, Boris 105
Jowitt, Kenneth 79–80
Judaism 169

Judd, Lord Frank 179, 180
judicial system 52, 107, 108–9, 122
judo 4, 14, 32, 265n

Kabardino-Balkaria 132
Kadyrov, Akhmad 177, 178
Kalamanov, Vladimir 111
Kalinin 166
Kaliningrad 133, 134, 154, 212
Kalmykia 135
Kalugin, Oleg 103
Kalyuzhny, Viktor 18, 65
Kamchatka 154
Karachaevo-Cherkessia 131
Karaganov, Sergei 48–51, 224
Karasin, Grigory 227
Karelia 134
Karimov, Islam 20, 231
Kartashkin, Vladimir 110
Kaspe, S. I. 41, 79
Kasyanov, Mikhail 48, 63, 65, 71, 154; economy 186, 190, 202; Slavneft 187
Kazakhstan 227, 230, 232
Kemerovo 30
Kerensky, Alexander 7, 42
Keynes, John Maynard 185
KGB 1, 6–7, 33, 43, 62, 65; Putin's career 8–10; *see also* FSB
Khakamada, Irina 22
Khakassia 131
Khasavyurt agreement 18, 171, 174, 177
Khasbulatov, Ruslan 178
Khattab 19, 171
Khinstein, Alexander 103–4
Khlebnikov, Pavel 50
Khloponin, Alexander 195
Khodorkovsky, Mikhail 100, *193*, 194, 199–200
Khrushchev, Nikita 6, 166, 265n
Kirienko, Sergei 16, 22, 142, 145, 183, 196
Kirkow, Peter 135
Kiselev, Yevgeny 103, 104–5
Klebanov, Ilya 72
Klyamkin, Igor 20–1, 83
Klyuchevsky, Vasily 130, 160
Kokh, Alfred 102
Kolakowski, Lesjek 242
Kolmakov, Sergei 191
Kolosov, V. A. 162, 163
Komi Republic 158, 195–6
Kommersant-Daily 74, 103
kommunal'no-zhilishchnoe kompleks (KZhK) 150

Komsomol 4, 245
Korzhakov, Alexander 21
Kosovo 134, 171, 213, 214, 216, 219
Kotenkov, Alexander 149
Kovalev, Sergei 20, 25, 237
Kozak, Dmitry 62, 64, 108, 125, 150
Kozak commission 156
Kozma, Petr 64
Kozyrev, Andrei 38, 210
Krasheninnikov, Pavel 144
Krasnodar *krai* 31
Krasnoyarsk *krai* 27, 195
Krasnoznammenyi Institute 8
Krupskaya, Nadezhda 2, 3
Kuchma, Leonid 220
Kudrin, Alexei 11, 12, 13, 122, 152
Kuibyshev 166
Kulakov, Vladimir 150
Kungaeva, Elza 176
Kursk (submarine) 72
Kursk *oblast* 154, 288n
Kvashnin, General 66
Kwasnieski, Alexander 229
Kyrgyzstan 171, 227, 232

Labour Code 122, 205
Land Code 122
Latvia 161, 212, 220
Latynina, Yulia 24–5, 159, 203
Latyshev, Petr 142–3
law 91, 107, 164, 203, 247; *see also*
    dictatorship of law
leadership 73–7, 82, 248–9
Lebanon war 221
Lebed, Alexander 16, 27, 31, 195
Lebedev, Vyacheslav 138
legislatures: regional 154–5; *see also*
    parliament
Lenin, Vladimir Ilyich viii, 7, 165, 265n,
    284n
Leningrad *see* St Petersburg
Leningrad State University (LGU) 6–8,
    10
Lesin, Mikhail 105–6
liberal authoritarianism 80
liberal conservatism 80–2, 164
liberal democracy 128
Liberal Democratic Party of Russia
    (LDPR) *22*, 26, 121, 200
liberal patriotism 244–5
Liberal Russia 75, 98, 99, 116
liberal statism 167
liberalism 37, 58–9, 78, 242
Lieven, Anatol 171

Linz, Juan J. 241
Lithuania 161, 212, 220
lobbying 200
local self-government 149–50
Locke, John 126
Logovaz 97
Lukashenko, Alexander 68, 74, 220–1,
    232
Lukin, Alexander 86
Lukin, Vladimir 167
Lukoil 97, 99, 187, 192, *193*, 195–6, 199,
    200, 222
Luzhkov, Yury 18, 22, 26, 27–8, 32, 77,
    153, 281–2n; Fatherland 21, 196;
    Federation Council 147; FICs 199;
    power base 62; tax code 152; Ukraine
    167

Macedonia 220
McFaul, Michael 40, 89
Machiavelli, Niccolò 234
Main Control Administration (GKU)
    12–13
Mainwaring, Scott 114
Makhashev, Kazbek 177
Malashenko, Igor 104
Maleva, Tatyana 68
Malta 212
Maly, Matvei 41
Mamut, Alexander 64, *193*
managed democracy 42, 122, 123, 124,
    127, 246
manipulated democracy 80
Margelov, Mikhail 223
market 183, 184, 190, 203–4, 206
Markov, Sergei 80, 88, 127
Maskhadov, Aslan 18, 19, 171, 174, 177,
    178, 181
Maslyukov, Yury 61
mass charisma 73, 74
Matvienko, Valentina 62, 74, 144
Mau, Vladimir 47
media 44, 57, 75, 125; freedom 89,
    103–7, 237; oligarchs 97, 99, 101–2
Media-Most 97, 99, 101, 102, 199
Medushevsky, Andrei 86
Medved see Unity
Medvedev, Dmitry 26, 62
Medvedev, Roi 25–6, 61, 123
middle class 68, 242, 272n
Mikhailov, Alexander 154
Mikhalkov, Nikita 165
Mikhalkov, Sergei 165
Miliband, Ralph 84

military 66–7, 74, 215, 221; alternative civilian service 110; Chechnya 174; and China 227; and regions 131, 142
Military Doctrine 214
Millennium Manifesto (Putin) 28, 43–7, 51, 56, 78, 89, 162, 163, 171, 251–62
Miller, Alexei 188, 199
Milosevič, Slobodan 161, 208
Ministry of Defence 13
Ministry of Natural Resources 204
Mironov, Oleg 111
Mironov, Sergei 122, 148
Mitrokhin, Sergei 32
Mitterand, François 83
Mityukov, Mikhail 140
modernisation viii–ix, 66, 122, 243
modernity viii
Modrow, Hans 9–10
Moldova 161, 173, 208, 230–1
Moltenskoi, Colonel General Vladimir 177
Mommsen, Margarita 37
Montenegro 220
Moore, Barrington 242
Mordashev, Alexei *193*
Moscow 46, 62, 132–3, 135, 281–2n
Moscow consensus 184–5, 186, 206
Moscow Helsinki Group 110
Moscow Treaty 218
Moslem Central Spiritual Board 134–5
motor industry 202–3
Movement for Civil Dignity 27
Mukhin, A. A. 15
Murrell, Peter 109
Muscovites 62
MVD 102, 131–2, 142, 143, 146, 176
My Lai 176

Nagorno-Karabakh 173, 229
Napoleon 60, 86, 249–50
Nash Dom – Rossiya (NDR) 11, 17, 21, 114–15, 199
nation building 161–70, 181
national anthem 164, 165, 284n
national identity 161
National Security Concept 106, 213–14
national values 162–4
nativisation 244–5
Nato 66, 213, 218–21, 224, 225, 227; enlargement 208, 211, 226, 230, 233
Nazdratenko, Yevgeny 15, 77, 135, 149, 153–4, 195
Nemtsov, Boris 16, 18, 22, 63, 101, 196; opposition parties 123, 124, 125

neo-liberalism 44
neo-Sovietism 36–7, 47, 104, 106, 165–6, 204, 235, 241, 249
Nevzlin, Leonid *193*
New International Information Order (NIIO) 106
newspapers 107
Nezavisimaya gazeta 54
NGOs 126, 127
Niccolo-M 200
Nietzsche, Friedrich 34
Nikitin, Alexander 103, 110, 205
Nizhny Novgorod 142
Norilsk Nickel 97, 99, 100, 102, *193*, 195
normalcy 41–2
normalisation 42, 43, 54, 58, 207–15, 245
normality 40–3, 45, 47, 53–8, 245, 248
Northern Ireland 180
Novgorod 135
Novosibirsk 142
NTV 18, 97, 99, 100, 101, 104, 105, 199, 277n
nuclear industry 204–5
nuclear weapons 218, 228
Nye, Joseph 233

objective predetermination 54
Obshchaya gazeta 104
O'Donnell, Guillermo 42
oil 184, 186, 194, 222, 231
Okun'kov, Lev 47
oligarchical capitalism 183, 190–2, *193*, 194–201
oligarchs 18, 55, 64, 67, 128, 155, 235–6; Fatherland 21, 28; media 107; Nemtsov 125; new rules 100–3; and Putin 68, 73, 88, 96–100, 242–3
Omsk 196
'On Counteracting Extremist Activity' 116–17
'On the Principles of Dividing Power between the Russian Federation Government and the Regions' 133
Open Letter by Vladimir Putin to the Russian Voters 28
opinion polls 69, 70–2
opposition 122–5
order 43, 53, 57, 79, 93
Ordnungspolitik 43
Organisation of Entrepreneurs' Organisations of Russia (OPORA) 198
Organisation of Petroleum Exporting Countries (OPEC) 184, 222

Organisation for Security and Co-
operation in Europe (OSCE) 213, 214,
224, 229, 231
ORT 97, 98, 104, 107
Orthodox Church 3, 62, 169–70
Ostrow, Joel M. 120
Otechestvo see Fatherland
Our Home is Russia (NDR) 11, 17, 21,
114–15, 199
OVR *see* Fatherland – All Russia

Pain, Emil 174
Pakistan 224
Pamfilova, Ella 27, *29*, 110–11
Pappe, Yakov 191
parliament: realignment 119–22; *see also*
Duma; Federation Council
Parliamentary Assembly of the Council of
Europe (PACE) 110, 111, 179, 180
parties 113–18, 155, 199–200
Party of Life 122
Pasko, Grigorii 110
Pastukhov, Vladimir 109, 203
patriotism 46, 163, 166–8, 244–5
patronage 128
Patrushev, Nikolai 14, 66
Pavlovsky, Gleb 26, 58, 69, 88, 168, 237;
civil society 125–6, 127; *siloviki* and
family 64, 65
Pechenev, Vadim 43, 269n
Pelshe, Arvid 13
People's Deputy 121
People's Party 122
perestroika 34, 38
Perm 135
Peter the Great viii, 40–1, 46, 76
Petrov, Nikolai 20, 158
Pioneers 4, 245
Piontovsky, Andrei 201
Pitery 62, 66, 67, 68, 87, 241–2
Plato 1
Plekhanov, Georgy 25–6
pluralism 37
pluralistic statism 89, 136
pochvennichestvo 244
Podberezkin, Alexei 27, *29*, 166
Poland 38, 190, 192, 208, 212, 219, 229
political parties 113–18, 155, 199–200
polpredy 130, 141, 142, 143, 146, 195
Poltavchenko, Georgy 144, 145
populism 67–8
poryadok 43
post-Sovietism 36–7, 47, 104, 204, 235,
241, 249

Potanin, Vladimir *193*; government
career 100–1, 196; Interros 99, 195;
Norilsk Nickel 97, 102; Sidanko 194
power vertical 129, 159–60, 237
pragmatism 55, 208–9, 211, 233, 247, 249
Pravda, Alex 217
predopredelennosti 54
presidency 83–4, 86, 96, 119, 128, 246–7
Presidential Archive 166
presidential elections: 1991 10, 30, 32;
1996 31, 32; 1999 43; 2000 25–33, *29*,
79, 166; turnout 69
Presidential Human Rights Commission
110–11
press *see* media
Prikhodko, Sergei 223
Primakov, Yevgeny 18, 26, 27, 32, 77, 198;
1999 Duma election 21, 22; centrism
78; Chechnya 180; foreign policy 208,
210, 215, 217, 227–8; and oligarchs 61,
97; prime minister 16, 196
Primorsky *krai* 50, 135, 183, 195
privatisation 55, 186, 187
Prokhorov, Mikhail *193*
property rights 122, 140, 195
Protestantism 169
Prusak, Mikhail 122
Pskov 134
Pugachev, Sergei 62, 170
Putin, Spiridon Ivanovich (grandfather)
2
Putin, Vladimir viii–ix, 234–5, 265n; 1999
Duma election 20–2; 2000 presidential
election 25–33, *29*, 268n; at Leningrad
State University 6–8; beyond transition
240–1; birth 2; bloc 61–8; business-
state relations 197–8; centrism 78–80,
82; character 14–15; Chechnya 171–81;
childhood and youth 3–6; as city
functionary 10–12; civil society 127–8,
129; as consolidator 60; contradictions
241–4; democracy 113; destiny and
decision 248–50; and Duma 121, 122;
economy 182, 186–90, *187*, 195, 201–6;
federal reforms 146–52; FICs 199,
200–1; foreign policy 207–33, 247;
Germany 9–10; judicial reform and
human rights 107–11; KGB 8–9;
leadership and style 73–7; liberal
patriotism 244–5; and media 103–7;
nation building 162–8, 181; and
oligarchs 96–103, 191; opposition
parties 123–5; Orthodoxy 170; party
system 114–18; pathways 78; and the

Putin, Vladimir – *contd.*
  people 68–73; personality and
  leadership 35–7, 82; politics of
  normality 41–3, 53–8, 59, 245, 247–8;
  premiership 16–20; regime to
  governance 245–7; regions 133,
  135–40, 141–6, 152–60, 238–9; rise to
  power 1, 33; roots 2–3; rules 235–6;
  Russia at the Turn of the Millennium
  43–7, 251–62; state 83, 85–6, 88–91,
  93–4, 95, 96, 110–11; state-of-the-
  nation speeches 51–3, 161, 234; as state
  official 12–14; state reconstitution or
  reconcentration 236–8; universal
  citizenship 239–40; use of think tanks
  47–51; Yeltsin's resignation and
  succession 23–5
Putin, Vladimir Spiridonovich (father)
  2–3, 5, 17, 170
Putina, Lyudmila (Shkrebneva) 7–8, 29,
  170
Putina, Maria Ivanovna (mother) 2–3, 6,
  17, 170

quasi-centre 79, 80

radio 105
Raeff, Marc 76
Raikov, Gennady 122
Rakhimov, Murtaza 156, 283n
Rakhlin, Anatoly 4
Rebirth of Russia 120
reconcentration *see* state reconcentration
reconstitution *see* state reconstitution
Red Banner Institute 8
Reddaway, Peter 39, 61
referendum, April 1993 32
regime politics 86–8, 93, 122–5, 135,
  245–7
regime type 241
regions 13, 27, 62–3, 91–2, 159–60, 235;
  beyond segmented regionalism 238–9;
  federal districts 141–6; federal reforms
  146–52; FICs 195–6; governors and
  legislatures 152–5; media 106; political
  parties 115; Putin's reforms 88, 89,
  135–40; state reconstitution and
  federalism 155–9
religion 168–70
Remington, Thomas 120
Renan, Ernest 162
revolution 39–40, 55–7, 81, 235, 240–1,
  249
Robertson, Lord George 66

Rodionov, P. 199
Rogozin, Dmitry 180, 184, 185
Roketskii, Leonid 154
Roman Catholic Church 169
Romania 212, 220
Rosagropromstroi 200
Rose, Richard 71, 248
Rossel, Eduard 142–3
Rossiya, Delovaya 198
Rosvooreuzheniya 13
rule of law *see* law
Rushailo, Vladimir 18
Russia 34, 37, 161–2, 181; extraordinary
  politics 37–9; history 43–7, 57–8;
  leadership 73; national values 162–4;
  normality 40–3; patriotism and images
  of the nation 166–8; religion 168–70;
  revolution from above 39–40; symbols
  and symbolism 164–6; third way 80–2
Russia at the Turn of the Millennium
  (Putin) 28, 43–7, 51, 56, 78, 89, 162,
  163, 171, 251–62
Russian Aluminium *193*, 197, 199
Russian Chamber of Commerce and
  Industry 77, 198
Russian Orthodox Church (ROC) 3, 62,
  169–70
Russian Union of Industrialists and
  Entrepreneurs (RUIE) 197, 236
Russia's Choice 21, 78, 114
Russia's Democratic Choice 78
Russia's Regions 121, 199
Russkii dom (*Russian House*) 170
Rutskoi, Alexander 119, 154
Ryabov, Andrei 64, 73, 147

St Petersburg viii, 1, 2–3, 46, 166, 271n;
  2000 gubernatorial election 74; 2000
  presidential election 31; 2003
  gubernatovial election 144; crime 11;
  Putin's career 10–12, 36–7; regime
  135, 144; *see also* Pitery
St Petersburg Mining Institute 12
Sakhalin 225
Sakharov, Andrei 37
Samara 30, 135, 142, 166
sambo 4, 7, 14
Samoilov, Sergei 148
Saratov 30
Savostyanov, Yevgeny 27
Sberbank 192
SBS Agro-Bank 200
Schmitt, Carl 246
Schroeder, Gerhard 209

Schumpeter, Joseph A. 15, 41, 73
Sechin, Igor 62
security: Chechnya 173; and foreign
    policy 210, 213–14
Security Council (SC) 66, 106, 107, 142,
    154
security establishment 66–7, 74; *see also*
    military
segmented regionalism 130–5, 136, 158,
    238
Seleznev, Gennady 17, 67, 120, 121, 123
semibankirshchina 190–1
semidesyatnik 6, 57
Semigin, Gennady 123
Semnadsat' mgnovenii vesny 6
September 11 (9/11) 215, 216–18, 219,
    220
Serbia 161, 213, 219, 220
Sevastopol 167
Seventeen Moments of Spring 6
Severstal' *193*
Shabdurasulov, Igor 22, 26, 98
Shaimiev, Mintimir 21, 134, 137, 150,
    153, 157
Shakhrai, Sergei 16, 133
sham constitutionalism 88
Shamanov, General Vladimir 154
Shanghai Co-operation Organisation
    (SCO) 227
Sharlet, Robert 107
Shchit i mech 6
Sheinis, Victor 79
shestdesyatniki 6, 56–7
Shestopal, Elena 72
Shevchenko, Yury 8
Shevtsova, Lilia 20–1, 83, 127
Shmakov, Mikhail 197
Shoigu, Sergei 21, 71
Shpigun, Major-General Gennady 18–19
Shumeiko, Vladimir 16
Shvidler, Yevgeny *193*
Siberian Accord 142
Siberian Aluminium *193*, 196, 203
Sibneft 97, 99, 187, *193*, 194, 196, 199
Sidanko 194
siloviki 62, 63, 64, 68, 125, 146, 154, 242
Simbirsk 166
Simonsen, Sven Gunnar 167
Sistema 192, *193*, 195
Skuratov, Yury 27, *29*, 97
Skyner, Louis 203
Slavneft 187, 201
Slavophile Russia 81
Slavyanskaya Hotel 27

Slovakia 212, 220
Slovenia 212, 220
small and medium enterprises (SMEs)
    190, 198, 206
Smirnov, Igor 231
Smirnyagin, Leonid 131
Smith, Adam 185
Smolensk *oblast* 139
Smolensky, Alexander 97
Sobchak, Anatoly 1, 7, 10–12, 13, 17
Sobyanin, Sergei 154
social solidarity 46, 163, 164
soft power 214–15, 233
Sokolov, A. 191, 196–7
Solzhenitsyn, Alexander 35, 45, 143, 149,
    244
sootechestvennik 230
Sorokina, Svetlana 105
Soskovets, Oleg 16, 191
South Korea 192, 201, 243
South Ossetia 173
sovereignty 130, 131, 135–6, 139–40, 158,
    208; Chechnya 173, 180
Soviet Union 55, 161, 168
Spiritual Heritage 27, 166
SPS (*Soyuz pravykh sil*) 121, 122, 124, 221;
    1999 Duma election 22, *22*; funding
    199, 200
stability 43, 53, 57, 80, 93
stagnation 81, 243
Stalin, Joseph viii, 2, 265n
Stalingrad 166
Stankevich, Sergei 167
state 83, 110–11; and civil society 128;
    and development 84–6; pluralistic or
    compacted statism 88–90; politics and
    law 90–6; reconstitution or
    reconcentration 236–8; and regime
    83–4, 86–8
State Bank 111
State Committee for Environmental
    Protection 204
State Committee on Forestry 204
State Council 147, 148, 150
State Duma *see* Duma
State in a Changing World, The (World
    Bank) 85
State Press Committee 105
state reconcentration 37, 89–90, 92, 111,
    236–8, 241
state reconstitution 37, 89, 92–3, 111,
    130, 236–8, 241, 247; economy 186;
    and federalism 136–7, 155–9, 239; and
    universal citizenship 239–40

statism 37, 46, 128, 136, 213, 242, 243;
   pluralistic or compacted 88–90
Stepan, Alfred 241
Stepashin, Sergei 16, 18–19, 21, 30, 102
Stiglitz, Joseph 184
Stolypin, Peter 51, 111, 244
Strategic Offensive Reduction Treaty 218
strategic planning 12
Strategy for Russia (Karaganov) 48–51
Stroev, Yegor 148, 157
Struve, Peter 81, 244
Sukhanov, Yury 187
Sultygov, Abdul-Khakim 111
Surgutneftegaz 97, 187, *193*
Surkov, Vladislav 26, 62
Sutyagin, Igor 110
Svyazinvest 100–1
Sword and Shield 6
symbols 164–6
system management 54–5

Taiwan 226
Tajikistan 232
Talanov, Viktor 15
Tang Jiaxuan 227
Tatarstan 131, 132, 133, 134, 137, 153,
   156, 157, 195
Tatneft 195, 199
Tatum, Paul 27
taxation 133, 151–2, 183, 187, 202
television 103–5, 125
terrorism 19, 53, 166–7, 173, 175, 266n;
   September 11 215, 216–18
third way 45–7, 79, 80–2, 235, 243;
   foreign policy 210–11, 215
Tikhon 170
Tilly, Charles 162
timber industry 203, 205
Titov, Konstantin 27, *29*, 30, 153
TNK 100, 187, *193*, 194, 200, 288n
Tocqueville, Alexis de 128
Toynbee, Polly 82
trade unions 197, 205
transactional leadership 74
Transdniestria 173, 208, 231
transformational leadership 74
transition 38–40, 240–1
Transparency International 50
trasformismo 129
Treisman, Daniel 134
Trenin, Dmitry 229
Tretyakov, Vitaly 54, 57, 95, 101, 102
Troshev, General Gennady 77, 176
Tsaritsyn 166

Tsuladze, Avtandil 72
Tula *oblast* 133
Tuleev, Aman 26–7, *29*, 30
TV6 105
TV Centre (TVS) 105
Tver 166
Tyumen *oblast* 50, 154
Tyumen Oil Company 100, 187, *193*, 194,
   200, 288n

Udmurtia 135
Ukraine 31, 58, 161, 167, 168, 180–1,
   211, 220, 230–1
Ulyanovsk 154, 166
Umazheva, Malika 176
Unified Energy Systems (UES) 55, 86,
   102, 188–9, 191, 196, 199, 200
Union of Rightist Forces *see* SPS
United Kingdom 243
United Nations (UN) 214, 218, 222, 224,
   229; Security Council 207; Universal
   Charter of Human Rights 247
United Russia 62, 75, 90, 117, 121, 122,
   199; *see also* Fatherland; Unity
United States 214, 221–4; companies 192;
   federalism 159; geopolitics 229; Iraq
   213; media 105; Missile Defence
   scheme 228; Putin's visits 14; return to
   normalcy 41; and Russia 231, 232, 233;
   State Department 54; war on terrorism
   173, 216–18, 230
Unity 62, 75, 98, 113, 199; 1999 Duma
   election 21, 22, *22*, 23; in Duma 120,
   121; *see also* United Russia
Universal Charter of Human Rights 247
universalism 247–8
Uss, Alexander 195
USSR 55, 161, 168
Ustinov, Vladimir 64–5
Uzbekistan 171, 224, 227, 230–1, 232

Vainstok, Semyon *193*
Vekselberg, Viktor *193*
Velichko, Valery 67
Vershbow, Alexander 223
Veshnyakov, Alexander 199
Vidamov, Victor 200
Vietnam 218
virtù 234
virtual politics 68
Volgograd 166
Voloshin, Alexander 16, 62, 64, 142, 223,
   272n
Volsky, Arkady 197, 199

Von Mises, Ludwig 81
Voronezh 150, 154
Vsya Rossiya see All Russia
Vyakhirev, Rem 99, 199
Vybor Rossii 21, 78, 114
Vybory 118

Washington consensus 184–5, 186
Weber, Max 88, 248
Westernisation 248
Williamson, John 184–5
Wolf, Marcus 9
World Bank 85, 190
World Trade Organisation (WTO)
    185–6, 194, 202–3, 210

Yabloko 30, 121, 122, 123, 124, 167,
    199–200; 1999 Duma election *22*, 27
Yakovlev, Vladimir 11, 12, 21, 62, 74, 144
Yakutia 131
Yanov, Alexander 81
Yasin, Yevgeny 47
Yastrzhembsky, Sergei 174
Yavlinsky, Grigory 27, *29*, 30, 122, 123–4
Yegorov, Nikolai 12
Yeltsin, Boris 6, 25, 34, 96, 249, 265n;
    1991 presidential election 10, 30; 1996
    presidential election 12, 31; coalition-
    building 63; economy 182; elite 63–6;
    foreign policy 208, 228; and media
    104; Moscow bombings 166–7;
    national anthem 165; and oligarchs 97,
    190, 191, 196; presidency 246–7;

presidential elections 26; privatisations
    55; and Putin 35–6, 75; Putin's
    premiership 19, 20.16–18; reforms viii,
    ix; regime politics 86–7, 90; regions
    62–3, 91, 133, 143, 152, 155, 156, 158;
    religion 169; resignation 1, 23–4, 32,
    43; revolution 38–9, 56, 240–1; Russia
    161, 163, 168; segmented regionalism
    130–1; state 237; support base 31–2;
    tax concessions 151; 'working on
    documents' 70
Yevtushenkov, Vladimir *193*
Young Pioneers 4, 245
Yuditskaya, Mina Moiseevna 4
Yukos 100, *193*, 194, 199–200, 288n
Yumashev, Valentin 16, 64

zachistki 177
Zakaev, Akhmed 178, 179
Zakaria, Fareed 42
zemli 143
zemlyachestvo 62
zemstva 149
zero-option 60, 65
Zhirinovsky Bloc *22*, 26, 121, 200
Zhirinovsky, Vladimir 26, *29*, 71, 121,
    143, 200
Zinoviev, Alexander 24, 35, 237
Zyazikov, Murat 153
Zyuganov, Gennady 46, 71, 121, 123, 166;
    1996 presidential election 31; 2000
    presidential election 26–7, *29*, 30, 31,
    32, 168